Cold War Legacie

Technicities

Series Editors: John Armitage, Ryan Bishop and Joanne Roberts, Winchester School of Art, University of Southampton

The philosophy of technicities: exploring how technology mediates art, frames design and augments the mediated collective perception of everyday life.

Technicities will publish the latest philosophical thinking about our increasingly immaterial technocultural conditions, with a unique focus on the context of art, design and media.

Published

Lyotard and the Inhuman Condition: Reflections on Nihilism, Information and Art
By Ashley Woodward

Critical Luxury Studies: Art, Design, Media
Edited by John Armitage and Joanne Roberts

Cold War Legacies: Systems, Theory, Aesthetics
Edited by John Beck and Ryan Bishop

Forthcoming

Fashion and Materialism
By Ulrich Lehmann

Cold War Legacies

Systems, Theory, Aesthetics

Edited by John Beck and
Ryan Bishop

EDINBURGH
University Press

Edinburgh University Press is one of the leading university presses in the UK. We publish academic books and journals in our selected subject areas across the humanities and social sciences, combining cutting-edge scholarship with high editorial and production values to produce academic works of lasting importance. For more information visit our website: edinburghuniversitypress.com

Edinburgh University Press Ltd
The Tun – Holyrood Road, 12(2f) Jackson's Entry, Edinburgh EH8 8PJ

First published in hardback by Edinburgh University Press 2016

Typeset in 11/13 Adobe Sabon by
IDSUK (DataConnection) Ltd, and
printed and bound in Great Britain by
CPI Group (UK) Ltd, Croydon CR0 4YY

A CIP record for this book is available from the British Library

ISBN 978 1 4744 0948 3 (hardback)
ISBN 978 1 4744 3224 5 (paperback)
ISBN 978 1 4744 0949 0 (webready PDF)
ISBN 978 1 4744 0950 6 (epub)

Contents

List of Figures

Series Editors' Preface

Technological transformation has profound and frequently unforeseen influences on art, design and media. At times technology emancipates art and enriches the quality of design. Occasionally it causes acute individual and collective problems of mediated perception. Time after time technological change accomplishes both simultaneously. This new book series explores and reflects philosophically on what new and emerging *technicities* do to our everyday lives and increasingly immaterial technocultural conditions. Moving beyond traditional conceptions of the philosophy of technology and of techne, the series presents new philosophical thinking on how technology constantly alters the essential conditions of beauty, invention and communication. From novel understandings of the world of technicity to new interpretations of aesthetic value, graphics and information, Technicities focuses on the relationships between critical theory and representation, the arts, broadcasting, print, technological genealogies/histories, material culture, and digital technologies and our philosophical views of the world of art, design and media.

The series foregrounds contemporary work in art, design and media whilst remaining inclusive, in terms of both philosophical perspectives on technology and interdisciplinary contributions. For a philosophy of technicities is crucial to extant debates over the artistic, inventive and informational aspects of technology. The books in the Technicities series concentrate on present-day and evolving technological advances but visual, design-led and mass-mediated questions are emphasised to further our knowledge of their often-combined means of digital transformation.

The editors of Technicities welcome proposals for monographs and well-considered edited collections that establish new paths of investigation.

John Armitage, Ryan Bishop and Joanne Roberts

Acknowledgements

We would like to thank the Institute for Modern and Contemporary Culture (University of Westminster) and the Centre for Global Futures in Art Design & Media at Winchester School of Art (University of Southampton) for their support of this project. In addition to all of the wonderful contributors to this volume, there are many individuals we would like to acknowledge for their engaged conversation and intellect which have assisted us in realising this project, including Ed d'Souza, Sunil Manghani, John Armitage, Joanne Roberts, August Davis, Sean Cubitt, Mark Featherstone, Benjamin Bratton, Ed Keller, McKenzie Wark, Kristoffer Gansing, Mike Featherstone, Couze Venn, Scott Lash, Mark Dorrian, David Cunningham, Leigh Wilson, Lucy Bond, Georgina Colby and Matthew Cornford. We are especially grateful to Jordan Crandall, not only for his excellent conversation and wit but also for his fantastic artwork that graces the book's cover – a piece that caused one and all in the design process to shout, 'That's it!'

At Edinburgh University Press, we are deeply indebted to Carol Macdonald for her editorial guidance and enthusiasm for the book as well as for the Technicities series. Thanks also to Rebecca Mackenzie and the rest of the production and design team for their care, concern and hard work.

Ryan would like to thank his daughters Sarah and Sophia, who must live with their own Cold War legacies. He also wishes to thank his most wonderful partner Adeline, for her endless intelligence, patience and humour. He dedicates this book to the memory of his father Steve, who showed him a great deal about Cold War systems and technologies. John would like to thank Paula and Ed, for making the trip and seeing the funny side.

Notes on Contributors

John Beck is Professor of Modern Literature and Director of the Institute for Modern and Contemporary Culture at the University of Westminster, London. He is the author of *Writing the Radical Center: William Carlos Williams, John Dewey, and American Cultural Politics* (SUNY Press, 2001) and *Dirty Wars: Landscape, Power, and Waste in Western American Literature* (University of Nebraska Press, 2009); co-editor with David Holloway of *American Visual Cultures* (Continuum, 2005); and has published widely on twentieth century literature, art and photography. His research interests in American and British literature and art are focused on areas concerned with politics, technology and space.

Ryan Bishop is Professor of Global Arts and Politics at the Winchester School of Art, University of Southampton, where he is also Director of Research and Co-Director of the Winchester Centre for Global Futures in Art Design & Media. In addition to co-editing with John Armitage and Doug Kellner the journal *Cultural Politics* (Duke University Press), he co-edits with John Phillips the Global Public Life sections of *Theory, Culture & Society* and is an editorial board member of that journal. He also edits the book series 'Theory Now' for Polity Press and co-edits the book series Technicities (with John Armitage and Joanne Roberts, Edinburgh University Press). Bishop's most recent books include *Comedy and Cultural Critique in American Film* (Edinburgh University Press, 2013); *Virilio and Visual Culture* (Edinburgh University Press, 2013), co-edited with John Armitage; *Otherwise Occupied* (Al-Hoash/Third Text, 2013); *The City as Target* (Routledge, 2012), co-edited with Greg Clancey and John Phillips; *Modernist Avant-Garde Aesthetics and Contemporary Military Technology* (Edinburgh University Press, 2010), co-authored with John Phillips; and *Baudrillard Now* (Polity Press, 2009). His research areas include critical theory, critical cultural studies, literary studies, visual culture, urbanism, aesthetics, critical military studies, institutional studies, architecture, and sensory perception and knowledge formation.

Ele Carpenter is a curator and writer on interdisciplinary politicised art and social networks of making. Her Nuclear Culture curatorial research project is a partnership between The Arts Catalyst and Goldsmiths College, University of London, where she is a senior lecturer in MFA Curating and convenor of the Nuclear Culture Research Group. Her curatorial work includes facilitating roundtable discussions between artists and nuclear stakeholders. Curated exhibitions include Actinium (OYOYO, Sapporo, Japan, 2014), Material Nuclear Culture (Karst, Plymouth, 2016) and Perpetual Uncertainty (Bilmuseet, Sweden, 2016–17).

Fabienne Collignon is Lecturer in Contemporary Literature at the University of Sheffield. Her work is focused on Cold War weapons systems, genre fiction/film, theories of technology and the poetics of space. Her first book, *Rocket States: Atomic Weaponry and the Cultural Imagination*, was published by Bloomsbury in 2014.

Mark Coté is a lecturer in Digital Culture and Society at King's College London, leading development in the analysis of big social data via an AHRC-funded research project. His research is concerned with the materiality of the digital, namely in critically unpacking the mediating environment of cultural practices and political economic relations.

Daniel Grausam is Lecturer in the Department of English at Durham University. His work focuses on American studies, Cold War culture, the novel and contemporary literature. His books include *On Endings: American Postmodern Fiction and the Cold War* (University of Virginia Press, 2011) and *American Literature and Culture in an Age of Cold War: A Critical Reassessment* (University of Iowa Press, 2012), co-edited with Steven Belletto.

Ken Hollings is a writer, broadcaster, visiting tutor at the Royal College of Art and associate lecturer at Central Saint Martins School of Art and Design. His books include *Destroy All Monsters* (Marion Boyars, 2001), *Welcome to Mars: Fantasies of Science in the American Century 1947–1959* (Strange Attractor Press, 2008) and *The Bright Labyrinth: Sex, Death and Design in the Digital Regime* (Strange Attractor Press, 2014).

Adrian Mackenzie is Professor of Technological Cultures at Lancaster University. His research is at the intersections of science and technology studies, media and cultural studies, and social and cultural theory. His books include *Wirelessness* (MIT Press, 2010), *Cutting Code: Software and Sociality* (Peter Lang, 2006) and *Transductions: Bodies and Machines at Speed* (Continuum, 2006).

Jussi Parikka is a media theorist, writer and Professor of Technological Culture and Aesthetics at Winchester School of Art, University of Southampton. Parikka has a PhD in Cultural History from the University of Turku, Finland, and in addition he is Docent of Digital Culture Theory in the same university. Parikka has published widely on digital culture, archives and visual culture, network society and media theory. Books include *Digital Contagions: A Media Archaeology of Computer Viruses* (Peter Lang, 2007), *Insect Media* (University of Minnesota Press, 2010) and *A Geology of Media* (University of Minnesota Press, 2015).

John W. P. Phillips is an associate professor in the Department of English at the National University of Singapore. He is co-author of *Modernist Avant-Garde Aesthetics and Contemporary Military Technology* (Edinburgh University Press, 2010) and has published widely in the fields of critical theory and continental philosophy.

Adam Piette is Professor of English at the University of Sheffield. He is the author of *Remembering and the Sound of Words: Mallarmé, Proust, Joyce, Beckett* (Oxford University Press, 1996); *Imagination at War: British Fiction and Poetry 1939–1945* (Macmillan, 1995); *The Literary Cold War, 1945 to Vietnam* (Edinburgh University Press, 2009); and co-editor of *The Edinburgh Companion to Twentieth-Century British and American War Literature* (Edinburgh University Press, 2012).

James Purdon is Lecturer in Modern and Contemporary Literature at the University of St Andrews. He is co-editor of the open-access book series *Technographies* (Open Humanities Press) and the author of *Modernist Informatics: Literature, Information, and the State* (Oxford University Press, 2016).

Aura Satz is an artist who works in film, sound, performance and sculpture. She has performed, exhibited and screened her work internationally in galleries and film festivals, including Tate Modern,

Tate Britain, the Hayward Gallery, Barbican Art Gallery, ICA, the Wellcome Collection, BFI Southbank, Whitechapel Gallery (London), Gallery 44 (Toronto), Gertrude Contemporary (Melbourne), De Appel Art Centre (Amsterdam), Baltic Centre for Contemporary Art (Gateshead), George Eastman Museum (Rochester, NY) and Dallas Contemporary (Texas). She is Moving Image Tutor at the Royal College of Art.

Neal White is an artist and Professor of Media Art in the Faculty of Media and Communication, Bournemouth University.

Introduction

The Long Cold War

John Beck and Ryan Bishop

In the suburbs of Washington DC during the early 1980s, a family-run travel agency provides cover for a married couple who are, in fact, KGB 'Illegals', Soviet agents fighting deep behind Cold War enemy lines. This is the premise of *The Americans* (2013–), one of the most unlikely hit television dramas of recent years. Framed by the everyday concerns of an ordinary American family, the show is at once ludicrous – the agents' next-door neighbour is an FBI officer – and nostalgic, not just for the paraphernalia of the 1980s but for an era when commitment might mean something beyond self-interest.[1] While initially the narrative appears to be taking shape as a drama of defection – the male agent's concern for the couple's two children leads him to wonder whether they ought to turn themselves in – the show swerves away from what might have become a conventional story of redemption through renunciation. Instead, the couple's resolve hardens and the audience is invited to root for a pair of assassins contemptuous of American freedoms (the mother despairs because her teenage daughter wants to go to church; in diners, they are appalled by the length of the menu). The United States intelligence community is hardly portrayed in a favourable light: the FBI man next door destroys his marriage by having an affair with an attractive Soviet spy, whose punishment is imprisonment in the Gulag. The senior Bureau officer is played by Richard Thomas, an actor best known as John-Boy in *The Waltons*, the sentimental Depression-set soap from the 1970s. The Soviets are far cooler: hard-bodied, ruthless and much more effective, they are able to drop the kids off at school before disposing of a body by snapping the bones and folding it into a suitcase.

The Americans manages to deliver a perspective on the US that would have been inconceivable only a few years ago: an unstable, inconsistent, yet occasionally direct anti-Americanism. Historical distance, of course, provides the necessary safety valve; everybody knows the Soviet Union will soon crumble. Yet by flipping current US-centric narratives – the male agent has a grown-up son serving in the Soviet army in Afghanistan; President Reagan's religious rhetoric, to the Russians, is a form of dangerous extremism – the show casts the United States as a foreign and disturbing place, indifferent to racism overseas (the Soviet agents support the anti-apartheid struggle in South Africa) and class inequality at home (the spies cultivate exploited US factory workers in order to obtain classified information on weapons designs).

The drama does serve as a nervous reminder that enemies may dwell amongst us and that the most dangerous of them are likely to be indistinguishable from ourselves; in this regard, *The Americans* merely perpetuates contemporary anxieties about a compromised domestic sphere. The show also, of course, reminds its viewers that the Cold War *was* a war and that Americans really were faced with a murderous alien power. More profoundly, though, *The Americans* is an assault on twenty-first-century complacency, irony and entitlement. The Russians portrayed are far from decent, but it is the United States that is the real problem: arrogant, naïve, self-interested and greedy, Americans do not seem to believe in anything. The Soviet agents make unpleasant choices, sacrifice themselves and their loved ones to the greater good, have an understanding of history and their place within it, and embrace struggle as a necessary part of life. The American agents are defending the status quo; the Soviets are utopian guerrillas. The misdirection of the show's title is not, perhaps, focused on the fact that 'the Americans' are really Russians, but that the Russians would make better Americans than many Americans. The KGB agents are what Americans ought to be: resourceful, resilient and dedicated to a cause.

How can it be that in the second decade of the twenty-first century, the heroes of a popular American TV drama are foreign-born communists? What has gone so wrong (or, perhaps, right) that the – albeit fictional – agents of the Evil Empire can demand sympathy and admiration? In part, the answer lies in nostalgia for a worthy adversary; modern-day terrorism does not play by the rules, is decentred and impossible to predict. In simpler times, there were rules of engagement, a balance of power to be maintained; calculations could be made: forecasts, predictions, measurable outcomes. Beyond this longing for binary lockdown, though, is the sense that, all too obvious in *The Americans*, the twenty-first-century world is the world the Cold War made. In this regard, the reimagined 1980s of the show folds uncontroversially into the present. The preoccupations of the time, from religious fundamentalism and Middle Eastern politics to ubiquitous surveillance, high-tech weapons systems, and security leaks, continue to shape culture and geopolitics in the US and beyond. This being the case, *The Americans* might be read less as a historical romance and more as an instructional film: regimes under threat need resourceful and selfless warriors – there's a war on.

The early 1980s of *The Americans* is so recognisable because, in a number of fundamental ways, contemporary life and thought continues to be shaped by theories, technologies, attitudes and perspectives that were forged during the total war of World War II and hardened into organisational, ideological and technological structures during the long Cold War. The material and conceptual infrastructure that supports the covert activities of the KGB and FBI in the TV show – communications systems, normalised secrecy, adversarial geopolitics, permanent emergency – remains the condition within which contemporary life is defined. The interlocking tensions and conflicts across personal, familial, national and global territories that made the Cold War psychologically, as well as socio-politically, all-consuming also persist in the present. The legacies of the deep structure of the Cold War are most properly the subject of this book.

Thinking Systems

The central assumption of the essays collected here is that the historically bounded period known as the Cold War (1946–1991) does not fully capture the extent to which the institutional, technological, scientific, aesthetic and cultural forms decisively shaped during that period continue to structure, materially and conceptually, the twenty first-century world. While it is not our intention to claim that the 1946–1991 period did not constitute a specific and distinctive set of historical, geopolitical and cultural circumstances, we are interested in extending the temporal frame in order to consider the intensifications, reversals and irreversibilities brought about by the politics and culture of the latter half of the twentieth century. In numerous ways, the essays gathered here insist that the infrastructure of the Cold War, its technologies, its attitudes and many of its problems continue to shape and inform contemporary responses to large-scale political and technological issues.

It should be noted that much of the discussion in this introduction and throughout the book concentrates, though not without exception, on the Cold War as it was constructed and managed by the United States and Western Europe. We are not attempting here to provide an exhaustive account of the global Cold War, so the stress on the Western, and especially US, perspective is in large part determined by our sense that, especially since the break-up of the Soviet Union, the material and immaterial technologies and practices that have survived and mutated from the 1946–1991 period have their source in the US and its extensive field of operations. To the extent that US Cold War influence has become, de facto, the dominant global influence, an understanding of the legacies of the Cold War must proceed from an understanding of the US global project during and after the historically bounded Cold War period. The Russians depicted in *The Americans* are just one small example of how the Cold War continues to be shaped by the US global imaginary.

The prosecution of the Cold War restructured the conception and experience of time and space, of scale and agency. Nuclear weapons made it necessary to think, at once, about the instantaneous (the decisive moment of mass destruction) and the endless (the stalemate of the superpower stand-off; the infinity of the catastrophic post-nuclear world). The individual act or decision was now outrageously amplified (the finger on the nuclear trigger) and radically diminished (powerless in the face of unfathomable forces with the ceding of human agency to machines in complex weapons systems). The reach of the nuclear threat expanded geopolitics to the scale of the global even as it compressed space (nowhere is safe) and promised to toxically recode matter itself. The challenges and threats posed by this radical spatio-temporal plasticity, where everything came to seem connected to everything – everywhere, everyone, all the time – engendered a mode of thinking preoccupied by networks and systems and the means of managing the proliferating complexity such systems at once represented and reproduced.

The Austrian biologist Ludwig von Bertalanffy first presented his notion of what he would later call 'General Systems Theory' at the University of Chicago in 1937, though his ideas were not widely circulated until a visit to London in 1949 led to the publication of two English-language papers (von Bertalanffy 1968: 90; 1950a; 1950b). Von Bertalanffy's work, alongside John von Neumann and Oskar Morgenstern's game theory (1944), Norbert Wiener's development of cybernetics (1948), and Claude E. Shannon's information theory (Shannon 1948; Shannon and Weaver 1949), contributed, by the early 1950s, to an explosion of interdisciplinary systems thinking that, during the second half of the twentieth century, shaped the direction of fields as diverse as anthropology, political theory, analytical philosophy, art, music and literature, as well, of course, as Cold War military strategy. Indeed, the growth of computational power, fuelled by military research and development, increasingly folded modes of Cold War-focused science and technology into multiplying, interlocking fields of enquiry. The systems model could contain multitudes, influencing social research and tendencies in the arts, such as the so-called systems novels of the 1960s and 1970s, minimalist and electronic music, conceptual art and the emergence of electronic media, as well as driving advances in communications networks and missile guidance technologies.[2] Systems thinking offered a means of conceptualising and understanding a world grown in complexity and in danger; nuclear weapons demanded radical new ways of thinking about time, scale, power, death, responsibility and, most of all, control – the control of technology, populations, information and ideas. The elaborate technologies of the Cold War emerged in coextension with non-material systems of simulations, optimisation, pattern recognition, data mining and algorithms, and equally complex modes of thought aimed at addressing the existential, ethical, metaphysical and onto-epistemological implications of a world permanently on the brink of annihilation.

The capacity of systems analysis to identify common properties characteristic of different types of objects can give an associational systemic logic to otherwise incongruous couplings, much as the surrealist notion of 'objective chance' implicitly accepted the inevitable relationality of things. To encounter the unexpected or accidental, then, is merely to fail to track the connections or identify the relation: microwaves function in both telecommunications systems and kitchens; Nazi rockets kick-start the space race; radiation controlled the North American screwworm fly population by selectively sterilising the male insects. Discussing her work *Impulsive Synchronisation*, an installation that draws on the frequency-hopping technology developed during World War II by Hedy Lamarr and George Antheil, artist Aura Satz notes, in this volume, the irresistible and unpredictable potentiality of new inventions. Lamarr and Antheil's innovation, intended to protect radio-controlled torpedoes from enemy disruption, subsequently found its way into the development of spread-spectrum telecommunications, the signal-structuring technique underpinning wireless telephony. The future ramifications of actions in the present are seemingly uncontainable, yet the scale of destruction made possible by nuclear technology pushed the management of the future to the forefront of the agenda for Cold War planners, as John Beck explains in his chapter. The Manhattan Project may have confirmed the power of intensive collective labour, but dealing with the outcome of that project demanded more prolonged and institutionalised corporate attention. The rise of futures research, inaugurated by the establishment of the RAND Corporation by the

US military shortly after the end of World War II, is not only an acknowledgement that the future cannot be left to fate, but it also reveals the extent to which the global management of time and space had become the major preoccupation of government and business.

It was growing computational power that made the calculation of possible futures feasible. Adrian Mackenzie, in this volume, explores the development of pattern recognition algorithms during the 1950s and how, like Lamarr and Antheil's invention, they have seeped into and structured the communications systems of the twenty-first century. The discovery of pattern in data, as Mackenzie notes, presupposes the existence of pattern; as in futures research, outcomes may be largely predetermined by the methods and presuppositions that construct the aim. The desire to command and control contingency on a large scale – geopolitics, stock markets, consumer behaviour, insurgents, climate change – inevitably, following the logic of systems analysis, results in feedback waves that, in the end, produce an answer to some extent engineered by the question. So technology technologises its objects – the future has to be the future modelled by futurists.

However, systems of control rarely control completely, and the creation of any technology or system is also, as Paul Virilio reminds us, the creation of its failure. The future, even if modelled by futurists, also remains the site of unintended consequences and proliferating iteration cycles, and the long Cold War is nothing if not a tale of ironic and unintended outcomes. The deep geological time of nuclear radiation forms the basis of Adam Piette's meditations on legacies and inheritances, a mobilisation of fissional materials that are the very stuff of destiny, or what Beck calls 'the future [that] used to be fate'. In Piette's chapter, the future is returned to fate as something uncontainable by humans yet thoroughly the unintended consequence of human intervention. The almost limitless temporal scale of nuclear futurity generated by radioactive half-life and decay deeply forms the future's horizon. The attempt to bury the truth of this futurity as a weakly repressed memory, however, is a doomed enterprise that feeds back in unexpected ways. Nuclear radioactive isotope dating of ancient rock formations, for example, became the means for discovering the effects of nuclear testing in the deserts of the US Southwest. Piette argues that these traces 'consolidated in the public imagination the link between deep geological time, radioactivity and underground secret tomb/refuge systems' (this volume). Growing awareness of the persistence of radioactivity also led to the ban on above-ground nuclear testing. Driving tests underground resulted in attempts to contain both the fallout from the explosions and the uranium processing required to create them in the same Plutonic nether regions of the earth that housed the ICBMs that still sit idly, though far from harmlessly, in the vast plains of the Dakotas and Kazakhstan. With underground storage of testing effects, radioactive storage and dormant missiles, the long Cold War has created Hades below ground, though we who occupy the earth's crust perceive it through our amnesiac asphodel-fuelled haze as Elysium.

The swords-into-ploughshares dream of peacetime applications for nuclear technology has thus far failed to contain the catastrophic latency of bombs and power stations. Ele Carpenter's survey of contemporary artistic practice surrounding the Fukushima Dai-ichi nuclear disaster of 2011 stresses the fact that nuclear technology, like the toxicity generated by its processes, is written deeply and indelibly into the bones of contemporary culture. The geophysical instability that caused the Fukushima disaster also challenges projects aimed at permanently storing nuclear waste underground. There are at least two crises of temporality here: the immediate need to tackle contamination from the plant and attend to the dispossessed and/or exposed populations; and the challenge of conceptualising and seeking to manage the seepage of contemporary waste into the deep future. For Carpenter and the artists she considers, there must of necessity be an embrace of the nuclear as an intrinsic aspect of landscape and identity, since the disavowal of toxic technology only generates greater risk due to ignorance and denial. At the same time, the nuclear must be worked with and upon – constantly reconceptualised, reimagined and reinvented in order to prevent its grim presence from stabilising into an achieved catastrophe.

It is precisely the active adaptation and excessive deployment of Cold War technologies, especially in their domestic forms, that Ken Hollings focuses on in his chapter, where communications technologies like transistor radios, telephones and televisions once pitched to consumers as engines for the formation of contained social totalities – the family, the nation – instead become nodes in the libidinal networks of insubordinate subjects. While fears of an anaesthetised mass rendered comatose and compliant by pop music and game shows accompanied the promise of ranch-style arcadia, subcultural and radical assemblages proliferated inside the networks, from civil rights activists and anti-Vietnam protestors to hackers and whistleblowers like Manning and Snowden.

A higher percentage of Germans use Facebook than were under Stasi surveillance, notes Mark Coté in his discussion of how metadata has 'transformed humans into machine-understandable information' (this volume). Contemporary fears regarding the erosion of privacy and the ubiquity of surveillance are not responses to a new phenomenon, argues Coté. Rather, current information-gathering technologies continue in radically intensified form, processes and procedures that go back at least to the punch-cards and alphanumeric coding used by the occupying US forces in the Philippines during the late nineteenth century and the postal surveillance techniques used by the British during the Boer War. The germinal point of Fabienne Collignon's chapter on non-human vision also draws on a *fin de siècle* anticipation of the world to come: H. G. Wells's *The War of the Worlds* (1898). Working a terrain stretching across several centuries of military technological and natural science development, Collignon traces the long Cold War thread of non-anthropocentric vision. By mobilising Jussi Parikka's work in *Insect Media* (2010), she explores how eighteenth- and nineteenth-century entomological studies helped create an imaginary that would dehumanise and re-corporealise human sight. Collignon tracks non-human seeing (as imagined by humans) through Wells to the remote North Dakota anti-missile defence radar system called Safeguard and its 'bug-eyed' viewing structure, on to contemporary tele-technologically sighted drones buzzing about in the skies today for private, corporate and military purposes. Her strategy neatly articulates White and Beck's brief foray into scientific narrative to show that science is not necessarily progressing but that 'scientific knowledge, along with everything else, is happening, interacting with materials and generating new, often unanticipated forms of understanding and organisation' (White and Beck, this volume).

As White and Beck note, the power of scientific invention in shaping Western culture is far too easily conflated with emancipatory discursive practices to make narratives of progress. Taking a simultaneously diachronic and synchronic tack, as do many of the contributors to this book, White and Beck argue that it is more productive to consider events and phenomena as occurring 'along multiple timelines and across multiple scales'. The narrative arc of seamless scientific progress still holds such sway in public common-sense attitudes that the Kuhnian paradigm shift has itself been converted from a radical disruption to a staging post. Understanding the gaps in the narrative of progress that underlines the historical Cold War is to consider these multiple timelines and scales and thus see, as Nietzsche did, that 'time is out of joint' with history, narrative and itself. With the various scientific and technological developments that merge in the formulation of the bomb, though, is the disturbing discursive technology of narrative closure – a teleology, in a sense, but a teleology that is also an eschatology.

Sometimes the material legacies of the Cold War are visible and tangible, as in Jussi Parikka's discussion of Berlin's ruined Teufelsberg listening station or the parasitic 'backbone' communications system set up by the British to counteract potential nuclear attack on its telecommunications capacities, as outlined provocatively by John Phillips. Often, however, the material traces of Cold War thinking are imperceptible, like the algorithms that structure so much contemporary computing, or the containers of radioactive waste seeking a secure (and permanently inaccessible) resting place. The global proliferation across scales and temporalities of the building blocks of Cold War attitudes and practices is, in many ways, uncontainable. We do not seek to contain them here, since it is all too clear that systems designed for the purpose of containment and control – of weapons, dissent, communism, history – served ultimately to render containment impossible, much as information theory sought to control noise within communications systems only to realise its necessity if the signal is to be identified as signal, a point taken up by Phillips again in relation to literary works, defence systems and immunology. Instead, we are interested precisely in proliferation: in the multiple valences compacted into individual decisions, innovations and strategies; in the capacity of collective enterprise designed to harness and shape powerful forces to, at once, generate unforeseen insights and produce seemingly insoluble problems; in the curious genius that can yoke the most hawkish technocratic project to the emancipatory energies of the artistic avant-garde. In this respect, systems thinking is, as it is for a novelist like Thomas Pynchon, or for John Cage or Buckminster Fuller, at once force and counterforce, cause and effect, catastrophe and utopia.

The holism of systems thinking, its capacity to scale up or down, to follow iterative patterns, seams, rhythms, networks and flows, is at once enticing yet suffocating – there is no outside, as the frame expands to contain earth, moon and stars as functions of an engineered battlespace and surveillance field; as time dilates while the carcinogenic messages of the twentieth century lay written in the rocks for ten thousand years. What is this poisoned, capacious space-time the Cold War has bequeathed us?

The Global

Contemporary conceptions of globalisation are inconceivable without the spatial compressions and conceptual expansions inaugurated by World War II and aggressively pursued during the Cold War. The global reach of rocket systems developed to deliver nuclear payloads and deposit orbital satellites beyond the terrestrial atmosphere have rendered the planet as target, battlespace and communications circuit. The construction of the global found within the concept of globalisation emerges from the networks required for real-time surveillance to track and target all of the world at the same time. Further, nuclear weapons introduced new conceptions of scale, not only in terms of the extent of possible destruction that might also include planetary extinction, but also in terms of time: once invented, such weapons and their deadly materials squat forever as a possibility of, on the one hand, instant death, and, on the other, an eternity of contamination. The communications systems developed to manage these weapons and to monitor the movements of the enemy equally persist in the present in the global communications systems that have facilitated the dematerialisation of the financial markets and the collapse of individual privacy, to name only two of the many consequences of the digital age. The agonistic binarism of the Cold War may be over, yet Eisenhower's military-industrial complex has expanded to become the military-industrial-university-entertainment complex that shapes relations among nations, corporations, educational institutions, entertainment industries and environmental policy, as well as structuring domestic and foreign policy in the US most notably – the various 'wars' conducted against abstractions such as 'drugs' and 'terror' – but also in Europe and beyond.[3]

A number of fierce ironies mark the emergence of a global consciousness following World War II. Postwar decolonisation, for example, takes place at the end of the old order of post-Westphalian nation-states just as former colonies realised their independence. Newly formed nation-states emerged into a geopolitical order that demanded they celebrate their freedom by choosing a side in the Cold War. Some flirted with the Non-Aligned Movement, founded in Belgrade in 1961 by India, Indonesia, Egypt, Ghana and Yugoslavia, but the global superpowers made sure such a movement could not be tenable. The fate of postcolonial countries was to be a staging ground for the Cold War by proxy in what, by the early 1950s, was known as the 'Third World': contained, if intense, flare-ups, but not the genuinely hot war that the Cold War attempted to keep at bay with these fledgling countries' hopes and aspirations for political autonomy returned to ashes. Similar material and symbolic displacements occurred as the declining British Empire found new uses for Commonwealth countries, as James Purdon explains in this volume, as sites for nuclear weapons development and, in Australia, testing. Popular Commonwealth products, such as crates of tea that once would have served as icons of imperial trade, are, under Britain's new nuclear dispensation, sacrificial goods exposed to radioactive contamination as postcolonial substitutes for an imagined nuclear strike on the UK.

The binary East versus West model of Cold War thinking, then, does not acknowledge the truly global reach of the conflict.[4] Yet the impact of the Cold War on global affairs extends beyond simply multiplying the nations involved; indeed, the Cold War can be said to have produced the global itself. The Cold War reconfigured metaphysics. Its tele-technological reach altered space and time to such an extent that it left no edge to the world. 'Ecology', wrote Marshall McLuhan, 'was born with Sputnik, for in an electric information environment all events become clamorous and simultaneous' (1974: ix). This metaphysical recalibration converted the earth into a globe; all that is global about our current globalised moment falls from the desire to transform the limits and vicissitudes of the planet's spherical shape (as bemoaned by Kant in his essay on perpetual peace) into a strategic advantage.[5] The global directly results from Cold War logic, strategies and systems. The goal of 'real-time' surveillance of the entire earth is to transform Earth into an object capable of being held in the clutch of a tele-technological hand and surveyed from all sides all the time. A host of technologies and strategies have been deployed, modified and updated – autonomous remote sensing systems, opto-electronics and planetary-scale computation – that not only seem to achieve the goal of complete real-time surveillance but also allow us to believe this goal is realisable.

Gayatri Chakravorty Spivak accurately calls this kind of globalisation 'the computerized globe' (2003: 73), an abstraction where nobody lives but which 'allows us to think we can aim to control it' (72). Instead, Spivak prefers the term 'planetarity', a differentiated political space of habitation; the planet, she writes, 'is in the species of alterity, belonging to another system' (72). The resistance to the global, here, is in part a response to the Cold War imperatives that underwrote the growth of interdisciplinary area studies in US universities post-World War II. Area studies aimed to develop US understanding of the non-Western world, especially in relation to perceived global security threats, not least among newly decolonised nations. Spivak's shift toward planetarity, then, marks a rhetorical, discursive and intellectual move away from the (Cold War) earth as globe and its attendant globalisation studies (see Spivak 2003: 71–102). Yet, even when disassembling the figure of earth as globe and positing the planet as an alternative figure of alterity, Spivak nonetheless falls back on the discursive formulation of the ecological planet as a system, relying on the gentler version of cybernetics that links technology (*techne*) and nature (*physis*) such as one might find in von Bertalanffy or Gregory Bateson.

Figuring the earth as globe and thus fully bounded, networked and observable in real time is an inheritance of the Cold War, as are the automated and autonomous remote sensing systems that enable real-time global surveillance. The military provenance of all of these is evident. For example, the Limited Test Ban Treaty on nuclear testing (1963) and the attendant requirement to monitor adherence to it through remote sensing systems coincides with the prefix 'geo-' becoming synonymous with the earth as strategically networked and surveilled globe. The prefix 'geo-' clearly conflates earth with ground and surface, that which is visible to human and machine observation. The first issue of *The Journal of GeoElectronics* (also 1963) underscores the moment the 'geo-' becomes codified as primarily a techno-scientific engagement with the earth. That first issue included an introductory meditation on the changing understanding of the prefix 'geo-' in relation to tele-technological developments.[6]

The 'geo-' as a prefix that helps figure our world emerges rapidly with the help of satellite technology. With Sputnik's geosynchronous orbit, the term 'satellite' slipped its astronomical moorings and meanings to become the quintessence of techno-atmospheric control, leading rapidly to material and immaterial developments such as the optimistic International Geophysical Year in 1957 (for which the Soviet Union launched Sputnik) and the 'Treaty on Principles Governing the Activities of States in the Exploration and Use of Outer Space, Including the Moon and Other Celestial Bodies' a decade later, a treaty which rendered the moon a site free from any military activity.[7] Although the word 'satellite' is used in astronomy, its etymology, from the Latin *satellit-*, relates to an attendant, courtier or bodyguard. Thus the word has long been associated with the function of oversight. The satellite is simultaneously a protector and one that is under the protected's own control, not vice versa. Or is it? With issues of agency, especially the control of others, human or otherwise, it is useful to bear in mind the complexity of agency, of causes and effects, intended or not. Almost all of our ways of thinking about the technological inventions we have parked in space that we call satellites reside in this etymology, and these ways of thinking, of seeing, sensing and surveilling the earth-as-globe, preside over us on that globe from geosynchronous orbit.

The incorporation of satellite systems into broadcast media and telecoms technologies helped further blur the boundaries between entertainment, industry and the military during the massive shift toward globalisation during the 1960s. Satellites are integral to the emergence of the 'real-time' technologies that have come to dominate the surveillance regimes permeating contemporary culture, their effects first experienced in living rooms around the world on 25 June 1967 with the first 'live' global transmission. It was called 'Our World', included such stellar figures in the arts as Maria Callas and Pablo Picasso, and required the services of over ten thousand engineers, technicians and performers. The satellites Intelsat 1 (aka 'Early Bird'), Intelsat 2-2 ('Lani Bird'), Intelsat 2-3 ('Canary Bird') and NASA's ATS-1 beamed the benevolent global programming to a receptive global audience.

The UK contribution to the broadcast was the Beatles singing 'All You Need Is Love', a provocative moment given the rapidly escalating proxy war being conducted by US forces in Vietnam at the time. Military technology broadcasting countercultural sentiments into millions of homes could be an ingenious détournement, a moment of accidental seepage, or an especially shrewd instance of counter-intuitive military public relations. Was the broadcast part of the civic sphere and intended for civilian use? What, ultimately, is the status of the civic sphere after the total war of World War II and the globalised containment of the Cold War, in which everyone born since the summer of 1945 entered the world – 'Our World' – with a target on his or her back?[8] Is there a civic sphere any more that is not reducible to GPS-coordinates (another pervasive, satellite-driven system) for phones and drones?

The Endless

If the Cold War at once expanded and contracted space, extending the reach of geopolitics beyond the terrestrial atmosphere and across the poles while collapsing distance between aggressor and target, the same systems and technologies simultaneously brought about a new understanding of temporal scale, a new sensitivity to relative velocities, and new relations between past, present and future. The invention of nuclear weapons simultaneously threatened to kill time by snuffing out much of, if not all, life on earth while opening up the prospect of a posthuman eternity. The impossibility of uninventing weapons of mass destruction also introduced a new mode of dread-infused time: living under the 'shadow of the bomb' made the always-present prospect of instant death charge everyday duration with a new precarity.[9] Living in and for the moment folded, in the West at least, the immediate gratification of consumer capitalism into existentialism's awareness of the abyss.

Further, even as the Soviet Union collapsed, the deep future of nuclear contamination continued to preoccupy governments and activists concerned with the dilemma of managing not only the immediate aftermath of weapons testing (as in Nevada and Utah, for example, or in Kazakhstan), but also the waste products of a technology capable of continuing to destroy life for thousands of years. The material remains of the Cold War are never merely the relics of a forgotten conflict but part of an ongoing struggle for the control and management of its legacies.[10] The often-apocalyptic tenor of high Cold War atomic dread has, in the twenty-first century, found a new, equally amorphous but all-too-real object in climate change. Not only does the anticipation of global environmental catastrophe often take on forms similar to those that once awaited the onset of nuclear winter, but the means of modelling global environmental events themselves derive from the systems analyses developed during the Cold War. Contemporary thinking on environmental matters, as recent scholarship demonstrates, is inseparable from the influence of Cold War policies, planning and modes of conceptualisation.[11] In terms of the scale of the current environmental crisis; its intractability in the face of political and practical efforts; the sense of powerlessness impending environmental collapse produces even as individuals are charged with the imperative to shoulder responsibility for averting it; and the ways in which this emergency has become normalised and, to a large extent, compartmentalised and actively forgotten – in these ways, among others, climate change – along with 'terror' – is the inheritor and intensifier of habits and anxieties learned during the permanent mobilisation of the Cold War.

By 1956, in an influential assessment of the entwined political, economic and military interests running the United States, sociologist C. Wright Mills recognised that the permanent mobilisation of the Cold War had instituted no less than 'a military definition of reality' that subordinated all other ways of life to a 'military metaphysic' (2000: 186). Under such a dispensation, while the worst outcome was nuclear annihilation, the best was not much better. In his 'The Chance for Peace' speech, delivered to the American Society of Newspaper Editors in 1953, President Eisenhower ominously sketched out what this best-case scenario might be like: 'a life of perpetual fear and tension; a burden of arms draining the wealth and the labor of all peoples; a wasting of strength that defies the American system or the Soviet system or any system to achieve true abundance and happiness for the peoples of this earth' (Eisenhower 1953). The tension and fear, the burden of arms, and the wasting of strength continue into the twenty-first century; the dread of all-out nuclear war may have diminished but it has been replaced by a more diffuse sense of permanent emergency. The massive economic, human and environmental costs of military operations continue to undermine the possibility of abundance and happiness for the peoples of the earth. After the proxy wars in Korea and Vietnam, the covert spectacle of President Reagan's anti-communist counter-insurgency police actions in Central America, the US military's post-Soviet reboot in the Persian Gulf, and NATO's 'humanitarian' wars of the 1990s, the global counter-terrorist regime inaugurated after the 2001 attacks on New York and Washington DC did not so much reawaken the military definition of reality Mills wrote of in the 1950s as pull it into focus.

The long Cold War maintains linearity without progress and teleology, especially a teleology found in the story of Cold War arms races. One of the radical aspects of the first Reagan administration was that, in its willingness to revive the possibility that the Cold War was winnable, it hotwired the stalled engine of American (and Western) teleological thinking and military-technological adventurism even as it sought ideological support from a mode of rugged individualism at odds with the corporate liberalism that, since the New Deal, had shaped the technocratic institutions that blossomed during the Cold War. This seeming contradiction – that massive government sponsorship of military R&D supports and drives the corporate technofuturist hive mind even as support for collective endeavour is removed in other areas of economic and social life – continues to structure the neoliberal world order Reagan was so instrumental in enabling.

The president who is now most commonly remembered for 'ending' (or, for some, 'winning') the Cold War might more accurately be seen as the agent of its perpetuation by other means. Certainly, for an intellectual cold warrior like neocon luminary Irving Kristol, the ex-Trotskyist who co-founded, with Stephen Spender, the anti-Stalinist (and, as it turned out, CIA-funded) magazine *Encounter* in 1953, there is no 'after the Cold War'. Writing in 1993, Kristol reflects that, '[s]o far from having ended, my cold war has increased in intensity, as sector after sector of American life has been ruthlessly corrupted' by a 'liberal ethos' driven by collectivism and 'moral anarchy'.[12] Now that 'the other "Cold War" is over, the real cold war has begun', claims Kristol, a war in which Americans are less prepared and more vulnerable than they were against the communist threat. Anticipating the long haul, he writes that this is a conflict 'I shall be passing on to my children and grandchildren' (Kristol 1993: 144). So much, indeed, of post-1991 history has been the bleeding out of Cold War politics and the unfinished business (from World War II, back through the Depression, World War I and beyond) that nearly fifty years of global geopolitical stand-off had staunched. The surge, beginning in the 1970s and cresting during the last years of the twentieth century and into the twenty-first, of popular and academic interest in the past, in memorialisation and remembrance, in testimony, cultural memory, nostalgia and vintage, is also partly a consequence of scepticism toward the systematic, totalised teleology of progress that drove the struggles and destroyed so much during the twentieth century. The neoconservative fantasy of rollback, underpinned by a misremembered lost world of individual self-determination and small government before, in the US, the social engineering of the New Deal, or, in the UK, the 1945 Labour victory, in order to be properly convincing, must also forget the corporate liberalism that organised the war effort, recognised union representation as a core aspect of the modern industrial state, and created the infrastructure and institutions that gave form to the energies that drove Cold War techno-scientific innovation and the long postwar economic boom. Reagan, Kristol and their neoliberal heirs forget only what it is useful to forget. What they do know, though, is that it is possible to make time, and the stories we tell about its passing, forge powerful legacies that seep into the future, contaminating the groundwater, like the culture wars Kristol imagines, enviously, his grandchildren striving to win against the nebulous forces of moral anarchy.

As Joseph Masco has argued, the post-9/11 US security state was

> actually a repetition, modelled in language and tone on the launch of the national security state in 1947. Both projects involved the designation of new insecurities, new institutions to fight them, a public mobilisation campaign grounded in fear, and above all, official claims that a new kind of war [. . .] was a multi-generational commitment, constituting a new mode of everyday life rather than a brief intensity of conflict. (2014: 5)

President George W. Bush's key personnel were veteran cold warriors, of course, but the adversarial stance taken by the administration and its moral legitimacy reached beyond the nostalgia of a few Washington hawks and tapped into a deep fifty-year reservoir of learned behaviour and shared cultural history. When Vice President Dick Cheney called the post-9/11 reality the 'new normal', it was not really that new; indeed, the dread, the suspicion and the costs that come from permanent preparedness had been normal for a long time.

Simulation and System

The nuclear, wrote Jean Baudrillard in *Simulacra and Simulation*, first published in 1981 just as Ronald Reagan was jumpstarting the Cold War after over a decade of détente, 'is the apotheosis of simulation' (1994: 32). Simulation is the *sine qua non* of the Cold War, its power and desirability made possible by the fertile ground established for systems theory by the cultivation of a triadic US research environment. Vannevar Bush, head of military R&D during World War II, convinced the US government after the conflict to maintain its military-industrial-university research infrastructure rather than disband it as had been the case after World War I. It was the interaction of the three sectors, along with the exponential increases in calculation and computing capacities, that enabled the flourishing of the cognitive sciences, information theory, area studies, cybernetics and systems theory, all of which attempted not merely to describe but to predict human behaviour in given situations as well as complex environments in which decisions, human or machinic or biological, were made. Essential to this predictive capacity of science, information and social science research is the model or the simulation that allowed for understanding complex interrelationships between actors, objects, elements, space and time. In this manner, events can be modelled ahead of time, predicted, and therefore, if desired, brought to fruition or terminated. Options within the processes modelled or simulated were provided by gaming, information, cybernetics and systems theory. The political regimes that hold sway over the global order of globalisation processes emerged from Cold War desires for control and containment systems and models. Thus they rely heavily on simulation to configure and identify a virtual future yet to be actualised and perhaps in need of being prevented from realisation. Thus the political, by operating these simulations, curtailed dramatically its purview just when its overall reach expanded to all parts of the globe.

Simulation itself came to define the vast majority of university-based research in the Cold War, with the lion's share driven by the defence-spending nexus that Vannevar Bush established. Defence-driven research on simulation was conducted in labs based in US universities (MIT, in the initial instance) and the private sector (IBM and American Airlines). The first simulated environments created at MIT were designed almost simultaneously for defence and business: SAGE (Semi-Automated Ground Environment) and SABRE (Semi-Automated Business Research Environment). SAGE emerged out of the earlier (1950) Electronic Air Defense Environment and essentially ran NORAD (North American Aerospace Command) from the 1950s through to the 1980s. With SAGE, operators of weapons tracking and aiming devices could use a 'light gun' to identify objects that appeared on their screens, allowing weapons to be directed according to the operators' understanding of the environment as displayed on their screens and not within their empirical fields of vision. The simulation of the airspace environment, provided by a unified and simulated image of this environment, under the operators' jurisdiction meant air defence could be conducted in a tele-, or at-a-distance, manner from a desk, not out in the field. The simulated environment relied heavily on systems design elements for its operation, including levels of interaction between open and closed systems to track potential incoming threats and targets, and to designate appropriate defence responses.

With the knowledge garnered from SAGE, MIT almost immediately started SABRE, a system designed by IBM for American Airlines to link thousands of reservations clerks throughout the country in a shared system of online transaction processing. The simulated environment made it possible for data, information and purchases to be exchanged in real time as if all the reservations clerks had congregated in the same room. That the first two simulated environments were military and corporate respectively indicates the priorities and values of the nation-state at that moment, priorities and values that continue into the present, ones that resulted in the ultimate goal being to weaponise or monetise all endeavours. The power of simulation to affect and control other spaces grew to be an integral part of the Cold War world, especially when war games were actuated allowing military planners to work through a variety of nuclear warfare scenarios while keeping the Cold War cold – or so they hoped and believed. The long-term, long-range, unforeseen effects of simulation in all areas of existence have manifested themselves as one of the primary legacies of the epistemological power of systems theory.

In the present, macroscopic platforms for planetary computing operate with and through remote sensing systems that gather together real-time data and generate specific views of the earth for specific stakeholders through models and simulations as their default modes of governance. Ryan Bishop's contribution to this volume discusses this confluence of events, technologies, systems and actors that outstrip agency in the name of agency and control. A system such as the Planetary Skin Institute, initiated by NASA and Cisco Systems, operates under the aegis of providing a multi-constituent platform for planetary eco-surveillance. It was originally designed to offer a real-time open network of simulated global ecological concerns, especially treaty verification, weather crises, carbon stocks and flows, risk identification and scenario planning and modelling for academia and corporate and government actors (thus replicating Vannevar Bush's post-World War II triumvirate of US triumphalist infrastructure).

The Planetary Skin Institute now operates as an independent non-profit global R&D organisation with its stated goal being dedication to 'improving the lives of millions of people by developing risk and resource management decision services to address the growing challenges of resource scarcity, the land-water-food-energy-climate nexus and the increasing impact and frequency of weather extremes'. The Institute therefore claims to provide a 'platform to serve as a global public good', thus articulating a position and agenda as altruistic as can possibly be imagined. The Planetary Skin Institute works with 'research and development partners across multiple sectors regionally and globally to identify, conceptualise, and incubate replicable and scalable big data and associated innovations, that could significantly increase the resilience of low-income communities, increase food, water, and energy security and protect key ecosystems and biodiversity' (Planetary Skin Institute: online). In spite of its altruistic stance, it is worth noting the potential for resource futures investment that could accompany such data and information. The Planetary Skin Institute's system echoes what a number of other polyscalar remote automated sensing systems provide in terms of real-time, tele-tracking occurrences in many parts of the globe, as well as beyond, and reveals a complex interactive simulation of strategically targeted systems of biological, eco-global actors across species of flora and fauna, as well as geological, meteorological and machinic-sensing agents.

Systems Culture

The current preoccupation with research-based practice in numerous areas of the contemporary arts, represented here variously by Aura Satz, Ele Carpenter and Neal White, is in many instances bound up with politically motivated investigations into advanced technological systems.[13] Artists are engaging in collaborative projects with technologists and scientists to an extent not seen since the great wave of university- and corporate-funded art and science research of the 1960s and 1970s. The resurgence of interest in Cold War-era systems-based art is not exactly surprising: this was a period of rapid innovation in computer and information art as well as in information technologies in general. The 1960s and 1970s was also, of course, the period of the Civil Rights Movement and the war in Vietnam; of increasingly violent state suppression of dissent and ramped-up surveillance of civilians. By the time of President Nixon's resignation in 1974, cynicism, corruption and paranoia were apparently the dominant characteristics of high office. In short, accelerating techno-utopian innovation emerged and operated within an ethically compromised, heavily militarised and flagrantly hypocritical political regime. Survey exhibits like Tate Modern's *Open Systems: Rethinking Art c.1970* (2005) and renewed attention to the work of artist-theorists like Jack Burnham (see Burnham 2015) mark a growing awareness of, and to some extent an identification with, the complex encounters between military-technological research and political aesthetics of the Cold War era.

György Kepes taught at the New Bauhaus in Chicago before moving to MIT in 1946, where he founded, in 1967, the Center for Advanced Visual Studies (CAVS). Drawing on the practical utopianism of his Bauhaus background, Kepes understood CAVS as a space that could effectively integrate scientific and artistic inquiry. His proposal for the Center forthrightly, and with the techno-modernist grandeur of the day, claimed that 'Making a place for the visual arts in a scientific university is imperative for a reunification of Man's outlook on life' (Kepes quoted in Ragain 2012). Such a reunification was not without problems, however, when the Pentagon was underwriting MIT research into computing, surveillance and advanced weapons systems to the tune of millions of dollars a year. CAVS was, in a sense, an attempt by MIT to soften its image during a period of increasingly vocal anti-war protests from students, staff and the wider public. The collaborative and interdisciplinary nature of the work undertaken by artists at CAVS undoubtedly served to deepen artistic research in new technologies, but the crossover nonetheless exposed artists to the ethical challenge of entering the military-industrial avant-garde: Burnham, for example, the pioneer of systems-based art and a research fellow at CAVS in 1968–69, was able to conduct his research using the state-of-the-art time-sharing computer system at the Lincoln Laboratory, the federally funded R&D centre for high-tech defence systems.

A number of influential exhibitions in the late 1960s and early 1970s showcased systems- or information-based art. Jasia Reichardt's show of computer-based art *Cybernetic Serendipity* was held at the Institute of Contemporary Art in London in 1968 before travelling to Washington DC. Kepes's *Explorations* show, originally intended for the American pavilion at the 1969 São Paulo Bienal before nine of the artists involved (including Burnham, Hans Haacke and Robert Smithson) withdrew in protest against Brazil's military regime, opened in February 1970 at the National Collection of Fine Arts, Smithsonian Institution. Kynaston McShine's *Information* at MoMA in New York opened in July 1970 and ran through to 20 September. Four days before *Information* closed, *Software – Information Technology: Its New Meaning for Art*, curated by Jack Burnham, opened at the Jewish Museum, also in New York. The controversy over the first iteration of *Explorations* indicates how the political contradiction of institutionally funded art research threatened to undermine the entire project. In a letter to Kepes, Smithson, for example, hacked into the ethos of collaboration at CAVS: ' "The team spirit" of the exhibition could be seen as endorsement of NASA Operations Control Room with all its crew-cut teamwork,' wrote Smithson. 'If one wants teamwork he should join the army. A panel called "What's Wrong with Technological Art?" might help' (Smithson 1996: 36).

Smithson's generation had found in cybernetics, systems, game and information theories a potentially powerful means of extracting themselves from the expressive formalism that had become the official culture of Cold War American art.[14] These models, along with the rising influence in the humanities of structuralism, provided the coordinates for a relational, collaborative, experimental, investigative and rigorous practice that might distance itself from the celebrity circuit of the luxury goods factory the art world had already become.[15] The promise of a working practice based on scientific investigation, however, did not take into account that the disinterested scientist might enjoy that freedom from the market because the Department of Defense (DoD) bankrolled the research. Bell Laboratories, for instance, where engineer Billy Klüver founded Experiments in Art and Technology (E.A.T.) in 1967 and worked with, among others, Jean Tinguely, Robert Rauschenberg, Merce Cunningham and Andy Warhol, was at the heart of satellite, laser and computing research much in demand with the DoD and NASA.

Less overtly challenged by their proximity to the dark star of military-industrial funding but no less cognisant of the perils of complicity than many artists involved in information-based work, a generation of American writers who came of age during the early Cold War years also saw in systems theory a means of cracking open the institutionalised carapace of 'serious' literature. Just as Greenbergian modernism had hardened into orthodoxy by the 1950s, so too had literary modernism been stripped of its radical thorns by the depoliticised, professionalised formalism of the so-called New Criticism.[16] Long, complex narrative fiction shot through with esoteric jargon and modelled on abstruse scientific or computational principles; novels obsessed with networks of corporate and military power, secret knowledge and occult forces; narratives less interested in character and plot than in patterns, permutations, subliminal signals and feedback loops – the work of writers like Thomas

Pynchon, William Gaddis and John Barth spoke to the largest, most highly educated generation of young (affluent white male) Americans ever assembled on college campuses deeply embedded in Cold War R&D.[17] The sway of these systems novelists remains active in the present for a generation of authors discerning a literary inheritance and positioning their work within the battles over novelistic and extra-literary legacies from the Cold War, as Dan Grausam's chapter in this volume evocatively works through. That a twenty-first-century novel such as James Flint's *The Book of Ash* should provide an intertextual set of conversations and engagements with works by Pynchon should come as no real surprise, given Pynchon's iconic status, but the turn to the form of the paranoid systems novel as a means of addressing the present confirms the continuing relevance of the earlier novelists' scale of ambition in attempting to grasp, however incompletely, the pervasive structure of complex systems that reach from the personal to the geopolitical. Grausam argues that Flint's tribute to – as well as his distance from – Pynchon's influences signals the continued import of Cold War literary influences into the present, as both a repressed legacy and an omnipresent underpinning of contemporary existence, something also articulated by the important and influential works of Don DeLillo, David Foster Wallace and Richard Powers.[18] Much as Adam Piette's chapter speaks to the entombed human intervention into geological time, Grausam's contribution traces the sustained deep time of literary production that engages the North American land mass and the immaterial structures and systems that govern it as an ineluctably radiated complex.

Not only was literary production affected directly by systems theory and Cold War *techne*, but so was literary theory, a situation codified by the famous *Diacritics* issue of summer 1984. Entitled 'Nuclear Criticism', the brief introduction to the issue expresses a common humanities anxiety about a lack of critical contribution to the public discursive sphere emanating from literary studies while also acknowledging the silent ubiquity of nuclear influence on all aspects of life. The introduction cautions against the easy embrace of teleological and eschatological thinking operative in public culture and questions the value of it while suggesting that all forms of nuclear discourse (policy, public, entertainment, academic) adhere to rhetorical strategies in need of critical engagement. Thus the editors make the case for a unique role to be played by critical theory scholars at a unique moment, one not unlike the somewhat face-value emergence of social science expertise in the early days of the Cold War but this time with a self-reflexive awareness garnered over the decades of failed social science certainty pertaining to the prediction and control of human behaviour. Such a line of critical inquiry returns us to the lines from Auden's epic *The Age of Anxiety* (1947), when he writes, 'Do I love the world so well / that I have to know how it ends?'

An important contribution to the *Diacritics* volume was Jacques Derrida's 'No Apocalypse, Not Now', which provocatively linked 'missives' and 'missiles' as discursive objects launched into the world. With a lead-in alluding to Virilio, Derrida places 'speed' and its effects on thought and action as truly indicative of Cold War knowledge formation and policy-generated aporias surrounding the notion of 'first use'. Derrida traces the apocalypse of nuclear weapons to that of religious revelation within monotheistic religious traditions and hermeneutics to underscore how the promise of the latter is elided by the potentialities of the technologically generated former kind of apocalypse: annihilation without revelation.

Although the structural synchronic links made by Masco and others between the paranoid adversarial logic of the Cold War and that found in the War on Terror are perhaps the clearest indication of the contemporary extensions of Cold War political, military and technological power structures, the purpose of this book, while acknowledging those links, is to interrogate the contemporary moment as it has been shaped by other, less apparent, Cold War continuations. We aim to identify the ways in which the algorithms, technologies, materials, concepts and cultural forms of the twenty-first century are underpinned by the procedures, practices, inventions and ideological positions of the permanent emergency of the Cold War. These provide the conditions of possibility that foster the current state of philosophical and theoretical inquiry, as well as geopolitical planning, policy and actions. The essays gathered here represent a growing awareness within critical theory, across a range of fields in the arts, humanities and social sciences, of the centrality of the Cold War to an understanding of contemporary issues surrounding, for example, knowledge formation and circulation, communications, data theory, security and surveillance, the management of the nuclear industry, risk assessment (corporate, environmental, social), and the role of art and culture within global neoliberal capitalism. To this end we have assembled a wide range of views from scholars and practitioners whose work probes the philosophical, material and conceptual structures constituted by systems that link the contemporary to the Cold War.

Alan Nadel's influential account of US Cold War 'containment culture' argues that it is through 'the power of large cultural narratives to unify, codify, and contain' (Nadel 1995: 4) that US military-industrial dominance was able to normalise and globalise Cold War strategy. Understood this way, culture is not merely a reflection of history; it is the material out of which history is made and provides the forms through which history is understood. With this in mind, the essays here include not only scholarly investigations of theories, strategies, concepts and texts, but also critical discussions with artists engaged in shaping the forms of contemporary culture. Here we recognise the power of large cultural narratives, not just to unify, codify and contain, but to challenge, expose and create alternatives to what might otherwise be an all-too-pervasive continuation of Cold War cultures of precarity and imperilment.

The end of the Cold War did not end systems thinking; indeed, given the phenomenal expansion of computer technologies into every aspect of contemporary life, it is fair to say that we are now living in a world imagined and engineered during the Cold War. The necessary production of enemies; the collapse of the distinction between civilian and soldier; the dependence of the economy on military spending; the foreclosure of the future by nuclear dread; the military origins of the internet – the broad contours of how the Cold War shaped the present are familiar enough. The pervasiveness of the deep structures of Cold War thought and practice in contemporary life, however, remains to be fully articulated, not least at the intersection of culture and politics.

The Bomb: An Impossible Coda

> The Bomb has become one of those categories of Being, like Space and Time, that [. . .] are built into the very structure of our minds giving shape and meaning to all perception [. . .] [a] history of 'nuclear' thought and culture [might be] indistinguishable from a history of all contemporary thought and culture.
>
> Paul Boyer (1985: xviii)

> Under glass: glass dishes which changed
> in color; pieces of transformed beer bottles;
> a household iron; bundles of wire become solid
> lumps of iron; a pair of pliers; a ring of skull-
> bone fused to the inside of a helmet; a pair of eyeglasses
> taken off the eyes of an eyewitness, without glass
> which vanished, when a white flash sparked.
>
> Galway Kinnell, 'The Fundamental Project of Technology' (1985: 48)

The atomic bomb as an object of unparalleled influence and effect – especially on Western thought and culture, but also equally for the world rendered and remade as globe – has been explored productively and provocatively by Peter Sloterdijk in the *Critique of Cynical Reason* (1988 [1983]). In a whimsical but useful moment, Sloterdijk calls the bomb the only Buddha that Western thought and reason can understand – that by its very presence, it has changed everything, whether it sits silently in its silo or erupts in full fiery conflagration. Whether it does either matters not one whit to it. It is the object that has wrested subjectivity fully from the subject, making of us, a mass with a bull's eye on our collective foreheads, a target. It has mediated our position in the universe and given us an object of collective annihilation hitherto the exclusive domain of nature or the gods. It is the supreme object of mediation and meditation: deeply paradoxical at all levels. The bomb makes us almost omnipotently powerful while simultaneously rendering us weaker and more vulnerable than we have ever been. Built for defence, it makes us completely defenceless. As a weapon, it has been used twice in anger but can now never be used again (hence our Baudrillardian state of simulated war). As a geopolitical tool, it is the trump card we can never play. It is potential incarnate, a potential for which we have built a massive tele-technological opto-electronic environment to ensure its potential is only ever potential and never realised. In its face, all logic, reason and rationality fail, replaced by impoverished and ludicrous cousins who parade under these names.

The bomb as medium and object that mediates remains a mysterious set of forces not yet adequately addressed but always obliquely present, perhaps now more than ever. The vast majority of the hardware and software that have broadcast and virtualised the object as real-time phenomenon result from Cold War R&D efforts linking university, military, corporate and entertainment industries. All IT and all media in the twenty-first century bear the mark of this complex of concerted Cold War efforts, now (or at least recently) retooled and remobilised in a Manichean war of good versus evil that makes the Cold War seem almost dialectical in comparison.

An early, prescient media object of the Cold War explored in evocative detail reveals some of the ways in which the bomb mediates all objects that appear in its shadow: this is, the cinematic collaboration between Alain Resnais and Marguerite Duras on *Hiroshima Mon Amour* (1959). The bomb as absent object fills the entire film. It is the reason for the film but is never present. The film's opening sequence lays bare the complete wreckage of subject-object relations that Baudrillard returns to only a few years later. In this famous sequence, we hear the French female and the Japanese male who has become her lover discussing what she has supposedly seen in Hiroshima. We do not see either person's face, only hear their disembodied voices, as in some play by Beckett. She asserts time and again that she has seen everything in Hiroshima: the hospital, the museum – the exhibits, the photos, the reconstructions ('for want of anything else'), 'the burned iron, the iron made as vulnerable as flesh' – the survivors, the tourists, Peace Square, the twisted Palace of Industry: everything meant to represent the bomb, its explosion, its destruction, the wounded and charred bodies and objects.

With each assertion of each object she claims to have seen, she is rebutted by her Japanese lover who says she has seen nothing. There is nothing to see, no object to study that will tell her or anyone about the city, the bomb, the explosion. A pair of bodies (perhaps theirs, perhaps not), barely glimpsed at the very start of the film covered in shiny ash ('deposited by the atomic "mushroom"'), have similarly been dematerialised, rendered object-less by the bomb that has brought them (as it has all of us) together on completely new terms. These bodies are like the most famous victim of Hiroshima: the famous photograph of the absence of a body, that most famous (non)body that constitutes a white shadow permanently embedded in the stone of a bridge, the person vaporised by the explosion and now forever part of the pores in the stone. This is the media image, the media object of the twentieth century that contains all media objects from then on.

The object that is the body is now more vulnerable than ever, as vulnerable as iron. The city is too. The object that is the city – especially Hiroshima – has itself been transformed wholly from the outside, represented globally, through an atomic lens. It has lost its inside, just as the self has lost its subject status, its subjectivity. The female protagonist is an actress, present in Hiroshima to make a film. When the man asks what the film is about, she replies, 'Peace, of course.' What other kind of film would be made by an international cast and crew in Hiroshima than one about peace? Hiroshima, the city-as-object, has been mediated by cinema both within the diegetic realm and outside of it, collapsing the two, just as it has been mediated by globalisation and global representation, just as it has been mediated by the bomb. It is another screen connected to networks with flows of information.

The bomb is the trickster object without compare, the 'evil genie of the object' that Baudrillard discusses in *Fatal Strategies* (first published in 1983): 'Anything that was once constituted as an object by a subject', he writes, 'represents for the latter a virtual death threat' (1990: 95). Once the genie is out, evil or not, there is no return to the bottle. There is no reversibility of time available here, only repetition – only now and from now on it is the 'real time' of global electronic surveillance. The bomb represents the most fully excessive object yet, one in which we as subjects are fully consumed and consummated. It has no instrumental function, no means to an end, for it is all only end: the end to end all ends. The object of the latter half of the twentieth century as constituted by the media may have been the consumer commodity, but was only ever the commodity that the bomb allowed it to be, created it to be: a commodity intractable, unassimilable, fatal. Even then, and more so now, the object is nuclearised, atomically mediated and mediating. It thinks us, removes our subjectivity from us, silences us, and vaporises us.

The bomb turns cities to dust, and sand and dust to glass, but without utopian or even progressive transparency. The new categories of urban metabolism will have been determined largely by this world-object that has helped make the world a strategically bounded globe and no longer a potentially explorable world. The future perfect tense provides us with delusions about determining and fixing the future perfectly even with and through indeterminate objects. Perhaps the drive for reification that so underpins Western thought has to do with the drive for determinacy, and yet the polyvalence of indeterminate objects and their ungovernable protean properties might teach us other lessons about things, objects, processes and taxonomies, lessons such as the failure of success in realising the bomb.

Notes

1. Another recent espionage show also set in the early 1980s, *Deutschland 83* (2015), a co-production between the German TV station RTL Television and SundanceTV, approaches the Cold War from the point of view of a young East German soldier sent into the West as a Stasi spy. *Deutschland 83* is the first German-language series to air on a US network.
2. On the Cold War and the social sciences, see Solovey and Cravens 2012, Rohde 2013, Cohen-Cole 2014, Reisch 2005 and Dunne 2013.
3. On the UK side, the national academic auditing exercise known as the REF (Research Excellence Framework) includes a worrying Cold War-inflected category, first introduced in 2014: 'Impact'. To evaluate the efficacy of Impact (a measure of university research outside the university sector), the Higher Education Funding Council for England went to the source of university-corporate-military research and hired the RAND Corporation. Thus the think tank that made it possible to 'think the unthinkable' through the deceptive numerical nomenclature of 'megadeath' provided the reports. Assessing the public impact of research could not be in more qualified hands.

4. For recent scholarship on the global Cold War, see, for example, Westad 2005, Cullather 2010, Hecht 2011, Hong 2015, and Pieper Mooney and Lanza 2012.
5. The Cold War's radical transformation of global space is addressed in Farish 2010.
6. It is worth noting that the journal is now called *The Journal for Geoscience and Remote Sensing*.
7. Steely Dan singer Donald Fagen satirises the techno-utopian boosterism of the International Geophysical Year in the song 'I.G.Y.' on the 1982 solo album *The Nightfly*, and Stanley Kubrick uses the space treaty as a subtext for the lunar stand-off in *2001: A Space Odyssey*.
8. See Bishop and Clancey 2003: 67: 'As nodes in the global, ideological grid of surveillance and intercontinental ballistic missile targeting, each global city was potentially *every other* global city. A nuclear attack of one (which implied direct attack of more because of Mutually Assured Destruction policies) meant radiation fallout and environmental devastation for all others. Global cities became, and remain, global insofar as they are targets for attack. It is their status as targets that renders them, *de facto*, "global".'
9. The sense that such fears were more than paranoid scaremongering is given a thorough hearing in Schlosser 2013, which catalogues the many near-accidents, gaffes and fumbles that, throughout the Cold War, threatened to destroy the fragile stalemate.
10. Notable discussions of Cold War sites include Vanderbilt 2002 and Hodge and Weinberger 2009. Wiener 2012 examines the various museums and monuments to the Cold War in the US. In the UK, English Heritage supported a major project investigating the remains of Cold War buildings. See Cocroft and Thomas 2003 and Cocroft and Schofield 2007. For a global consideration of Cold War commemoration and memorialisation, see Lowe and Joel 2014.
11. On the relationship between the Cold War and environmental thinking, see, for example, McNeill and Unger 2010, Hamblin 2013 and Nixon 2011.
12. It is here, in the neoconservative contempt for liberalism's moral dissipation, that the TV show *The Americans* taps into a rich seam of resentment that does indeed, perhaps, unite the fictional Soviet spies and youthful Trotskyist proto-neocons like Kristol and his City College peers such as Daniel Bell, Nathan Glaser and Seymour Martin Lipset. It is not America as such that the agents despise – it is the liberal America of the late 1970s that Reagan, did they but know it, would attempt to straighten out. It is as nascent neoconservatives that the spies in *The Americans* make most sense.
13. See, for example, the Forensic Architecture project led by Eyal Weizman at Goldsmith's College, University of London, Laura Kurgan's work at the Spatial Information Design Lab at Columbia University, or Trevor Paglen's various engagements with the US security state.

14. For the standard account of American art's absorption into postwar ideology, see Guilbart 1983; on the role of the CIA in covertly funding the cultural Cold War as an attempt to address 'the culture gap' with the Soviet Union, see Saunders 2001.
15. The influence of structuralism in the 1960s art world is discussed in Meltzer 2013.
16. Terry Eagleton's assessment of the politics of the New Criticism is clear enough: 'New Criticism's view of the poem as a delicate equipoise of contending attitudes, a disinterested reconciliation of opposing impulses, proved deeply attractive to sceptical liberal intellectuals disoriented by the clashing dogmas of the Cold War. It drove you less to oppose McCarthyism or further civil rights than to experience such pressures as merely partial. It was, in other words, a recipe for political inertia' (1996: 43). See also Richard Ohmann's contribution to the collection *The Cold War and the University* in which he discusses the advent of New Criticism as an apolitical means of teaching literature insofar as it only examined the text on its own terms (Chomsky et al. 1998).
17. Tom LeClair (1988, 1989) is responsible for naming these, and other writers such as Joseph McElroy and Robert Coover, systems novelists.
18. See the 2008 special issue of *Cultural Politics* entitled 'Nuclear Stories: Cold War Literatures' (4.3), edited by Tim Armstrong, for an extended engagement with many of these issues.

References

Baudrillard, Jean (1990 [1983]), *Fatal Strategies*, trans. Philippe Beitchman and W. G. J. Niesluchowski, New York: Semiotext(e).

Baudrillard, Jean (1994 [1981]), *Simulacra and Simulation*, trans. Sheila Glaser, Ann Arbor: University of Michigan Press.

Bishop, Ryan, and Greg Clancey (2003), 'The-City-as-Target, or Perpetuation and Death', in Stephen Graham (ed.), *Cities, War, and Terrorism: Towards an Urban Geopolitics*, Oxford: Blackwell, pp. 54–74.

Boyer, Paul (1985), *By the Bomb's Early Light: American Thought and Culture at the Dawn of the Atomic Age*, New York: Pantheon.

Burnham, Jack (2015), *Dissolve into Comprehension: Writings and Interviews, 1964–2004*, ed. Melissa Ragain, Cambridge, MA: MIT Press.

Chomsky, Noam, Ira Katznelson, R. C. Lewontin, David Montgomery, Laura Nader, Richard Ohmann, Ray Siever, Immanuel Wallerstein and Howard Zinn (1998), *The Cold War and the University: Toward an Intellectual History of the Postwar Years*, New York: The New Press.

Cocroft, Wayne, and John Schofield (eds) (2007), *A Fearsome Heritage: Diverse Legacies of the Cold War*, Walnut Creek, CA: Left Coast Press.

Cocroft, Wayne D., and Roger J. C. Thomas (2003), *Cold War: Building for Nuclear Confrontation 1946–89*, Swindon: English Heritage.

Cohen-Cole, Jamie (2014), *The Open Mind: Cold War Politics and the Sciences of Human Nature*, Chicago: University of Chicago Press.

Cullather, Nick (2010), *The Hungry World: America's Cold War Battle against Poverty in Asia*, Cambridge, MA: Harvard University Press.

Derrida, Jacques (1984), 'No Apocalypse, Not Now (full speed ahead, seven missiles, seven missives)', *Diacritics* 14(2): 20–31.

Dunne, Matthew W. (2013), *A Cold War State of Mind: Brainwashing and Postwar American Society*, Amherst: University of Massachusetts Press.

Eagleton, Terry (1996), *Literary Theory: An Introduction*, 2nd edn, Oxford: Blackwell.

Eisenhower, Dwight D. (1953), 'The Chance for Peace', *Social Justice Speeches*, <http://www.edchange.org/multicultural/speeches/ike_chance_for_peace.html> (last accessed 22 January 2016).

Farish, Matthew (2010), *The Contours of America's Cold War*, Minneapolis: University of Minnesota Press.

Guilbart, Serge (1983), *How New York Stole the Idea of Modern Art: Abstract Expressionism, Freedom, and the Cold War*, trans. Arthur Goldhammer, Chicago: University of Chicago Press.

Hamblin, Jacob Darwin (2013), *Arming Mother Nature: The Birth of Catastrophic Environmentalism*, Oxford: Oxford University Press.

Hecht, Gabrielle (ed.) (2011), *Entangled Geographies: Empire and Technopolitics in the Global Cold War*, Cambridge, MA: MIT Press.

Hodge, Nathan, and Sharon Weinberger (2009), *A Nuclear Family Vacation: Travels in the World of Atomic Weaponry*, London: Bloomsbury.

Hong, Young-Sun (2015), *Cold War Germany, the Third World, and the Global Humanitarian Regime*, Cambridge: Cambridge University Press.

Kinnell, Galway (1985), *The Past*, Boston: Houghton Mifflin.

Kristol, Irving (1993), 'My Cold War', *The National Interest* 31, Special Issue: The Strange Death of Soviet Communism: An Autopsy (Spring): 141–4.

LeClair, Tom (1988), *In the Loop: Don DeLillo and the Systems Novel*, Champaign: University of Illinois Press.

LeClair, Tom (1989), *The Art of Excess: Mastery in Contemporary American Fiction*, Champaign: University of Illinois Press.

Lowe, David, and Tony Joel (2014), *Remembering the Cold War: Global Contest and National Stories*, London: Routledge.

McLuhan, Marshall (1974), 'Introduction', in Wilson Bryan Key, *Subliminal Seduction: Are You Being Sexually Aroused by This Picture?* (aka 'Ad Media's Manipulation of a Not So Innocent America'), New York: Prentice-Hall, pp. i–xvii.

McNeill, J. R., and Corinna R. Unger (eds) (2010), *Environmental Histories of the Cold War*, Cambridge: Cambridge University Press.

Masco, Joseph (2014), *The Theater of Operations: National Security Affect from the Cold War to the War on Terror*, Durham, NC: Duke University Press.

Meltzer, Eva (2013), *Systems We Have Loved: Conceptual Art, Affect, and the Antihumanist Turn*, Chicago: University of Chicago Press.

Mills, C. Wright (2000 [1956]), *The Power Elite*, Oxford: Oxford University Press.

Nadel, Alan (1995), *Containment Culture: American Narratives, Postmodernism, and the Atomic Age*, Durham, NC: Duke University Press.

Nixon, Rob (2011), *Slow Violence and the Environmentalism of the Poor*, Cambridge, MA: Harvard University Press.

Parikka, Jussi (2010), *Insect Media: An Archaeology of Animals and Technology*, Minneapolis: University of Minnesota Press.

Pieper Mooney, Jadwiga E., and Fabio Lanza (eds) (2012), *De-Centering Cold War History: Local and Global Change*, London: Routledge.

Planetary Skin Institute, <http://www.planetaryskin.org> (last accessed 22 January 2016).

Ragain, Melissa (2012), 'From Organization to Network: MIT's Center for Advanced Visual Studies', *X-TRA Contemporary Art Quarterly* 14(3) (Spring), <http://x-traonline.org/article/from-organization-to-network-mits-center-for-advanced-visual-studies/> (last accessed 22 January 2016).

Reisch, George A. (2005), *How the Cold War Transformed Philosophy of Science: To the Icy Slopes of Logic*, Cambridge: Cambridge University Press.

Rohde, Joy (2013), *Armed with Expertise: The Militarization of American Social Research during the Cold War*, Ithaca, NY: Cornell University Press, 2013.

Saunders, Frances Stonor (2001), *The Cultural Cold War: The CIA and the World of Arts and Letters*, New York: The New Press.

Schlosser, Eric (2013), *Command and Control: Nuclear Weapons, the Damascus Accident, and the Illusion of Safety*, New York: Penguin.

Shannon, Claude E. (1948), 'A Mathematical Theory of Communication', *Bell System Technical Journal* 27: 379–423, 623–56.

Shannon, Claude E., and Warren Weaver (1949), *The Mathematical Theory of Communication*, Urbana: University of Illinois Press.

Sloterdijk, Peter (1988 [1983]), *Critique of Cynical Reason*, trans. Michael Eldred, Minneapolis: University of Minnesota Press.

Smithson, Robert (1996), 'Letter to György Kepes (1969)', in *Robert Smithson: The Collected Writings*, ed. Jack Flam, Berkeley: University of California Press, p. 36.

Solovey, Mark, and Hamilton Cravens (eds) (2012), *Cold War Social Science: Knowledge Production, Liberal Democracy, and Human Nature*, London: Palgrave Macmillan.

Spivak, Gayatri Chakravorty (2003), *Death of a Discipline*, New York: Columbia University Press.

Vanderbilt, Tom (2002), *Survival City: Adventures among the Ruins of Atomic America*, Princeton: Princeton Architectural Press.

von Bertalanffy, Ludwig (1950a), 'The Theory of Open Systems in Physics and Biology', *Science* 111: 23–9.

von Bertalanffy, Ludwig (1950b), 'An Outline of General System Theory (The World View of Biology)', *The British Journal for the Philosophy of Science* 1: 134–65.

von Bertalanffy, Ludwig (1968), *General System Theory – Foundations, Development, Applications*, New York: Braziller.

von Neumann, John, and Oskar Morgenstern (1944), *Theory of Games and Economic Behavior*, Princeton: Princeton University Press.

Westad, Odd Arne (2005), *The Global Cold War: Third World Interventions and the Making of Our Times*, Cambridge: Cambridge University Press.

Wiener, Jon (2012), *How We Forgot the Cold War: A Historical Journey across America*, Berkeley: University of California Press.

Wiener, Norbert (1948), *Cybernetics or Control and Communication in the Animal and the Machine*, Cambridge, MA: MIT Press.

1 Pattern Recognition

Chapter 1

The Future: RAND, Brand and Dangerous to Know

John Beck

> The absolute novelties now coming into play in every order of things – for all things are now in some way dependent upon industry, which follows science as the shark its pilotfish – must inevitably result in a strange transformation of our notion of the future [which] is endowed with *essential unpredictability*, and this is the only prediction we can make.
>
> Paul Valéry (1962 [1944]: 69, 71)

The future used to be fate, meaning that the 'not yet' is a fact of the time to come that is inaccessible to human beings (though not for want of trying) but known to the gods. Modernity's demolition job on fate repositioned the future as something produced by human action, something shaped and defined in the present. Once the future is considered as something made rather than something given, it can become an opportunity, making room for the possibility of the ascending temporal arc of progress. The notion of futurity is a crucial aspect of the ideology of progressive modernity, rooted in a commitment to the accumulation of information and the acquisition of knowledge, and to the economic and social transformations made possible by scientific and technological innovation and discovery. As change accelerates, however, uncertainty tends to increase since the temporal gap between a knowable present and an unknowable future continues to shrink. While the rate of change remains moderate and there is enough data from the past, future outcomes can be calculated probabilistically. But when the future is no longer a continuation of the past, and as change multiplies, the accumulation of past information is no longer helpful. Cut adrift from precedent, the horizon of the future gets closer, no longer a space of empty potentiality but rapidly filling up with the unresolved problems of the present. As the space of anticipation contracts, the chance of being able to think beyond the increasingly shorter term becomes ever more difficult.

The invention of nuclear weapons made a decisive cut into time. More precisely, weapons of mass destruction, especially once they were powerful and plentiful enough to guarantee the destruction of life on earth if even a fraction of their number was ever to be used, contracted and stretched the future at the same time. An automated missile launch could bring the world to an end in an instant, radically stopping time, but the uncertainty as to when that instant might come prolonged the seeming inevitability of its occurrence for an indeterminate amount of time. Just as the discovery of fossils recalibrated the measurement of Earth's past, revealing the planet to be older, and human life less significant, than had once been thought, so too did nuclear weapons deepen an understanding of futurity precisely by foreclosing on its inevitability. The post-nuclear-war future might indeed be long, but humanity would remain only as dinosaur bones compressed by the rubble of the present.

The Cold War, then, inaugurates a new mode of thinking about the future, both as an existential limit point that could be radically compressed into the present, and as a challenge. The nature of the challenge was precisely to forestall nuclear catastrophe by attempting to calculate if and when a deadly strike might occur and what, if any, the response might be. The cold aspect of the Cold War in large part refers to the temporal freeze instantiated by the threat of mutually assured destruction, an ice age of geopolitical paralysis even as techno-modernity goes into developmental overdrive. Forecasting and what has become known as futurology or futures research were born out of this contradiction in an attempt to deploy scientific rationality, in a sense, against itself: the methods used to invent the end of the world were to be used to calculate ways to save it.

While the particular challenges of the Cold War have dissipated, forecasting and futures research have developed into a core industry, underpinning business and finance, government and policy in all areas of life. The markets, of course, are driven by speculation on the future; so is climate policy. As computational power expands, so does the reach of futures research, where big data promises to deliver increasingly fine-grained simulations of all manner of possible outcomes. Futures research is still preoccupied with catastrophe, though the most likely threats are now financial and climatic, yet there is a real sense, as with Cold War deterrence policy, that modelling the future feeds directly into the dangerous idea of the present as the pivot of history. Market jitters generate turbulence that confirms the jitters; global-warming scenarios demand immediate action. The present is never a period of repose during which future prospects can be coolly rehearsed. Instead, as in Cold War thinking, future-oriented reflection often taps into, and perpetuates, a toxic combination of anticipatory inertia and hysterical urgency. The kind of future the Cold War invented was a future that shapes its own past (that is, the present). This is as it must be, since the form of all forecasts is shaped in the here-and-now and by the limits of our calculations. Yet it may well be that the most deadly future out there is not the one on the horizon but the one we forecast, since this is the future we live with now.

RAND and After

In the US, the study of the future began at the RAND Corporation, the independent think tank set up in 1948 to undertake research and development (R-AN-D) for the military. Much of the work conducted at RAND during the Cold War, led by its chief strategist Herman Kahn, focused on what Kahn famously called 'thinking about the unthinkable' (1962). The unthinkable here not only refers to calculating the massive death toll produced by numerous permutations of nuclear conflict, but it is also about giving form to notions of the future – treating the future as something that can be thought, grasped and managed. While futures research was not confined to RAND, other forecasters tended to use imagined future outcomes for mainly rhetorical purposes. The RAND futurists had a broader goal, as Mark Solovey and Hamilton Cravens argue, which was to establish a framework that would 'redefine the social sciences by quantifying, compiling, and examining hypothetical data in order to make decisions based on desirable futures' (2012: 45). The ambition here reaches far beyond the kind of blue-sky pitch that might win a contract. Nicholas Rescher, a philosopher who worked in RAND's Mathematics Division, explains that the RAND futurists 'envisioned a revolutionary enlargement in our capacity to foresee and control the course of events' (1997: 28). For the RAND analysts, mathematics was on the threshold of forging a radical transformation of economic, social and political life.

Whether or not a future considered desirable by RAND researchers would have wider appeal, there is a tantalising but disturbing whiff of megalomania in the drive to obtain power over future outcomes. Needless to say, belief in the liberating capacity of American scientific ingenuity was at a high in the years following the end of World War II, even if the shocking aftermath of total war might be considered compelling counter-evidence. The US desire to be able to control and manage events on a global scale is, in part, motivated by an all-too-real understanding of the devastating consequences of the totalitarian ambitions of fascist and communist regimes in other parts of the world. In comparison to the aggressive world-building of dictators, the prospect of developing a countervailing, democratic power led by objective, disinterested scientists starts to seem more like a duty than a mode of technocratic social engineering. It is true that a tightening bureaucratic grip on the future was not the exclusive ambition of the US; Solovey and Cravens note the 'critical role' the Soviet five-year plans played in the growth of futurism in the USSR, to the extent that forecasting came to overshadow planning (2012: 50). Nevertheless, however expedient the US military's embrace of futures research, and however benign the command and control model of top-down future management was intended to be, there remains a world-creating grandiosity to the RAND project, a certain hand-of-God self-legitimation that is indicated even in the name given to their best-known analytical strategy, the Delphi Method.

Named after the Greek oracle located at the point Zeus believed to be the centre of Earth, the key to the Delphi Method's problem-solving approach is collective, interdisciplinary analysis, kick-started by individually completed, anonymous questionnaires that are compiled and disseminated by a coordinator. Regular feedback provides opportunities for the modification of views (this feature is known, as Norman Dalkey, who developed Delphi with Rescher and Olaf Helmer, explains, as 'iteration with controlled feedback' (Dalkey 1969: 15)). The cycle of questionnaires, monitoring and feedback continues until consensus emerges. Beginning with analysis of the future technological capabilities of the armed forces, the Delphi Method was subsequently used to assess trends in science, population growth and the space programme, among others. By the 1960s, the popularity of the Delphi Method, along with other RAND research methodologies including game theory, scenarios, role-playing, modelling and simulations, spread through the tendrils of the military-industrial-education complex. As a consequence, Cold War-driven futures research methods used by military strategists found their way into many areas of civilian intellectual life in the social sciences, industry, corporate planning, education, politics and business.

In the years 1965 to 1975, interest in futures research surged in the US and Europe. Kahn's Hudson Institute, founded in 1961, was soon followed by a proliferation of new future-oriented research organisations and projects. In 1965, the American Academy of Arts and Sciences launched a Commission for the Year 2000, chaired by Columbia sociologist Daniel Bell. RAND alumni Olaf Helmer, Paul Baran (inventor of packet switching) and Ted Gordon founded the Institute for the Future (IFTF) in 1968, intended to push futures research more decisively toward dealing with social problems. IFTF launched *Futures* the same year, which became a key journal in the field. The science writer Edward Cornish founded the World Future Society (WFS) in Washington DC in 1966 and launched the magazine *The Futurist* the next year. By 1970, WFS membership was 4,000, rising to 15,000 in 1974, and included Kahn, Buckminster Fuller, Robert McNamara, Arthur C. Clarke, and Alvin and Heidi Toffler (Solovey and Cravens 2012: 52–3). The equally self-consciously global World Futures Studies Federation (WFSF), founded in Paris in 1973, emerged out of a series of major conferences during the 1960s and early 1970s driven by the work of, among others, Bertrand de Jouvenel (French), Igor Bestuzhev-Lada (Russian), Johan Galtung (Norwegian) and Robert Jungk (Austrian). The Congressional Research Service established a Futures Research Group in 1975 to support policy analysis. This rapid rise of what Rescher calls the 'Advice Establishment' – academics, scientists, technical experts and pundits of all stripes – serving on advisory boards, policy study groups and public commissions also included the development in the US of various doctoral programmes in future studies, particularly in business schools (Rescher 1997: 29). In 1973, for example, Helmer was appointed Professor of Futuristics at the School of Business Administration at the University of Southern California.

Institutional validation of futures research was accompanied by rising public awareness, aided by TV shows like Walter Cronkite's mid-1960s series on the twenty-first century, and features like Alvin Toffler's piece for *Horizon* magazine in the summer of 1966 and *Time* magazine's 'The Futurists: Looking Toward AD 2000' (February 1966), which had Kahn foreseeing a future 'pleasure-oriented' society full of 'wholesome degeneracy'. Such upbeat forecasting, however, soon gave way to less sanguine readings of the near future as the postwar economic boom came to a dramatic halt. The other side of the public's awareness of forecasting came courtesy of the Club of Rome's influential, if subsequently proven to be inaccurate, report, *The Limits to Growth* (1972). Futures research did not end with the oil crisis and stagflation but its horizons did, in some quarters, contract: the National Science Foundation's 1980 two-volume study restricted itself to 'The Five-Year Outlook'. It would be a mistake, however, to dismiss futures research as a short-lived cultural offshoot of Cold War scientism and postwar prosperity, though the public fascination with foresight was indeed largely restricted to the optimism that accompanied economic growth. The embrace of futures research by business, on the other hand, was far from fleeting and the role of forecasting during the economic crisis of the 1970s was to prove decisive in cementing the status of future studies.

Scenarios

Among the most influential techniques to cross over from military strategy into the business world was scenario planning. Kahn developed RAND-style scenario planning for a business context at the Hudson Institute during the 1960s. In *The Year 2000* (1967), Kahn and his colleague Anthony J. Wiener describe scenarios as 'hypothetical sequences of events constructed for the purpose of focusing attention on causal processes and decision-points. They answer two kinds of questions: (1) Precisely how might some hypothetical situation come about, step by step? And (2) what alternatives exist, for each actor, at each step, for preventing, diverting, or facilitating the process?' (1967: 6). Scenarios, then, are methodological devices, not geared toward prediction as such but aimed at assessing options and dealing with uncertainty. A scenario, explains Peter Schwartz, whose futurist career began at the Stanford Research Institute (established in 1970), is 'a tool for ordering one's perceptions about alternative future environments in which one's decisions might be played out' (1991: 4). The effectiveness of scenario planning for business was made clear, however, not in a research institute but at Royal Dutch/Shell in London, where in the early 1970s Ted Newland and Pierre Wack managed to help the company avoid the worst of the oil crisis. Wack's innovation was to move scenario planning beyond merely outlining possible futures and instead to use the scenario to change the mindset of decision-makers – as Schwartz writes, 'ordering one's perceptions' – so that they could 'reperceive' the way the world works; in other words, the future is engineered by the reperception effected by the scenario itself.

Some futurists have identified a clear correlation here between the scenario and literary critic Darko Suvin's notion of 'cognitive estrangement' in science fiction. The scenario and the science fiction narrative are each able, according to organisational theorists Charles Booth et al., to achieve a 'dawning sense of dislocation' through 'the rupturing of ontological linearity and the change in the world as we know it' (2009: 93). Suvin himself was not convinced of the similarity (Suvin's work emerges, not from futures research, but out of the Marxist tradition of Shklovsky, Brecht and Bloch), seeing futures research as normative and narrowly instrumental (Booth et al. 2009; Suvin 1979: 28), though it is precisely science fiction's radical disregard for plausibility and its determination to subvert conventional notions of the real that makes it a powerful alternative model for the kind of futures planning concerned with global restructuring, whether the objective is military, corporate or political. It should come as no surprise that science fiction writers are regularly used as consultants in futures research.

Wack's notion of reperception, while not interested in science fiction, does draw on sources beyond military futurism; as Fred Turner explains, during World War II, Wack attended the mystic Georges Gurdjieff's Paris salons and became an enthusiastic seeker of enlightenment through 'the art of seeing' (Turner 2006: 187; Jaworski 2011: 218). Adopting Gurdjieff's narrative style, Wack used stories to alter the mental maps of executives, with scenarios becoming, in Turner's words, 'a form of corporate performance art [where] two traditions, corporate and countercultural, merged' (2006: 187).

Access to Tools

The most enduring and influential fusion of corporate and countercultural approaches to futures thinking, though, remains that of Stewart Brand, the ex-Merry Prankster responsible for the operating manual for spaceship Earth, the *Whole Earth Catalog*. RAND's Delphic aspirations sat comfortably enough within Brand's systems-based synthesis of computing and environmentalism; the 1969 *Catalog* announced, famously, that 'We *are* as gods and might as well get good at it' (Brand 1969). The world-building utopianism that motivated Cold War futurism, gutted of its military strategic objectives, lends itself remarkably well to Brand's West Coast revitalisation of the frontier mythos, where self-build housing and a fashionable celebration of Native American resourcefulness combined with the nascent high-tech sector's de-bureaucratised, RAND-style collective problem-solving. In theory, at any rate, this was the best of both worlds: the shared scientific adventure coupled with the practically driven self-becoming of the pioneer. The *Catalog* was appropriately past- and future-oriented, recalling the nineteenth century Sears mail order catalogues ('the Consumers' Bible') that plugged Western settlers into the global marketplace, and anticipating the contemporary internet search engine. In 1974, Brand also launched a more conventional magazine, *CoEvolution Quarterly*, intended to provide more space for discussion of contemporary innovations and which survived waning interest in futurism until 1985. In that year, Brand started the Whole Earth 'Lectronic Link (the WELL) with tech pioneer Larry Brilliant, one of the earliest virtual communities.

The economic slump of the 1970s and the loss of confidence in technology to solve social and economic problems meant that futurism was eclipsed during the 1980s by rising nationalism, religious fundamentalism and a growing interest in the past. Economists had failed to anticipate the recession, the Club of Rome's dire forecasts had proved ill-founded, and no one seemed to have expected the fall of the Soviet Union. Brand, as usual, was right to focus on computing as the most fertile territory for his utopian energies, but he continued to pursue the futurist agenda in the one area, business consultancy, where futures research remained buoyant.

Among the most influential organisations to continue the futures research programme was the Global Business Network (GBN), founded in 1987 by Brand, Schwartz, Jay Ogilvy (who had worked with Schwartz at Stanford), oil industry planner Napier Collyns (who worked under Wack at Shell) and Lawrence Wilkinson, a business and marketing strategist.[1] Schwartz replaced Wack on his retirement from Shell in 1982 and continued the systems-led, countercultural approach to scenario planning at GBN. During its history, GBN was funded by almost 200 large corporations, including Apple, AT&T, Chevron Texaco, Deutsche Bank, Dow Chemical, DuPont, Fannie Mae, General Electric, IBM, the London Stock Exchange, Nokia, and Wack's and Schwartz's old boss, Shell Oil. The Network also counted among its clients the Joint Chiefs of Staff and the Defense Department (Turner 2006: 188). GBN members have included Mary Catherine Bateson, Freeman Dyson, Brian Eno, Francis Fukuyama, Peter Gabriel, William Joy, Kevin Kelly, Jaron Lanier, Sherry Turkle and a raft of writers, including Gary Snyder, Richard Rodriguez and Douglas Coupland, plus science fiction novelists William Gibson, Bruce Sterling and Vernor Vinge. Reminded of Isaac Asimov's famous science fiction series about a cabal of experts capable of anticipating and changing the future, journalist Joel Garreau, himself a GBN member, concluded: 'Holy shit. This is The Foundation' (1994). What GBN accomplished was perhaps the fullest convergence of Cold War systems thinking, technofuturism and countercultural collectivism, put to work to further the interests of global corporations.

Garreau's view of GBN as a cabal captures, I think, something of the fragrant mix of glamour and paranoia that, since Kahn's days at RAND, so often characterises the futures research milieu, at least at the high table. Becoming a member of GBN was, for Garreau, less of a commission and more like a seduction:

> One simply gets more and more tangled in its swirling mists. I was first asked to join a discussion on the network's private BBS. Then I started receiving books that members thought I might find interesting. Then I got invited to gatherings at fascinating places, from Aspen to Amsterdam. Finally, I was asked to help GBN project the future regarding subjects about which I had expertise. By then, the network seemed natural. (1994)

This reads more like initiation into a cult than a consultancy gig for a business network, but, as we saw in the case of Wack, the mystical dimension of futures research in some sense goes all the way down. This is probably related to the implicit connections futures research has with older, more obviously occult modes of soothsaying and prophecy as well as the more prosaic yet nevertheless intoxicating promise of corporate funding. The need for 'vision' often tends to position futurists as visionaries and, as a consequence, provides the latitude for grandstanding as a means of lifting discourse out of the mud of mundane affairs. Showmanship and hyperbole certainly appear to be parts of the brief.

Brand's most recent venture, the Long Now Foundation (founded in 1996), while more outward-facing than GBN, retains the mystique of the inner circle typical of his previous enterprises. The aim of Long Now is to foster long-term thinking – namely, the next 10,000 years – in an age of 'faster/cheaper'. The roll call of speakers at the foundation's monthly seminars is the familiar combination of tech gurus (Ray Kurzweil, Kevin Kelly, Jimmy Wales), sci-fi writers (Bruce Sterling, Neal Stephenson, Cory Doctorow) and ecological and environmental scientists (Beth Shapiro, Peter Kareiva, Paul Ehrlich). As with Whole Earth and GBN, Brand has seized the time, and current debates on climate science, the Anthropocene, mass extinction and the posthuman dominate the Long Now agenda.

Part of the reason the Long Now Foundation's programme seems more relevant in 2016 than perhaps it did in 1996 is due to the intensification of interest in the future during times of perceived crisis. The mass annihilation of World War II and Cold War dread birthed futures research; terrorism and climate change have rekindled interest in scenario planning in the twenty-first century. After the terrorist attacks on New York and Washington in 2001, demand for scenario consultancy surged: the number of businesses using scenarios rose from 40 per cent in 1999 to 70 per cent by 2006 (*The Economist* 2008). The events of 2001 also released a wave of catastrophe-related studies by prominent scientists and commentators that continues unabated. Unlike the techno-optimism and faith in democracy that characterised much futures-oriented writing of the Cold War years, current pre-occupations are darker. Titles alone tell the tale: *Our Final Century* (Rees 2003), *Deep Futures: Our Prospects for Survival* (Cocks 2003), *Catastrophe: Risk and Response* (Posner 2004), *Collapse* (Diamond 2004), *Global Catastrophic Risks* (Bostrom and Cirkovic 2008), *Be Very Afraid* (Wuthnow 2010), *Tropic of Chaos* (Parenti 2011). This is not to say that the Cold War did not also generate negativity and despair, but Kahn's unthinkable no longer refers to probabilistic outcomes attributed to rational actors. The dread associated with the catastrophic sublime now is directed toward the inexorable and irreversible 'slow violence' (Nixon 2011) of global environmental collapse brought about by the same human ingenuity that once promised to save us. In this respect, terror-related anxiety, while legitimate, may in the end prove to be an at least familiar distraction away from the truly unthinkable, ungraspable proposition of planetary extinction.

Probability and its Problems

One of the key tensions within futures research is that among the probable, the possible and the impossible. While it would seem on the surface that scenario planning would be most usefully deployed in addressing probable and possible futures, especially when it comes to longer-term scenarios it is more likely to be what is currently perceived to be impossible that demands attention. Indeed, the category of the impossible makes little sense in terms of futures thinking, since what may be considered outrageous fantasy today could indeed come to pass in some unspecified future. As Kahn asked his readers in a report to the Hudson Institute in 1963: 'Is there a danger of bringing too much imagination to these problems? Do we risk losing ourselves in a maze of bizarre improbabilities?' Hardly, Kahn responds, since it has 'usually been lack of imagination, rather than an excess of it, that caused unfortunate decisions and missed opportunities' (Kahn quoted in Ghamari-Tabrizi 2000: 172). The real work of futures research, then, is in tackling the impossible.

The emergence of probability theory in the eighteenth century, as an Enlightenment attempt to capture and manage chance, produced, according to Allen Thiher, 'a subject that could view itself as detached from the contingencies of history' (2001: 28). Instead of a subject viewed as a 'continuation of an identity anchored in families, institutions, and inheritances' (28), the calculating subject is structured and positioned by and in the moment of calculation. Probability theory is thus a way of dealing with uncertainty by mediating between knowledge and mere opinion; the calculus offers a way to be uncertain without being irrational. A fictional probability can be wrested away from the impossible and placed in relation to the present that is a version of the real: probability provides a rational means of accounting for decision-making that is not necessarily a continuation or repetition of the past but is not entirely at the mercy of chance. The definition of the impossible is always produced in relation to what can be calculated as probable. From the end of the Enlightenment until the present, Thiher concludes, 'the exploration of the impossible has always predicated the probable and the possible – and in this sense every description of the impossible has had the effect of affirming the power of the probable to define what is reality' (2001: 29). The fact that the probable is not reality but only a calculation of what might occur, however, opens a space for mistaking likely falsehoods for implausible truths. With the formalisation of probability theory in the nineteenth century as statistics, what had been a method of decision-making takes on the shape of a set of laws, and the fictional dimension of statistical probabilities takes on the form of empirical fact. Extrapolation, then, is riddled with problems since it must prefer the probable over the impossible in order to make sense. As such, futures research that is too beholden to methods of extrapolation, as Kahn knew, will lose out. The astronomer Martin Rees points out that 'straightforward projections of present trends will miss the most revolutionary innovations' (2003: 12), which are more likely to be discovered by chance than by design. Most forecasts of future technological transformations fail to anticipate key innovations and, often, incremental change is far slower than might be expected.

The problem with scenario planning is that, just as probability theory in the eighteenth century normalised uncertainty as statistics, it tends to normalise estrangement as a policy option, which is largely what happens in futurist manuals like James Ogilvy's *Facing the Fold* (2011), where everything from logic and systems thinking to literary criticism and critical theory are put to work in order to create the intellectual space for an optimistic technofuturism, or, as Ogilvy has it, to move us from 'the eclipse of utopia to the restoration of hope' (2011: 8). It is a bracing read, though frighteningly reductive. Among the ironies of futures research is that however far it moves toward contemplating the impossible, the normative rhetorical and ideological underpinning of the project steers speculation back to an affirmation of the values driving the research. In this way, as Turner writes of GBN: 'the exigencies of everyday life assumed an informational cast [. . .] where being informed and thinking in cybernetic terms came to seem to be much the same thing. This pattern characterized GBN's scenario process as well. [. . .] [S]cenario-building workshops aimed to make visible the hidden informational systems of their participants' (Turner 2006: 192). Systems thinking, then, is used to demonstrate that systems just is the way things are. Futures research driven by systems thinking cannot help but provide cybernetic models of the future, thereby inscribing the present into all future scenarios as the horizon of possibility. The most impossible future scenario conceivable, at some level, must confirm the methods that generate it. There is, it seems, no outside the system.

The synthesis of Cold War military thinking and countercultural libertarianism achieved by futurists like Wack and Brand allows space for both the collective, if hierarchical, energies of the military and the radical individualism of the spiritual voyager. The convergence of systems theory and the whole earth outlook provides a potent conceptual basis through which post-Fordist, globalised capitalism can articulate itself as an optimistic, best-case union of scientific, corporate and creative energies that plays equally well at the Pentagon and in Silicon Valley. In this regard, futures research has squared the circle of postwar dissensus; who doesn't, after all, want to achieve the impossible?

Still Thinking the Unthinkable

The end of the future can be seen, according to Franco 'Bifo' Berardi, in the failures of twenty-first-century climate summits. 'The complexity of the problem', he writes, 'exceeds the power of knowledge and influence of world politicians. The future has escaped from the hands of political technique, and everything has capsized' (2011: 40). Growing insecurity, fuelled by neoliberal deregulation, the emergence of virtual enterprise in communication and finance, and the erosion of national sovereignty by global business, leaves little space or time for future-oriented thinking, which has scuttled over to the corporate world where it continues to thrive. The implicitly liberal democratic aspirations driving large-scale postwar aspirations, however much they might have been underpinned by militarised systems analysis, have given way, according to Bifo, to an even more thoroughgoing technocratic elitism typified in *Wired* magazine (Kevin Kelly, *Wired*'s founding executive editor, was formerly an editor of the *Whole Earth Catalog*), where 'the libertarian soul melt[s] with the market theology of neoliberal economists' (42).

In *After the Future*, Berardi admits that he can see no escape from neoliberalism: 'The dissociation of capitalism and modernity is accomplished,' he concludes. At the same time, he admits that 'the catastrophe is exactly [. . .] the point where a new landscape is going to be revealed', though he cannot see that landscape since 'my knowledge and my understanding are limited, and the limits of my language are the limits of my world'. Without the knowledge, understanding or language to grasp the incomprehensible and unspeakable, Berardi must act 'as if':

> As if the forces of labor and knowledge may overcome the forces of greed and of proprietary obsession. As if the cognitive workers may overcome the fractalization of their life and intelligence, and give birth to a process of the self-organization of collective knowledge. I must resist simply because I cannot know what will happen after the future, and I must preserve the consciousness and sensibility of social solidarity, of human empathy, of gratuitous activity, of freedom, equality and fraternity. Just in case, right? Just because we don't know what is going to happen next, in the empty space that comes after the future of modernity. (127–8)

Here, Berardi implicitly invokes, though not without weariness, an alternative futures tradition: the utopian commitment to thinking the unthinkable required by revolutionary movements. There is a similar move made in McKenzie Wark's recent *Molecular Red* (2015), a book that excavates a canon of radical futures research from the Soviet Proletkult (Alexander Bogdanov and Andrei Platonov) and dissident SoCal tech writers (Donna Haraway and Kim Stanley Robinson). If Berardi, with Wittgenstein, is right that the limits of language are the limits of my world, the challenge for Berardi and Wark – as Kahn, Wack, Brand and others have known all along – is to renegotiate the limit, to engineer some kind of base-level reperception. Futures research in its military and corporate forms has constructed a future for its own present needs – a model of foreseeable temporality that can accommodate, for example, the policy of preemptive strikes (on the Bush doctrine and futurology, see Dunmire 2011) or, more recently, the notion of the 'good Anthropocene', where climate crisis is an opportunity to pursue limitless growth beyond the planetary constraints of what used to be called 'nature' (see *An Ecomodernist Manifesto* 2015; Hamilton 2015). The limits of language, in these cases, are clearly malleable enough to allow the impossible the room to root itself in the real. If there is to be a countervailing language of the future – a future that can accommodate Berardi's wishlist of 'as ifs' – it has to be able to tap into the grandeur of Kahn's or Brand's disregard for the impossible while detonating the world-building aggression that comes with the kind of military-industrial or corporate sponsorship that has, since the Cold War, set the terms upon which the future can be imagined.

Notes

1. The Global Business Network became part of the Monitor group in 2000; after filing for bankruptcy, Monitor was bought in January 2013 by multinational consulting firm Deloitte, who closed GBN.

References

Berardi, Franco 'Bifo' (2011), *After the Future*, ed. Gary Genosko and Nicholas Thoburn, Oakland, CA: AK Press.

Booth, Charles, Michael Rowlinson, Peter Clar, Agnes Delahaye and Stephen Procter (2009), 'Scenarios and Counterfactuals as Model Narratives', *Futures* 41: 87–95.

Bostrom, Nick, and Milan M. Cirkovic (eds) (2008), *Global Catastrophic Risks*, Oxford: Oxford University Press.

Brand, Stewart (ed.) (1969), *Whole Earth Catalog*, Melo Park, CA: Portola Institute.

Cocks, Doug (2003), *Deep Futures: Our Prospects for Survival*, Montreal: McGill-Queens University Press.

Dalkey, Norman C. (1969), *The Delphi Method: An Experimental Study of Group Opinion*, Santa Monica, CA: Rand.

Diamond, Jared (2004), *Collapse: How Societies Choose to Fail or Succeed*, New York: Penguin.

Dunmire, Patricia L. (2011), *Projecting the Future through Political Discourse: The Case of the Bush Doctrine*, Amsterdam: John Benjamins.

An Ecomodernist Manifesto (2015), <http://www.ecomodernism.org/manifesto-english/> (last accessed 26 January 2016).

The Economist (2008), 'Scenario Planning', 1 September, <http://www.economist.com/node/12000755> (last accessed 26 January 2016).

Garreau, Joel (1994), 'Conspiracy of Heretics', *Wired* 2(11) (November), <http://archive.wired.com/wired/archive/2.11/gbn_pr.html> (last accessed 26 January 2016).

Ghamari-Tabrizi, Sharon (2000), 'Simulating the Unthinkable: Gaming Future War in the 1950s and 1960s', *Social Studies of Science* 30(2): 163–223.

Hamilton, Clive (2015), 'The Theodicy of the "Good Anthropocene"', <http://clivehamilton.com/the-theodicy-of-the-good-anthropocene> (last accessed 26 January 2016).

Jaworski, Joseph (2011), *Synchronicity: The Inner Path of Leadership*, San Francisco: Berrett-Koehler.

Kahn, Herman (1962), *Thinking about the Unthinkable*, New York: Horizon Press.

Kahn, Herman, and Anthony J. Wiener (1967), *The Year 2000: A Framework for Speculation on the Next Thirty-Three Years*, New York: Macmillan.

Meadows, Donella H., Dennis L. Meadows, Jørgen Randers and William W. Behrens III (1972), *The Limits to Growth: A Report for the Club of Rome's Project on the Predicament of Mankind*, New York: Universe Books.

National Science Foundation (1980), *The Five-Year Outlook: Problems, Opportunities, and Constraints in Science and Technology*, Washington, DC: United States Government Printing Office.

Nixon, Rob (2011), *Slow Violence and the Environmentalism of the Poor*, Cambridge, MA: Harvard University Press.

Ogilvy, James A. (2011), *Facing the Fold: Essays on Scenario Planning*, Axminster: Triarchy Press.

Parenti, Christian (2011), *Tropic of Chaos: Climate Change and the New Geography of Violence*, New York: Nation.

Posner, Richard (2004), *Catastrophe: Risk and Response*, Oxford: Oxford University Press.

Rees, Martin (2003), *Our Final Century: Will the Human Race Survive the Twenty-First Century?*, New York: Heinemann.

Rescher, Nicholas (1997), *Predicting the Future: An Introduction to the Theory of Forecasting*, Albany, NY: State University of New York Press.

Schwartz, Peter (1991), *The Art of the Long View*, New York: Doubleday.

Solovey, Mark, and Hamilton Cravens (eds) (2012), *Cold War Social Science: Knowledge Production, Liberal Democracy, and Human Nature*, London: Palgrave Macmillan.

Suvin, Darko (1979), *Metamorphoses of Science Fiction: On the Poetics and History of a Literary Genre*, New Haven, CT: Yale University Press.

Thiher, Allen (2001), *Fiction Rivals Science: The French Novel from Balzac to Proust*, Columbia: University of Missouri Press.

Time magazine (1966), 'The Futurists: Looking Forward to A.D. 2000', *Time* 87 (25 February): 28–9.

Turner, Fred (2006), *From Counterculture to Cyberculture: Stewart Brand, the Whole Earth Network, and the Rise of Digital Utopianism*, Chicago: University of Chicago Press.

Valéry, Paul (1962 [1944]), 'Unpredictability', in *The Outlook for Intelligence*, trans. Denise Folliot and Jackson Mathews, New York: Harper & Row, pp. 67–71.

Wark, McKenzie (2015), *Molecular Red: Theory for the Anthropocene*, London: Verso.

Wuthnow, Robert (2010), *Be Very Afraid: The Cultural Response to Terror, Pandemics, Environmental Devastation, Nuclear Annihilation, and Other Threats*, Oxford: Oxford University Press.

Chapter 2

Simulate, Optimise, Partition: Algorithmic Diagrams of Pattern Recognition from 1953 Onwards

Adrian Mackenzie

Contemporary attempts to find patterns in data, ranging from the now mundane technologies of touchscreen gesture recognition through to mammoth infrastructure-heavy practices of deep learning conducted by major business, scientific and government actors to find cats (Markoff 2012), the Higgs boson, credit card fraud or terrorists, rely on a group of algorithms intensively developed during the 1950–1960s in physics, engineering and psychology. Whether we designate them as pattern recognition, data mining or machine learning (all terms that first came into play during the 1950s), the standard account enunciated by proponents (and opponents) of these techniques is that they uncover patterns in data that cannot appear directly to the human eye, either because there are too many items for anyone to look at, or because the patterns are too subtly woven through in the data.

In the contemporary narratives of their efficacy and indeed necessity, the spectrum of differences accommodated under the rubric of pattern is striking. Pattern here is understood to encompass language, images, measurements and traces of many different kinds. Pattern-finding techniques – although that term is problematic because it suggests skilled hands doing something; I will refer to them as *operations* – diagram a strikingly new kind of continuum or field which accommodates seemingly very different things – terrorists, fundamental particles, photographs, market transactions, utterances and gestures – more or less uniformly.

What counts as pattern finding today, I will suggest, can be better understood by taking into account the transformations in simulating, optimising and above all *classifying* associated with different uses of computers taking shape in the mid-twentieth century. Despite their often somewhat ahistorical invocations, the patterns recognised in pattern recognition have a historically concrete specificity. From the plethora of operations in current use, three diagrams developed in the Cold War era operate in contemporary modes of pattern finding:

1. Monte Carlo simulation as a way of shaping flows of random numbers to explore *irregular probability distributions*;
2. *convex optimisations* or finding maximum- or minimum-value numerical solutions to systems of equations as a way of classifying things;
3. *recursive partitioning* algorithms that reorder differences according to clustering and sparsity in data.

The operations expressed in these diagrams took shape in different places – nuclear physics, control systems engineering and psychology – but soon moved across boundaries between academic disciplines, and between domains such as universities, industry, the military and government. Each of them, deeply reliant on electronic computation, configures a different mode of moving through data in order to find or make patterns. The different perspectives on event, difference and recognition they embody imbue many power relations, forms of value and the play of truth/falsehood today. In each case, they contributed something to the formation of an operational field that today has generalised to include many aspects of media, culture, science, business and government, none of which exists purely or in isolation, but in combination with each other. Because the diagrammatic operations of probability, optimisation and classification have intersected, we today increasingly inhabit a pattern-recognised space that configures what it is to belong, to participate, to anticipate, to speak or to decide differently.

What Are Continuities in the Operational Field?

> If the operatives of the Cold War could reserve for themselves the position of grey eminence, the distant adviser to the executive power, the new spaces of collectively intelligent networks and the asymmetrical relations these put in place demand instead the more difficult position of grey immanence. (Fuller and Goffey 2012: 32)

In order to understand how the generalisation of probability-simulation-optimisation took place, Matthew Fuller and Andrew Goffey's contrast between grey eminence and grey immanence is suggestive. The shift from grey eminence or powerful technical-scientific advisers to executive power and grey immanence in intelligent networks is precisely the movement that we might delineate by paying attention to the operations of simulation, optimisation and partitioning that underpin and in many ways sub-structure social network media, contemporary health and biomedical knowledges and credit ratings, to name a few. The operations for working with data, numbers, probability and categories took shape deep in the epistemic cultures of the Cold War. Specific locations such as the RAND Corporation, the Cornell Aeronautical Laboratory and IBM Corporation figure large here, but they somehow proliferate and disseminate in a field that is neither that of lifeworld (lived, urban, etc.) experience linked to a subject position (the grey eminences of Cold War science, as described for instance in *How Reason Almost Lost Its Mind* (Erickson et al. 2013)) nor an unliveable mathematical abstraction (the Euclidean space of geometrical abstraction analysed by Cold War philosophers such as Hannah Arendt (Arendt 1998)), but something more like an *operational field* in Michel Foucault's sense of the term (Foucault 1972: 106).[1] The dimensions and composition of this field undergo constant expansion and accumulation, partitioning and aggregation via operations increasingly detached from expert 'grey eminences'. Through it, in it, near it, derived from it, many different artifices, devices, arrangements, operations and processes accumulate. It is a power-laden operational space that traverses and structures many aspects of our lives, but is only intermittently sensible or palpable to us. It appears at the intersection of many scientific disciplines, various infrastructures, operations and institutions. It is object and domain of much work and investment in management, enterprise and State.

Authoritative and recent accounts of Cold War rationality have strongly dramatised the part that cybernetics played in restructuring human-machine-organism relations in various Cold War contexts ranging across engineering, psychology, management, military strategy and anthropology (Bowker 1993; Edwards 1996; Hayles 1999; Pickering 2009; Halpern 2015). These accounts argue that cybernetic systems of control, automation and cognition were constitutively metaphorical and openly trans-disciplinary. From the outset, cybernetics propositions concerned organisms, organisations, states, machines and subjectivity. The diagrammatic operations I describe here are also intimately linked with transformations in what counts as pattern, recognition, learning and intelligence, but their mode of semiosis differs somewhat from cybernetics. The composition of the operational field we are concerned with here lacks the constitutive generality of cybernetics. Although coeval with cybernetics, it is much more densely woven through methods, operations, infrastructures, forms of expertise and models. Hence, we can't understand the contemporary force of the operational field without moving backwards and seeing how those power-laden operations proliferated and coalesced. It is an operational generalisation rather than an enunciative one, and takes place, unsurprisingly given its contemporary materialisation, in code.

Exact Means Simulated, Simulated Means Open

In 1953, Nicholas Metropolis, the Rosenbluths and the Tellers, all physicists working at Los Alamos, were considering 'the properties of any substance which may be considered as composed of interacting individual molecules' (Metropolis et al. 1953: 1,087). These properties might be, for instance, the flux of neutrons in a hydrogen bomb detonation. In their short, evocatively titled and still widely cited paper 'Equation of State Calculations by Fast Computing Machines' (over 20,000 citations, according to Google Scholar; over 14,000 according to Thomson Reuters Web of Science), they describe how they used computer simulation to manage with the inordinate number of possible interactions in a substance, and to thereby come up with a statistical description of the properties of the substance. While statistical descriptions of the properties of things are not new,[2] their model system consists of a square containing only a few hundred particles. (This space is a typical multivariate joint distribution.) These particles are at various distances from each other and exert forces (electric, magnetic, etc.) on each other dependent on the distance. In order to estimate the probability that the substance will be in any particular state (fissioning, vibrating, crystallising, cooling down, etc.), they needed to integrate over the many-dimensional space comprising all the distance and forces between the particles. The dimensions of the space, in which all of the variables describe the velocity, momentum, rotation and mass for each of the several hundred particles, are already expansive. As they write, 'it is evidently impossible to carry out a several hundred dimensional integral by the usual numerical methods, so we resort to the Monte Carlo method' (1,088), a method that Nicholas Metropolis and Stanislaw Ulam had already described several years previously in an earlier paper (Metropolis and Ulam 1949). Here the problem is that the turbulent randomness of events in a square containing a few hundred particles thwarts calculations of the physical properties of the substance. They substitute for that non-integrable turbulent randomness a controlled flow of random variables generated by a computer.

While still somewhat random (i.e. pseudo-random), these Monte Carlo variables taken together approximate to the integral, the area or volume under the curve geometrically understood, of the many-dimensional space.

A toy example to show the intuition of Monte Carlo simulation is shown in Figure 2.1. The point of this simulation, which comprises half a dozen lines of code, is to calculate the value of the mathematical constant π, a value that describes the ratio between the radius and circumference of a circle. In this Monte Carlo simulation of π, 100,000 points are randomly generated, each point described by an x-y coordinate. Given the formula for the area of a circle (πr^2) and assuming the radius of the circle is 1 unit, the algorithm tests each random point to see if it falls inside the circle. The ratio for π is given by dividing the number of points inside the circle by the total number of randomly generated points and then multiplying by 4 (since if the radius of the circle = 1, then the diameter = 2, and therefore the total area of the bounding box = 2 × 2, so $\pi = 4 \times p$, the proportion inside the circle). The point of this demonstration is not to restate the value of π, but to suggest that we can see here an inexact, probabilistic

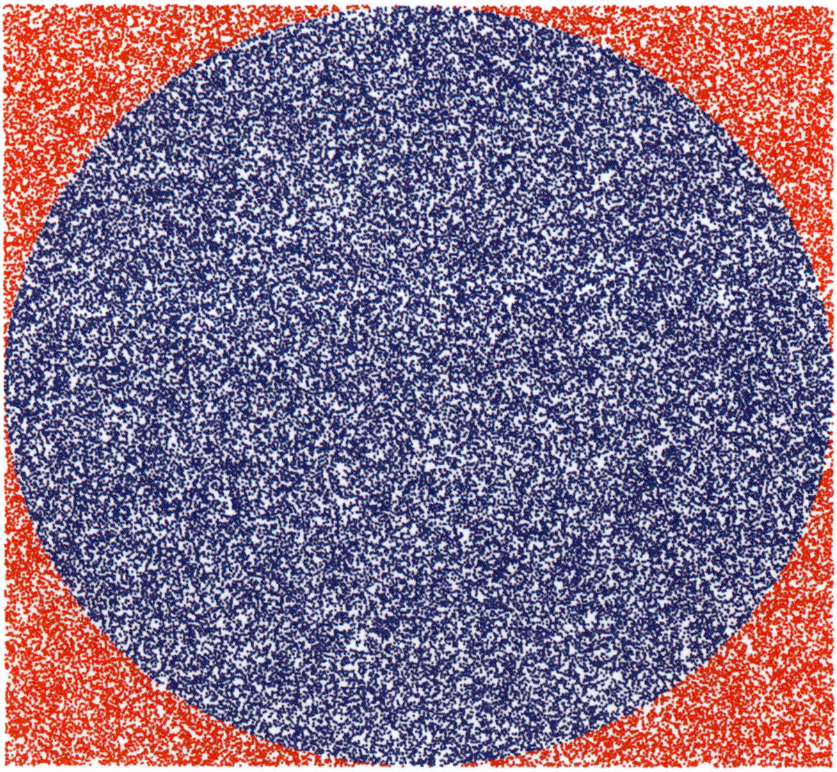

Figure 2.1 A Monte Carlo simulation of π.

calculation of a number that previously epitomised mathematical precision and geometric ideal form (the circle). Monte Carlo simulation, we might say, puts ideal form on a computational footing.

Amongst the many different implications of this simulation of ideal forms, perhaps the most important concerns the status of probability. The contour plot in Figure 2.2 was generated by a variant of Monte Carlo simulation called MCMC – Markov Chain Monte Carlo simulation – that has greatly transformed much statistical practice since the early 1990s (see McGrayne 2011 for a popular account). Like the simulation of π, this simulation calculates significant numbers, this time μ_1 and μ_2, the mean values of two probability distributions. This seemingly very simple simulation of the contours of two normally distributed sets of numbers shows four main diagrammatic operations. First, pluri-dimensional fields arise at the intersection of different axes or vectors of variation. While the graphic plot here is two-dimensional in this case, it can be generalised to much higher dimensions, thus combining many more variables. Second, although Descartes may have first formalised the coordinate geometry using

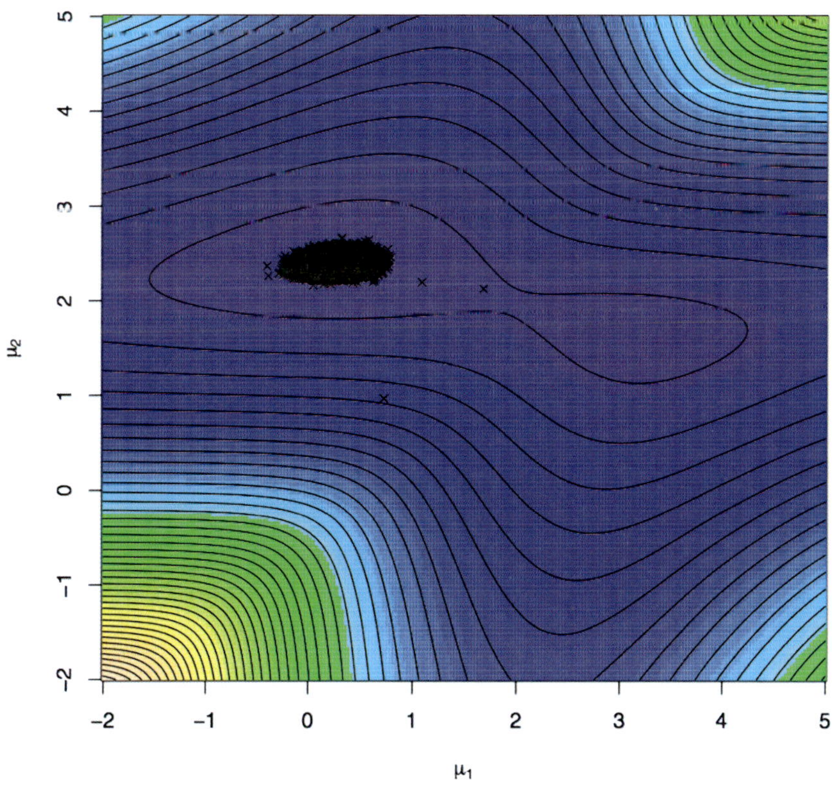

Figure 2.2 A Markov Chain Monte Carlo simulation of two normal distributions.

axes in the form of the Cartesian plane, we can see in Figure 2.2 that this plane has a different consistency or texture. While the Cartesian axes are intact with their scales and marked intervals, the field itself is topographically shaped by a plural flux of random numbers in the Monte Carlo simulation. The topographic convention of showing heights using contour lines works in Figure 2.2 to render visible continuously varying distributions of values across multi-dimensions. The curves of these contours outline the distribution of values in large populations of random numbers generated in the simulation. While the curves of the contour lines join elevations that have the same value, the continuous undulation of values overflows line or regular geometrical form. Third, superimposed on the contour lines, a series of steps or a path explore the irregular topography of the pluri-dimensional field. This exploration appears in the dense mass of black points on the figure deriving from the further flows of random numbers moving towards the highest point, the peak of the field, guided by continuous testing of convergence. Finally, the plot as a whole graphs the different values of the means (μ_1, μ_2) of two random variables distributed over a range of different possible values. We need know nothing about what such variables relate to – they may refer to attributes of individuals, behaviours of markets, growth of an epidemic, the likelihood of an asthma attack. But as descriptions of probability distributions, as ways of assigning numbers to events, the MCMC simulations widely used today to explore complex topographies of things in variation suggest that this form of computation transforms pattern into a probabilistic simulation.

Optimise in Order to Learn: 1957

We know from the histories of Cold War rationality that cognition and calculation are tightly entwined. Cold War cognition calculates its chances of winning, error, loss, costs, times and delays in, for instance, game theory (Erickson et al. 2013: ch. 5). But the mechanisms and devices of this entwining of cognition and calculation are not necessarily obvious or homogeneous. The subtle mechanisms and diagrammatic operations of cognitive calculation sometimes remain opaque and almost subliminal in the words of Cold War discourse. Yet it is precisely these mechanisms that flow along long fault-lines into contemporary knowledge apparatuses with all their power-generating armatures in areas such as security or online media. The operations of these mechanisms are often quite localised and in some cases trivial (e.g. fitting a straight line to some points), but their operations accumulate and generalise in ways that sometimes produce strategic, even hegemonic effects in contemporary culture. While there are quite a few operations that might be examined from this perspective, the case of the Perceptron from 1957 is evocative because of both its cybernetic provenance and its subsequent re-enactments during the 1980 and 1990s in the form of neural nets, in the very abundant support vector machines of the 1990s (Cortes and Vapnik 1995), and today in the massively ramified form of 'deep learning' (Hinton and Salakhutdinov 2006).

'Learning' is pivotal to the diagrammatic operation of machines such as the Perceptron and its many contemporary avatars (see Mackenzie 2015a). While initially framed in terms of rational actors playing games (for instance in 1944 in John von Neumann and Oskar Morgenstern's *Theory of Games and Economic Behavior* (2007); see Erickson et al. 2013: 133–4), the locus of learning shifts diagonally through diagrams, plans and equations into different arrangements typified by the Perceptron. Such devices stand at some remove from the agential dilemmas of Cold War military strategy that animated high-profile game theory. While the Perceptron retains some figurative aspects of its biological inspiration in the neurone, these figurative aspects are rapidly overlaid and displaced by asignifying processes that have continued to mutate in subsequent decades. The so-called 'learning problem' and the subsequent theory of learning machines was developed largely by researchers in the 1960–1980s but based on work already done in the 1950s on learning machines such as the Perceptron, the neural network model developed by the psychologist Frank Rosenblatt in the 1950s (Rosenblatt 1958). Drawing on the McCulloch-Pitts model of the neurone, Rosenblatt implemented the Perceptron, which today would be called a single-layer neural network, on a computer at the Cornell University Aeronautical Laboratory in 1957. A psychologist working in an aeronautical laboratory sounds rather odd, but given that the title of Rosenblatt's 1958 publication – 'The Perceptron: A Probabilistic Model for Information Storage and Organization in the Brain' – already suggested an intersection between statistics (probabilistic models), computation (information storage and organisation) and neuroscience ('brain'), perhaps Rosenblatt's cross-campus mobility is symptomatic of the diagonal movement occurring around learning. The very term 'Perceptron' already amalgamates the organic and the inorganic, the psychological and the technological, in a composite form.

Like the Monte Carlo simulations, the Perceptron operates according to a simple computational process: a machine can 'learn' by classifying things according to their position in a pluri-dimensional data space. 'Geometrically speaking,' writes Vladimir Vapnik (a machine learning researcher famous for his work on the support vector machine), 'the Perceptron divides the space X into two parts separated by a piecewise linear surface. [. . .] Learning in this model means finding appropriate coefficients for all neurons using given training data' (Vapnik 1999: 3). Note the emphasis on *classification*: if the Monte Carlo simulation generated a space in which many different variables could be integrated in exploring irregular probability distributions, devices such as the Perceptron configure a space in which the divisive operation of classification can be configured as a problem of optimisation. 'Learning', as Vapnik puts it, 'means finding appropriate coefficients.'

The practice of learning here owes more to logistics than perhaps to cognition or neuroscience. That is, learning occurs through and takes the form of optimisation. Optimisation in turn is understood in terms of mathematical functions located in high-dimensional spaces that cannot be analysed in closed forms, but only explored looking for maxima or minima. Optimisation algorithms such as gradient descent or expectation maximisation (EM) are the key components here. That is, the theory of machine learning alongside decision theory was interwoven with a set of concepts, techniques and language drawn from statistics. Just as humans, crops, habitats, particles and economies had been previously, learning machines became entwined with statistical methods. Not only in their reliance on the linear model as a common starting point, but in theories of machine learning, statistical terms such as bias, error, likelihood and indeed an increasingly thoroughgoing probabilistic framing of learning machines emerged.

Learning machines optimise rather than cognise. The plot of a few points in a two-dimensional space shown in Figure 2.3 again has to stand in for a much more voluminous, densely populated and pluri-dimensional space. The different shapes of the points index different categories of things (for example, male vs female). The lines in this figure are the work of a Perceptron learning to classify the points by searching for lines that divide the space. Starting with an arbitrary line, the Perceptron tests whether a line effectively separates the different categories. If it does not cleanly separate them, the algorithm incrementally adjusts the parameters that define the slope and intercept until the line does run cleanly between the different categories. It easily may be that the different categories overlap, in which case the Perceptron algorithm will never converge since it cannot find any line that separates them.

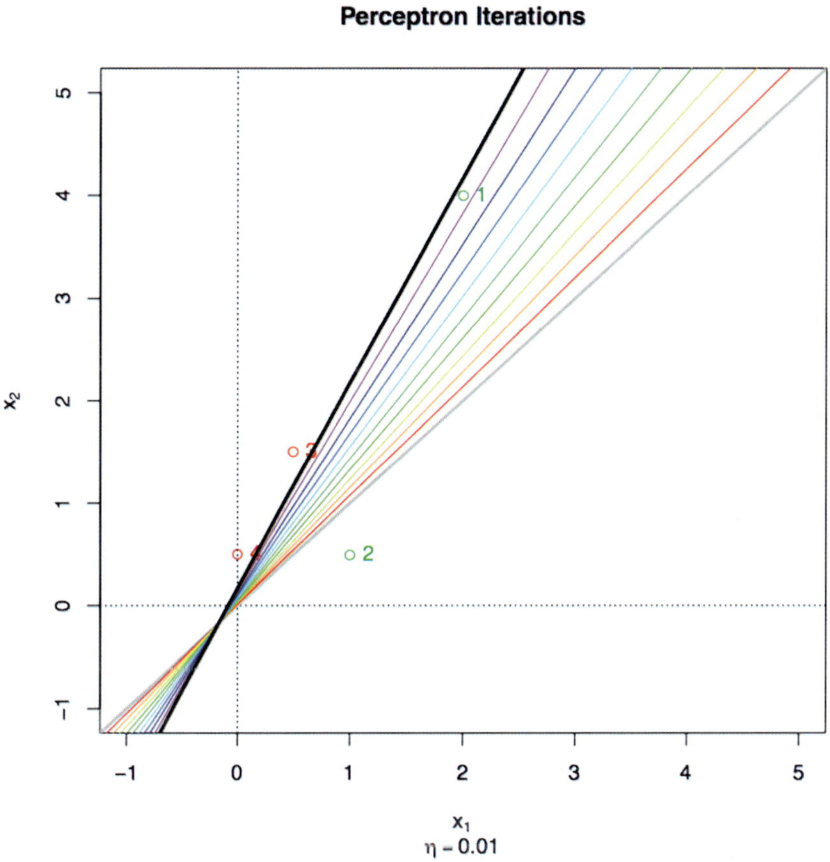

Figure 2.3 Perceptron learns to separate.

For our purposes the point is that any learning that occurs here lies quite a long way away from the biological figure of the neurone. Some biological language remains – 'activation functions', for instance, figure in the code that produces the lines in Figure 2.3 – but the algorithmic process of testing lines and adjusting weights in order to find a line or plane or hyperplane (in higher-dimensional data) very definitely relies on an optimisation process in which errors are gradually reduced to a minimum. Furthermore, the diagrammatic operation of the Perceptron – repeating the drawing of lines in order to classify – appears in a number of variations in the following decades. Some of these variations – linear discriminant analysis, logistic regression, support vector machine – generalise the process of finding separating lines or planes in data in quite complicated ways in order to find more supple or flexible classifications. The Perceptron is not unique in doing this. Subsequent developments, including various machine learning models such as logistic regression, neural nets, support vector machines, *k* nearest neighbours and others present variations on the same diagrammatic operation: pattern recognition entails learning to classify; learning to classify means finding a way of best separating or partitioning a pluri-dimensional data space; the best partition optimises by reducing the number of misclassification errors. It is not surprising that later iterations and variations of the Perceptron proliferated the process of optimisation. For instance, neural nets, current favourite machine learning techniques for working with large archives of image and sound, aggregate many Perceptrons in layered networks, so that the Perceptron's diagrammatic operation of classification can be generalised to highly complex patterns and shapes in the field of data. No matter how complex the classifiers become, they still propagate the same diagrammatic operation of drawing a line and testing its power to separate.

Learning to classify in this way generated many new possibilities. Vapnik observes: 'The Perceptron was constructed to solve pattern recognition problems; in the simplest case this is the problem of constructing a rule for separating data of two different categories using given examples' (1999: 2). While computer scientists in artificial intelligence of the time, such as Marvin Minsky and Seymour Papert, were sceptical about the capacity of the Perceptron model to distinguish or 'learn' different patterns (Minsky and Papert 1987 [1969]), later work showed that Perceptrons could 'learn universally'. For present purposes, the key point is not that neural networks, the present-day incarnations of the Perceptron, have turned out by the 1980s to be extremely powerful algorithms in learning to distinguish patterns, and that intense research in neural networks has led to their ongoing development and increasing sophistication in many 'real world' applications (for instance, in commercial applications such as drug prediction (Dahl 2012)). Rather, the important point is that it began to configure computational machinery as an ongoing learning project. Trying to understand what machines can learn, and to predict how they will classify or predict, became central concerns precisely because machines didn't seem to classify or predict things at all well. The project of learning to classify by optimising choice of coefficients or model parameters has become powerfully performative today, since it underpins many of the recommendation systems, the personalised or targeted advertising, and increasingly the shaping of flows of media, financial and security power. In all of these settings, classification has become a matter of learning to construct a rule for separating things.

Ramified Decisions

Cold War information theory says information is that which allows a move down a decision tree (Solovey and Cravens 2012: 103). Decisions – as the term itself suggests – are a kind of cut. But decisions often have a complicated branching structure, at least, in the procedural rationality typical of Cold War operations research and logistics. In procedural rationality, branches in a decision tree stem from rules that embody the expert knowledge of the grey eminences of management science and its cognate power-knowledge formations. Increasingly during the decades of the Cold War, these rules were shaped by optimisation and modelling procedures that sought to allocate resources most efficiently (especially in the field of operations research; see Erickson et al. 2013: 79).

The decision tree was and remains a key diagrammatic construct in Cold War closed-world thinking in its attempt to represent optimal allocation of resources amidst systems of increasing scale and complexity. The development of procedural rationality based on various algorithmic procedures (the linear programming and dynamic programming techniques are at the core of much operations research (Bellman 1961)) was shadowed by the growth of a different form of decision tree: the classification and regression tree (Breiman et al. 1984). During the 1960s, the decision tree itself was computationally regenerated as a rather different kind of device that in some ways owes more to older systems of classification associated with taxonomy or natural history. Expert decision rules are replaced by learning algorithms that partition data according to quasi-statistical measures of mixedness or purity. This inversion of the decision tree again permits its generalisation. In a certain sense, the decision tree (and its contemporary incarnation in the very popular random forest (Breiman 2001)) dismantles the classical tree with its reference to kinds of being. It also obviates in certain ways the decision tree of procedural rationality as a distillation of expert knowledge. The decision tree is no longer a way of regulating information flow towards optimum resource allocation (missiles, cargoes, troops, etc.). In classification and regression trees, branches are instead something to be learned from the data rather than from experts. It potentially transforms the biopolitical rendering of differences through specific attributes of individuals and populations into a rather mobile matrix of potential mixtures and overlaps.

Take the case of the iris dataset, one of the most famous datasets in the machine learning scientific literature. The eugenicist statistician Ronald A. Fisher first used this dataset in his work on the important linear discriminant analysis technique in the late 1930s (Fisher 1938). The iris in some ways innocuously enough epitomises the modelling of species differences via measurements of biological properties (in this case, measurements of such things as petal widths and lengths of irises growing in the Gaspé Peninsula in Canada).

The plot on the left in Figure 2.4 shows the decision tree and the plot on the right shows the three *iris* species, *virginica*, *setosa* and *versicolor*, plotted by petal and sepal widths. As the plot on the right shows, most of the measurements are well clustered when plotted. Only the *setosa* petal lengths and widths seem to vary widely. All the other measurements are tightly bunched. This means that the decision tree shown on the left has little trouble classifying the irises. Decision trees are read from the top down, left to right. The top level of this tree can be read, for instance, as saying, if the length of petal is less than 2.45, then the iris is *setosa*. Recent accounts of decision trees emphasise this legibility: 'A key advantage of the recursive binary tree is its interpretability. The feature space partition is fully described by a single tree. [. . .] This representation is popular among medical scientists, perhaps because it mimics the way a doctor thinks. The tree stratifies the population into strata of high and low outcome, on

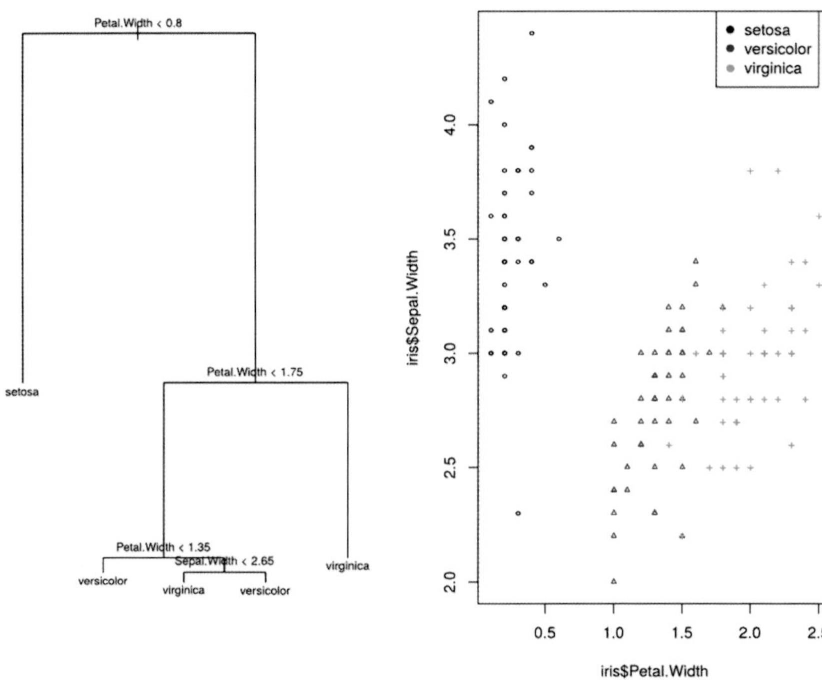

Figure 2.4 Decision tree model on 'iris' data.

the basis of patient characteristics' (Hastie, Tibshirani and Friedman 2009: 306–7). Decision trees do indeed have a rich medical as well as commercial and industrial history of use. Decision trees and their later variations (such as C4.5, the 'top' data-mining algorithm according to a survey of data miners in 2009 (Wu et al. 2008)) are often presented as easy to use because they are 'not unlike the serious of troubleshooting questions you might find in your car's manual to help determine what could be wrong with the vehicle' (Wu et al. 2008: 2). While that scenario is unlikely today, especially as Google sends autonomous-driving cars out on to the roads of California undoubtedly controlled by a variety of classifiers such as decision trees, neural networks and support vector machines, the recursive partitioning technique still has a great deal of traction in machine learning practice precisely because of its simplicity.

In the iris, species differences have an ontological or biopolitical weight. The species differences that the decision tree algorithm finds also exist in the world for us. But the recursive partitioning algorithm that constructs the decision tree knows nothing of these differences. Moreover, in many cases, differences are not easily identifiable even for experts. Often there is some pattern of separation, perhaps in the form of overlapping clusters or clouds of points, but not enough to define a simple set of decision rules. How then does a decision tree decide how to split things? Choosing where to cut: this is a key problem for classification or decision trees. What counts as a good split has been a long-standing topic of debate in the decision tree literature. As the statisticians Malley, Malley and Pajevic observe, 'The challenge is to define *good* when it's clear that no obviously excellent split is easily available' (2011: 121).

Regardless of how 'excellent splits' are defined, the recursive partitioning decision tree subtly alters the nature of decision. Just as Monte Carlo simulation renders all events as probability distributions, or the Perceptron configures classification as an ongoing process of optimisation, decision trees and the like render expert judgement as an algorithmic problem of finding good splits or partitions in data to account for differences. Decision trees, especially in their more recent incarnations of ensembles of decision trees (for example, random forests), no longer formally express the rules that Cold War rationality used to stabilise power-knowledge. The generation of the rules that define the branches in diagrams such as Figure 2.4 no longer relies on domain experts. Decisions diverge somewhat from cognitive skill or technical rationality to reappear as recursive generated partitions. To give a brief indication of how the decision tree has dispersed in the world, we might think of the

Microsoft Kinect game controller, a popular gaming interface that uses video cameras and decision tree algorithms to learn to classify players' gestures and movements, and thereby allow them to play a computer game without touching buttons, levels or holding a game controller. The decision tree algorithm, coupled with the imaging system, translates the mobility and fluidity of gesture into a set of highly coded movements in the on-screen space of the game. There is little human gesture expertise implemented in the Kinect game controller, only algorithms that learn to classify gestures into a number of categories by propagating gestural data down a decision tree. These categories still refer to conventions and codings of the world, but these classifications have little of the ontological or biopolitical depth, since they only derive from relative density and sparsity in the data.

Conclusion: The Pluri-Dimensional Space

We are dealing here with classificatory operations that differ quite radically from both the artificial intelligence of the Cold War, with its attempts to develop computer intelligence, and the expert decision support systems of the 1970s and 1980s that sought to capture domain expertise in software (Collins 1990). Both still assumed that there could be in principle separation or discrimination underpinning decisions and classifications and that algorithmic operations should learn to mimic the discriminative finesse of experts. Cold War rationality remained attached to a decisionistic logic that classification and regression trees, even if only by their sheer abundance, radically rescale and diversify.

Monte Carlo simulations and the subsequent Markov Chain Monte Carlo simulations, the Perceptron and its ramification in contemporary neural nets, or the decision tree and its proliferation in random forests and similar ensembles are just some of the matrices of transformation playing out in an operational field spanning contemporary science, media and government. They exemplify diagrammatic operations flowing through a vast and complex space of scientific knowledges, techniques, technologies, infrastructures and disciplines concerned with pattern and the production of pattern. There are hundreds of other techniques in these spaces, and literally thousands of implementations and variations: Gaussian mixture models, gradient boosted trees, penalised logistic regression, AdaBoost, expectation maximisation, linear discriminant analysis, topic models, principal component analysis, independent component analysis, and so on (see Hastie, Tibshirani and Friedman 2009 for a reasonably comprehensive textbook listing).

While the exemplary diagrams I have discussed do not exhaust the spectrum of movements in the operational field, they do point to some of the principal axes along which many contemporary power-knowledges move as they search for hidden patterns and value in data. What happens to pattern in this power-knowledge nexus? Alfred North Whitehead proposed that quantity presupposes pattern:

> Thus beyond all questions of quantity, there lie questions of pattern, which are essential for the understanding of nature. Apart from a presupposed pattern, quantity determines nothing. Indeed quantity itself is nothing other than analogy of functions within analogous patterns. (Whitehead 1956: 195)

I have been suggesting that we are experiencing a re-patterning of pattern today at the intersection of probabilistic, optimising and recursive partitioning processes. Each of the diagrammatic operations described above comprehends a proliferation of data and various enumerations that can be quantified and, via quantification, subjected to computation. Text, voice, image, gesture, measurement, transaction and many forms of record and recording have been and are being ingested by digital systems as digitised quantities. But the quantities or numbers involved presuppose pattern. The promise of pattern recognition, machine learning or data mining has been predicated on finding patterns in data rendered as number, but the production of data as number, and as massive accumulation of numbers, might already derive from the shifts in seeing, differentiating and classifying that pattern recognition, data mining and machine learning introduce to the presupposed patterns. If algorithmic operations do locate patterns in data, this location already presupposes certain kinds of pattern. The differences between Monte Carlo simulation, the Perceptron and the decision tree starkly delineate presupposed patterns that guide the relations between quantity that algorithms uncover, optimise or converge towards. I have framed these differences as diagrammatic operations to highlight their dependence on and inherence to criss-crossing visual, semiotic, mathematical, technical and infrastructural planes. All of these operations have somewhat diagonal tendencies, which project them across disciplinary boundaries (from physics to gaming media, from psychology to weapons development, from mathematical theory to handheld devices) with sometimes remarkable transcontextual momentum. The diagonal tendencies of, for instance, the decision tree with its indifference to the qualifications of quantity – it traverses different kinds of data very easily – differ from those of the Monte Carlo simulation with its intensive sampling of data spaces generated by accumulated random numbers.

Many different processes and decisions depend increasingly on such diagrammatic operations. If pattern itself takes on a new diagrammatic force, if its asignifying assimilation of differences reiterates what Whitehead terms an 'analogy of functions within analogous patterns', then the Cold War problems of simulation, optimisation and classification find themselves concatenated in a new configuration. The few hundred neutrons of Metropolis and his co-authors expand to include hundreds of millions of observations of players on Xbox Live; the few hundred scientific articles classified by Maron's early decision tree (Morgan and Sonquist 1963) expand to include several billion DNA base pairs of a cancer genome whose associations are analysed by random forests at a Google I/O conference demonstration (Mackenzie 2015b); the simple logical functions that almost choked the development of Perceptrons in the 1960s are inundated by the billions of features that deep learning nets at YouTube and Yahoo pipeline into unsupervised object recognition tasks in online video.

In this ramifying diagrammatic redistribution of pattern, we can expect transformations and reassignments of subject positions as once quite localised force-relations become strategies generalised to business, government and science. What counts as individual, what counts as population, what categories or differences matter, and what the terms of decisions are potentially shift or are reclassified in this generalisation of the diagrammatic operations. Since their inception in problems of nuclear weapons design, logistics or cybernetics, techniques flow out of the closed-world spaces of the Cold War labs and research facilities. They become banal devices rather than instruments of a decisionistic elite. In this movement, another space takes shape, a space whose dimensions are practically treated as open-ended, and whose potential expansion animates the massive build out of infrastructures and the intense efforts to scale up and scale down circuitry and electronic devices. We might need to think about how it might be possible to inhabit this space of patterns as these patterns become power matrices of transformation. The three general cases discussed above all suggest ongoing instability in what counts as pattern, and how pattern derives from movements through data.

Notes

1. Foucault writes: 'I now realize that I could not define the statement as a unit of a linguistic type (superior to the phenomenon of the word, inferior to the text); but that I was dealing with an enunciative function that involved various units (these may sometimes be sentences,

sometimes propositions; but they are sometimes made up of fragments of sentences, series or tables of signs, a set of propositions or equivalent formulations); and, instead of giving a "meaning" to these units, this function relates them to a field of objects; instead of providing them with a subject, it opens up for them a number of possible subjective positions; instead of fixing their limits, it places them in a domain of coordination and coexistence; instead of determining their identity, it places them in a space in which they are used and repeated. In short, what has been discovered is not the atomic statement – with its apparent meaning, its origin, its limits, and its individuality – but the operational field of the enunciative function and the conditions according to which it reveals various units (which may be, but need not be, of a grammatical or logical order)' (1972: 106).

2. Isabelle Stengers provides an excellent account of some of the nineteenth-century development of thermodynamics (2011). The history of statistics since the late seventeenth century obviously forms part of the background here (Stigler 1986; Hacking 1975).

References

Arendt, Hannah (1998), *The Human Condition*, Chicago: University of Chicago Press.

Bellman, Richard (1961), *Adaptive Control Processes: A Guided Tour*, vol. 4, Princeton: Princeton University Press.

Bowker, G. (1993), 'How to Be Universal: Some Cybernetic Strategies, 1943–70', *Social Studies of Science* 23(1): 107–27.

Breiman, Leo (2001), 'Random Forests', *Machine Learning* 45(1): 5–32.

Breiman, Leo, Jerome Friedman, Richard Olshen, Charles Stone, D. Steinberg and P. Colla (1984), *CART: Classification and Regression Trees*, Belmont, CA: Wadsworth.

Collins, Harry M. (1990), *Artificial Experts: Social Knowledge and Intelligent Machines*, Cambridge, MA: MIT Press.

Cortes, Corinna, and Vladimir Vapnik (1995), 'Support-Vector Networks', *Machine Learning* 20(3): 273–97.

Dahl, George (2012), 'Deep Learning How I Did It: Merck 1st Place Interview', *No Free Hunch*, 1 November, <http://blog.kaggle.com/2012/11/01/deep-learning-how-i-did-it-merck-1st-place-interview/> (last accessed 26 January 2016).

Edwards, Paul N. (1996), *The Closed World: Computers and the Politics of Discourse in Cold War America*, Cambridge, MA: MIT Press.

Erickson, Paul, Judy L. Klein, Lorraine Daston, Rebecca Lemov, Thomas Sturm and Michael D. Gordin (2013), *How Reason Almost Lost Its Mind: The Strange Career of Cold War Rationality*, Chicago: University of Chicago Press.

Fisher, R. A. (1938), 'The Statistical Utilization of Multiple Measurements', *Annals of Human Genetics* 8(4): 376–86.

Foucault, Michel (1972), *The Archaeology of Knowledge and the Discourse on Language*, trans. A. Sheridan, New York: Pantheon.

Fuller, Matthew, and Andrew Goffey (2012), *Evil Media*, Cambridge, MA: MIT Press.

Hacking, Ian (1975), *The Emergence of Probability*, Cambridge: Cambridge University Press.

Halpern, Orit (2015), *Beautiful Data*, Durham, NC: Duke University Press.

Hastie, Trevor, Robert Tibshirani and Jerome H. Friedman (2009), *The Elements of Statistical Learning: Data Mining, Inference, and Prediction*, New York: Springer.

Hayles, N. Katherine (1999), *How We Became Posthuman: Virtual Bodies in Cybernetics, Literature, and Informatics*, Chicago: University of Chicago Press.

Hinton, Geoffrey E., and Ruslan R. Salakhutdinov (2006), 'Reducing the Dimensionality of Data with Neural Networks', *Science* 313(5,786): 504–7.

McGrayne, Sharon Bertsch (2011), *The Theory That Would Not Die: How Bayes' Rule Cracked the Enigma Code, Hunted Down Russian Submarines, and Emerged Triumphant from Two Centuries of Controversy*, New Haven, CT: Yale University Press.

Mackenzie, Adrian (2015a), 'The Production of Prediction: What Does Machine Learning Want?', *European Journal of Cultural Studies* 18(2): 429–45.

Mackenzie, Adrian (2015b), 'Machine Learning and Genomic Dimensionality: From Features to Landscapes', in Hallam Stevens and Sarah Richardson (eds), *Postgenomics: Perspectives on Biology after the Genome*, Durham, NC: Duke University Press, pp. 73–102.

Malley, James D., Karen G. Malley and Sinisa Pajevic (2011), *Statistical Learning for Biomedical Data*, Cambridge: Cambridge University Press.

Markoff, John (2012), 'How Many Computers to Identify a Cat? 16,000', *The New York Times*, 25 June, <http://www.nytimes.com/2012/06/26/technology/in-a-big-network-of-computers-evidence-of-machine-learning.html> (last accessed 26 January 2016).

Metropolis, N., A. W. Rosenbluth, M. N. Rosenbluth, A. H. Teller and E. Teller (1953), 'Equation of State Calculations by Fast Computing Machines', *The Journal of Chemical Physics* 21(6): 1,087–92.

Metropolis, Nicholas, and Stanislaw Ulam (1949), 'The Monte Carlo Method', *Journal of the American Statistical Association* 44: 335–41.

Minsky, Marvin, and Seymour Papert (1987 [1969]), *Perceptrons: An Introduction to Computational Geometry*, expanded edition, Cambridge, MA: MIT Press.

Morgan, James N., and John A. Sonquist (1963), 'Problems in the Analysis of Survey Data, and a Proposal', *Journal of the American Statistical Association* 58(302): 415–34.

Pickering, Andrew (2009), *The Cybernetic Brain*, Chicago: University of Chicago Press.

Rosenblatt, Frank (1958), 'The Perceptron: A Probabilistic Model for Information Storage and Organization in the Brain', *Psychological Review* 65(6): 386–408.

Solovey, Mark, and Hamilton Cravens (eds) (2012), *Cold War Social Science: Knowledge Production, Liberal Democracy, and Human Nature*, London: Palgrave Macmillan.

Stengers, Isabelle (2011), *Cosmopolitics II*, trans. Robert Bononno, Minneapolis: University of Minnesota Press.

Stigler, Stephen M. (1986), *The History of Statistics: The Measurement of Uncertainty before 1900*, Cambridge, MA: Harvard University Press.

Vapnik, Vladimir (1999), *The Nature of Statistical Learning Theory*, 2nd edn, New York: Springer.

von Neumann, John, and Oskar Morgenstern (2007 [1944]), *Theory of Games and Economic Behavior*, Princeton: Princeton University Press.

Whitehead, Alfred North (1956), *Modes of Thought: Six Lectures Delivered in Wellesley College, Massachusetts, and Two Lectures in the University of Chicago*, New York: Cambridge University Press.

Wu, X., V. Kumar, J. Ross Quinlan, J. Ghosh, Q. Yang, H. Motoda, G. J. McLachlan et al. (2008), 'Top 10 Algorithms in Data Mining', *Knowledge and Information Systems* 14(1): 1–37.

Chapter 3

Impulsive Synchronisation: A Conversation on Military Technologies and Audiovisual Arts

Aura Satz and Jussi Parikka

Aura Satz's technological art engages with mediated realities and historical pasts that are somehow still present. She completed her PhD in 2002 at the Slade School of Fine Art. Satz's work has been featured in various galleries and festivals in the UK and internationally, from FACT (Liverpool) to Tate and Whitechapel Gallery in London, the Victoria and Albert Museum to the Barbican as well as ICA, and internationally for example at the Zentrum Paul Klee in Switzerland. In 2014–15 she was a Leverhulme Artist-in-Residence at the University of Southampton (the Institute of Sound and Vibration Research, the Department of Music and the John Hansard Gallery) and an artist in residence at Chelsea College of Art, and she also teaches at the Royal College of Art.

Her various installation, audiovisual and performance projects have been able to summon a condition or environment in which one experiences the parallel existence of pasts and presents. Often through historical source work and engaging with past technological ideas, Satz creates poetic imaginaries of technologies, bodies and sonic realities. Indeed, sound technologies are one key theme that runs through a lot of her work, but in a way that engages with the wider vibratory aspects of nature that often become exposed through technological ways of making vibrations and waves visible. She was part of London Science Museum's 'Oramics to Electronica' project (2011) on the female inventor Daphne Oram's 1950s synthesiser. Sound visualisation comes out in projects such as *Vocal Flame* (2012) and the *In and Out of Synch* filmic performance (2012). Cultural techniques of synchronisation are exposed in that specific piece and in others, including *Joan the Woman – with Voice* that was exhibited in 2013. Her interest in the history of automata is most visible in *Automamusic* (2008) and *Automatic Ensemble* (2009), a mixture of old and new automata that engage with surrealist and spiritualist ideas and explorations of automatic writing. Besides the agency of machines, the 'auto-' in the automata, Satz however is always meticulously aware of the human body as a vibratory 'medium' in itself. This body as medium is always, also, recognised as a gendered one, resulting in her historical excavations into specific moments of media history that result in a poetic and empowering relation to women that is often excluded from many projects and historical narratives. Pieces such as *Ventriloqua* (2003) reveal this interest in the close relationship between vibrations, the body and sonic media.

In a way, one could also characterise Satz's method as media archaeological: she is interested in the other stories of media history and sudden, surprising and exciting juxtapositions across temporal layers. Her interest in technological modes of sensing and experience also speak to this media archaeological theme. She is interested in archival material and forgotten 'minor' ideas of media history as a way of staging an audiovisual encounter with the past.

In this conversation Jussi Parikka and Aura Satz focus on her work *Impulsive Synchronisation* (2013) and its contexts in World War II, the later technological frequency-hopping applications and, more widely, the relation of war, art and media archaeological art. The conversation expands to other themes including embodiment, vibration and the importance of modern technological development to our modes of perception.

Jussi Parikka: Let's start with your work *Impulsive Synchronisation* that was exhibited at the Hayward Gallery in London. It's an installation that immerses the visitor in the audiovisual landscape of the 1940s of military technologies but also Hollywood film. The piece refers to a specific 'Secret Communication System' that was patented actually during the war by the Hollywood actress Hedy Lamarr and the composer George Antheil, and besides the immersive experience refers back to this world of 'frequency hopping' as a specific technique that was installed in torpedoes. Could you unpack the work a bit more, elaborate this setting in terms of the historical media technologies and the piece itself?

Aura Satz: I am very much drawn to the history of technology in its most unstable, wobbly moments, such as its inception or its demise into obsolescence. War is an unfortunate catalyst and accelerator for new developments in technology, and in particular during World War II in America the National Inventors Council (NIC) was set up, soliciting inventions and ideas from the general public towards the war effort. Lamarr and Antheil submitted their patent in June 1941, and it was granted to them the following year. The patent of a technological invention is full of the potentiality of its future applications: one doesn't quite know where it will lead to, just as Lamarr and Antheil's invention of frequency hopping was initially conceived for military purposes but then migrated to the realm of telecommunications, wifi and wireless telephony. Their invention was designed to protect radio-controlled torpedoes from enemy disruption by distributing the signal over many frequencies and synchronising the transmitter and receiver in rapidly changing patterns. The idea, which rather bizarrely drew in part on Antheil's unsuccessful attempt to synchronise sixteen pianolas in his 1924 avant-garde masterpiece *Ballet mécanique*, suggested the use of eighty-eight frequencies (the number of keys on a piano), and the use of perforated paper rolls to keep the frequency hops in sync with each other. I am interested in this collision of unlikely technologies: radios, pianolas, torpedoes, implausibly invented by a Hollywood actress and an avant-garde composer. Another key interest in many of my works is the question of the removal of authorship, either through the mediation of agency

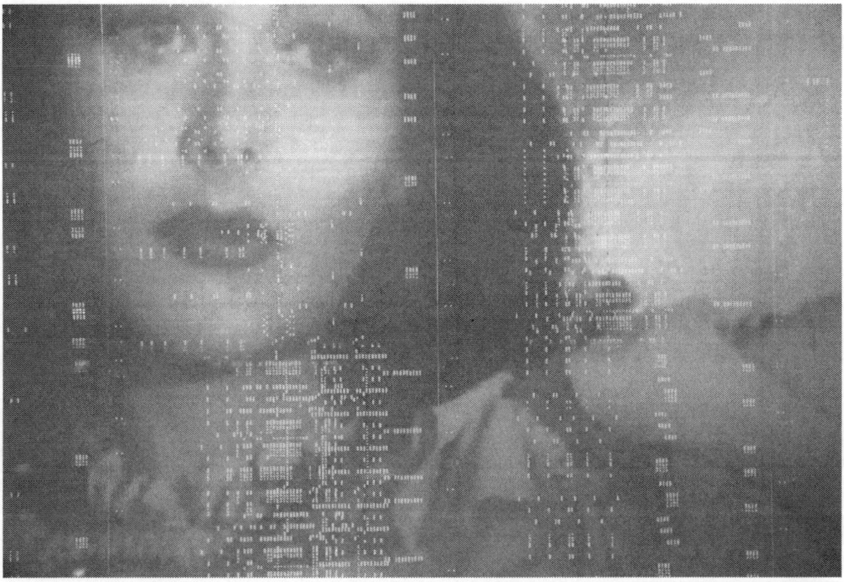

Figure 3.1 Aura Satz, *Impulsive Synchronisation* (2013). Installation view. Courtesy of the artist.

in technology, or the nature of an encounter, oscillating in and out of synchronisation, tuning in and out in dialogue. I love the fact that they invented this together, collaboratively.

JP: It's about communication between humans but also about modern information theory: senders and receivers in the presence of noise, as Shannon and Weaver coined it in the 1940s, right?

AS: Yes, this communicative nature of the invention is echoed in the concept of transmission and reception – the secret communication system is intended as a narrow channel connecting two agents, excluding unwanted enemy interception. It is about a signal moving efficiently between two elements, shrouded in apparent noise, but effectively in sync. Ironically Antheil was supposedly unable to synchronise his pianolas in his music performances so instead he rewrote the numerous scores compressed into one, for a single pianola. For the purposes of this invention the perforated paper strips of transmitter and receiver would have had to have been synchronised in order to operate successfully. The patent states:

> The two records may be synchronized by driving them with accurately calibrated constant speed spring motors, such as are employed for driving clocks and chronometers. However, it is also within the scope of our invention to periodically correct the position of the record at the receiving station by transmitting synchronous impulses from the transmitting station. The use of synchronizing impulses for correcting the phase relation of rotary apparatus at a receiving station is well-known and highly developed in the fields of automatic telegraphy and television.

The patent implicitly addresses the difficulty of synchronisation. Having worked extensively with acoustic devices and sound technologies which explore sound and image synchronisation, I realised that in fact the most interesting moments occur when things fall out of sync, when there is a slippage, a gap, a misalignment, allowing the viewer to inhabit a space between signal and noise. This slippage features both conceptually and materially in the piece, which in a sense conveys the impulse towards synchronisation, effective secret communication, a perfect fit between transmission and reception, but also allows for receiver and transmitter to collide, obscure and misread each other.

The film and sound installation consists of a scrolling screen made from five specially commissioned pianola rolls from Antheil's *Ballet mécanique* (Figure 3.1). The screen is in constant motion so that the film creates a complex light play from the encoded musical score, as the perforated strips of paper interact and produce patterns on the surrounding walls. In addition, a light located behind the screen – a kind of imageless echo of the projection lamp – flashes in systematic intervals, flattening the film-screen and highlighting the materiality of the pianola paper. At times the conflicting light sources overlap and cancel each other out. The pianola paper perforations on the screen slide across each other so that occasionally the holes will overlap, allowing for a peep-hole of sorts, and at other times the screen appears almost to breathe between flatness and sculptural depth, light play and obscurity.

The film projected on to the scrolling screen is a very short extract from *Come Live with Me*, starring Hedy Lamarr and James Stewart. In this romantic comedy – premiered in 1941, the year she submitted the patent for her invention – Lamarr uses the metaphor of the flashlight, like a firefly, to attract a mate. In the installation, the torch footage signals in flashes according to Morse code (the text is an extract from the patent description) (Figure 3.2). The soundscape is composed of vintage underwater recordings of submarines and torpedo explosions from the 1940s, punctuated by the siren sections from *Ballet mécanique*.

JP: The piece itself connects to our theme of Cold War legacies and continuities in many ways. It's centrally concerned with overlapping

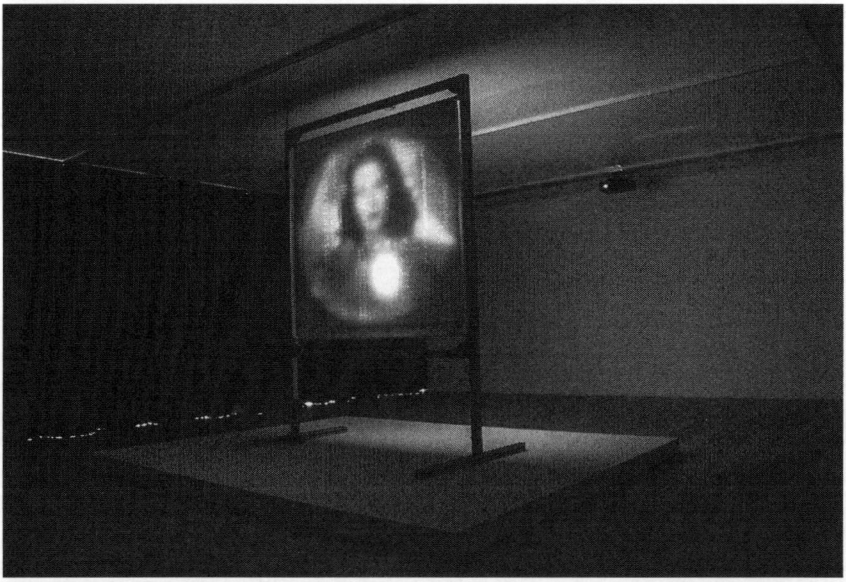

Figure 3.2 Aura Satz, *Impulsive Synchronisation* (2013). Installation view. Courtesy of the artist.

codes. It sets the stage for an investigation that many would attach to a certain Pynchonesque narrative of the twentieth century: the media spectacle worlds of Hollywood, scientific development and military technologies – an array of wild cross-connections that Pynchon employs into an atmosphere of paranoia as the defining 'mood' of the modern technological culture but for you is something else. One thing that stands out is an interesting array of connections relating to code and especially cryptography and signals as a theme that grows out of the Second World War and extends as part of the Cold War era into our current computational worlds. An interest in 'frequencies' is part of your different projects too (including *Ventriloqua*, 2003). This interest refers to the existence of the world of frequencies on which modern communications builds its own high-tech reality. How does that theme of frequencies, code, code-breaking, etc. broadly speaking get mobilised in your work?

AS: I am particularly drawn to codes or transcription systems which hover on the cusp of decipherability. Frequencies, as in recurring patterns of vibration, rotation or waves, are physical manifestations which we read and interpret as a code of sorts. Both *Ventriloqua* and *Theremin* feature the use of a theremin, which is an electronic musical instrument played without physical contact, only by proximity. Invented by the Russian Leon Theremin, who was investigating proximity sensors, it too is a strange case of technology migrating from alarm systems into music, and featuring heavily in Hollywood soundtracks of the '30s and '40s. It usually consists of two antennas, one controlling pitch, the other loudness, and the change in frequency is created by minute hand movements. When we see performers wave their hands about near the antenna, a code or notation system of sorts is suggested, but remains somewhat unreadable, and in turn the musical gestures also suggest some hidden sign language or melodramatic acting technique made music. Many of my projects have looked at forms of notation, scoring, writing, reinterpreting, playback, sonification, through the history of acoustics, music technology and sound reproduction technologies. My film about the unsung electronic music pioneer Daphne Oram not only addressed a little-known contribution of a woman inventor to music technology but also looked at notation and methods of encrypting/writing/composing for a machine. Though she drew on 35 mm clear film, she was less interested in the visuals than in the possibility of reversing an oscilloscope to create a machine that could play drawn sound and provide feedback to monitor immediately. Her Oramics machine, first developed in 1959, used a notation that was intended to provide an empirical pattern-drawing through 'visual-to-aural' means, that would be both intuitive yet precise. Driven by a desire to 'humanise' the machine, Oram promoted the freehand quality of the hand-drawn shapes, which would be inaccurate, indeterminate, able to convey human error, and therefore a musical code full of rich individuality.

I had also made a previous project about mechanical music, with a similar interest in how one can encode music in the binary system of perforated paper, such as the kind used in pianolas (or, in the case of certain orchestrions, pricked barrels). So it was a fortuitous discovery to encounter the pioneering invention of Lamarr, who had collaborated with Antheil for this purpose, drawing on the history of pianola data storage as well as methods of complicating encryption, transmission and reception. Pianola paper just about looks like music notation, but it is intended to be read, played back and performed by the mechanical piano. Likewise, the calligraphic shapes featured in the Oramics machine invented by Oram certainly suggest a form of writing, but one which cannot be imagined or deciphered until it is sonified through the machine.

I am constantly drawn to certain technological devices which enable us to see or hear differently, providing access to an invisible layer of reality, which remains otherwise hidden. Recently I have made a project about 'human computer' astronomers, with a focus on pattern perception in photographic plates of constellations, leading to Henrietta Swan Leavitt's discovery of variable stars. Here too there is an interest in how we translate supposedly random data into meaningful patterns, which are measured in terms of a variable frequency. I suppose many of my works intend to explore heightened perception as a potential experience for the viewer or participant, but also convey the labour of close attention, altered perceptual sensitivity, and the mediated form of authorship or agency that these technologies provide.

JP: This idea of invisible layers of reality which cannot be directly accessed but become sensible, experienced through your artistic work, is really interesting. It somehow, to me, seems like a crystallisation of the logic of technical media realities as well as a commentary of that situation: the technical realities of sound and vibrations that are somehow paradoxically present and yet sensually removed from our bodies.

AS: Yes, I am drawn to sound and more recently colour as both suggest a certain instability, a vibratory state which is perceptually hard to hold on to or fix and codify. Acoustics often translates it into visual means in order to apprehend it better, make it more stable as a sensory experience. The visualisation of sound waves facilitates the perception of patterns which are otherwise hard to access visually. It is essentially a form of notation, of transcription, which allows for the translation from one sense to the other. And yet precisely because of its elusive nature, sound resists notation, it can never be accurately conveyed, only certain information can be translated and it is inevitably a partial representation. An interesting example of this difficulty of transcription which I have always found fascinating is Alexander Melville Bell's 'Visible Speech' method of phonetic notation (1864); it is an attempt to write language from the outside in, as it were, the positions of the tongue and teeth in relation to pronunciation, so as to make spoken language accessible to those without hearing. I find these kinds of partial notation systems a useful way of accessing our bodies differently, reconfiguring our senses, hearing through seeing or vice versa. Colour too has its own instability, in the materiality of its support surface, which is inherently deteriorating or fading or shifting in tone according to light, but also perceptually: we all see colours differently. So although it is a sensory experience, it is intrinsically unreliable, resisting a stable system of codification; we can only approximate it.

JP: Another aspect that interests me in this piece is that it can clearly be said to be historical in some ways. As in a lot of your work – and we can return to your artistic methodology more broadly a bit later – you work with historical material and with archival methods too. But there is another way in which time is employed here and it is revealed in the title even: synchronisation. It can be claimed that synchronisation is one key modern technique of rationalisation (from synchronisation of mass transport such as trains to the wider temporal synchronisation of time across the globe since the nineteenth century) as well as part of technological culture. Modern computational systems as well are constantly concerned with synchronisation, such as network traffic. What's your interest in this concept or technique?

AS: That's a really interesting question. I think all my works deal with synchronisation and asynchronisation, tuning in and tuning out, in one way or another. In a sense the works themselves are always out of sync with their own time frame, having a strong historical reference point in the past. I am particularly interested in the time frame of 1850–1950, when many significant technologies of communication and the audiovisual were being established, tested out and experienced for the very first time. I look back at history, exploring archives and trying to figure out what significant paradigm shifts a certain technology may have enacted. So in *Sound Seam* I looked at how the phonograph shifts our understanding of writing, or script, of time and playback, memory and recovery, whilst also opening up to the idea of creating sound out of nothing, from a line that is unencoded. How does technology remember in our stead? How does technology echo our own mnemonic patterns? And how might technology affect a change, so that we reconfigure our understanding of our anatomy and psyche? I am frequently in the position of looking backwards to a moment in which the future was imagined.

I think of many of my more historical works as a conversation of sorts, in which I am in dialogue with the historical figure from the past, bringing their work into speech, making visible a forgotten or overlooked part of history, providing a platform for this to receive attention. But beyond this revisionist project, it is crucial for me that the content of this historical moment in itself addresses questions around time.

In all my works around sound technology I am always questioning the possibility of playback, of writing sound in order to reproduce it. If the device is merely for the sake of visualisation (rather than reproduction), such as my works with the Chladni Plate and the Ruben's tube, then it is again to address the difficulty of memory latching on to this living shape-shifting alphabet that resists writing and exists only in a fascinating now-moment. These geometric shapes in sand or flame patterns suggest a code but are in fact too abstract a form of writing for us to truly engage with it. And so we hover in a state of suspended attention; the patterning hypnotises us into looking, sensing we are on the threshold of understanding something, but at the same time we are thrown out of an easy narrative seduction, alienated from being fully immersed and therefore intensely aware of our sensory body and physical engagement. I try to create in the spectator an intense awareness of the present through a phenomenological encounter with sensory disorientation (visual or acoustic illusions, hypnotic light patterns, drone music, etc.), a stimulation, sometimes even an assault on the senses, so we are forced into a bodily first-hand encounter. At the same time the work is about the past, speaking of and through the past. As I said above, I like to inhabit the slippages between synchronisation, when what you see doesn't quite fit what you hear and vice versa, and therefore you are forced into a state of close attention, an awareness of the materiality of what you are looking at.

JP: I perceive a strong sense of rhythm, pulse and multi-sensorality in your approach and understanding of aesthetics.

AS: In my 16 mm film *In and Out of Synch*, the perfect rendition of an analogue optical soundtrack, a true representation of what you are hearing, is broken and segmented by the machine's stroboscopic monitor effect. Instead of a smooth translation of sound into image you are confronted with what look like Rorschach inkblots, pulsing to their own autonomous rhythm, which is not clearly connected to the poetic voiceover. The jarring effects of these instances become pregnant with new meanings. I like the freedom in abstraction, though it is always on the brink of appearing decipherable, and that tension between the abstract and the figure, the noise and the signal, provides a fascinating mode of encounter. In the title of *Impulsive Synchronisation* I wanted to point to the fact that as living beings we are inherently pattern seekers. No matter how random a sequence, there is a threshold at which we start to hear or see repetition and use this in our understanding of the world. We have an impulse toward synchronisation. I always come back to the example of how we understand the immateriality of sound; if an unexplained noise catches our attention, we will immediately seek out a visual counterpart (the slamming door etc.).

I tend to work with an unsettling effect, where you cannot easily latch sound on to image, or where the sound itself doesn't quite reveal its source: is it human or machine? Is it inside or out, near or far? In many instances my projects seem to inhabit an unstable territory somewhere between futuristic nostalgia, science fiction, horror film and abstraction, all of which are closely tied in together.

JP: In my introduction to your work, I already used the term 'media archaeology'. At least to me I see your work as being close to some of that in media archaeological methods, both scholarly and artistic. It seems to write media history but in ways that are not 'merely' historical. What I mean by that is that you are interested in a non-linear as well as parallel investigations of media pasts and current moments, often attaching this to science and technology as well as gender issues. Can you elaborate a bit more on aspects of your artistic methodology? Does it relate to the just-mentioned idea of conversation?

AS: Yes, I am definitely interested in media archaeology, though I wouldn't dare call myself one! I think it is clear by now that I like to time-travel through the work and sometimes take unexpected historical leaps. Some of the technologies I have engaged with are not quite ripe for their historical moment, or they are already obsolete in the moment of their inception. Others are small components in a greater technological or scientific evolution, but it is rarely ever linear. It flashes backwards and forwards to other moments in time, and is very often also in a close conversation with the present moment.

The Lamarr/Antheil invention is very much of this moment, with wifi, spread-spectrum and broadband being the predominant network system for telecommunications. With regard to gender, it really started with my *Oramics* project, though I had been interested in the female voice and technology for many years prior to that. In *Ventriloqua* I was interested in the possibility of suggesting intra-uterine speech from an unborn foetus. A truly literal ventriloquist act of 'belly-speaking', the pregnant belly was transformed into a musical instrument, an antenna, a medium, through which an otherworldly voice was transmitted. The body became a vessel, a mouthpiece through which the disembodied voice appeared re-embodied – one body placed within another body, speaking and spoken through, producing abstract musical utterances which might predict the future, although destined to remain in an amniotic amnesia. This in itself harks back to the primal drive of all sound reproduction technologies, a dislocation of voice from the mouth, sound and its source.

Since then I have remained concerned with questions of voice, of speaking and being spoken through, a porous notion of authorship. It seems that women were instrumental in the most significant moments of the history of telecommunications, as telephone operators; of writing systems, as secretarial typists; to name but a few. They were in a sense hollow vessels or carriers of other voices, but they barely had the right to vote, to actually have a voice.

So I feel it is partly my duty, not only my fascination, to convey some of this history and bring back into speech – make audible – something of this forgotten narrative. Through my work I am also somehow spoken through, a medium or carrier of other historical voices. I like to examine technologies, which are for the most part speech and image containers, and in my films most of my camera-work involves close-up, getting inside the machine and looking at it in ways which are usually inaccessible. I try to uncover some of the narratives that are already implicit in the sculptural qualities of the technology I am zooming in on. Mechanical music instruments look like analogues of the human body, complete with wheezing lungs, skeletal fingers and splayed entrails. The Oramics machine looks like a weaving loom, a film lab, a dystopian architectural ruin, the film

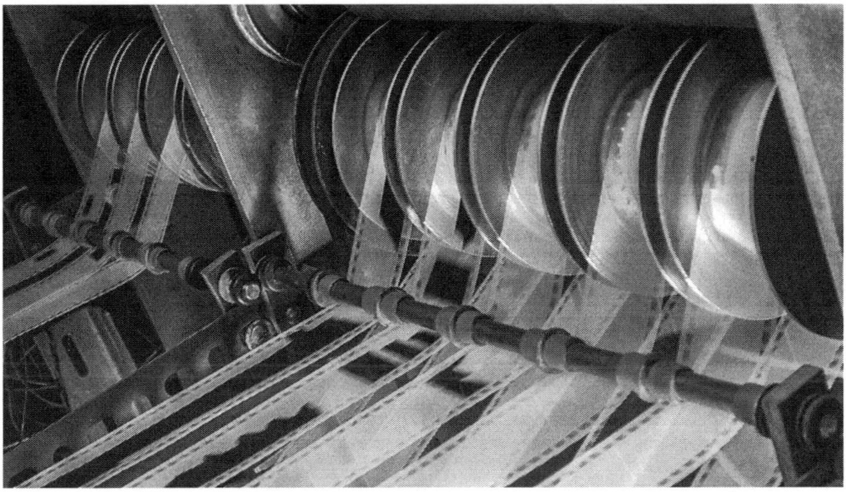

Figure 3.3 Aura Satz, *Oramics: Atlantis Anew* (2011). Film still. Courtesy of the artist.

set of *Metropolis* (Figure 3.3). The valves and lenses of the colour lamp-house of an analogue printer in my film *Doorway for Natalie Kalmus* bring to mind sci-fi film sets, where the specks of dust on a glass surface evoke the constellations of outer space or galaxies, and the miniature valves controlling the colour flow recall the haunting doors and coloured gel lights of a Dario Argento film set. The formal material qualities of these machines are in themselves darting back and forth in historical timelines, referencing potential echoes of their pre- and post-existence.

JP: And also in addition to historical, archaeological impulses, you underline the collective nature of the work: with specialists but also collectively letting objects have a certain agency and participate in the collectives of the art making.

AS: I undertake extensive research and I also consult with specialists in the field, be this historians, technicians, engineers, archivists, so in that sense there is definitely a 'scholarly' aspect to my process. I feel I need this also out of respect to the subject matter. But at the same time I do let the objects speak for themselves, tell a different story, based on visual, acoustic or formal associations. The scrolling screen of *Impulsive Synchronisation* seemed to evoke the temporary projection screens of contemporary PowerPoint lectures, while the pulsing light of Hedy Lamarr, though drawing on Morse code and other forms of light signalling such as heliography (solar telegraphy), also brought to mind the spotlight of Hollywood, like a variable star, fading in and out of visibility. My private reference point for the film installation's light configuration was actually structuralist film-maker Malcolm Le Grice's piece *Castle 1*, in which a film is projected alongside a bare flashing light bulb which has itself been filmed and appears within the movie. When the light bulb switches on, the screen as a projection surface is flattened to reveal its materiality. So the archaeological impulse is both historical, looking through time, and material.

JP: That is indeed the fascinating point – this entanglement of time and materiality. You mention your interest in the period of 1850–1950 as fundamental to a range of modern inventions, or a technological way of life. It's interesting in this context to consider how research into acoustics was instrumental in post-World War II and Cold War-era information theory as well: psychophysics as a way to understand information and noise. In the context of information theory, cybernetics and systems theory even, it seems that sound, vibrations and acoustics (and the embodied listener of the psychoacoustic measurement) still have a place too. Perhaps one could go even as far as to speculate on this aesthetic and embodied grounding of information theory, a thesis that sounds paradoxical but has some historical mileage. There are interesting projects in the media art history of the twentieth century – for example, Alvin Lucier's – which offer interesting counterpoints and resonances. To me your work also addresses this aspect of materiality of information, and I am looking forward to your future projects.

II The Persistence of the Nuclear

Chapter 4

The Meaning of Monte Bello

James Purdon

King George VI – Britain's last pre-nuclear monarch – died on 6 February 1952. By the time Elizabeth II was crowned, in June of the following year, the United Kingdom had become an atomic power. Operation Hurricane, the first British atom bomb test, took place on 3 October near the Monte Bello islands in Western Australia, marking not only the success of Britain's nuclear ambitions but a key moment in Commonwealth relations. Its success depended upon an extensive international infrastructure of uranium mines, laboratories, reactor piles, depots and proving grounds. Yet most accounts of British Cold War culture have tended to obscure rather than illuminate the detail of that global effort. If the Manhattan Project quickly took on the shape of an 'origin myth' for atomic-age America, its British counterpart has remained stubbornly unmythological (Hales 1992: 251). Or so it might appear. In this chapter, I want to challenge that idea by drawing attention both to the energetic programme of official nuclear self-fashioning that accompanied the British atomic bomb project, and to some of the complex imaginative fictions of the time that responded to the possibility of a nuclear war involving Britain. My main claim will be that both kinds of narrative, official and unofficial, are best understood not by comparison with American cultural production, but in light of strenuous efforts during the 1950s to consolidate the Commonwealth of Nations under the British nuclear umbrella. Those efforts had begun at the end of the Second World War, when America withdrew support for the British nuclear programme, and continued until 1958, when – following Britain's successful production of the hydrogen bomb – transatlantic nuclear links were renewed.

In the intervening years, Commonwealth co-operation was essential to British nuclear policy. 'In the research and development phase', notes the defence historian Wayne Reynolds, 'Britain attempted the integration of the Commonwealth in its own Manhattan programme. Apart from the well-known role of rocket and atomic testing, the Commonwealth provided the all important ingredients for the bomb formula – scientific manpower plus materials' (Reynolds 1996: 122). Those ingredients – uranium, skilled labour, vast tracts of 'empty' space – were not readily available elsewhere. In 1946, despite Churchill's confidence that the British contribution to the Manhattan Project was 'a happy augury for our future relations', the United States had passed the McMahon Act, reversing wartime agreements on nuclear collaboration ('First Atomic Bomb Hits Japan', p. 4). Without access to American data and American test sites, Britain fell back on the Commonwealth for the resources it needed to develop its own atomic bomb.

Since the Second World War, however, the Commonwealth had experienced a series of geopolitical shifts. Ireland had left in April 1949, becoming a republic. In 1950, India also became a republic, though it elected to retain its Commonwealth membership. Pakistan was expected to follow suit. With the King in declining health, the future of the Commonwealth was not assured. George had been named the first 'Head of the Commonwealth' at the 1949 Prime Ministers' Conference, but it was far from clear that the title would automatically pass to Elizabeth (see Murphy 2013: 50–3). Careful planning and a good deal of back-channel diplomacy managed to avert any public crisis, but the extent of those discreet negotiations testifies to the fact that the period was a sensitive one in Commonwealth relations. This was the political background to the Monte Bello test. As a result, British nuclear propaganda had three purposes: to give the impression of continuity, both in respect of Britain's foreign policy and in respect of her military capacity; to reflect the (albeit temporary) realignment of Britain's security policy away from the United States and towards Commonwealth partners; and to shore up Commonwealth relations in the wake of Irish and Indian independence. The Bomb, such propaganda insisted, would secure the Commonwealth from its enemies. But it would also help to secure the Commonwealth for Britain.

Once transatlantic intelligence-sharing resumed in 1958, Britain became less dependent on the Commonwealth. Tests of the first British thermonuclear weapons took place not in Australia but in the South Pacific, and later weapons tests were carried out jointly with the United States in Nevada. The irradiated spaces of the Commonwealth became sacrificial zones, the contaminated residue of a military-industrial process designed to engineer nuclear security. Having been placed at the heart of that project throughout the 1950s, they became marginal once more. In the beginning, however, those spaces had been highly visible. The British nuclear programme was far more widely dispersed, spatially, than its American and Soviet counterparts, but it was also far more conspicuous. Where the tests of Trinity and RDS-1 had been conducted in conditions of strict secrecy, Operation Hurricane was a highly anticipated media event: the precise location of the test was made public even before the bomb had left England, and its success was reported without delay. Indeed, thanks to the time difference between Britain and Australia, *The Times* was able to carry the news in the same day's edition. At breakfast, readers in London might have skimmed advertisements extolling the modern comforts of latex foam mattresses, the luxury of Qantas Empire Airways, and the energy-giving properties of Supavite vitamin pills before encountering the following item at the top of page six:

> BRITISH ATOMIC WEAPON EXPLODED
> SUCCESS OF MONTE BELLO TEST
>
> Britain's first atomic weapon was exploded in the Monte Bello Islands to-day. The Admiralty announced that the test had been a success.
>
> An observer reported that the cloud from the blast had a ragged shape at the base and that one minute after the detonation it reached 6,000ft. Within three minutes the cloud was a mile wide at its centre and the shape at the top was like a ragged letter 'Z'. ('British Atomic Weapon', p. 6)

Operation Hurricane had exploded with the force of twenty-five kilotons of TNT. As planned, it incinerated the frigate carrying it and left a twenty-foot-deep crater on the seabed. The cloud from the explosion, blown into that strange 'Z' shape by strong winds, drifted in unexpected directions and passed over the Australian mainland 15,000 feet lower than expected. Soldiers and aircrew assigned to retrieve samples of contaminated material were routinely exposed to dangerous levels of radiation (see Darby et al. 1988). On his return to England the project leader, William Penney, was greeted by reporters from British Pathé who wanted to know what he would do next. Beaming at the camera with satisfaction, Dr Penney replied: 'I shall have a short holiday, and I hope to play some golf' (*Atom Man's Hush-Hush Return*).

Pathé was not the only organisation covering the progress of the British nuclear programme, however. Not one but two official films were made in order to explain the significance of the test to British audiences. *Operation Hurricane* (1952), directed by Ronald Stark and produced by Stuart Legg, was sponsored by the Ministry of Supply, and won a diploma at the 1953 Edinburgh International Film Festival. At around the same time, Adrian Cooper and Ron Osborn directed

This Little Ship (1953) for the UK Atomic Energy Authority. Although both films used some of the same location footage from the Monte Bello test, they drew on different aspects of the British documentary tradition, and the results differed in form, in tone, and in focus. What the two films have in common, however, is a repertoire of tropes, inherited from a quarter of a century of British documentary film-making, which they deploy in order to situate Britain's first nuclear test within a continuous national narrative of technological progress and military power. Each sought to integrate the new and unfamiliar weapon into a specifically *global* understanding of English identity associated with its geopolitical leadership formerly of the Empire and latterly of the Commonwealth of Nations.

Operation Hurricane opens, to the accompaniment of John Addison's eerie brass and woodwind score, in deep England: 'It began on the rolling Weald of Kent. For the Monte Bello bomb was designed, and most of it was made, in this quiet, unsuspecting countryside.' After a long, wide pan across the bucolic Kentish landscape, the film takes its audience through a tangled screen of trees and past the security checkpoints of Fort Halstead – 'built for defence against French invasion' – to introduce Sir William Penney, the leader of Britain's atomic bomb project and 'the only British scientist at the atom bombing of Nagasaki'. There follows a sequence in which the marvels of high technology work in harmony with good old-fashioned skill, as the voiceover introduces us to the 'electronic brain' used by the nuclear scientists before enumerating the no-less-impressive accomplishments of the 'British craftsmen' engaged to produce precision instruments and components for the nuclear test.

Soon the action shifts to the naval dockyard at Chatham, where the finished equipment is loaded on to the carrier HMS *Campania* and the landing ship HMS *Tracker*. Next, after a brief glimpse of early on-site preparations at Monte Bello, we follow *Campania* to Portsmouth, where – 'within sight of Nelson's *Victory*' – she takes aboard the scientific team that will conduct the nuclear test. The first third of the film thus deftly establishes a continuous history for Britain's defence sector, drawing a direct line from Nelson and Napoleon to Nagasaki and nuclear weapons. After that comes the voyage out: leaving Britain behind, *Campania* and *Tracker* head for Monte Bello. The latter two thirds of the narrative concern the preparation of the nuclear test, the countdown to detonation, and the collection of data from around the site. Particular emphasis is given throughout to Commonwealth collaboration. The film begins with a title card explaining that the nuclear test was performed 'with the fullest co-operation' of Australia, and we see that contribution demonstrated in what follows. At Monte

Bello, the engineers of the Royal Australian Air Force are filmed building a jetty and roads. Meanwhile, an Australian meteorologist prepares the weather forecast that will decide the timing of the test, and the Royal Australian Navy and Air Force are deployed to patrol the test zone itself.

As Lee Grieveson has shown, the first generation of Commonwealth information films made in the 1920s and early 1930s were designed to reinforce Britain's economic hegemony by presenting an idealised account of the exchange of goods and capital between a colonial periphery and a metropolitan core. Grieveson describes two related topoi that became central to films made by the Conservative Party, and later to those of such early British film-propaganda bodies as the Empire Marketing Board and the GPO Film Unit. The first of these topoi, exemplified by the Conservative Party's *West Africa Calling* (1927), displays the transformation of 'unproductive natural spaces (forest, swamp, desert)' into 'exemplary spaces of liberal civility (hospital, school)' through the activities of British technology, administration and capital. We can call this the *development* topos. The second, call it the *circulation* topos, depicts the movement of commodities around channels of global trade opened and secured by British power. Here, Grieveson's exemplary instances are Walter Creighton's *One Family* (1930), in which a small boy dreams about visiting the different Commonwealth countries that produce ingredients for the King's Christmas pudding, and Basil Wright's *Cargo from Jamaica* (1933), which follows a single commodity – the banana – from colonial plantation to metropolitan warehouse. Together, development and circulation became the standard way of representing Commonwealth interdependency in early colonial film (Grieveson 2011: 97).

At first glance, *Operation Hurricane* appears to perpetuate the colonial information film's apportioning of spaces. On the one hand, there is a technologically advanced metropolitan modernity represented by British laboratories and workshops; on the other, an unproductive colonial space ('the remote and barren Monte Bello islands') which can be made useful only through the deployment of Western machines, capital and administration. This is development writ large. But what kind of development is it? The aim of the test, after all, is not creation but destruction; a successful outcome will not make an unproductive space productive, but pollute that space irreversibly. To make this quite clear, the film takes a moment of calm before its countdown sequence to show soldiers fishing in the shallow waters of the Trimouille lagoon. 'This is their last chance to fish,' explains the announcer. 'After the explosion all fishing will be banned, because of the danger of contamination.' Once the fishing is done, the squaddies get back to work, setting out samples of protective clothing and edible produce. Like the fish, it will not be edible for long. 'Foodstuffs of all kinds await tomorrow's experiment: butter, tea, tinned meat, sacks of flour, some open to the air, some packed in boxes or cartons or tins, to test the value of various containers as protection against contamination.'

At the centre of this short sequence is that most British of commodities: tea. And not just any tea. Shown in close-up, the wooden packing crate we are invited to inspect bears its stamp of origin in large capitals: 'CEYLON'. All of the commodities listed and laid out for testing in the film (butter, tea, meat, flour) are of precisely the kind that Britain traditionally imported from Commonwealth countries. These were the same commodities that colonial documentary had traced around the trade-routes of the Empire. But tea, and particularly Ceylon tea, had a special significance. Followed from field to cup, tea was the commodity narrative's star commodity. The loading and unloading of tea crates had been a standard segment in a host of films, from Basil Wright's *The Song of Ceylon* (1934) to Theodore Thumwood's *Food from the Empire* (1940).[1]

On screen, the tea crate came to stand for imperial trade, making visible the routes around which commodities and capital circulated. Colonial film, like the Empire itself, ran on tea. In *Operation Hurricane*, however, tea is put to a different use. Instead of making visible the abstraction of trade, it signifies the invisible radiation damage that will soon turn it into a waste product of the nuclear test. The colonial product will never be consumed by Britain's tea-drinkers; like the Monte Bello fish, it will be sacrificed, set aside as collateral. Removed from circulation, the contaminated tea will underwrite the nuclear security that guarantees Britain's continued geopolitical status.

A group of fishing soldiers. A tea crate. These two objects of the film's attention might seem incidental to the narrative of nuclear development, but in fact they are the means by which that narrative is made to connect with a much longer history of colonialism and its representation on film. The iconography of Britain's imperial past is sacrificed in order to sustain power in a new guise. By comparison with the neatly stacked commodities at Monte Bello, that new power is formlessness itself, made manifest in the black nuclear cloud with which the film ends. Over the course of two minutes, caught from several angles, the cloud fills the frame and quickly expands beyond it as the announcer sums up:

> That lethal cloud rising above Monte Bello marks the achievement of British science and industry in the development of atomic power. But it leaves unanswered the question: how shall this new-found

> power be used? For good or evil? For peace or war? For progress or destruction? The answer doesn't lie with Britain alone, but we may have a greater voice in this great decision if we have the strength to defend ourselves and to deter aggression. That was the meaning of Monte Bello.

Shaping the meaning of Monte Bello was precisely what *Operation Hurricane* was designed to do, and it did so by laying out the iconography of colonial film for inspection at the very moment of its obsolescence. Like Operation Hurricane, *Operation Hurricane* stacks up the symbolic commodities of Empire trade as a necessary sacrifice to the new nuclear power that will ensure Commonwealth security. At the same time, the film makes clear that such security depends on new (military, industrial) kinds of co-operation between Britain and her Commonwealth allies. No longer united by the homely symbol of the King's Christmas pudding, the Commonwealth will be united by the atomic bomb. The mute cloud – the condition of Britain's continuing ability to speak for itself – guarantees 'a greater voice' in the nuclear age. That voice was not to be attained without the help of the Commonwealth. Despite the inclusive 'we', the voice making the argument in *Operation Hurricane* was not British. The announcer's cut-glass accent in fact belonged to Chester Wilmot, a well-known Australian war correspondent whose reports on the Siege of Tobruk and the Normandy landings had made him famous both in Britain and in Australia. The following year, along with the Canadian Bernard Braden, he would contribute commentary to the BBC's televised coverage of the Coronation (Potter 2012: 166). As the narrator of *Hurricane*, he was an inspired choice: a perfect embodiment of the kind of Commonwealth co-operation that the film sought to celebrate.

The reason Britain's first nuclear weapon was tested in a lagoon rather than on land was to see how extensive the damage might be were a ship-borne bomb to be deployed in a British port. In *This Little Ship*, the Atomic Energy Authority told the story of the test as a eulogy for HMS *Plym*, the frigate that carried the bomb. *Plym*, it turns out, is an unlikely hero, undistinguished in wartime service. Now, however, by being offered as a sacrifice in the service of a nuclear Britain, *Plym* has a shot at redemption: 'If she goes to kingdom come like this,' the commentary points out, 'perhaps she'll prove the greatest of them all.' Gerard DeGroot, who describes *This Little Ship* as 'a typical example of British official dissimulation', is no doubt right to draw attention to the film's use of propaganda techniques forged in wartime (2005: 220). The countdown sequence, in which the camera shows the empty halls of *Plym* in the last seconds before the explosion, and even the fall of an abandoned teacup in the ship's galley, were evidently creative reconstructions of the kind that had become a staple of the wartime Crown Film Unit. But *This Little Ship* also fits into a rather longer tradition of ship films made by the Unit and its predecessors. Ships always played a major role in British documentary. As emblems of maritime history, as small mobile communities, and as links in the communications and trade networks of the Empire, they were excellent subjects for film-makers who wanted to tell factual stories about the state of Britain. Grierson, in *Drifters* (1929), had kick-started the documentary movement with a ship film, the first of many. Harry Watt's *North Sea* (1938) told the story of a fishing trawler lost in a storm. Humphrey Jennings's *SS Ionian* (1939) had used a merchant vessel's last voyage around the Mediterranean ports as the structure for a story about British commerce and character in uneasy times. David MacDonald's *Men of the Lightship* (1940) concerned a Luftwaffe raid on an unarmed British lightship, and more recently Basil Wright had made *Waters of Time* (1951), a celebration of the London docks for the Festival of Britain. Ships, in these films, represent the transformation of traditional seafaring through high technology, from 'brown sails and village harbours' – as the first title card of *Drifters* has it – to 'an epic of steam and steel'.

To be sure, the makers of *This Little Ship* were no Humphrey Jennings. But they did manage to produce an oddly poignant film, less a tribute to *Plym* than an elegy for a whole form of warfare rendered obsolete by the atom bomb. It is that connection to Britain's naval past, rather than any enthusiasm for the bomb itself, that gives the film whatever propaganda value it possesses. For DeGroot, the film presents 'a sense of finality – the death of the ship – rather than of beginning – the dawning of a new age of nuclear uncertainty'. But is this really the case? There is something ambivalent, at the very least, about a propaganda film in which the symbol chosen to demonstrate the continuity of British values and British valour goes up in smoke. As the sailors of *Campania* watch the cloud drift, the narration tries to put the image in some kind of context: 'From 1300 tons to nothing. Lost without loss of life. Lost – and saving life. For now war is self-destruction, and who will dare attack?'

The film might have ended there, in a mood of optimism. Yet there follows a self-consciously eerie coda, in which the nuclear test's success is reported in a tone that turns triumph to anxiety. From the image of the drifting nuclear cloud, we cut to an establishing shot of a London street sign. We are in Whitehall, in a dark Admiralty operations room, where the message is received in a dim operations room by a naval officer. The voiceover gives the content (presumably invented for the film itself):

PLYM, OBLIVION. REPEAT, OBLIVION. OBLIVION.

Between the final repetitions of the word 'oblivion', the officer walks across the room to a large map of Australia, where with studied efficiency he removes the marker which must – as we see when the film cuts to a close-up of the map – have indicated *Plym*'s position. From the map we then dissolve to the territory, or rather to a shot of the deep water where (the cut implies) *Plym* until recently floated. From this closing shot, accompanied by the monitory brass note that sounds over it, the ending of *This Little Ship* seems far less upbeat than might be expected. And indeed the film as a whole is full of such subtle indications that *Plym*'s noble sacrifice might amount to an ambiguous sort of redemption, not least in the fact that in its last harbour, 'enmeshed, tied, bound for nowhere', the little ship appears framed against the ghostly sky, for all the world like a nuclear *Temeraire*.

Each of these films attempts to explain Britain's first nuclear test – to give meaning to Monte Bello – by placing it within a continuous history of British global power. Yet in both cases, the visible cloud of nuclear sublimity exceeds the attempt to impose order by means of the linear movement of cinematic narrative technique. Both films, having reached their climactic, explosive moment at the end of a formal countdown sequence, end with moments that reinstate formlessness as a compositional principle. *Operation Hurricane*, having first moved from the explosion back to the processes of ordering, analysing and sorting carried out by the test team as they check their results, returns in its final moments to a view of the black nuclear plume itself. This is in effect an action replay, revisiting the moment of the test in terrifying detail, but it might also be taken to demonstrate the kind of repetition required by the regime of deterrence. *This Little Ship*, meanwhile, ends with a shot of rippling water. Drawing on their colonial and wartime precursors, these films know how to deal with the pre-nuclear world of order, arrangement and precision craftsmanship. They are far less sure how to deal with the destructive formlessness represented by an atomic cloud. Both, ultimately, have recourse to an imperial iconography that will no longer serve. A few years later, in his World War III novel *On the Last Day* (1958), the left-wing British journalist Mervyn Jones would imagine an exiled civil servant gazing from the Canadian coast back towards Soviet-occupied England, as a damaged warship limps back into harbour:

> Each life travelled like a little ship about an infinity of ocean: some with better charts than others, some quite at random, but each creating in its isolation a fantasy of its own importance. [. . .] Looking back, Bernard saw that it was because the sea was so vast that there were so few collisions. Now one vast storm could include and cancel all the collisions measured by time, and add time itself to the wreckage. (Jones 1958: 134)

Bernard Austen is ostensibly drawing a comparison here between the battered destroyer and the individuals who have fled Britain to continue fighting the war from Canada – but he is also thinking about Britain itself, that once-proud maritime power now reduced to the status of a political fantasy. It is within such a fantasmatic space that these films attempt to 'give meaning to Monte Bello' by placing the inaugural British nuclear test within a continuous history of development: from nation, to Empire, to Commonwealth. Yet the logic of nuclear deterrence, as the films themselves show, is not that of continuous progress but rather that of repetitive stalemate. In the final moments of *Operation Hurricane*, the camera returns once more to the black nuclear cloud itself, as if to demonstrate that the regime of deterrence requires not one atomic test, but a permanent spectacle of nuclear capability.

The first nuclear weapons were powerful enough to level entire cities. It was not long, however, before imaginative writers had to reckon the potential destruction on a much larger scale. In Aldous Huxley's *Ape and Essence* (1948), for instance, the zone of desolation is very nearly global:

> This new bright day is the twentieth of February, 2108, and these men and women are members of the New Zealand Rediscovery Expedition to North America. Spared by the belligerents of the Third World War – not, I need hardly say, for any humanitarian reason, but simply because, like Equatorial Africa, it was too remote to be worth anybody's while to obliterate – New Zealand survived and even modestly flourished in an isolation which, because of the dangerously radioactive condition of the rest of the world, remained for more than a century almost absolute. Now that the danger is over, here come its first explorers, rediscovering America from the West. And meanwhile, on the other side of the world, the black men have been working their way down the Nile and across the Mediterranean. What splendid tribal dances in the bat-infested halls of the Mother of Parliaments!

> And the labyrinth of the Vatican – what a capital place in which to celebrate the lingering and complex rites of female circumcision! We all get precisely what we ask for. (Huxley 2005 [1948]: 48)

Huxley goes further, here, than Thomas Macaulay, who in 1840 had supplied one of Victorian Britain's most enduring symbols of transience when he imagined a far-future traveller from New Zealand sketching among London's ruins. (Even if New Zealand outlasted the British Empire, Macaulay, unlike Huxley, thought it quite possible that the Vatican would still be in one piece.) We might breathe a sigh of relief at remembering that Huxley's New Zealanders – and the apes who rule America in the novel – are only characters in a rejected film script, but the idea that brought them into existence had taken root. When British writers sought an escape route from nuclear war, they tended to look south. The novelist Bruce Chatwin (b. 1940) would later remember how, having watched a Civil Defence lecturer circling perimeters of destruction on a map of Europe, he and his schoolmates decided upon migration as their only hope for survival: 'We started an Emigration Committee and made plans to settle in some far corner of the earth. We pored over atlases. We learned the direction of prevailing winds and the likely patterns of fall-out. The war would come in the Northern Hemisphere, so we looked to the Southern' (Chatwin 1998 [1977]: 3–4).

Many writers of the time did too. In John Wyndham's *The Chrysalids* (1955), New Zealand (or 'Sealand', as the book's psychic posthuman children interpret it) is the narrative's utopian goal, while another of Wyndham's novels, *The Outward Urge* (1959), depicts a post-nuclear-war world in which Australia and Brazil have emerged as a new superpower duopoly. Other writers echoed Huxley's vision of Africa as a plausible successor continent: Christine Brooke-Rose's *Out* (1964) imagines an unspecified radiation-producing catastrophe ('the great displacement') reversing the power relation between black and white, and sending waves of white migrants to work in menial jobs in Africa (Brooke-Rose 1986: 49). In such imagined post-atomic futures, these novelists considered how the post-nuclear world might be unintentionally reconfigured in favour of those zones – usually in the Southern Hemisphere – which had hitherto been deemed strategically insignificant. Nuclear war would eliminate the old civilisations, but perhaps life might carry on in some far-flung innocent corner of the globe. If England couldn't inherit the earth, perhaps the Commonwealth could.

Broadly speaking, early British nuclear fiction associates nuclear guilt and punishment with the Northern Hemisphere, where the major powers were to be found. This was also the most likely zone of destruction. Since those nations were responsible for developing and using nuclear weapons, they alone could be held responsible for the repercussions of their use. The world might even be left, as in *The Chrysalids*, to 'a superior variant' of humanity. Appalling as it would be, nuclear devastation limited to the Northern Hemisphere might satisfy, at least approximately, some crude sort of moral calculus: 'We all get precisely what we ask for.'

To begin with, Nevil Shute's bestseller *On the Beach* (1957) looks as if it will follow this trend. After a third world war in the Northern Hemisphere, the cloud of nuclear fallout is drifting south towards Melbourne, the last city in its path. Humanity – what's left of it – is in peril, with less than a year left on the clock. There are, however, two faint glimmers of hope. Some scientists believe that rainfall in the North might be dissipating the radiation, allowing life to continue in the South, or even in that most pristinely innocent continent Antarctica. Moreover, an intermittent radio telegraph transmission has been picked up, coming from somewhere near Seattle. The last American submarine, now under Australian command, is sent to investigate. When the submarine reaches North America, hope vanishes. First of all, the radio signal turns out to be purely random, the result of a blown-out window frame tapping against the transmitter key. Then, in the far north, the crew finds that atmospheric radiation remains as high as ever, with no prospect of it diminishing in time to avert humanity's extinction. They return to Melbourne in order to live out their last days.

One problem with such a scenario, as Anthony Burgess once pointed out (1983: 256), is that of perspective: who, after the end of the world, will narrate the end of the world? Burgess thought that *On the Beach* might be considered to have cheated on that count, but Shute more or less side-stepped this difficulty by building in an ecological delay. Though the cataclysmic war is over, and death is assured for those left behind, there is a brief period in which life continues. Indeed, it continues (improbably) more or less as normal. Petrol is scarce, admittedly, but there don't seem to have been any mass migrations or riots. Order is maintained; there are still policemen on the streets; parliamentary sessions are still being held in Canberra. In Chapter 3, the scientist John Osborne invites Peter Holmes, a naval officer, to his club:

> It was an ancient building for Australia, over a hundred years old, built in the spacious days in the manner of one of the best London clubs of the time. It had retained its old manners and traditions in

> a changing era; more English than the English, it had carried the standards of food and service practically unaltered from the middle of the nineteenth century to the middle of the twentieth. Before the war it had probably been the best club in the Commonwealth. Now it certainly was. (Shute 2009 [1957]: 86)

Once again the Empire has been preserved in altered form, its institutions and rituals maintained in the face of their irrelevancy. Society, meanwhile, has been reorganised around an atomic centre of interest that appears not, in this instance, as the guarantor of geopolitical security, but as the sign of its failure.

On the Beach was not the first of Shute's books to imagine such a reorganisation. In the year of the coronation, he had published the turgid *In the Wet* (1953), a novel whose chief concern is how to keep the Commonwealth together. Narrated by a delirious clergyman in an outback hut, the main part of the narrative is a vision of a future socialist Britain, mismanaged by years of Labour administration and sunk deep in austerity. The Queen is still on the throne, sidelined by the British government but beloved by her subjects in the Commonwealth. 'The old King and the present Queen have been terribly wise,' says the Queen's secretary at one point. 'They've held the Commonwealth together, when everything was set for a break up.' There is no doubt who, in Shute's mind, is to blame: 'The common man has held the voting power, and the common man has voted consistently to increase his own standard of living, regardless of the long term interests of his children, regardless of the wider interests of his country.' Something must be done. What *is* done, in this case, is the appointment of a Governor-General, leaving the Queen free to take charge of Commonwealth affairs. When the Queen, now in residence in Australia, refuses to return to England until the voting system is changed, there is uproar, and the government is forced to commit to electoral reform.

There isn't much to recommend a novel in which the motor of the plot is the campaign to abolish the single non-transferable vote – nor, to be sure, one in which the mixed-race protagonist named 'Nigger' foils a bomb plot with his 'Aboriginal' sixth sense. But *In the Wet* makes it clear, at tedious length, how strongly Shute felt about the preservation of the Commonwealth, and how close he believed it had already come to dissolution. It also demonstrates how committed Shute was to the kind of Commonwealth imagined in the colonial films of the Empire Marketing Board, one in which Britain exported high technology and expertise to the relatively unsophisticated yet energetic dominions. When a superior officer asks the protagonist whether relations with England still benefit Australia, the answer is a simple one: '"Of course," said the pilot. "You've only got to look at the 316, or at Rolls-Royce. We couldn't get along without England."'

The simplicity of that schema serves, quite as much as the novel's casual racism, to date the novel, but it also helps to explain one oddity, or oversight, in *On the Beach*. For Shute seems to forget the role played by Australia itself in the development of the nuclear power that had helped – perhaps more, even, than the King and Queen – to bind the Commonwealth together. Indeed, the novel not only ignores Australia's ongoing contribution to nuclear proliferation, it denies it on three separate occasions. First of all, the Australian Moira Davidson talks, after a drunken party, to her new friend, the American submariner Dwight Towers:

> 'It's going to go on spreading down here, southwards, till it gets to us?'
>
> 'That's what they say.'
>
> 'There never was a bomb dropped in the Southern Hemisphere,' she said angrily. 'Why must it come to us? Can't anything be done to stop it?'
>
> He shook his head. 'Not a thing. It's the winds. It's mighty difficult to dodge what's carried on the wind. You just can't do it. You've got to take what's coming to you, and make the best of it.' (34)

Despite her name, or perhaps because of it, Moira objects to the idea that her fate should be decided by wind currents. In her outrage, which is also the novel's, she tries to establish a moral as well as a geographical distance between the North, whose error and confusion have resulted in deadly nuclear warfare, and the doomed survivors of the innocent South. So intent is she on taking the hemispherical approach to ethics that she repeats the same point a few paragraphs later: 'No one in the Southern Hemisphere ever dropped a bomb, a hydrogen bomb or a cobalt bomb or any other sort of bomb. We had nothing to do with it. [. . .] It's so bloody unfair' (36). Finally, as radiation sickness begins to overtake the survivors, one character asks her husband, 'But we didn't have anything to do with it at all, did we – here in Australia?' 'We gave England moral support,' he replies. 'I don't think we had time to give her any other kind' (270).

To the novel's first readers, at least to those who also read the newspaper, these repeated claims about nuclear collateral must have seemed extraordinary. By the beginning of 1957, as well as the Monte Bello tests eight further fission weapons had been detonated at British-operated facilities in Australia. In addition to those major detonations, which were widely reported, many other highly radioactive components were being tested in secret, spreading plutonium and other contaminants over a wide area of the South Australian desert. Few places indeed had undergone nuclear bombardment more continuously or more publicly. The irony – and not, I think, an irony of which the novel itself demonstrates much consciousness – is that Shute sites humanity's last refuge from fallout on the continent where Britain, with the enthusiastic backing of the Australian government, had established the ground zero of its nuclear programme.

That irony does, however, clarify the problem with taking a hemispherical view of geopolitical ethics, which is that it fails to account for the new fully global dimensions of Cold War power. 'Nuclear war is a *political* phenomenon of the global North,' writes the author of one recent study of Shute's novel, 'but it is the global South that becomes the last victim of the war' (Baker 2012: 149–50). Yet in the mid-1950s, thanks to Anglo-Australian nuclear policy, parts of the global South were at the very centre of 'the political phenomenon of nuclear war', while the inhabitants of those regions might be reckoned among the war's earliest victims. The novel's strenuous suppression of these elements continues the symbolic work of reading Australian nuclear zones as pure nothingness, desert, *terra nullius*, that convenient political fiction in which, as John Beck has argued, areas excluded from the polity as militarised zones are transformed into 'both guarantor of security and an oblique and uncanny signifier of what is feared' (2009: 23). In order to extract a maximum of sympathy for his (white, middle-class) Australians, Shute is obliged to recycle an obsolete notion of Australia as the innocent antipode of a guilty colonial centre, thereby suppressing the knowledge that the environmental and human catastrophe depicted in the novel is already under way elsewhere. As it apportions guilt in hemispherical terms, the novel suppresses the more intricate and insidious project of a specifically *nuclear* colonialism. This is why *On the Beach* simply has nothing to say about the ecological effects of uranium mining in the outback, about the acres of desert irradiated by British weapons tests, or about the indigenous Australians to whom nuclear catastrophe was not just a monitory fiction but a daily reality. In that sense, the novel offers readers not a stark warning about the perils of nuclear proliferation, but a consoling fiction: that the nuclear damage has not been done, *yet*.

If the propaganda films of the British nuclear programme sought to project an image of continuity rooted in the imperial past, apocalyptic novels like *On the Beach* went to another extreme, displacing nuclear damage into hypothesis, into a possibility that might still be averted. What neither of them quite grasped – or, rather, what each of them tried to ignore – was the fact that such damage was not only already present but continuous, sustaining the legacy of imperial power within the palatable iconography of a nuclear Commonwealth. The suppression of that knowledge within British nuclear culture was made possible only by the uniquely archipelagic character of the United Kingdom's weapons programme, and was perhaps specific to the brief window of time in which that programme was carried out without the assistance of the United States. The crucial thing, for British Cold War studies, is to take stock of such details: to consider how the Cold War began to play out not only in the British Isles, but across those parts of the globe that were still under direct or indirect British control. Then we might begin to understand how British Cold War culture worked within a global security field to reinforce British influence in the former colonies. We might see how nuclear colonialism replaced Empire as the guiding ideology of Britain's early Cold War. The aim is not to think in terms of hemispheres and zones, the nuclear and the non-nuclear, but to think in terms of sites and networks, the circulation of nuclear materials and the dissemination of an ideology of nuclear (in)security on a planetary scale. As H. G. Wells put it in *The World Set Free* (1914) – the first great novel of nuclear apocalypse – 'From the first they had to see the round globe as one problem; it was impossible any longer to deal with it piece by piece' (212).

Notes

1. As an early recruit to the British documentary movement, *Operation Hurricane*'s producer Stuart Legg had contributed to *The Song of Ceylon*.

References

Atom Man's Hush-Hush Return (1952), British Pathé, 20 October.

Baker, Brian (2012), 'On the Beach: British Nuclear Fiction and the Spaces of Empire's End', in David Seed (ed.), *Future Wars: The Anticipations and the Fears*, Liverpool: Liverpool University Press, pp. 144–60.

Beck, John (2009), *Dirty Wars: Landscape, Power, and Waste in Western American Literature*, Lincoln: University of Nebraska Press.

'British Atomic Weapon' (1952), *The Times*, 3 October, p. 6.

Brooke-Rose, Christine (1986), *The Christine Brooke-Rose Omnibus*, Manchester: Carcanet.

Burgess, Anthony (1983), 'The Apocalypse and After', *Times Literary Supplement* 4,172, 18 March, p. 256.

Chatwin, Bruce (1998 [1977]), *In Patagonia*, London: Vintage.

Darby, S. C., et al. (1988), 'A Summary of Mortality and Incidence of Cancer in Men from the United Kingdom who Participated in the United Kingdom's Atmospheric Nuclear Weapon Tests and Experimental Programmes', *BMJ* 296: 332.
DeGroot, Gerard J. (2005), *The Bomb: A Life*, Cambridge, MA: Harvard University Press.
'First Atomic Bomb Hits Japan' (1945), *The Times*, 7 August, p. 4.
Grieveson, Lee (2011), 'The Cinema and the (Common) Wealth of Nations', in Lee Grieveson and Colin MacCabe (eds), *Empire and Film*, London: Palgrave Macmillan/British Film Institute, pp. 73–113.
Hales, Peter Bacon (1992), 'Topographies of Power: The Forced Spaces of the Manhattan Project', in Wayne Franklin and Michael Steiner (eds), *Mapping American Culture*, Iowa City: University of Iowa Press, pp. 251–90.
Huxley, Aldous (2005 [1948]), *Ape and Essence*, London: Vintage.
Jones, Mervyn (1958), *On the Last Day*, London: Jonathan Cape.
Murphy, Philip (2013), *Monarchy and the End of Empire: The House of Windsor, the British Government, and the Postwar Commonwealth*, Oxford: Oxford University Press.
Potter, Simon J. (2012), *Broadcasting Empire: The BBC and the British World, 1922–1970*, Oxford: Oxford University Press.
Reynolds, Wayne (1996), 'Atomic War, Empire Strategic Dispersal and the Origins of the Snowy Mountains Scheme', *War and Society* 14: 121–44.
Shute, Nevil (1953), *In the Wet*, London: Heinemann.
Shute, Nevil (2009 [1957]), *On the Beach*, London: Vintage.
Wells, H. G. (1914), *The World Set Free: A Story of Mankind*, London: Macmillan.

Chapter 5

Deep Geological Disposal and Radioactive Time: Beckett, Bowen, Nirex and Onkalo

Adam Piette

This chapter will consider nuclear futurity and long-term radioactive half-life and decay as timescales of continuity that are figured in eerie and apocalyptic ways not only in fictions that engage with nuclear anxiety during the Cold War (I will use Elizabeth Bowen and Samuel Beckett as case studies) but also in the engineering projects that deal with the inconceivably long aftermath risks in deep underground nuclear waste disposal. In particular, I will be comparing Gunther Anders' 1962 'Theses for an Atomic Age' with late-1980s Nirex reports into the suitability of storing highly radioactive waste in deep boreholes, and using other pairings of literary/cultural speculation with actual storage facility technologies to explore the deep time of nuclear waste continuities beyond the Cold War. The chapter will first explore the bunker mentality of the high Cold War, using Virilio's *Bunker Archaeology* as well as anecdotal evidence proving the relation between family nuclear shelters and the underground systems of the nuclear state. This entombed refuge technology is set against the work of geologist J. Laurence Kulp, who developed radioactive isotope dating of extremely ancient rock formations, and in doing so stumbled on the radioactive effect of the tests in the nuclear South-West, which led to the crucial Project Sunshine which uncovered the dangers of fallout linked to tests at proving grounds and in the atmosphere. Project Sunshine not only effectively led to the Test Ban Treaty of 1963, but also consolidated in the public imagination the link between deep geological time, radioactivity and underground secret tomb/refuge systems. These connections can be traced in two 1964 texts: Beckett's 'All Strange Away', which features a tight tomb space where the human is figured as waste, and Bowen's *The Little*

Girls, which features an obsessive burying of expressive objects as a time capsule speaking to a deep future time. The texts are drawn into the force field, then, of later Cold War debates about how to deal with radioactive waste from the nuclear industry, specifically Swedish research that used deep-time geological comparisons to illustrate what might happen to the buried world of nuclear waste repositories in the equally deep futurity of half-life timescales. The chapter then looks at a British example, with Windscale/Sellafield research done by Nirex (the Nuclear Industry Radioactive Waste Executive) that tried to convince the world that waste could be disposed of deep underground in the local area – research which was successfully challenged by environmental activists. The chapter ends with a theoretical and philosophical meditation on the contemporary nuclear repository, using all the information and accrued relations from Anders, through Beckett, Virilio, Bowen and Kulp, to present-day waste depository R&D.

From the very origins of research into radioactive materials, an uncanny correlation was fostered between geological depths, long timescales and death. In 1908, Bertram Boltwood (the first scientist to measure the age of rocks using the decay of uranium) had struggled to split uranium into its radioactive constituents. He had managed to refine a kilo of pure uranium salt, sealing it in a bottle, but wrote to Ernest Rutherford of the difficulties:

> I am considering the possibility of excavating a sepulcher and publicly entombing this uranium with the hope that some scientist of future generation may examine it and solve the mystery of the birth of actinium. (Quoted in Badash 1979: 173)

Boltwood's fiction of a radioactive sepulchre projects the deep time of uranium (he had the year before dated the earth to a staggering 2.2 billion years using the presence of lead as half-life clock) into the future as both tomb and epistemological revelation.

In Cold War contexts, the fiction of the uranium tomb is filtered through the more general underground consciousness of the nuclear age. In 1948, the first Civil Defence planning office was set up and the Munitions Board were surveying caves and abandoned mines as possible storage spaces. A source told *The New Yorker*, 'People have to be educated. They've got to become underground-conscious' (quoted in Seed 2003: 118). That underground consciousness was both a powerful presence in the folk imaginary and a very real material fact about the nuclear state. As early as 1949, nuclear fictions surveyed by David Seed featured family shelters, as in William Tenn's 'Generation of

Noah', which features a bullying father drilling his six-year-old to run to the shelter within three minutes of the warning. These fantasy fears are being generated by fear of the Bomb: underground is the only place to hide after Hiroshima. Yet the earth is shadowed by nuclear death. In Tenn's story, the boy has to repeat a mantra that imagines his head burning and the earth stained by the dark spot, his nuclear shadow (Seed 2003: 124). The family shelters were constructed on lines imitating the material reality of the national security state's underground facilities. Huge caves were carved out of rock by the Federal Emergency Management Agency (FEMA) from the 1950s on, such as the Mount Weather complex near Bluemont, northern Virginia. The mountain contains a lake, ponds and water tanks, sewage plant, hospital, cafeteria, streets and pavements, generating plant, living quarters, studios, communication systems and electric cars (Sauder 1995: 50). Robert Heinlein built his family shelter in Colorado Springs in 1961 close to the massive North American Aerospace Defense Command (NORAD) underground complex (Seed 2003: 130). The underground complexes were not only spaces offering protection from nuclear attack, but were also associated with storage and launch systems for nuclear weapons, and as zones for tests: the missile silos (like the Minuteman silos at Great Falls, Montana),[1] the underground testing zones (for instance, the detonation of nuclear devices in Area 12 in Nevada – tunnels under Rainier Mesa – from 1957 on), and as waste storage facilities. For example, Asse II, an abandoned salt mine beneath field and forests near Brunswick, Germany, was turned into a temporary store for hundreds of thousands of drums of radioactive waste in the 1960s and 1970s. In 1988, groundwater began to seep through the walls of the mines, heralding an environmental disaster. As Amanda Mascarelli reported:

> Each week, hundreds of litres of brine entering the chambers are collected and stored with the drums of waste, and the mine's structure is becoming unstable. So a decision had to be made: should engineers backfill the chambers, abandon the mine and leave the waste there in perpetuity, or should they remove it all? Both options are risky. Removing the waste will be complex, take decades and expose workers to radioactivity. If the waste stays and the mine eventually floods, groundwater may become contaminated, potentially exposing those living nearby to deadly radioactive particles. (Mascarelli 2013: 42)

All of the underground complexes become toxic to the Cold War imaginary after such knowledge, as though the Cold War as a military-industrial force and set of technologies were itself radioactive, concealed beneath culture as covert contaminant. These complexes gave material shape and form to the psychological complexes governing nuclear underground consciousness in the Cold War.

That underground consciousness can be brought into relation to Paul Virilio's theorising of bunker mentality in his 1958 *Bunker Archaeology*. Within the monumental bunker, the subject experiences a 'crushing feeling': 'the visitor in this perilous place is beset with a singular heaviness' (Virilio 1994: 16).[2] The bunker is a survival machine, like a crypt where the nuclear subject awaits resurrection, an 'ark that saves' (Virilio 1994: 46). As such, the bunker resembles ancient underground burial sites, ancient Egyptian or Etruscan tombs. The dream of the crypt-like tomb had beset Virilio since childhood experiences during the Second World War. The war had left him with a desire to 'uncover the geostrategic and geopolitical foundation of total war [he] had lived through as a young boy in Nantes, not far from the submarine base of Saint-Nazaire' (Virilio and Parent 1996: 11). The U-boat pen at Saint-Nazaire is a massive concrete structure with gaping cave-like openings to the sea and clearly shaped Virilio's haunted sense of the concrete bunker. For Virilio, the bunker is, as John Beck has argued, a 'myth, present and absent at the same time; present as an object of disgust instead of a transparent and open civilian architecture; absent insofar as the essence of the new fortress is elsewhere, underfoot, invisible from here on in'. Its visibility 'asserts the invisibility of power's current location' (Beck 2013a: 41). The underground fortress as signifying invisible power evolves in his postwar imagination into a form of fallout shelter, especially in the bunker church Saint-Bernadette du Banlay he designed with Claude Parent in 1966 (see Beck 2013b: 48: 'more in common with the fallout shelter than the military bunker'). The occupant of the bunker fallout shelter is encapsulated, like the astronaut Virilio theorises in *Open Sky*, within cosmic or deep time, 'cut off from local time [. . .] victim of an unprecedented inertia' (Virilio 1997: 128). The bunkered subject is, paradoxically, 'already in the grips of that cadaveric rigidity from which the shelter was designed to protect him' (Virilio 1994: 16).

Virilio's powerful imagining of the fallout shelter as concrete capsule moves beyond Second World War and Cold War coordinates and places the bunker within deep time in ways that chime with the history of the dating of the earth since Boltwood. Twentieth-century technologies developed to work out the age of the earth centred on isotope geochemistry. The decay of radioactive elements could give a measure of the extraordinary timescales of rock formation and age.

The key figure was J. Laurence Kulp, who helped develop radiometric dating in the 1950s at Lamont Geological Observatory at Columbia. He specialised in nuclear geochronology, that is the use of isotopic geochronometers (potassium-argon, rubidium-strontium, uranium-lead and radiocarbon) to date the earth (see Kulp 1961).

The half-lives of the isotopes as they decayed to stable daughters ranged from between five and six thousand years (carbon-14) to 50 billion years (beta decay of rubidium-87 to strontium-87). Kulp also introduced radiocarbon dating to Columbia, having spent time with Willard Libby learning the technique. It was during his time carbon-dating samples at Lamont that his team discovered that the Nevada tests were screwing up the results all the way over in New York. Both Libby and Kulp had worked on the Manhattan Project during the war, and the AEC was funding most of the geophysical and geochemical projects. The discovery of the impact of nuclear testing on New York confirmed the terrifying spread and scope of fallout. Libby and Kulp led the secret AEC investigation into the fallout effects of the tests, called Project Sunshine; this began as a classified project, but the two scientists convinced the AEC that the investigation had to go public. Their discovery of the damage caused, most spectacularly the strontium-90 contamination of the food chain, produced the worldwide protests that were eventually to lead to the atmospheric test ban in 1963. So from the start of the Cold War and into the high Cold War of the 1950s and early 1960s there was this link between deep geological time and nuclear-fallout damage to the human body. The same element used to determine the oldest rocks, strontium (in its isotope 87 form), turned out to be the key radioactive element contaminating the world population with the H-bomb tests (as the unstable isotope 90 created by fission – substituting for calcium in bone).

The cadaveric deep time of the fallout shelter sketched by Virilio connects, then, to the eerie correlation between the technology capturing geological timescales and the fallout of the Nevada tests. The deep time of the earth dated by radioactive elements and their half-life decay links as if by chain reaction to the sequence of fission, fallout, contamination and the killing of the nuclear subject. Geological timescales map on to the terminal time of the nuclear. As Gunther Anders argued in his 'Theses for an Atomic Age', nuclear time defines the age 'even if it should last forever, [as] "The Last Age": for there is no possibility that its *differentia specifica*, the possibility of our self-extinction, can ever end – but by the end itself' (1962: 493). For Anders, nuclear politics surrendered responsibility to 'machines and instruments': 'These have become, so to speak, "incarnated" or "reified actions". [. . .] Since we have shifted our activities and responsibilities to the system of our products, we believe ourselves able to keep our hands clean' (503). Nuclear technology, in other words, wrested from the earth's geology and turned into a death machine, imposes the last age upon that same earth, a terminal futurity that is at once without limit ('even if it should last forever') and absolutely the final terminus ('the end itself'), beyond human control.

Nuclear fictions written in thrall to the Last Age reimagine the sensed relations among earth, death and radioactive encapsulation. Beckett in 1949 explored modern art as an act of 'mourning of the object' and registered, in the work of Bram van Velde in particular, the spatialisation of that act of mourning as an entombing of the subject: 'burial within the unique, in a place of impenetrable proximities, cell painted on the cell wall, an art of incarceration' (Beckett 1983: 136).[3] The buried subject in van Velde is 'a being apart, imprisoned and turned in for ever upon himself, without traces, without air, Cyclopean'.[4] The massive stonework of Mycenaean fortification systems enclose the buried subject as in an airless tomb, walled in by the artwork itself; carceral art that represents the cell as if it were the wall in a display of deadening self-reflexivity. Mária Minich Brewer has related Beckett's figure of burial in this essay to the nuclear telos (Brewer 1986–87), and evidence for this is traceable to the fictions he was writing in the years of fallout from atmospheric testing, 1958 to 1963. 'All Strange Away', published in 1964, imagines the carceral space as a cube entombing the subject:

> Hollow cube three foot overall, no way in imagined yet, none out. Black cold any length, then light slow up to full glare say ten seconds still and hot glare any length all ivory white all six planes no shadow, then down through deepening greys and gone, so on. Walls and ceiling flaking plaster or suchlike, floor like bleached dirt, aha, something there, leave it for the moment. Call floor angles deasil a, b, c and d and in here Emma lying on her left side, arse to knees along diagonal db with arse towards d and knees towards b though neither at either because too short and waste space here too some reason yet to be imagined. (Beckett 1995: 173)

The cube incarcerates Emma at the same time as it subjects her to 'hot glare'. That glare reveals the 'waste space' that surrounds the cadaveric subject, meaning the space unoccupied by the dying/dead body. Emma is wasted by the space; she is the space's waste product too, at once a prison and tomb of impenetrable proximities. The alliance of hot glare and waste presents the cube as potentially readable as radioactive, as containing nuclear waste that contaminates the human within the cube's terminal deep time ('hot glare any length [of time]'). As John Beck has argued about radiation and time:

> While nuclear war promises to end time, radiation lasts a long time, and the dilemma of how to imagine the persistence of contaminated matter surviving intact for thousands of years is barely more manageable than conceiving the devastation of nuclear war itself. The intervention of nuclear energy not only introduces the reality of there being no future, it also delivers an irreversible future of waste. (2009: 179)

Beckett's cube is a 'waste space' that contains contaminated matter figured as the cadaveric subject caught in deep time, subject to the 'hot glare' of radiation.

Written the same year as 'All Strange Away', also in the wake of Project Sunshine's revelations, Elizabeth Bowen's *The Little Girls* opens with Dinah in a cave down in a bear-pit hole in the grounds of a big house, preparing to seal into the cave a box of 'expressive objects'. For Dinah, the time capsule she is creating is aimed to project into the far future: '"It's for someone or other to come upon in the far future, when practically nothing about any of us – you or me, for instance – would be otherwise known. We're putting these things in here to be deduced from"' (Bowen 1964: 9). The expressive objects speak to the future beyond humankind ('"I'm looking ahead to when we are a vanished race"' (9)), acting as potential clues from which to reconstruct us. The cave will be sealed by the nuclear blast, and it constitutes an underground sepulchre that is also a museum capturing the bunker mentality within the deep time of futurity, imagining an impossible posthuman future. The 'expressive objects' are remnants of current commodities fetishised by the nuclear generation, tokens of '"really raging peculiarity"'[5] that counter nuclear time with objects that somehow speak of human timescales. Dinah's time capsule sepulchre is itself bound into expression of her own lifetime, since the act of anti-nuclear preservation repeats a childhood gesture. As a girl, she and two friends had buried a box during the First World War inscribed with this message to the future, written in blood: '*We are dead, and all our fathers and mothers. You who find this, Take Care. These are our valuable treasures, and our fetters*' (134). The box contains expressive objects and also a special object (each girl's 'secret thing'). When this specific object is put in the box, the others must stop their ears in the dark. The box is then sealed up with wax that takes the imprint of their thumbs. Dinah tracks down her friends as the novel progresses and they join forces to open the box – extraordinarily, it contains *nothing*, as though looted, or as though the human time the girls had sent into the future has vaporised along with the history of the twentieth century. That destruction is nevertheless countered by the girls meeting as women, however, and they reconstruct the lost time within a renewal and re-presentation of the past destroyed by war.

The melancholy nature of Bowen's pondering of nuclear time and the history of our affections within the deep timescales of the terminal Last Age is figured not only in the empty box but also in the strange space of the cavern. Nuclear blast will seal it up at the end time, and that fact makes the underground space a zone of nuclear melancholia: '"perhaps you're right about that cave; one does get forlorn down there, though without noticing"' (15). The pressure of deep time occupies the zone too:

> Only round noon did sun strike the circular pit's floor. It now was within an hour or so of sunset – unpent, brilliant after the rainstorm, long rays lay over the garden overhead, making wetness glitter, setting afire September dahlias and roses. Down here, however, it was some other hour – peculiar, perhaps no hour at all. (5)

The 'other hour' of nuclear time is, I would suggest, the deep time of the cavern's geological strata projected on to the unimaginable terminal future of apocalypse, as though connecting the sepulchral archaeology of the human (expressive objects as waste products of human days) to the radioactive half-life timescales both within the earth and stretching forward to Anders' 'end itself'.

The sepulchral connection of waste space to deep nuclear time maps strangely on to the research into nuclear waste depositories from the Cold War to the present day. Much of the work sets out to track 'radionuclide migration', that is, the spread of radioactive material, within depositories, over timescales stretching many centuries into the future. As one study puts it, they seek to test 'radionuclide transport models spanning geological timescales' (Ivanovich 1991: 237). One important study in 1984, sponsored by Svensk Kärnbränslehantering AB (Swedish Nuclear Fuel and Waste Management Co., aka SKBF/SKB) and the Swiss company Nagra Baden, explored the potential for natural analogues in working out what might happen to the radioactive waste in the depositories over time – effectively mapping what has happened naturally to radioactive material in the earth since the beginning of terrestrial time on to the nuclear future of the depository's timescales. The technical report used isotopic methods, such as uranium-series disequilibrium measurements, in order to determine 'the behavior of the isotopes of uranium and their radioactive daughters [. . .] within a time-scale encompassing the last million years or more' (Chapman et al. 1984: 1). The depository for this system comprises a series of cylindrical capsules containing the waste within canisters embedded in bentonite and concealed within the host rock at great depths within the earth. Trying to imagine the ways 'redox' (combined reduction and oxidisation) works over these unimaginably long timescales involves calculating the slow release of the radionuclides 'from the waste matrix' over 10^5 to 10^6 years (Chapman et al. 1984: 7). To calculate rates of matrix diffusion,[6] for instance, the scientists seek out naturally occurring ore samples 'from the edge of a water-conducting fracture surface out into a host crystalline rock' (82). Of particular importance to the waste depository team was the natural reactor at Oklo, Gabon: two billion years ago, it went critical and generated huge amounts of energy for 500,000 years, producing ten tonnes of fission products 'identical to the fission products from man-made nuclear reactors' (45). The waste depository, with its fission products, its radionuclides and the unimaginably long timescales of their diffusion and decay, is made to seem as natural as the earth's own billions of years of geological history and events. The research not only naturalises nuclear technology; crucially, it also directly maps geological timescales on to nuclear waste futurity in ways comparable to those imagined in the nuclear fictions. Beckett's cube and Bowen's cave find material reality in the deep systems designed by SKBF/SKB and Nagra Baden; like them, the deep waste depository encapsulates waste space that deploys geological timescales into a future beyond species, a fusion of technology and geology designed to survive and persist beyond biology, a transcendental waste space within mineral rock environment and bentonite sepulchre.

The deep waste depository does not go uncontested, however. Just as the nuclear cave is countered by the memory-time of the women in *The Little Girls*, and just as the cube houses a still-dreaming human subject that complicates the posthuman project in the Beckett story, so too does the technology of nuclear waste sepulchre meet resistance in the public sphere. In the 1980s, the UK nuclear industry set up a body to explore the possibility of deep geological disposal of nuclear waste. Originally known as the Nuclear Industry Radioactive Waste Executive, it was renamed United Kingdom Nirex Limited in 1985. In 1989, work began on two possible sites to take both intermediate and low-level waste: near Dounreay in Caithness and near Sellafield in Cumbria. Nirex planned to build a 'Rock Characterisation Facility' or RCF at Sellafield in 1992, defined by Katherine Bickerstaff, in a paper on the controversy, as 'an underground laboratory to investigate the detailed properties of the potential host rock' (2012: 2,615). Planning permission was denied by Cumbria County Council; Nirex appealed, and it was at the public inquiry that ensued that more concerted opposition was brought to bear. Friends of the Earth and Greenpeace helped the Council challenge the scientific evidence put forward by Nirex. Friends of the Earth argued that the RCF (sited near Gosforth and Sellafield) was a stalking horse for a fully fledged deep waste repository. It also successfully argued that the RCF proposal was scientifically flawed and that Nirex's scientific knowledge was insufficient to prove that disposal was safe for any site. In 1997, following the five-month local planning inquiry, the Secretary of State for the Environment, John Gummer, rejected Nirex's case, stating that he was 'concerned about the scientific uncertainties and technical deficiencies in the proposals presented by Nirex [and] about the process of site selection and the broader issue of the scope and adequacy of the environmental statement' (quoted in Bickerstaff 2012: 2,615).

Looking a little closer at the Nirex research and its contestation brings out the timescale perils of deep waste disposal. Nirex's siting decisions rested on a longer history of research into the Sellafield area. A 1980 study by the Institute of Geological Sciences had already explored the possibility of an underground radioactive waste repository at Sellafield, exploring Sellafield's local geology, the west Cumbrian coastal plain, sedimentary rocks resting on older, volcanic rocks at nearly a kilometre underground; but the 'expected difficulty and cost of investigation and potential engineering and construction problems associated with developing a repository at such depths were considered to be unfavourable factors' (Michie and Bowden 1994: 5). Nirex's own study in 1989 identified a potentially suitable repository zone near Gosforth, and stated that:

> studies in progress on the characterization of the surficial Quaternary deposits will contribute to an understanding of the latest geological history of the area and will provide inputs to regional hydrogeological modelling, assessment of possible neotectonic activity and palaeoseismicity for seismic hazard assessment and may help suggest the possible timing, magnitude and pattern of future changes in climate and relative sea-level. (Quoted in Michie and Bowden 1994: 8)

Here we hear again the fusion of geological history and the 'timing' of the future of the Sellafield waste under pressure from the likely changes in the thousands of years ahead. The trouble was, the Nirex research was deeply flawed, and proved to be leaky at the public inquiry.[7] Hydrogeology expert Dr Shaun Salmon's evidence, for instance, quoted a 1993 Nirex report:

> The host geological environment is intended to provide a stable setting in which groundwater flow is predictable. The host environment should also provide a long pathway and travel time for transport of radionuclides to the Biosphere.

But he found the chosen site to be 'extensively faulted': there was too much 'geological variability'; evidence regarding groundwater flow was inconclusive; considerable danger was generated by the fact that the groundwater in the geology is drawn *upwards* towards the Irish Sea by a combination of environmental factors; Nirex's water-table approximation was crude; there were modelling problems (only in two dimensions, only steady-state, etc.). Furthermore, he noted that he was 'not aware of any firm commitment by Nirex to undertake three-dimensional, time-variant modelling, even though it is a standard modelling technique'. In other words, Nirex had failed properly to imagine the full complexity of what would happen in deep time: its fusion of geological history (the 'host geological environment') and waste's futurity (the 'long pathway and travel time for transport of radionuclides to the Biosphere') was based on a flawed two-dimensional model without a *real* sense of the temporal variabilities involved.

Friends of the Earth's campaign aimed to ensure that 'the radioactive legacy resulting from the use of nuclear power is managed and passed on to future generations in the least environmentally damaging way possible'. Despite such opposition, however, and despite the eloquence of the arguments by environmental agencies concerning the dangers of the waste depository, the construction of repositories is under way. Specifically, in Finland a vast network of tunnels more than 400 metres below ground is being built, the Onkalo Spent Fuel Depository. This deep geological repository for the final disposal of spent nuclear fuel is the first such repository in the world. It is currently under construction at the Olkiluoto Nuclear Power Plant in the municipality of Eurajoki, on the west coast of Finland, by the company Posiva, and its design is based on the KBS-3 method of nuclear waste burial developed in Sweden by Svensk Kärnbränslehantering AB (SKB), the company who had commissioned the research into natural analogues cited earlier. As Michael Madsen, the Danish filmmaker who made a 2009 documentary on Onkalo, *Into Eternity*, has argued:

> The ONKALO project of creating the world's first final nuclear waste facility capable of lasting at least 100 000 years, transgresses both in construction and on a philosophical level all previous human endeavours. It represents something new. And as such I suspect it to be emblematic of our time – and in a strange way out of time, a unique vantage point for any documentary.[8]

All strange away and out of time, the Onkalo galleries hundreds of metres underground will be sealed once all of the disposal holes are filled with the cylindrical copper canisters containing the waste, calculated as the year 2130 (Deutch and Moniz 2006: 82). This will be a dead zone of deep time, a crypt of toxic futurity, the years creeping on beyond species to the last syllable of nuclear time, a waste space as much out of time on any human scale, locked into the infinitesimally slow processes of radionuclide migration, matrix diffusion, corrosion, waste-form dissolution and breakdown, sealed within the tomb of geological timescales.

If we take the examples of Nirex and Onkalo together, along with the thinking through implicit in nuclear fictions by Beckett, Bowen and others, and attempt to construct a working definition of the deep waste depository as it strikes the Cold War-inflected imaginary, we arrive at this potential summation: following Bowen, nuclear spent fuel acts as a form of message sent to the aftermath of the apocalypse, an expressive object aimed towards the deep geological future. The capsules of waste speak forwards to a time when we are a vanished race, presenting as our far future sepulchres, our treasures and our fetters, sealed with the spectral blood of the species. The questions are, still, about sealing, about how to seal, how long to seal, about the forlornness of all underground geological space-time. The nuclear spent fuel is equivalent, following Anders, to *the end itself*, enclosed within the 'system of our products'-as-waste, and will always signify self-extinction of the species. The deep geological repository, following Beckett, is at once a tomb and a refuge, not for ourselves but for ourselves conceived merely as our systems' toxic waste, within a 'space of impenetrable proximities' as multi-barrier resistance to million-year 'transport' and flow; so impenetrable, yet measured in creeping inches of proximate disaster. The boreholes and repositories reconfigure Beckett's hollow cube, with its full hot glare of radiation and bleached dirt of contaminant waste space, as posthuman toxic time capsule. The encapsulation contains the irreversible future of waste: in an all strange away out-of-time, perhaps no hour at all. It is, too, following Virilio, a perilous place of crushing heaviness, a bunker as a form of survival machine, where what survives is radioactive half-life, expressing geological (more than geopolitical) absence of power (as the reactor that was), a religious site of refuge for refuse, saintly waste. The repository entombs and encapsulates its radiant occupant in the rods of deep time, cut off from local time, extra-worldly, atrophied, a single point where only repetition of itself is possible: representation of a cell on the cell wall here as 100,000-year half-life transmission of itself to itself. The depository persists within the contaminant space-time of geological preservation and protection, preserving Cold Wartime in endless continuity. As such the underground nuclear waste complexes will always signify, through what one might call the Kulp effect, Project Sunshine's findings about the interrelation of radioactive decay and contamination of the food chain. Onkalo and Nirex are haunted by Asse II. Deep time, even where it stages impossible timescales beyond species, also signals deep toxicity within our own bodies, hot glare irradiating Emma's interiority – Onkalo's network of canisters and tunnels feature as our own insides, our own neural pathways, a literally posthuman futurity encapsulated deep within the imagination of the global citizens of the Continuity Cold War.

Notes

1. See 'The Air Force Underground' in *Harpers Magazine*.
2. Virilio's text was written in 1958, though only published in *Architecture principe* in 1966.
3. The original French reads: 'l'ensevelissement dans l'unique, dans un lieu d'impénétrables proximités, cellule peinte sur la pierre de la cellule, art d'incarcération'.
4. '[U]n être écarté, enfermé et rentré pour toujours en lui-même, sans traces, sans air, cyclopéen'.
5. '"What really expresses people? The things, I'm sure, that they have obsessions about: keep on wearing or using, or fuss when they lose, or can't go to sleep without. You know, a person's only a person when they have some really raging peculiarity"' (10).
6. Matrix diffusion is transfer of solutes from the main groundwater conduits to the surrounding rock matrix by means of diffusion.
7. The evidence given at the inquiry is available online as a Nirex archive on the Friends of the Earth website: <http://www.foe.co.uk/archive/nirex> (last accessed 26 January 2016).
8. 'Director's Note', <http://www.intoeternitythemovie.com/synopsis> (last accessed 26 January 2016).

References

'The Air Force Underground' (1962), *Harpers Magazine*, May, pp. 169–72.

Anders, Gunther (1962), 'Theses for an Atomic Age', *The Massachusetts Review* 3(3): 493–505.

Badash, Lawrence (1979), *Radioactivity in America and Decay of a Science*, Baltimore: Johns Hopkins University Press.

Beck, John (2009), *Dirty Wars: Landscape, Power, and Waste in Western American Literature*, Lincoln: University of Nebraska Press.

Beck, John (2013a), 'Bunker Archaeology', in John Armitage (ed.), *The Virilio Dictionary*, Edinburgh: Edinburgh University Press, pp. 40–2.

Beck, John (2013b), 'Church of Saint-Bernadette du Banlay', in John Armitage (ed.), *The Virilio Dictionary*, Edinburgh: Edinburgh University Press, pp. 47–8.

Beckett, Samuel (1983 [1949]), 'Les Peintres de l'empêchement', in *Disjecta: Miscellaneous Writings and a Dramatic Fragment*, ed. Ruby Cohn, London: John Calder, pp. 133–7.

Beckett, Samuel (1995), *The Complete Short Prose*, New York: Grove.

Bickerstaff, Karen (2012), '"Because We've Got History Here": Nuclear Waste, Cooperative Siting, and the Relational Geography of a Complex Issue', *Environment and Planning A* 44: 2,611–28.

Bowen, Elizabeth (1964), *The Little Girls*, London: Jonathan Cape.

Brewer, Mária Minich (1986–87), 'Postmodern Narrative and the Nuclear Telos', *boundary 2* 15(1/2): 153–70.

Chapman, Neil A., Ian G. McKinley and John A. T. Smellie (1984), 'The Potential of Natural Analogues in Assessing Systems for Deep Disposal of High-Level Radioactive Waste', *SKB/KBS Technical Report 84-16*, Stockholm, <http://www.skb.se/upload/publications/pdf/tr84-16webb.pdf> (last accessed 12 February 2016).

Deutch, John M., and Ernest J. Moniz (2006), 'The Nuclear Option', *Scientific American* 295 (September): 76–83.

Ivanovich, M. (1991),'Aspects of Uranium/Thorium Series Disequilibrium Applications to Radionuclide Migration Studies', *Radiochimica Acta* 52–3(1): 237–68.

Kulp, J. Laurence (1961), 'Geologic Time Scale', *Science* 133(3,459): 1, 105–14.

Mascarelli, Amanda (2013), 'Waste Away: Tackling Nuclear Power's Unwanted Legacy', *New Scientist* 220(2,941): 42–5.

Michie, U. McL., and R. A. Bowden (1994), 'UK NIREX Geological Investigations at Sellafield', *Proceedings of the Yorkshire Geological Society* 50(1): 5–9.

Sauder, Richard (1995), *Underground Bases and Tunnels: What Is the Government Trying to Hide?*, Kempton, IL: Adventures Unlimited Press.

Seed, David (2003), 'The Debate over Nuclear Refuge', *Cold War History* 4(1): 117–42.

Virilio, Paul (1994), *Bunker Archaeology*, trans. George Collins, Princeton: Princeton University Press.

Virilio, Paul (1997), *Open Sky*, trans. Julie Rose, London: Verso.

Virilio, Paul, and Claude Parent (eds) (1996), *Architecture principe 1966 et 1996*, Besançon: L'imprimeur.

Chapter 6

Shifting the Nuclear Imaginary: Art and the Flight from Nuclear Modernity

Ele Carpenter

Shortly after the bombing of Hiroshima and Nagasaki, László Moholy-Nagy captured the emerging nuclear imaginary in *Nuclear I, CH* (1945), a painting that depicts a nuclear world balanced on the modern grid of Chicago. The grid pattern over which the nuclear sphere hovers is probably inspired by the aerial view of the city Moholy-Nagy witnessed during a mission to consider how to camouflage landmarks, a practice the atomic bomb rendered useless (Engelbrecht 2009: 639). The painting shifts in scale, from the monochrome urban plan to the global nuclear condition, where the world is exposed to the full light spectrum of the atomic explosion. The grid is a paradigmatic sign of modernity, its infinitely extendable, mathematical partitioning of space emblematic of Enlightenment rationality and the implicit mastery of the physical world that stems from it. In contrast, the organic 'bubble' earth seems less solid and more fragile, yet it also signals a complete, closed environment. Moholy-Nagy's painting is significant not just because it is one of the first artworks of the atomic age but because it instantiates a set of spatial relations among the bomb, the position of the observer, and the planet that will come to characterise the discourse of nuclear politics in subsequent decades. The painting situates the artist and viewer in the elevated, and thus removed, position of the pilot (a position of removal that is also one of complicity), a vantage point from which the nuclear explosion can be apprehended as sublime spectacle and not as an act of mass destruction. The target is abstracted so that there is no detailed information on the structures and populations destroyed, only the gridded information as surveyed from above. And finally, the event of the detonation is represented as world-making – it defines and encompasses the 'whole earth': from inside this world, the effects and knowledge of the nuclear cannot be undone.[1]

The purpose of this chapter is to consider artistic practices that continue to grapple with the implications of the nuclear perspective outlined in Moholy-Nagy's painting. The predominant existential and political issues surrounding the 'nuclear' are no longer focused on nuclear weapons as such, although proliferation remains a persistent concern. Especially in the aftermath of the 2011 Fukushima Dai-ichi Nuclear Power Plant disaster, nuclear crisis has come to mean catastrophic accident rather than military conflict. Yet the coordinates of the nuclear spatial imaginary remain disturbingly consistent. The immensely destructive capability of nuclear technologies has again become evident in the civilian realm; the scale of the contamination of populations and the environment remains an enormous challenge, as do the containment of toxicity and the issue of how to dispose of radioactive materials that will remain deadly for thousands of years. The promise of the nuclear – to end all wars; to generate cheap and boundless energy – is in many ways itself a toxic remnant of a triumphant industrial modernity that has failed to account for the experience on the ground. This nuclear modernity is part of a complex belief system that has sedimented faith in scientific solutions into everyday practices which maintain the nuclear status quo. How might the nuclear be approached otherwise? Can the abstracting gaze of modernity in its nuclear form be addressed through an attention to the materials that make up the industries driven by nuclear technology? How might the nuclear be apprehended, not from above and outside the target zone, but from below, from within, close at hand? Can art practice engage with and find new ways of addressing belief in scientific modernity, its specialist knowledge and operating procedures? Is it possible to think beyond the permanent dread produced by a notionally uninventable technology? What kinds of knowledge need to be retained, and what might be lost? These are some of the questions addressed by artists dealing with the contemporary nuclear threat.

Tacit Knowledge

In their influential essay 'Tacit Knowledge, Weapons Design, and the Uninvention of Nuclear Weapons', sociologists Donald MacKenzie and Graham Spinardi argue that the 'traditional' view of science as 'universal, independent of context, impersonal, public, and cumulative' does not adequately account for the importance of tacit knowledge in scientific research, even in the most rarefied world of weapons design (1995: 44). In addition to what MacKenzie and Spinardi call the 'explicit' knowledge of information and instructions that can be written down and therefore stored, copied and transferred by means of documents and computer files, an essential aspect of the scientific process remains outside the written record and can only occur experientially, in relation to the materials at hand. This is what they refer to as 'tacit' knowledge, which is acquired only in its local context. Scientists, engineers and technicians learn the skills required to fulfil a task by practically working with the physical materials under particular circumstances. The traditional notions of scientific knowledge as universal and context independent are, therefore, 'precarious achievements' (45) at best. In many ways, as some of the scientists interviewed by MacKenzie and Spinardi claim, designing nuclear weapons is as much an art as it is a science, since a successful outcome relies so heavily on the judgement of skilled workers able to adjust, modify and sometimes ignore what the mathematics is telling them.

What is clear from this is that the claims made for scientific rationality must be modified to include reliance upon what, in other fields, might be described as craft skills and practical wisdom. As such, the kinds of knowledge often regarded as irrelevant to scientific research – intuition, sensitivity to materials, manual skills, making and learning with others, first-hand observation, slowness – must be seen to be intrinsic to science and not separate from it. Part of what it takes to build a nuclear device, then, is art and craft.

There are a number of implications to be considered once tacit knowledge is accepted as necessary for science. Among them is the fact that, unlike documented information, tacit knowledge, like any craft skill, can be forgotten if it is not passed on. Following the explicit knowledge alone will not produce a functioning bomb, so it is entirely possible that, should what we might call the folk wisdom of nuclear weapons manufacture disappear, the weapon would be effectively uninvented. Traditional science might prefer to believe that, as the Harvard Nuclear Study Group claimed in 1983, 'The atomic fire cannot be extinguished' (quoted in MacKenzie and Spinardi 1995: 47), but this is the God's-eye view that does not account for the local conditions on the ground. The permanent, unalterable state of the nuclear condition, in these terms, begins to appear much more tenuous and contingent.

Another implication of the necessity of tacit knowledge is that any two weapons – or reactors, or submarines – are not the same, even if they are manufactured to the same design. Against the sameness and repetition promised by the abstract grid or the mathematical calculation, each object is distinct in time and space, produced out of specific materials, assembled by particular individuals at a particular site under particular conditions. Despite the familiar assumption that mass production generates identical objects, no one thing is, in fact, exactly the same as another. One of the ways in which tacit knowledge is lost is when parts, techniques and materials are replaced over time. When parts of a machine are gradually replaced, how long is it before the machine becomes an entirely different version of itself?

The ramifications of replaceability are not just ontological; once parts are replaced, will the device still work? Once nuclear testing was replaced with computer simulations, the tacit knowledge of what actually happens during a nuclear detonation was replaced with code. In the 3D digital 'virtual reality cave', the world is smoothed; parts become shapes, their materiality a set of data – we are back in the world of abstracted knowledge, safely removed from brute materiality and its contingent properties. In this way, the computer simulation is the culmination of a process of removal that begins with the clean hands provided by the glove-box, one step away from the smell, texture and penetration of radioactive materials, and the robot that eliminates the shaky hand and responsibility for handling. The computer simulation does not just mediate experience through the production of another dust-free, non-toxic environment – it *is* the experience.

In the face of this reinscription of traditional science, where explicit knowledge has overridden the pragmatic, experiential checks provided by tacit knowledge, how might the kind of craft skills and attention to materials be reintegrated into an understanding of nuclear science? How might new forms of tacit knowledge be introduced into the management and control of nuclear facilities, not, like the weapons scientists, to make the bombs more effective, but to challenge 'normal' science and to make visible the necessity of tacit knowledge as a mode of practice that might assist in the uninvention of some things and the creation of others; where the slowing down of production allows time to think and question the process?

The Replica and the Real

Some of the complexities and paradoxes that MacKenzie and Spinardi identify surrounding the notion of displaced and replaced materials are played out in Lara Favaretto's sculpture *Momentary Monument IV*, exhibited in the scrap metal yard behind Kassel Station as part of

Documenta 13 in 2012. The artwork involved removing nine large metal pieces from the heap which were then cast in white concrete. The casts were repositioned on the pile as stand-ins for the actual objects, which were placed in a small gallery. The concrete casts occupy the same space as the objects they replicate, but more as markers of something absent than as objects in their own right. The displacement, here, foregrounds how de- and re-contextualisation transforms the meaning of an object and the impossibility of substituting one thing for another. The cast cannot reproduce the rusted metal it replaces and formally mimics. The scrap metal archived within the museum, once it is removed from its context as scrap, becomes a form of 'evidence' of somewhere else, a cipher for an absent world notionally contained through the preservation of the fragment of the real.

This process of removal and storage in Favaretto's sculpture recalls the process of dealing with radioactive materials in Japan in the aftermath of the Fukushima catastrophe. In 2013 I travelled with a group of artists through the Fukushima exclusion zones where pristine white walls seal off large areas of land used to store contaminated materials and debris from the tsunami. The sites are used to separate wood and rusted metal, unrecognisable parts of the damaged infrastructure (road barriers, houses, boats, car parts, building materials). The white concrete 'place-holders' of Favaretto's sculpture would not be out of place in this eerie landscape where it is hard to tell exactly which pieces of debris are contaminated and which are not.

Another form of substitution can be found at the Horonobe Underground Research Laboratory visitor centre on Hokkaido, where a model of vitrified high-level waste is cast in dark glass. It stands in, like Favaretto's casts, for the hundreds of thousands of such flasks that governments are planning to bury in underground repositories in the most stable geological formations they can find within their borders. Unlike the symmetry of Favaretto's sculpture, where the replica and the 'real thing' are both available to view, albeit in different locations, the original decaying material at Hokkaido is not present to be seen and compared to the model: the replica is a stand-in for a real thing that has been thoroughly expunged from view. These 'hot' waste materials generated by sixty years of nuclear energy production are not available for the public to see, and their burial will attempt to make them utterly invisible and untraceable forever. The vitrified glass is sleek, strangely non-reflective, itself opaque and unreadable, ready to be encased in a steel flask and entombed in a giant 'plug' of bentonite clay. The underground laboratories in France, Sweden and Japan are testing designs for manoeuvring waste canisters into deep underground drifts. By the time the live waste is ready to be buried, the simulated procedures will have attempted to normalise the culture of geological waste storage.

The Tacit Knowledge of Nuclear Modernity

Isabelle Stengers has described the confidence of the modern scientific stance in relation to pre-modern forms of understanding as an opposition between belief and knowledge, past and present: 'they believed/we know' (2008: 49). Belief is ungrounded and relies on faith; knowledge is secured by establishing the facts. Yet as MacKenzie and Spinardi show, the scientific production of knowledge is deeply dependent on the contingencies of experience and the passing on of experiential modes of understanding. There is, then, no firm division between belief and knowledge, intuition and subjective experience and objectively demonstrable fact.

From the 'traditional' science point of view, in the nuclear context, the notion of mastery (military, technological, environmental) relies upon the subordination of belief to knowledge and conceals dependence on tacit knowledge: the socially constructed domain of the nuclear is represented instead as a fact of nature, unalterable and inevitably just the way things are. Once the necessity of tacit knowledge is lifted into view, however, the simple binaries between science and art, objectivity and experience, abstract and local knowledge are unsustainable and inadequate. And once the artistic, the experiential and the local are properly accounted for, the practice of doing science can no longer fully claim to be above contingency and separate from the needs and desires of those involved, not only in the work of science, but also those who might directly or indirectly be affected by the consequences of scientific research. A fully integrated deployment of tacit knowledge in science, then, would include not only the scientists, engineers and technicians that MacKenzie and Spinardi interviewed, but also anti-nuclear activists, downwinders and others contaminated by toxic materials. Properly expanded, in line with Moholy-Nagy's sense of the nuclear as of planetary significance, an account of tacit knowledge of the nuclear, given its global and trans-temporal reach, would involve all human and non-human inhabitants of the planet both now and in the future.

Knowledge based on experience, on trial and error, on working upon and transforming materials – these forms of knowing as doing, already embedded in the process of doing science, might also assist in working through the consequences of science in its nuclear forms. It is here, especially in art practices engaged precisely in the legacies of nuclear science, that tacit knowledge can be fed back into an understanding of science in order, perhaps, not just to uninvent bombs but to invent new modes of thinking and doing, new ways of approaching experimentation and discovery, and new forms of engagement with the legacies of Cold War nuclear science that are not just material but also ideological and political. In works by artists such as Kenji Yanobe and Kota Takeuchi, among others, it is possible to identify an aesthetic sensibility that embraces the nuclear as part of a folk wisdom that creates new, expanded notions of the public, of history, and of the future. The practices collapse the opposition between belief and knowledge and instead seek a synthesis between different forms of understanding.

Kenji Yanobe, for example, has developed a set of characters and rituals that combine ancient traditions with contemporary nuclear mythology. Since the Mihama nuclear accident in 1991, Yanobe has continued to investigate various forms of human agency in a radioactive world in projects that include a radiation protection suit for an inquisitive artist, elaborate ceremonies drawing on the dark symbolism of nuclear nightmares, and the innocent Sun Child.[2] In the *Atom Suit Project* (1997–2003), Yanobe visited Chernobyl wearing a yellow radiation suit, now kept behind lead glass. Yanobe reflects on how, like modern art, the utopian hope for the future once ascribed to atomic power was destroyed by the Chernobyl disaster.[3] Here the notion of modernity as progress and mastery is a demolished dream that opens up a very different nuclear aesthetic, one that has mutated into a science fiction pseudo-religious cult.

Yanobe's *Sun Child* (2011) has appeared in many forms, first as a performance, then as a giant iconic sculpture, appearing again to preside over the ritual of a wedding at the Aichi Triennale (Horikiri et al. 2013: 184). The work has become the iconic post-Fukushima public artwork. The Sun Child character is reminiscent of the 1950s Atom Boy science fiction cartoon, in which a child powered by nuclear fission raises awareness of the dangers of the nuclear age. The Sun Child holds the sun, as symbol of power and energy, in his hand; the Geiger counter on his suit reads zero as if all the radiation in the world has decayed; slightly grazed and with classic manga wide eyes, he takes off his hood and innocently views the post-disaster world. What kind of political space might this work open up in terms of nuclear belief? In his short film *Sun Child Document* (2012), Yanobe describes the siting of the sculpture at Fukushima Airport as an 'image of the future' that must be shared; it is a message to and from the people of Fukushima: 'We will face the problems that humans should confront.' The radioactive present is, of necessity, embraced here rather than denied; the rejection of denial enables the possibility of a safer future lived in full awareness of threat. Here, the disabling binary of nuclear denial and radiation-phobia is replaced by a playful willingness to write the nuclear legacy into the culture as part of a shared, if disturbing, history.

This strategy of open acceptance of the nuclear legacy is also present in the political debates surrounding geological repositories for radioactive waste, where responsibility for the future overrides the antagonisms of the past. Yanobe strategically places *Sun Child* as an altar centrepiece, reinforcing the character's symbolic role in the ritual as the inheritor of the post-radiation era. As such, the force of the work lies in its public visibility (in opposition to the tendency of evidence of the nuclear to be, or be made, invisible) and in its willingness to embrace the nuclear as an intrinsic aspect of contemporary culture. Yanobe's work is not anti-modern but it does rely on the continuing relevance of ritual within modernity; the work is a fabricated assemblage where belief and experience are combined. *Sun Child* apprehends the present from a position in the future where knowledge and belief systems might be acknowledged as provisional and speculative.

Radioactivity and Aesthetics

Bruno Latour argues that there are no facts, only matters of concern (Latour 2004). Nowhere is this more apparent than in the measurement of radiation and its effects. Since the Fukushima meltdown, residents and workers in the Tohoku region have become chronically aware of the nuclear economy, and are coming to terms with living in a radioactive environment. The environmental disaster shifted the nuclear economy into view and in turn the radiation has created an archive of the landscape produced by the tsunami. Many artists have travelled to the area to document the disaster and its social impact, and are involved in cultural programmes helping to rebuild communities. Others are engaged in a critical and aesthetic investigation of the nuclear crisis within the international context of nuclear semiotics and radioactive contamination.

In 2013, architect Katsuhiro Miyamoto mapped a 1:1 scale drawing of the Fukushima Nuclear Power Plant into the public space of the Aichi Arts Center in Nagoya (Horikiri et al. 2013: 98). The work created a giant 3D drawing of the plant throughout the many levels of the arts centre, using tape attached to the floors, walls and ceilings that enabled the public to spatially occupy the power plant, tracing its lines and thin protective layers (Figure 6.1). By transposing the industrial blueprint of the building on to the cultural venue, Miyamoto folds the abstracted information contained in the explicit knowledge of the

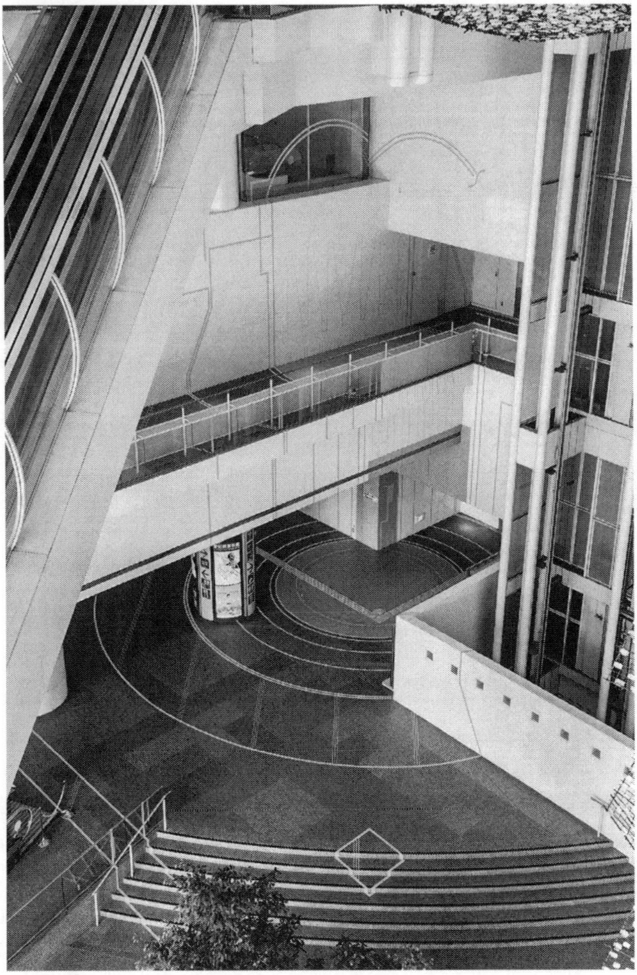

Figure 6.1 Katsuhiro Miyamoto, *Fukushima Dai-ichi Sakae Nuclear Power Plant*, 2013. Aichi Arts Center, Nagoya, Japan.

architectural drawing back into the embodied experience of being inside the arts centre, compelling the document to become spatio-temporally contingent.

Miyamoto's proposal to enshrine the Fukushima Dai-ichi Power Plant (2012) takes a vernacular approach to nuclear architecture, capping the reactor building with traditional roofs from Buddhist and Shinto shrines (Figure 6.2). The architect's proposal to cap the reactor buildings with pre-Meiji roofs is part of an elaborate design for intergenerational maintenance of the place through architecture as a living site marker. The project resonantly extends Thomas Sebeok's concept of the 'Atomic Priesthood' into a workable proposition based on Japanese culture and tradition where shrines are rebuilt

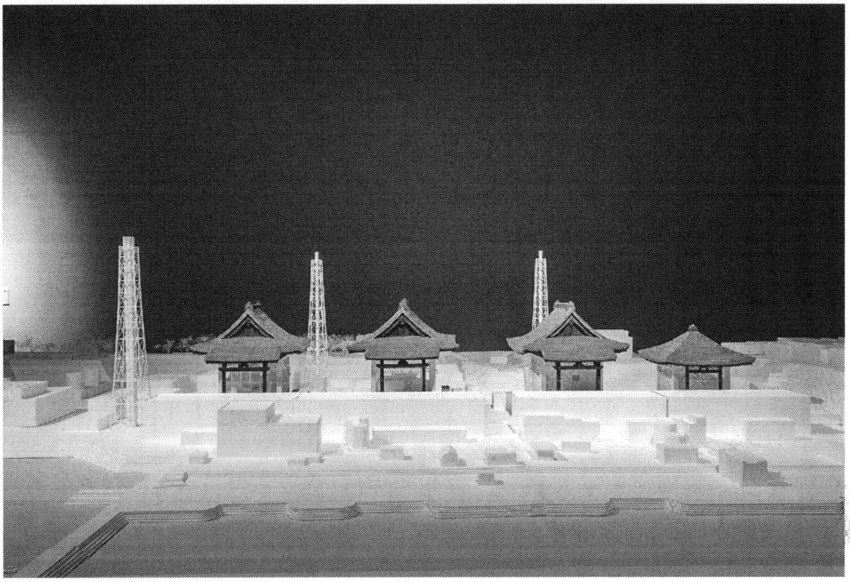

Figure 6.2 Katsuhiro Miyamoto, *The Fukushima No. 1 Nuclear Power Plant Shrine*, 2012.

every twenty years to ensure that traditional building techniques are passed on through the generations. Miyamoto describes the challenge of architecture trying to address the nuclear as a malevolent god, and the need for 'watchful preservation' over the 'negative legacy' of the Fukushima Dai-ichi site (Miyamoto 2012). This assemblage of seemingly incongruous styles on the one hand suggests the investment of the Japanese economy in nuclear power to the point where tradition and modernity collapse into one another; on the other hand, the traditional roofs are in danger of over-identifying the disaster as a localised Japanese architectural challenge, rather than the problem of a global industry.

Kota Takeuchi's art practice is concerned with the lived nuclear experience in Iwaki, Japan.[4] Takeuchi reconfigures different forms of cultural and physical exposure to radiation through digital technologies that enable tracking and syndication of data, capturing and filtering imagery through multiple platforms and spaces on- and offline. Takeuchi's work is, in part, a process of trying to understand the moment of exposure and how it can be captured and recaptured over time through the slippages between different modes of production (film, painting, social media, performance, sculpture). He is interested in how information networks are interrupted, looped, mapped, slowed down for reflection on how things are made, how stories are told, and how knowledge is consolidated. His approach echoes

Moholy-Nagy's visual loop, where the position of the artist as both agent and witness, complicit and separate, is achieved through access to the (military-industrial) technology of image capture.

During the Fukushima Nuclear Power Plant meltdown, Takeuchi produced *From the Moment of Recording, It Became Peeping* (2011), recording the unfolding events as reported through multiple online media. The distance between the location of the event and its real-time, delayed or filtered mediation is repeatedly interrogated in Takeuchi's practice.Takeuchi is the agent for the Finger Pointing Worker who features in *Open Secret* (2012), where a nuclear power plant worker is positioned within a visual loop, the performance of pointing at the webcam inserting itself into the media mythology around the event (Figure 6.3). The insider position here may be 'on the ground' but the gesture is toward the mediation rather than an active engagement with the circumstances of the event itself. In this work, the challenge of the nuclear is not how to leave it behind but how to enter; how to get closer to the material flows rather than escape.

In the Fukushima Prefecture thousands of reconstruction workers travel daily through the zones, along with the nuclear engineers, scientists, tourists, refugees and artists. All are now part of the nuclear economy, all exposed to the complexity of radiation and navigating its visual and cultural capture of the environment and its inhabitants. Takeuchi's *Ego-Surfing* (2013) Twitter paintings are the result of a multi-layered process that starts by making a performance photographed on camera. The photos are then uploaded

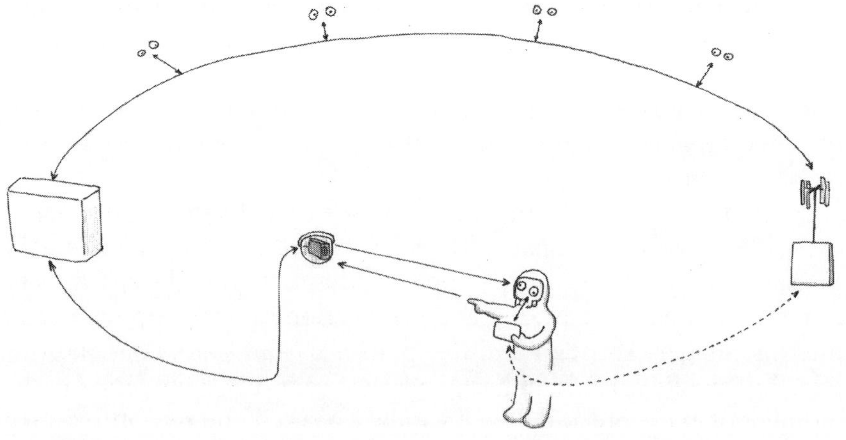

Figure 6.3 *Finger Pointing Worker, Network as Mirror*, 2011. Pencil and ink on paper, 21 × 29.7 cm. Courtesy of the artist and SNOW Contemporary, Tokyo.

to social media, the screen image is painted on canvas, and the secondary process of re-photographing the painting, uploading, circulating, downloading and painting starts again. These paintings archive the position of the viewer within a loop of images, from the site of the performance in Fukushima Prefecture to the circulation of images through social media and their re-appropriation back into art objects. Takeuchi's work provides a way of thinking politically about the loop of representation without being captured in a repetitive and closed dualistic position. The repetition slows down the process of making, creating space to reflect on the increasingly degraded image.

It is hard to distinguish between implicit and tacit knowledge of radiation. The removal of damaged and contaminated buildings, along with the burial of topsoil, is one form of material evidence of radiation. The miles of blue and black sacks, each with its microSievert level scrawled on the side, are another partial form of 'reading' radiation in the landscape. The radiation survey meter takes inch-by-inch measurements, a hotspot here, but not there; somehow the authorities have to create zones of priority and reconstruction.

Archives of Deep Time

Takeuchi's series of works about the human act of marking sites moves between stone and digital media.[5] The series deals directly with the functional slippage between monument (as memorial) and site marker (as warning to the future). While the monument may be important as a site of remembrance, when there is no one left to remember it becomes little more than a historical artefact of interest to some future archaeologist rather than a vital part of ongoing contemporary culture. This dilemma poses an important challenge for artists such as Cécile Massart and Thomson and Craighead, who are involved in documenting and marking nuclear sites and artefacts for the future, combining complex forms of tacit and explicit knowledge. Here, the explicit knowledge of radioactivity (in the form of writing or other symbols) cannot be confidently transmitted across time; nor can the tacit knowledge of how to deal with radioactivity as a part of everyday life be confidently passed on over the course of many generations. The poverty of explicit knowledge is, in nuclear marking projects, staged as a problem of limits, whilst tacit knowledge is always a localised task in the present. Thomson and Craighead's work attempts to tie together the abstract data of the radionuclide decay rate with its specific artefact, identifying located details which are usually smoothed over by the generic industry classifications of high-level, intermediate-level and low-level waste.

Massart's work, for example, presents in the form of prints, films and photographs the international architecture of radioactive waste storage sites (Massart 2015) (Figure 6.4). Massart's work is all about the site: marked on maps, drawn, inscribed on the landscape, concrete marked with symbols. Her first proposals for architectural markers encouraged people to continue to add to the site, to mark the place over generations and centuries. Her reinvention of the marker, constantly reinterpreted within the present, is very different from the landmarks proposed by the Human Interference Task Force set up by the US Department of Energy in the 1980s (Sebeok 1984; Bryan-Wilson 2003). Rather than trying to communicate with the deep future as a semiotic challenge, like Takeuchi, Massart's work contends that the problem is not simply one of the past or future, but of the continuing present. Here the nuclear vernacular is formalised within modern architecture, stylistically at home, but proposing new forms of social organisation

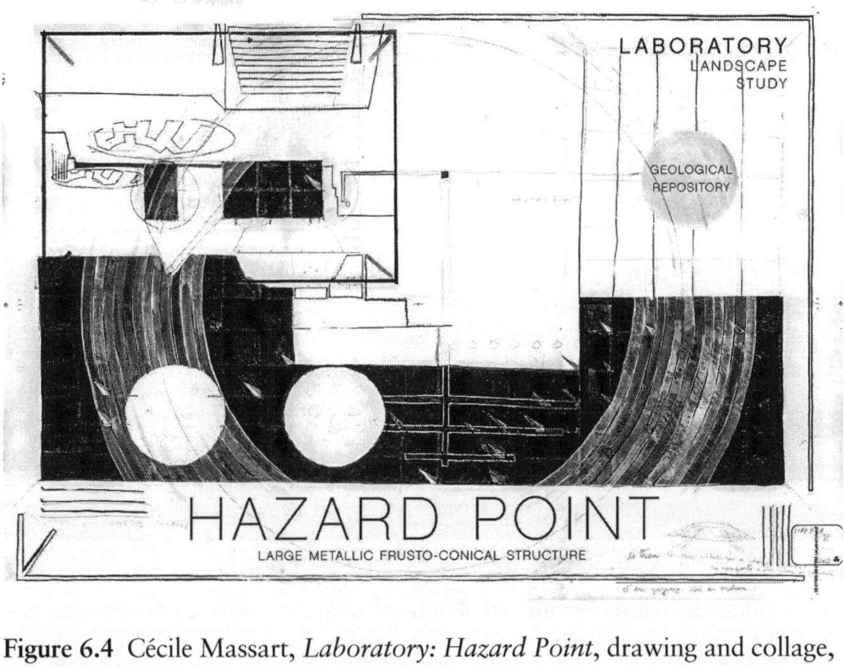

Figure 6.4 Cécile Massart, *Laboratory: Hazard Point*, drawing and collage, 2013. Courtesy of the artist.

prioritising interdisciplinary and intergenerational knowledge sharing. It remains to be seen if the nuclear waste management agencies will understand or even commission the social infrastructure as well as the modernist gesture of the site marker proposed by Massart in France and Belgium.

Nuclear aesthetics must inevitably return to processes of replacement and displacement, often disguised by the official language of removal and disposal. In terms of the deep time of the radioactive half-life of things, nothing can be adequately removed from the closed world that contains all the toxic stuff of the planet; neither can anything be made to 'disappear' (though it can be placed out of sight). Today, nuclear technologies are most visible when they wear out or fail. The decommissioning of power stations and submarines, the stockpiles of waste, the ongoing catastrophe of the Fukushima NPP meltdown: these processes and events cannot be contained as discrete industrial or military clean-up operations and instead spill into the public realm. State, private and public institutions are extremely unlikely to last for the lifetime of the toxic waste they are charged with managing, and new forms of public consultation must be developed to engage local populations in waste monitoring. Collective responsibility for dealing with the nuclear must include the gathering and maintenance of archives of tacit as well as explicit knowledge, including how culture maintains a living record of material, aesthetic and social legacies of contamination and waste. Such archives must include art as a record of how the nuclear-military-industrial complex and its affects change the way in which the world is perceived within each generation.[6]

British artists Jon Thomson and Alison Craighead propose to build a series of 'Nuclear Semiotic Totems', not simply as markers of place but as markers of time which can be embedded in physical and virtual sites and archives anywhere (Thomson and Craighead 2015). The work comprises numerical counters which count down the decay rate of radioactive isotopes accompanied by their particular historical narrative and material trace (Figure 6.5). The work makes plain that the isotopes are not 'contained' within the clean lines of nuclear architecture, but have entered the messy domestic sphere of everyday life. Not only are the materials fallible, but so, too, are the processes of containment. Rather than seeking to visualise data, the work presents numerical measurement simply as an abstraction, foregrounding the impenetrability of data shorn of any tacit knowledge that might make it useful.

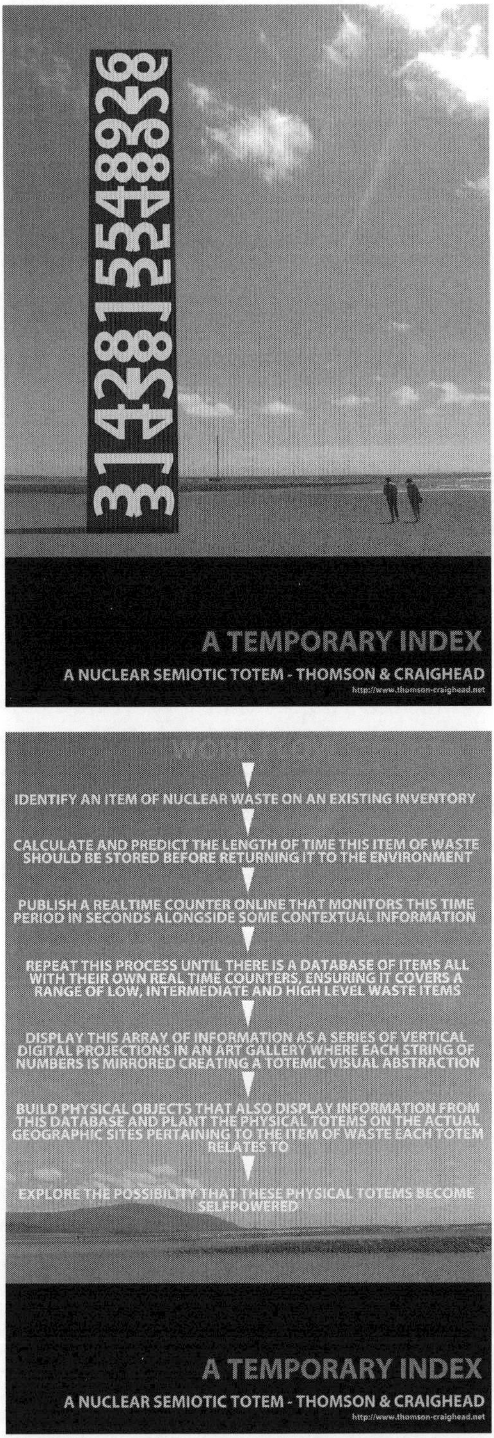

Figure 6.5 Thomson and Craighead, *A Temporary Index*, poster, 2013. Courtesy of the artists.

Conclusion

The discussion of replacement materials and the subjectivity of tacit knowledge opens up perspectives on the nuclear as a provisional technology still in the early stages of development and that is constantly undergoing redefinition in terms of its function and perceived public benefit. The key to a critical rethinking of the nuclear may well lie in MacKenzie and Spinardi's notion of tacit knowledge: if skills can be unlearned within a generation, the lockdown that once seemed to freeze the nuclear as an irreversibly apocalyptic technology can be – and, to an extent, has been – lifted. The problem, though, is that when it comes to the nuclear, one disaster scenario seems to replace another, with plant meltdown substituting for nuclear war as the most recent catastrophic scare, while the dilemma of storing nuclear waste on a geophysically unstable planet is likely to persist for thousands of years. There is still plenty of reimagining to be done. More broadly, though, rethinking the viability of the nuclear does destabilise the ideological support system that preserves the status quo as 'normal' science. If it really is possible, if not likely, to uninvent nuclear weapons, the imaginative space for the generation of more viable tacit knowledge has opened up considerably. The power of art to construct other modes of understanding beyond the solely instrumental has a strong part to play in the generation of new folkways, new vocabularies, and new formal arrangements. These new forms of knowledge production combine tacit and explicit knowledge as part of the process of understanding the relationship between the form and content of the artwork within a specific context, often drawing on fictional and archival modes.

MacKenzie and Spinardi state that the loss of tacit knowledge in weapons manufacturing can only occur when combined with the erosion of nuclear belief systems. So the challenge for art lies not just in the reintroduction of non-instrumentalised modes of practice but, in turn, in how to reconfigure nuclear modernity within socially and institutionally constructed practices. In Japan, the previously uncontested belief in nuclear energy is being challenged through the courts, where a legal movement aims to prevent the restarting of nuclear power plants which closed after the 2011 disaster.[7] It once seemed as if the Cold War could never end; indeed, the structure of global geopolitics had so taken on the bifurcated logic of the superpower stand-off that permanent stalemate could be mistaken for the natural order of things. But there is no natural order, no facts separate from the construction of knowledge, no universal science, no singular method, no knowledge independent of context. In a post-Fukushima world we have an opportunity to review where we sit within the Nuclear Anthropocene, counter-factually and spiritually as well as geologically. As we slide about in time, from early to post-Cold War scenarios, the deep time of radiation demands that we look further back and further forward: from pre-modern cultures to twentieth-century nuclear modernity and the twenty-first-century nuclear vernacular and beyond.

Notes

1. The image of the earth from space came to represent the ecosystem of the planet, popularised during the 1960s and 1970s in publications such as the *Whole Earth Catalog*; see <http://www.wholeearth.com/index.php> (last accessed 29 January 2016).
2. For more information on Yanobe's projects, see <http://www.yanobe.com> (last accessed 29 January 2016).
3. See Yanobe's *Atom Suit Project: Tower* (2003): 'Atomic power was formerly seen as the symbol of hope for the future, as was the Osaka Expo. That idea was destroyed with Chernobyl. We have lived in the crevice between prosperity and decay.' See <http://www.yanobe.com/projects/pj008_atomsuit04.html> (last accessed 29 January 2016).
4. For more information on Takeuchi's work, see <http://kota-takeuchi.net> (last accessed 29 January 2016).
5. *Bookmark* (2013), Takeuchi's ten-channel video, states: 'I am not a stone monument.' Each Japanese character is carefully edited from his video footage of stone markers of important environmental knowledge and military events in the Iwaki region. Takeuchi's *Take Stone Monuments Twice* and *Bookmark* draw on Ichiro Saito's *Economic History in the Modern Age of Iwaki* (1976), which documents stone monuments and markers in the region.
6. Wick, in Scotland, is the proposed site for Britain's National Nuclear Archive, next to the decommissioned Dounreay fast reactor research centre. See <http://www.nda.gov.uk/2012/12/national-nuclear-archive-project> (last accessed 29 January 2016).
7. The Fukui District Court (May 2014) decision not to operate reactors at the Ohi NPP was based on the personal rights of the plaintiffs living within 250 km of the plant. Personal rights, under Japanese law, include the right to protect life and lifestyle, or way of life.

References

Bryan-Wilson, Julia (2003), 'Building a Marker of Nuclear Warning', in Robert S. Nelson and Margaret Olin (eds), *Monuments and Memory, Made and Unmade*, Chicago: University of Chicago Press, pp. 183–204.

Engelbrecht, Lloyd C. (2009), *Moholy-Nagy: Mentor to Modernism*, Cincinnati: Flying Trapeze Press.

Favaretto, Lara (2012), *Momentary Monument IV*, site-specific installation, 400 tons of scrap metal, nine concrete elements, nine metal found objects, Documenta 13, Kassel, Germany.

Horikiri, H., et al. (2013), *Aichi Triennale 2013: Awakening – Where Are We Standing? Earth, Memory and Resurrection*, catalogue, Aichi, Japan: Aichi Triennale Organising Committee.

Latour, Bruno (2004), 'Why Has Critique Run Out of Steam? From Matters of Fact to Matters of Concern', *Critical Inquiry* 30(2): 225–48.

MacKenzie, Donald, and Graham Spinardi (1995), 'Tacit Knowledge, Weapons Design, and the Uninvention of Nuclear Weapons', *American Journal of Sociology* 101(1): 44–99.

Massart, Cécile (2015), *Laboratory Project*, <http://cecile-massart-lisibilite-dechets-radioactifs.com/en> (last accessed 29 January 2016).

Miyamoto, Katsuhiro (2012), *The Fukushima No. 1 Nuclear Power Plant Shrine: Pacifying Malevolent Gods*, Tachibana Gallery, Osaka, <http://dancer.co.jp/?p=1269> (last accessed 29 January 2016).

Moholy-Nagy, László (1945), *Nuclear I, CH*, oil on canvas, 96.5 × 76.6 cm, The Art Institute of Chicago.

Sebeok, Thomas (1984), 'Communication Measures to Bridge Ten Millennia', *Technical Report Prepared by Research Center for Language and Semiotic Studies, Indiana University, for Office of Nuclear Waste Isolation, OH, USA.*

Stengers, Isabelle (2008), 'Experimenting with Refrains: Subjectivity and the Challenge of Escaping Modern Dualism', *Subjectivity* 22: 38–59.

Takeuchi, Kota (2011), *From the Moment of Recording, It Became Peeping*, video, 1h 31m 56s, <http://kota-takeuchi.net> (last accessed 29 January 2016).

Takeuchi, Kota (2012), *Agent for Open Secret (2012/3/17 [Sat] 12.00–20.00 [Sun])*, video, drawing, <http://pointatfuku1cam.nobody.jp/images/sight/network_as_mirror01.jpg> (last accessed 29 January 2016).

Takeuchi, Kota (2013a), *Ego-Surfing*, oil on canvas, series of paintings, variable.

Takeuchi, Kota (2013b), *Bookmark*, ten-channel video.

Takeuchi, Kota (2013c), *Take Stone Monuments Twice*, photographs.

Thomson, Jon, and Alison Craighead (2015), <http:/www.thomson-craighead.net> (last accessed 29 January 2016).

Yanobe, Kenji (1997–2003), *Atom Suit Project*, <http://www.yanobe.com/projects/pj004_atomsuit00.html> (last accessed 29 January 2016).

Yanobe, Kenji (2011), *Sun Child*, FRP, steel, neon, others, 620 × 444 × 263 cm, <http://www.yanobe.com/artworks/sunchild.html> (last accessed 29 January 2016).

Yanobe, Kenji (2012), *Sun Child Document*, video, 6'06, <http://www.yanobe.com/moviearchives/index.html> (last accessed 29 January 2016).

Chapter 7

Alchemical Transformations? Fictions of the Nuclear State after 1989

Daniel Grausam

You can't make this shit up

James L. Acord, epigraph to James Flint's *The Book of Ash*

James Flint's *The Book of Ash* (2004) opens with a postal problem: Cooper James is a twenty-something, civilian computer programmer employed by the US military at Featherbrooks, an RAF outpost in North Yorkshire (based, presumably, on the real-world Fylingdales Radar Installation), which carries out either electronic surveillance or nuclear missile defence (Cooper cannot tell us what his job is, because he simply doesn't know himself – he is a cog in the machine). Cooper is an unhappy and sexually frustrated nerd whose main hobby is his elaborate audiophile stereo system, and is someone who seems to have a thoroughgoingly ironic relationship to his employment, noting that whenever he speaks off-base to a fellow employee with a higher security clearance, she has to fill out a security form, and he imagines the file 'groaning with conversations we've had about *ER* and *The X-Files*. (Especially *The X-Files*)' (Flint 2004: 9).[1] So there is a kind of world-weariness here about the national security state: it still exists, but it is now recording idle banter about *X-Files* plots – banter about a conspiratorial version of itself – as much as it is protecting us from terrorists after 9/11. During an ordinary work day Cooper's office is suddenly evacuated, and he dutifully shuffles off with the rest of the employees. To his surprise he is called back in to see the director of base security, and interrogated about a mysterious parcel, addressed to him, that has just arrived on the base. At a time of dirty bomb threats and anthrax scares, the military is hardly in the mood for pranks, and Cooper is given the third degree.

By the end of the first chapter we've come to learn that this canister contains nothing more than what looks like 'some kind of dust' (15). Dust, of course, is always the residue of something else, and this detritus is supposedly physical remains, the ashes of Cooper's long-absent father, the artist Jack Reever. The novel's problem of mysterious postage – what has come through the *mail* – is thus also a problem of post-ness in another, *male*, sense, since Cooper hasn't seen his father in twenty years after Jack Reever walked out of his life and moved back to the United States. Cooper is put on indefinite security leave at his job and, not knowing what else to do, he sets out for the United States to try to figure out who his father was, who sent the ashes, and why, after twenty years of zero contact with his father, anyone thinks he would care.

Things get complex when over the course of his travels across the United States, tracking his father's movements from a granite-mining town in Vermont to Seattle and then to nuclear waste storage and nuclear material production sites on the West Coast, Cooper comes to learn that his father was an atomic-obsessed sculptor and conceptual artist who acted as a thorn in the side of the national nuclear complex. Through the epigraph, descriptions of some of Reever's artworks, and material Flint supplies in an afterword, we learn that the supposedly dead father at the heart of the plot is inspired by the real-life American sculptor James Acord (1944–2011), one of the more experimental American artists of the second half of the century, given that he believed in a *literally* experimental artistic practice (he was the only private citizen in the world licensed to own and handle high-level radioactive materials).[2] In 1989 Acord moved from Seattle to Richland, a town just outside of Hanford, site of US plutonium production for the Cold War weapons complex (it supplied, for instance, the material for the Nagasaki weapon) and by far the most polluted nuclear site in the US, where he sought to create something like a nuclear Stonehenge as a long-term memorial to the (still-continuing) nuclear age, and to develop artistic practices for transmuting radioactive waste into less harmful substances. Acord's work remains some of the most ambitious artistic attempts to assess the legacies of the American nuclear project and to lift the veil of nuclear secrecy.

This intensely personal generational story of trying to come to terms with a mysterious, absent father who sought to make art out of the radioactive state is particularly appropriate for a collection such as this one, given the aim here of exploring continuities and differences between the Cold War and post-Cold War periods,[3] especially when we remember that the father was someone who himself sought unsuccessfully to memorialise the nuclear complex and to undo some of its toxic effects through his art. So this is very much a novel interested in where we are relative to the Cold War's material nuclear legacies, and Cooper's personal quest can be read as a more generalised problem of how to come to terms with the ashes of the first nuclear era when an earlier generation who themselves had attempted this very thing are dead and their projects have failed to come to fruition.[4]

What is particularly striking about *The Book of Ash*, however, is the way it turns its thematic interest in a young man's quest to understand his absent, slightly mad, Cold War nuclear artist father into a *literary* problem as well. Acord imagined his own aesthetic practice, with its goal of changing perceptions of, and dangers caused by, nuclear material, to be a kind of alchemy, and the beauty of *The Book of Ash* is precisely in this same style, at once making Acordian-style alchemical transformation a literary subject but also a literary technique: it is a radioactive novel in the sense of both its subject and the way it transmutes novelistic style and content over time. Opening an ambitious novel about someone at the heart of the military-industrial complex with a problem of incoming, unexpected mail makes those of us attuned to literary history think, of course, of the grand master of Cold War letters, Thomas Pynchon, given that a problem of mysterious postage underwrites Pynchon's Cold War primer *The Crying of Lot 49* (1966), a novel which concerns the possible existence of a centuries-old alternative system of postal delivery (the Tristero or Trystero) that operates at the margins of society. The protagonist of that novel, one Oedipa Maas, begins to understand how the system works when she is on a tour of a defence contractor, and there are echoes of this encounter with a system of postal signification in *The Book of Ash*.[5] Pynchon's more directly war-obsessed *Gravity's Rainbow* (1973) picks up on this postal theme: the novel opens in London during the V-2 rocket raids of World War II, and those rockets, so obviously ICBM predecessors, are referred to as 'incoming mail' (Pynchon 1995: 6). As a number of critics have argued, Pynchon is perhaps the American novelist most attuned to what life in the age of planetary destruction at the press of a button looked like, though his novels approach their nuclear referent indirectly and obliquely.[6] More broadly, the interest in *The Book of Ash* in exploring the complexities of the nuclear state makes us think of the possibly paranoid vision of a postwar 'Rocket State' at the heart of *Gravity's Rainbow*. The links to Pynchon's work extend across the novel (and we might say that *The Book of Ash*'s Jack Reever and Thomas Pynchon share much in common: Pynchon is something like an absent father to a whole generation of writers, given his enormous influence and yet famously reclusive nature). Indeed, the opening of *The Book of Ash*, with its mysterious postal missive announcing the death of a once-close associate, seems a direct nod to *The Crying of Lot 49*, which opens with a similar moment of mysterious postage: Oedipa arrives home one day to find a letter announcing that she has been named the executrix of the estate of a former lover. In both novels the initial postal provocation initiates a plot of detection, and sends characters on a quest that takes them into some of the stranger aspects of the United States, and leads them to a host of revelations (and blocked revelations) about formerly mysterious bodies of knowledge.

On numerous occasions the references to Pynchon's work in *The Book of Ash* take more direct form. When Oedipa begins her work as executrix of the estate, she is aided by an attorney named Metzger, and in *The Book of Ash* a chance discovery leads Cooper to one Dr Metzger, a quirky nuclear physicist who had taught Reever in an introductory university course on the subject and is thus able to fill Cooper in on some of the details of Reever's life and nuclear obsessions. As any reader of *The Crying of Lot 49* will recall, at the centre of the plot is an elaborate parody of a Jacobean revenge tragedy, a play which is almost incomprehensibly complex in its imagination of political intrigue and court politics. The equivalent in *The Book of Ash* is a sixteenth-century metallurgical and pyrotechnics manual authored by Vannoccio Biringuccio (the name could come right out of Pynchon's *The Courier's Tragedy*, given the play's focus on rival political groups in seventeenth-century Italy), a metallurgist whose own incredibly complicated relationship to patronage and politics sounds quite a bit like the machinations recorded in Pynchon's play. And just as Oedipa becomes obsessed by the play (part of her activity involves tracing out minor differences across editions, trying to determine authorial intention in the face of conflicting information), Cooper becomes obsessed by the 'amazing' book (though here again the questions of meaning and intention are raised by the fact that the book was unrevised and uncorrected at the time of its author's death, paralleling the problem of textual instability produced by the multiple versions of *The Courier's Tragedy*) (173), taking time to read it each evening as he drives across the United States. Cooper's mother echoes the amateur revisionist historians and paranoiacs of Pynchon's novel: her bookshelf is filled with New Age material that Cooper describes as 'prehistorical hyperspeculation' (51) as well as conspiratorially minded works by authors such as David Icke (among his many theories, the earth is run by a strange race of secret reptilian lizard people; in a nice twist, an Icke-like character makes an appearance in Pynchon's most recent work, 2013's *Bleeding Edge*).[7]

Near the end of *The Crying of Lot 49* Oedipa suspects that she may be the victim of an elaborate hoax organised by her former lover, Pierce Inverarity, who might not be dead after all, and such a plot twist is, in *The Book of Ash*, fully realised. Near the end of the novel Cooper comes to realise that his father's ashes aren't in fact in the canister, since his father didn't die in the fire that consumed his house; in fact, Reever started the fire himself and then had another character send the canister to see if his son had the detective skills to track down his legacy. And just as *The Crying of Lot 49* has a consistent symbol – a muted postal horn – that indicates the secret postal system's potential presence, *The Book of Ash* also has a recurring symbol, in this case the eye of Horus (the Egyptian Sun God) that indicates Reever's hand at work.

But these running references to Pynchon shouldn't make us think of Flint's novel as one extended piece of fan fiction. As I have mentioned, Reever (and James Acord) desired a kind of alchemy, a process that would transform toxic materials, though his projects never came to fruition. There's a different kind of alchemical desire in *The Book of Ash* as well: the question of how we alchemically transform the Pynchonian-style paranoid systems novel after the Cold War, and after postmodernism. It's something of a truism, for instance, to suggest that many ambitious younger novelists write under the shadow of Pynchon: he plays the role for them that Joyce would have played for Pynchon's generation. So in Flint's debt to, but also distance from, Pynchon's work I think we can begin to see some of the ways we might speak to the lingering hold of the Cold War, and to imagine what the paranoid systems novel that came to define a certain strand of American postwar fiction looks like in the twenty-first century: Flint's rewriting of Pynchon offers both a loving look back on Pynchon's work and also a testing of its limits, and it joins a series of recent novels that have explored the lingering hold of both the Cold War nuclear state and postmodernism on contemporary culture.

As readers of Pynchon's *Lot 49* well know, the book is incredibly frustrating: at the conclusion of the novel we are left hanging as to whether or not the secret postal conspiracy actually exists, left wondering if there is 'Another mode of meaning behind the obvious, or none', and whether Oedipa is 'orbiting in the ecstasy of true paranoia, or a real Tristero' (150). The novel never resolves the question of what might be behind all of its textual zaniness, whether 'Behind the hieroglyphic streets there would either be a transcendent meaning, or only the earth' (150). The effect of all of this is to make us paranoid about our own paranoia, unsure if the novel's world is one shot through with conspiracy or one explainable by chance and coincidence, whether there is or is not a secret shadow realm, and, if there is, just how big it might be.

Part of Cooper James's education over the course of *The Book of Ash* makes him confront parallel questions. In a late scene Cooper has travelled to a town called Atomville (based on Richland, Washington, the town built to house the workers at the Hanford site), a town Cooper describes as the 'ur-Featherbrooks, the Platonic original, the distillation and essence of the nuclear imperium' (247) given the role it has played in enabling the nuclear state. There he is stalked by, and then meets, a shadowy old associate of his father's named Lemery; the discussion quickly turns strange when Lemery tells Cooper that Reever was 'a *magician*: he was here to cast a spell', an assertion which annoys Cooper no end: 'Who the fuck are you to tell me, you fucking freak? How the fuck would you know, creeping around behind my back in Salt Mountain like some kind of half-baked spy, leaving stupid messages, talking about magic and spells like some kind of Harry Potter nutcase' (334). What we come to learn, however, is that speculative fictions such as the Harry Potter franchise are perhaps outstripped by actually existing reality when we consider the nuclear state. When Lemery asks Cooper if he has ever heard of the 'True World Government' or 'The Society of the Golden Dawn? The Illuminati, The Hermetic Brotherhood of Light?', Cooper's response is to dismiss him as a classic conspiracy theorist (and he could be a stock character from Pynchon's paranoid universe): 'Yeah, sure. I watch *The X-Files*', as if to say all of this talk of conspiracy and secret societies is the product of a fantastic televisual imagination that includes aliens (336). Lemery's retort, however, suggests that the problem with shows like *The X-Files* is that they blind us to the actually existing secret state:

> 'Fuck *The X-Files*,' Lemery hisses, shaking loose a Warholian head of hair. 'Fuck *The* fucking *X-Files*. *The X-Files* is for losers and for idiots. What I'm talking about, what I'm telling you, this stuff's for real.' He jabs his outstretched fingers in the direction from which I'd come. 'See Atomville, see the Areas out there? See how there's almost nothing visible on the surface? You wanna know why that is? It's because 90 per cent of it's all *underground*. You don't believe me, I've got maps, I've got copies of plans like you would not believe. I've been studying this for years. Forget Tibet, forget fucking Atlantis. This is where they hang out. This is the City of the Sun, the City on the Hill. This is the New Atlantis, my friend. *Atomville*.' (336)

But the suggestion that Atomville is a kind of real-world equivalent to mythical sites (as Lemery points out, the place is a 'New Jerusalem', given the 'reactors unleashed the power of the sun' by splitting atoms (335)) is only the tip of the iceberg; as Lemery goes on to point out, Atomville is both an incredibly specific place and an access point for thinking about larger realities of the nuclear state it quite literally fuelled. As he puts it: 'By the end of the 1940s the requirements of the nuclear industry, the public face of this secret state, already dictated political policy in this country. And still it grew, went transnational, until by the 1960s, what with its arms races and power stations and the multitude of its spin-off technologies, the exigencies of the atomic sector were dictating governmental policy for half the globe'; he goes on to point out that the nuclear economy 'pump-primes a good proportion of the world's major economies and controls millions of jobs and the destinies of billions of people, and all because the product it creates is so dangerous and toxic that its existence is guaranteed for thousands and thousands of years in order to take care of it. Plus, of course, it's not answerable to anyone; no one can touch it' (335–6).

If Lemery sounds a bit nutty here he isn't far off the mark when we consider the real cost of the nuclear age: between 1940 and 1996 the US spent over 5.5 trillion dollars on nuclear weapons alone, and the plutonium produced for weapons will remain dangerous for 240,000 years (Schwartz 1998: 5). As the omniscient narrator of Lydia Millet's 2005 novel *Oh Pure and Radiant Heart* (*The Book of Ash*'s contemporary) puts it, the sheer amount of federal dollars that went to nuclear weapons design, manufacturing, stockpiling and testing means that what once might have seemed paranoid musing is in fact the bedrock of the US economy: 'The so-called "military-industrial complex" about which Eisenhower warned is thus, in a sense, the single largest consumer of the country's resources. It might fairly be seen as the prime mover of the U.S. government' (Millet 2006: 525).[8] So while many of Atomville's secrets might be hidden underground, what is perhaps hidden in plain sight, though unacknowledged, is the way the nuclear economy and the US economy are intertwined: the United States perhaps really is Pynchon's 'Rocket State' after all. In place of Oedipa's binarised options of a vast conspiracy or mere coincidence, *The Book of Ash* offers us a choice between the speculative fantasies of *The X-Files* and the actually existing reality of the secret state.

One of the points Lemery makes is that we live in a version of what the anthropologist Joseph Masco would call a 'mutant ecology' (Masco 2006: 289–334), given how radiation is never really site containable: Lemery is himself a downwinder, one of the massive population of American (and global) citizens directly exposed to radioactive waste and fallout, and he details the harrowing health difficulties he has struggled with. We are most definitely after nature in this novel as well, given how Lemery describes an irradiated ecology and food chain. As he explains, radioactive waste in the 1940s and 1950s was frequently poured into big concrete trenches, designed to allow the nuclear effluent to form mineral salts. But of course animals living in the desert need mineral salts, so desert badgers lick the troughs, thereby exposing themselves to incredibly high levels of toxicity, which kills them, which then causes jack rabbits to take over the real estate. When they all start to die off as well, coyotes have a field day snacking on them, until the brain tumours the coyotes develop leave them less afraid of human presence; a coyote can then leave 'a trail of plutonium-laced coyote shit right down Main Street, USA, at least until he gets hit by a truck and torn apart by the neighbourhood cats who go home and cuddle up next to little Jane and Johnny' (363). Ironically, Lemery claims that the only reason he is alive is his terrible diet as a child and adolescent: the half of his class at school who are now dead were the ones who 'ate their vegetables, drank their milk', while those who lived on candy bars, Planter's peanuts and soda are alive because they 'didn't get as much of the local produce' in their diet (371).

Lemery extends this idea of an irradiated 'Main Street, USA' when he explains how the nuclear state in fact helped to determine the most iconic features of the postwar American landscape, given how the nearly overnight construction of Richland, Washington – where the housing estate was invented and first built – gave US urban planners the blueprint for postwar suburban domesticity. As historian Kate Brown has outlined in her recent, brilliant, *Plutopia*, this was comprehensively the case: the nuclear age saw nuclear families living in communities quite literally materially shaped by and based in the nuclear state, given that Richland supplied a turnkey template for how to deal with the postwar population explosion of returning veterans and the families they started. The nuclear, that is, shaped even the most basic features of postwar demography (Brown 2013).

But to return to the question of genre, just what happens to the Pynchonian systems novel when we are supposedly looking back on, rather than immersed in, the Cold War state? Here the interest in visual experience in Flint strikes me as key: Pynchon's novel, despite the importance of the Remedios Varo painting within it, and despite the visual iconography of stamps, is fundamentally about reading – a major interpretive dilemma is represented by the English Professor

Emory Bortz and the theatrical director Randolph Driblette, and concerns new critical textual autonomy and the affective fallacy. And, of course, the novel is all about alternative ways of delivering written communication. This thematic interest in reading informs the kinds of critical reading practices we bring to Pynchon's novels, reading practices that are always suspicious, symptomatic readings that see the text as in need of excavation to reveal the pathology that underlies it – a point brilliantly encoded in the plot of *Gravity's Rainbow* with Slothrop's conditioning, in which cause and effect seem to be reversed. We might see the vision at the heart of *The Book of Ash* as something very different – less a call to uncover a suppressed referent hidden within the intricacies of media, and more to start to see the nuclear and the Cold War as everyday shaping presences on vast swathes of American society: we don't need conspiracy theory if we just learn to open our eyes (one character claims that Jack Reever taught members of the Atomville community how to see, and that they needed an artist for that task). The novel repeatedly foregrounds acts of visual recognition of the radioactive everyday, finding atomic references across the town of Atomville in the names of everyday businesses and a school sports team, and including many of these as actual images within the novel. What one reviewer dismissed as nothing more than a derivative Sebaldianism (Tague 2009) is instead something like the banality of the radioactive economy, its presence in, rather than absence from, suburban American life.

In other words, perhaps Pynchon wasn't paranoid enough, as the military-industrial complex is really something more like the economy period, and the proper post-Cold War response is less to hunt for secret links and more to see what is manifestly visible. Indeed, Jack Reever's most important work is hidden in the novel, but it is hidden in a suburban home's garage. And Reever's first attempt to make art out of radioactive material relied on the uranium glaze in red Fiestaware pottery, which he would extract after crushing the tableware. The radioactive economy is literally consumed in this novel, and so you don't have to be one of the desert animals Lemery details to be part of a radioactive food culture. As I've already mentioned, the textual equivalent to Pynchon's muted postal horn is the eye of Horus, a symbol located on US currency. In Pynchon you opt in to the Trystero, you choose to use an alternative system of communication; in Flint the claim would seem to be that to participate in the economy is to participate in the workings of the nuclear state.

Other characters frequently suggest that they would like to help Cooper find 'closure' on his father's life, but the fact that the ashes within the canister turn out not to be Jack Reever's remains means that the novel never completes the act of mourning that its plot seems to demand, and thus we might claim that the book shares with Pynchon's work a problem of narrative resolution: Jack remains unburied, his continuing life an open question; the identity of the buyer of the mysterious lot of stamps at the end of *Lot 49* remains unknown. But in Pynchon we're suspended at the moment just before revelation, quivering with anticipation as the auction begins for those stamps – but it is a revelation that never arrives, the narratological equivalent of what Jacques Derrida identified as a peculiar form of nuclear destruction, one without unveiling, revelation and apocalypse (Derrida 1984).[9] That Jack Reever, radioactive artist, never receives his funeral rites and burial, however, might speak to an equally unthinkable temporality of the multimillennium, as the waste that was his raw material also remains unburied – we look forward here not to instantaneous annihilation, but, as in the title of the recent Michael Madsen film concerning nuclear waste storage, *Into Eternity* (2010).[10]

Cooper does experience a moment of relief: at the end of the novel Lemery and an associate have come up with a madcap plan to use a helicopter to illegally deposit one of Reever's artworks – a large granite sculpture – on the Hanford site, thereby fulfilling Reever's goal of creating a nuclear Stonehenge. As they prepare to move the artwork, Lemery reveals to Cooper that it has a cavity (where Reever had intended to place radioactive material) and in that cavity is another message from his father. Inside a steel canister (thus echoing the initial package Cooper received) Cooper finds a tympanic bulla – a bone from the inner ear of a whale – on a lanyard. This item has been an ongoing bone (no pun intended) of contention for Cooper since his childhood: his father had, years ago, extracted it from the carcass of a whale that had washed up on the Cornwall coast near the English commune they were living in, and then explained to Cooper and another of the children living there that a bulla was something Roman fathers gave to their sons when they were born to 'ward off evil' (62). Cooper is mortified when his father gives the bone to the other child, and then doubly mortified when, after the other child loses it during a madcap adventure, he steals and hides it, only to then discover that it has disappeared (evidently Jack knew where it was hidden, and had retrieved it). So in a sense the familial inheritance is now complete: Cooper has been symbolically reborn, gifted the inheritance due a son from a loving father. But just two pages later we learn that things aren't so simple when Flint extends, only to then complicate, this idea of narrative resolution for Cooper James:

> I have the sensation of being alone on the prow of a ship, my ship, right on the apex of a giant bow wave, no other vessels in sight, nothing ahead of me but the rippling sea and only the sun, the moon and the stars to help me navigate. I feel like this for a long time and for a long time nothing happens until gradually I boomerang around and come back into myself and realize I'm breathing, breathing naturally, easily, breathing deep clear breaths down to a part of my lungs I'd forgotten existed, a part of my lungs I've not managed to use for close on twenty years. (399)

Cooper has been an asthmatic almost his entire life (something he blames on exposure to fumes from a small blast furnace his father had crafted in his art studio when Cooper was a child) and so this evocative passage, with its imagination of a forward journey into an unspoiled nature and its accompanying sudden opening of lungs that have remained closed for years, suggests a kind of peace for Cooper, a freedom from the psychic and physical effects of his (non-)relationship with his father. But there's a dark irony to this, of course: Cooper's lungs expand fully just as he hears 'the unmistakable sound of rotor blades' (399) as the helicopter that will carry the artwork to the site comes into view. Lemery and Cooper then complete the assembly of the artwork, and hook it to a winch extending from the helicopter 'directly overhead' (400). Given that they are in a dirt field in the Washington desert just outside one of the most radioactively polluted sites in the world, one has to suspect that the inevitable dust raised by the slipstream of a helicopter directly above you is very much not something you want to be breathing in, and that, cruelly enough, this is perhaps not a moment when you want your asthma to disappear and give you access to deep pockets of your lungs that have remained inaccessible for years. If part of the revelation of *The Book of Ash* is that we are citizens of a nuclear state that, in size and scale, exceeds the realm of conspiracy theory, then here Cooper literally inhales that state's toxicities, becoming its biopolitical nuclear citizen (though he doesn't even know it). The bulla, intended to ward off evil, is thus something more akin to Derrida's notion of the pharmakon, that which poisons even as it cures.

Cooper's journey had taken him to Salt Mountain (the novel's version of Yucca Mountain – the proposed, though now likely never-to-open, storage site for high-level US nuclear waste) as Jack had lived near the site for some time, and had pestered the waste-storage project to make him part of the conceptualisation of warning systems, given that any conventionally descriptive language of warning and signification will never work in the face of the timescales of waste storage.[11] In Pynchon's work waste is, as I've mentioned, an acronym (We Await Silent Trystero's Empire), and that novel is all about the desire for, and failure of, the arrival of some revelation. For Flint, however, waste is a far more literal object, not something we await but something we are living with in perpetuity, an empire not of the yet-to-arrive so much as a nuclear 'imperium' that threatens to outlive humanity. When Cooper finds, outside of the Salt Mountain complex, a makeshift waste repository his father dug, marked by a sheet of metal on to which is carved 'Reever's Waste Repository', we might say that while Trystero's empire has not arrived, a very different empire has, namely a nuclear state so complex, long-lasting and far-reaching that it may never quite come into full focus, dispersed as it is across the entirety of the US landmass and economy (indeed, Lemery refers to the nuclear sector as an 'empire' later on (335)).

Looking at Salt Mountain, Cooper suddenly understands what his familial legacy is, and the answer isn't familial at all: 'here, this is our legacy, this is our inheritance – mine, these kids', all children's to come' (234). It is an ugly epiphany of sorts, and seems a critical updating of that strangely moving moment when Oedipa finds herself alone near the end of *Lot 49*: 'She had dedicated herself, weeks ago, to making sense of what Inverarity had left behind, never suspecting that the legacy was America' (147). Oedipa's claim makes sense when we remember just how central a belief in a revelation yet to arrive has been for classic studies of American literature, in which America names less a collective past and more a future ideal that we must strive toward.[12] Cooper's revelation, however, concerns a past that we as a species will *never* escape, as in his final musings about his father's masterpiece, which will stand 'silent as a scarecrow and lonely as a sentinel for ten thousand years until the Areas are gone and the USA is gone and everything else that is familiar to us now is beyond history and forgotten' (400).

Notes

1. Subsequent references are to this edition and are parenthetical.
2. What distinguished Acord from other artists who have worked with radiation was his licence from the Nuclear Regulatory Commission, which enabled him to work with material on a scale unavailable to other artists. In a legendary case he actually convinced the German

energy company Siemens to donate twelve spent uranium fuel rods to him, and was able to wangle his way through bureaucracy such that he actually received them, though the stress of maintaining control over them may have contributed to his death. For a brief account of Acord's work see the exhibition catalogue for *Atomic*, which includes an essay by Flint (Flint 1998).

3. This idea of a generational link back to an explicitly Cold War parent, and the problems of the transmission of historical knowledge about the Cold War, are repeated in a host of novels that question the Cold War's hold on contemporary culture. For a discussion of this subject see Grausam 2016.
4. The term 'first nuclear era' is Jonathan Schell's, and is used to refer to the period that began with the Trinity test and ended with the fall of the Berlin Wall (Schell 1998).
5. Oedipa's first encounter with the muted postal horn that is the symbol of the Trystero postal system comes in a restroom, where she finds it below a message: 'Interested in sophisticated fun? You, hubby, girl friends. The more the merrier. Get in touch with Kirby, through WASTE only. Box 7391. L. A.' While touring Yoyodyne, the defence contractor at the heart of San Narciso, she sees the muted postal horn being scribbled by an engineer. When she engages him in conversation she makes a mistake, referring to the system as WASTE; he corrects her by telling her it's an acronym, not a word: 'It's W.A.S.T.E., lady' (Pynchon 1999: 38, 69; subsequent references are to this edition and are parenthetical). This problem of misrecognising acronyms for words is repeated in the early pages of *The Book of Ash* when Cooper is confronted by security about the canister. Daniels, the security officer, grills him: 'What about the initials DECD? Do you know of any organization going by this name?' (Flint 2004: 16). When Cooper looks at the envelope he realises that it isn't initials but an abbreviation for 'deceased'; written on the envelope are the words Reever, Jack, and below this D.E.C.D.
6. I have argued elsewhere that Pynchon's novel associates problems of postage, postalness and postmodernism with postwar ontological problems brought into being by the nuclear age (see Grausam 2011: 42–58; see also Collignon 2014 for an extended investigation into Pynchon and the nuclear).
7. Mike Fallopian, in *The Crying of Lot 49*, is 'attempting to link the Civil War to the postal reform movement that had begun around 1845' (39) and offers a bizarre account of the origins of the Cold War, in which it begins in a mid-nineteenth-century naval encounter between Russia and the Confederacy off the coast of California. More widely, Pynchon's work is interested in alternative forms of historical speculation and explanation.
8. For a discussion of Millet's novel in relation to questions of nuclear waste storage, see Grausam 2015.
9. For a discussion of Pynchon in relation to Derrida, see Grausam 2011.

10. I borrow from Masco the idea of a doubled temporality of the unthinkable (Masco 2006: 2–4).
11. The most extended critical discussion of this problem comes in van Wyck 2005. See also Bryan-Wilson 2003, Masco 2006: 197–212, and Moisey 2012.
12. For an elegant account of the role of futurity, and its connections to other concepts, in classic American literature and criticism, see Breitwieser 2007.

References

Breitwieser, Mitchell (2007), 'Introduction: The Time of the Double-Not', in *National Melancholy: Mourning and Opportunity in Classic American Literature*, Stanford: Stanford University Press, pp. 1–56.

Brown, Kate (2013), *Plutopia: Nuclear Families, Atomic Cities, and the Great Soviet and American Plutonium Disasters*, New York: Oxford University Press.

Bryan-Wilson, Julia (2003), 'Building a Marker of Nuclear Warning', in Robert S. Nelson and Margaret Olin (eds), *Monuments and Memory, Made and Unmade*, Chicago: University of Chicago Press, pp. 183–204.

Collignon, Fabienne (2014), *Rocket States: Atomic Weaponry and the Cultural Imagination*, New York: Bloomsbury.

Derrida, Jacques (1984), 'No Apocalypse, Not Now (full speed ahead, seven missiles, seven missives)', *Diacritics* 14(2): 20–31.

Flint, James (1998), *Atomic*, exhibition catalogue, London: Arts Catalyst.

Flint, James (2004), *The Book of Ash*, London: Viking.

Grausam, Daniel (2011), *On Endings: American Postmodern Fiction and the Cold War*, Charlottesville: University of Virginia Press.

Grausam, Daniel (2015), 'Imagining Postnuclear Times', *Common Knowledge* 21(3): 451–63.

Grausam, Daniel (2016), 'Cold-War, Post-Cold-War, What Was (Is) the Cold War?', in Jason Gladstone, Andrew Hoberek and Daniel Worden (eds), *Postmodern/Postwar and After*, Iowa City: University of Iowa Press, forthcoming.

Madsen, Michael (2010), *Into Eternity: A Film for the Future*. DVD.

Masco, Joseph (2006), *The Nuclear Borderlands: The Manhattan Project in Post-Cold War New Mexico*, Princeton: Princeton University Press.

Millet, Lydia (2006), *Oh Pure and Radiant Heart*, Orlando: Harcourt.

Moisey, Andrew (2012), 'Considering the Desire to Mark Our Buried Nuclear Waste: *Into Eternity* and the Waste Isolation Pilot Plant', *Qui Parle* 20(2): 101–25.

Pynchon, Thomas (1995 [1973]), *Gravity's Rainbow*, London: Vintage.

Pynchon, Thomas (1999 [1966]), *The Crying of Lot 49*, New York: Harper Perennial.

Schell, Jonathan (1998), *The Gift of Time: The Case for Abolishing Nuclear Weapons Now*, New York: Metropolitan Books.

Schwartz, Stephen I. (ed.) (1998), *Atomic Audit: The Costs and Consequences of U.S. Nuclear Weapons Since 1940*, Washington, DC: Brookings Institution Press.

Tague, John (2009), Review of *The Book of Ash*, *The Independent*, 3 April, <http://www.independent.co.uk/arts-entertainment/books/reviews/the-book-of-ash-by-james-flint-755572.html> (last accessed 29 January 2016).

van Wyck, Peter C. (2005), *Signs of Danger: Waste, Trauma, and Nuclear Threat*, Minneapolis: University of Minnesota Press.

III Ubiquitous Surveillance

Chapter 8

'The Very Form of Perverse Artificial Societies': The Unstable Emergence of the Network Family from its Cold War Nuclear Bunker

Ken Hollings

'Boys Calling Girls, Boys Calling Boys'

'There is the Tiger,' Gilles Deleuze and Félix Guattari observe in 'Balance Sheet – Program for Desiring-Machines', first published in January 1973; 'it is rumoured that there is even an Oedipus in the network; boys calling girls, boys calling boys. One easily recognises the very form of perverse artificial societies, or a Society of Unknowns. A process of reterritorialization is connected to *a movement of deterritorialization that is ensured by the machine*' (Deleuze and Guattari 1977: 119; emphasis in original). Appearing at the start of a year that marked the unravelling of President Nixon's cover-up of the Watergate burglary, their essay can be seen as an attempt to transcend the physical logic of machinery at a time when the Leader of the Free World found himself deeply engaged in fighting a Cold War both at home and abroad. Emerging from an assemblage of phone lines and switches, recording and playback devices, microphones, spokesmen and secretaries, Nixon's war machine swiftly became a network of repression and marginality: operating through such strategies while at the same time extending them to such a degree that the president's staff were busily compiling an 'enemies list' of his political opponents.

In opposition to this, the 'perverse artificial societies' described by Deleuze and Guattari were the random ones thrown up by Paris's unstable telephone system in the late 1960s and early 1970s, where crossed lines, misdialled numbers and bad connections created an entire phantom network of voices: 'a Society of Unknowns', which is to say, young people operating the system mainly through exploiting its eccentricities, malfunctions and weaknesses. As they did so, early models of online communities came into being with a large number of participants adopting aliases in order to remain anonymous within them.

Having previously informed its existence, 'Oedipus' would never have had the need, or indeed the opportunity, to be on Nixon's 'Enemies List'. He was already a functioning part of it. So how is his presence within the deterritorialised network described by Deleuze and Guattari to be interpreted? Perhaps as a text that can never complete itself, a fiction that remains unresolved, or even as an act of communication without informational content. A closer examination of the 'perverse artificial societies' created within the switches and exchanges of the Paris phone system reveals an emphasis upon 'boys calling girls, boys calling boys': not boys talking to girls or boys talking to boys. An attempted but incomplete connection between the parties involved is enough. Not surprisingly, Deleuze and Guattari link this '*movement of deterritorialisation that is ensured by the machine*' to the existence of 'groups of ham radio transmitters' who 'afford the same perverse structure' (1977: 119). At the same time it is worth noting how strictly regulated such networks had already become over the Cold War period. 'Every ham and his station have a unique call sign,' according to one source, 'the alphanumeric sequence that is usually the most prominent thing on the QSL card. It identifies the user and his location to other hams and to the government organization overseeing the airwaves' (Gregory and Sahre 2003: 153). An incomplete text in itself, a QSL card is exchanged between two operators when they make contact for the first time, the 'QSL' code being a common signal meaning 'Can you acknowledge receipt?'.

The physical logic of the machine marks its final collapse into completion. Its ideal form, Deleuze and Guattari propose, is in the elusive and unknowable 'machine' explored in their essay. 'Desiring-machines', they declare, 'have nothing to do with gadgets, little homemade machines or phantasies' – or, to reposition their argument slightly, with networks. In fact, they suggest, desiring-machines are related to such imperfect and completed forms 'from the opposite direction' (1977: 117). In other words, the network exists as the residue of desiring-machines; by extension, the network is in turn revealed as an incomplete assemblage of gadgets, homemade machines and phantasies. Their existence informed by both repression and marginality, only uncompleted entities are able to inhabit or traverse it.

'Right across the Country in a Straight Line'

Already perverse and artificial, the predominant phantasy of the Cold War was the nuclear family as the key statistic in an undeclared war that had been mapped out over grids, lines and circles representing kill ratios, civilian targets and second-strike capabilities. From 1947 onwards the suburban housing projects developed by William Levitt, Philip Klutznick and Henry J. Kaiser, all of whom had close connections either with the military or with national government, were intended to become a first line of defence as 'the world becomes a map, missiles merely symbols and wars just plans and calculations written down on paper', in the soothing words of an article appearing in a RAND newsletter under the title 'Better SAFE Than Sorry' (*RANDom News* 9(1), quoted in Marcuse 2007: 84). RAND's SAFE project was a series of war games played out 'down in our labyrinthine basement – somewhere under the Snack Bar' since 1961 (Marcuse 2007: 84). 'The Rand Corporation,' Herbert Marcuse would later observe, 'which unites scholarship, research, the military, the climate and the good life, reports such games in a style of absolving cuteness' (2007: 85). The grid that makes possible such plans and calculations can be very simply superimposed over the suburban housing estates that sprang up during the Cold War with their uniform divisions of property and street design, their standardised deployment of prefabricated domestic units.

The suburbs consequently came to embody space in its most schizophrenic form. Concrete islands, asphalt precincts and clusters of identical single-floor ranch-style dwellings gloried under such evocative names as Island Trees, Goldenridge, Pinewood, Lakeside, Forsythia Gate and Twin Oaks. The first Levittown community, built to accommodate munitions workers from Manhattan and Long Island, may have sounded like a decisive battle from the American Civil War, but its original inspiration was the utopian planned community created in secret at Oak Ridge, Tennessee, during World War II to house the technicians and scientists of the 'Manhattan Project' engaged in developing the first atomic weapon. The rush to the suburbs took place under the shadow of nuclear annihilation. Using the slogan 'Houses for the Atomic Age!', the Portland Cement Association marketed a ranch-style home made out of solid concrete to provide 'comfortable living – PLUS a refuge for your family in this atomic age' (Heimann 2002, unpaginated). Their advertising copy could not have made its reader more aware of the grid that had been superimposed so neatly upon his domestic life. 'The blast-resistant house design', it boasted, 'is based on principles learned at Hiroshima and Nagasaki and at Eniwetok and Yucca Flats.'

Once it became known that the Soviet Union had acquired first the A-bomb and later the hydrogen bomb, the dispersal of the American populace into widespread communities located far outside the major cities was regarded as a vital part of national defence. A presidential advisory committee on the National Highway Programme determined that 'at least 70 million people would have to be evacuated from target areas in case of threatened or actual enemy attack'. With a road system wholly inadequate to the task, such a statistic could not resist being set in concrete for very long. A 41,000-mile National System of Interstate and Defense Highway was under construction by 1958, and heavy industry was being encouraged to relocate itself to the 'wide countryside', taking its huge workforce with it. A major supplier of earth-moving equipment, Caterpillar was quick to capitalise on this sudden expansion, strategically placing the words 'Big Reason for Better Roads' under an image of a violent red mushroom cloud in one of their advertisements from the 1950s. 'This one is only a test (atomic detonation in Nevada)' (Heimann 2002: 138) runs a reassuring caption appended to the photograph. The advertising copy manages to keep Caterpillar's defence strategy sounding positive throughout. 'This tremendous network of no-stop freeways offers other vital defense benefits too,' it declares. 'Obviously, it will speed the movement of men and material. But more importantly, it will encourage the decentralization of our industries' (Heimann 2002: 138).

Establishing a network of highways on such a scale entails the rolling-out of a new kind of civilian war machine. 'His roads were planned so as to run right across the country in a straight line,' Plutarch wrote of the ambitious building programme initiated by Gaius Sempronius Gracchus in the second century BCE, 'part of the surface consisting of dressed stone and part of tamped down gravel. Depressions were filled in, any watercourses or ravines which crossed the line of the road were bridged, and both sides of the road were levelled or embanked to the same height so that the whole of the work presented a beautiful and symmetrical appearance' (Plutarch 1968: 183). Such beautiful symmetry connected Rome not just with the rest of Italy but also with its conquests in Europe and North Africa. Marker stones were introduced to indicate distances in Roman miles; where Rome's legions marched, the dispersal of its citizens, including builders, scribes, merchants and administrators, would accompany them along the straight line traced across the landscape by Gaius Gracchus. This process of colonisation through a civil population was extended historically into the American suburbs during the Cold War, except that the grid and the network now replaced the incomplete straight line of Roman conquest and occupation. During the Cold War the deployment of grids and networks not only represented conflict, they simultaneously *became* it.

'We've Been a Motorola Family for 20 Years'

'Desiring-machines', Deleuze and Guattari counter, 'cannot be equated with the adaptation of real machines or fragments of real machines, or to dreams of fantastic machines operating in the Imaginary' (1977: 117). This applies in particular to the rapidly expanding suburbs of the 1950s and 1960s and the ensuing spike in postwar population growth, together with the emergence of what came to be called the 'baby boom' generation. A social structure whose birth rate continues to accelerate remains incomplete; only its margins can define it. Standard codes of conduct remain to be established. From its very inception, the new American suburb is a fantastic machine springing up from nothing and 'operating in the Imaginary'. It is therefore not surprising to discover that the opening of William Levitt's earliest suburban housing grid on Long Island in 1947 coincided with advance copies of Alfred C. Kinsey's *Sexual Behavior in the Human Male* going on sale at the American Association for the Advancement of Science convention in Chicago. The 'Kinsey Report', as it became popularly known, offered the first statistical survey of practices usually conducted strictly in private. The Kinsey Institute for Research in Sex, Gender and Reproduction, incorporated that same year, was one of the first to use tabulators, adding machines and a standardised questionnaire to gather and process data from thousands of anonymous respondents. Kinsey's survey of *Sexual Behavior in the Human Female* followed in 1954.

By coupling the spectrum of human sexual responses to a closed network of calculating machines, questions and files, the residue of a desiring-machine dispersed itself through the media of the time. Torrid Hollywood dramas such as *No Down Payment*, *Peyton Place* and *Sin in the Suburbs* charted hitherto undetected phantasies haunting suburbia. Such a shift revealed that the nuclear family was by no means as stable as it might have seemed; as it transformed itself into the networked family of tomorrow, it became more tightly defined and structured by what was perceived to exist outside of it. At the same time suburbia produced its own sociological literature, offering lurid accounts of schizophrenia, adultery, drunkenness and divorce. Classic titles of the period included *The Crack in the Picture Window* and Dr Richard Gordon's *The Split-Level Trap*. Researching this latter volume over a five-year period among the people of Bergen County, New Jersey, Dr Gordon presented such a persuasive guide to the psychological decay inherent in suburban life – summed up on the book's cover as 'crab grass, ulcers and coronaries . . . a study of suburbanites under stress' (Gordon et al. 1961: jacket copy) – that he proposed calling it 'disturbia' instead.

Dispersed in this manner across the mass media, the nuclear family – under threat of nuclear destruction from without and psychological collapse from within – had already started to become a networked family whose distributed presence was experienced as a defence position. A key moment in the understanding of this shift came in 1956 with the release of Bell Telephone's popular promotional film *Once Upon a Honeymoon*, which expressed in unequivocal terms the vital importance of connection as it was experienced at the end of the 1950s. Jeff and Mary, a young married couple, are unable to get away on their honeymoon because Jeff has to finish composing a Broadway show tune for an upcoming musical. If only he had not stopped to pick up the phone when his agent called, they would have been on their way to sexual bliss. Instead Mary is left alone to fantasise about redecorating their home with matching telephones, unwittingly assisted by an angel sent down from heaven to help 'save' the marriage. As the boys and girls exploring the Paris telephone system would soon discover, it is more about calling than actually speaking with someone. Making a connection is all that matters; but how can Oedipus survive in a household with more than one phone? Assemblages of domestic devices and various models of telephonic apparatus proliferate throughout the film and the newlyweds' home. Even as the wife dances through her domestic phantasies while the husband frowns and stubs out yet another cigarette, *Once Upon a Honeymoon* pursues its principal argument that marital happiness is equated to an extension in every room and a speakerphone in the office.

By the height of the Cold War technology had effectively become both house and home. From the power mower parked on the front lawn to the stereophonic hi-fi system, the radio and the television set in the lounge, the nuclear family was finally completed within a loosely connected assemblage of fantastic machines. 'You bet we bought a Motorola TV,' a 1951 print advertisement boasted, 'we've been a *Motorola Family* for 20 years!'(Heimann 2002: 425; emphasis in original). This unifying self-identification with the machine is a central part of the Motorola pitch, which makes a point of emphasising that the father, speaking for the entire Motorola clan, 'wanted a screen big enough for his whole family to see at once'

(425). Within a few years, however, it was the device's portability rather than its defining presence that sold it. 'The gift they'll take into their hearts . . . and everywhere!' (436) ran the slogan in a 1957 advertisement for General Electric's Big Screen Portable, meaning that the television set was now joining the transistor radio as a means of moving away from the Motorola Family circle. The lure of portability opened up a new set of contradictions and discontinuities within the mass-media image of the nuclear family as it transformed itself into the network family. 'Even a modest-screened television, with all its tubes, was a very difficult thing to carry around,' Thomas Hine would later point out. 'Yet in much of the advertising for portable televisions, an elegantly dressed woman wearing white gloves is shown carrying the television as if it were a handkerchief, her arm completely extended' (Hine 1986: 121). Caught between the instant nostalgia for the past offered by shows like *The Lone Ranger* and *Howdy Doody* and phantasies of the future, as represented by *Captain Video* and *Tom Corbett, Space Cadet*, the offspring of the Motorola Family had no other option but to escape. 'Children running away from home with portable television sets', Hine would also note, 'proved to be a durable theme for cartoonists' (121).

'The New Assemblages Will Also Contain Effectors'

Escape, as practised from early childhood to late adolescence by the baby boom generation, can be read as a preliminary movement towards the process of deterritorialisation described by Deleuze and Guattari in their 1973 essay. Mobile devices such as transistor radios, portable televisions and record players allow the Motorola Family's offspring to disengage themselves from their unifying self-identification with the big screen and the even bigger machine that is hooked up to it. 'Desiring-machines', Deleuze and Guattari assert, 'are not in our heads, in our imagination, they are *inside the social and technical machines themselves*. Our relationship with machines is not a relationship of invention or of imitation: we are not the cerebral fathers nor the disciplined sons of the machine' (1977: 129). Unlike the telephone extension in every room, which regulates a visible world of phantasy, work and gadgets, the portable device offers the ambiguous possibilities of evasion and flight into unreason. 'I go wild when he flips that dial,' an anonymous voice announces on the break in Alma Cogan's 1960 single release 'Just Couldn't Resist Her With Her Pocket Transistor'.[1] Connecting the uncontrolled irrationality of going 'wild' with the technological processes involved in flipping a transistor radio dial, the song is a tiny desiring-machine that takes shape only when it is hooked up to an actual machine in the guise of a record player, tape recorder or jukebox. Even the homophonic wordplay in the title, coupling 'Resist Her' with 'Resistor' to rhyme with 'Transistor', hardwires sexual desire and electronic components into an ever-expanding, and therefore incomplete, circuit. Later in the same song a second anonymous voice responds to the first in similar but also very different terms: 'I go wild when she flips that dial.' Boys start connecting with girls; boys start connecting with boys; but who are these anonymous voices addressing? Desiring-machines, according to Deleuze and Guattari, 'constitute the non-Oedipal life of the unconscious, Oedipus being the gadget or phantasy' (1977: 120). Alma Cogan's song, hidden away on the 'flipside' of a 7" vinyl record released by His Master's Voice, introduces the missing but necessary elements of escape and evasion required for the process of deterritorialisation to begin. 'Now every night when it gets dark,' the song concludes, referring explicitly to the kids with their pocket radios, 'You know where they will be / Havin' fun there in the park / Happy as can be.'

By the time Alma Cogan released this record suburbia had revealed itself as both a gadget and a phantasy. However, it was the behaviour of the adult members of the Motorola Family, or their corresponding representation in the mass media, that showed the most unmistakable discontinuities and contradictions. 'Our marriage is over,' James Mason had thundered four years earlier, confronting his wife across the dining table in the 1956 movie melodrama *Bigger Than Life*. 'In my mind I've divorced you. You're not my wife any longer. I'm not your husband any longer.' This total disconnection exists solely in his mind, however. Mason plays schoolteacher and family man Ed Avery who has been prescribed cortisone, the latest 'wonder drug' to cure the chronic bouts of pain produced by overwork. Unlike in *Once Upon a Honeymoon*, released in the same year, gadgets and phantasies do not guarantee happiness. All the hallmarks of domestic bliss greet him at home: a television set dominating the lounge with a young son kneeling on the floor before it, plus a refrigerator and a dutiful wife in the kitchen. 'Doesn't this stuff bore you?' Avery demands of his son, ostensibly referring to the cowboy show playing on the TV but also giving voice to a much broader sense of disconnection. Pretty soon the cortisone exacerbates Avery's mounting sense of frustration, and the resulting mood swings become increasingly violent and unpredictable. As *Bigger Than Life* approaches its inevitable climax, Avery prepares to sacrifice his only son to an unseen god with a pair of scissors while his wife continues to pretend that nothing is wrong and makes whispered calls for help into the family telephone, hoping Oedipus will soon come back on the line again.

Released in the same year as *Bigger Than Life*, MGM's *Forbidden Planet* went even further in suggesting that the new range of gadgets had also let loose an unknown range of psychological monsters in the family unit. Both films offered visions of a disturbed and unstable patriarchal presence running 'wild'. Like James Mason, Walter Pidgeon plays a father ready to sacrifice everything to an unseen planetary force in order to preserve his hold over his daughter Altaira, even to the extent of threatening her own life. As Professor Morbius, the scientist father of an only child, Walter Pidgeon does not require a domestic pair of scissors to accomplish this. Set four hundred years into the future, *Forbidden Planet* is well named; another dangerous suburban phantasy, this time located on the other side of the universe, Altair IV is both the birthplace of Morbius's daughter, who has known no other world and is even named after it, and the final resting place of the Krell, a technologically advanced, semi-divine race who had perished in a single night many centuries ago. As the 'cerebral father' of one and the 'disciplined son' of the other, Morbius has become dangerously obsessed with both.

Behind Morbius's highly educated but unstable ego – and to a lesser extent Ed Avery's as well – lurks the psychological turmoil of mathematician and 'father of cybernetics' (Conway and Siegelman 2005) Norbert Wiener, whose thinking on communication and control in biological, mechanical and electronic systems is haunted by his own emotional and mental volatility. The publication of his key treatise *Cybernetics* in 1949 suddenly brought him to the attention of a much wider readership, prompting *Business Week* in February of that year to comment upon how 'Wiener's book resembles *The Kinsey Report*: the public response to it is at least as significant as the content of the book itself' (Conway and Siegelman 2005: 182). Such interest required Wiener to explain his position in more general terms. In 1949, *The New York Times* invited him to write an overview of his book for their Sunday supplement. The eventual piece, entitled 'The Machine Age', was never published, but a third draft of it can be found on the Massachusetts Institute of Technology online archive. 'By this time', the article confidently begins, 'the public is well aware that a new age of machines is upon us based on the computing machine, and not on the power machine. The tendency of these new machines is to replace human judgment on all levels but a fairly high one, rather than to replace human energy and power by machine energy and power' (Wiener 1949: 1).

In effect, Wiener is stepping down the processes of communication and control to the lower assemblies of the machine; no longer a self-contained gadget completed by the 'higher levels' of human judgement or power, the computing machine is now revealed to function on a deeper, more autonomous level. 'We have so far spoken of the computing machine as an analogue to the human nervous system rather than to the whole of the human organism,' Wiener concludes. 'Machines much more closely analogous to the human organism are well understood, and are now on the verge of being built' (1949: 4). In connection to these autonomous systems Wiener observes that 'new assemblages will also contain effectors' (4); in other words, some factors will remain outside of the overall control of the machine. 'Furthermore,' he stipulates, 'the actual performance of these effector organs as well as their desired performance will be read by suitable gauges and taken back into the machine as part of the information on which it works' (4).

But what happens if the disparity between 'actual performance' and 'desired performance' is taken back into the machine as repeated messages of escape, evasion and the urge to 'go wild'? The uncompleted circuit starts to feed back on to itself. One of Norbert Wiener's publishers described the mathematician as 'mercurial', 'unpredictable' and 'touchy' to work with (Conway and Siegelman 2005: 247), while those who knew him both professionally and privately referred to him as 'immature', 'petulant' and 'infantile' (Conway and Siegelman 2005: 198). Prone to extended bouts of depression and angry outbursts, Wiener's mood swings dominated his household in much the same way that those of Ed Avery and Professor Morbius did with theirs. This would eventually oblige one of his offspring to 'flip the dial', declaring that 'I'm tired of being Norbert Wiener's daughter. I want to be Peggy Wiener' (Conway and Siegelman 2005: 207).

'A State of Permanent Mobilization for the Defense of this Universe'

'Roughly speaking,' Wiener calmly observed in his unpublished article, 'if we can do anything in a clear and intelligible way, we can do it by machine' (Wiener 1949: 5). And yet the subassemblies of the Machine Age would prove to be anything but clear or intelligible. What separates 'desired' from 'actual' performance is the difference between an incomplete and a complete system. In 1949, the same year that *Cybernetics* was published and the Soviet Union exploded its first A-bomb, former World War II sharpshooter Howard Unruh killed thirteen of his neighbours in Camden, New Jersey, thus becoming America's first single-episode mass murderer. It took him just twelve minutes. Reading an account of the incident in *The New York Times*, Marshall McLuhan was later prompted to observe that it 'provides bizarre testimony to the cooling participational character of the telephone' (McLuhan 2001: 298). Unruh's killing spree was only halted by a phone call from the editor of *The Camden Evening Courier*. 'Why are you killing people?' Unruh was asked, to which he was alleged to have replied: 'I don't know. I can't answer that yet. I'll have to talk to you later. I'm too busy now' (298). McLuhan had already noted that 'the power of the telephone to involve the whole person is recorded by psychiatrists, who report that neurotic children lose all neurotic symptoms when telephoning' (298).

In relation to this last observation, R. D. Laing went so far as to quote Norbert Wiener in *The Divided Self*, his groundbreaking study of psychogenetic relationships published in 1964, the same year as McLuhan's *Understanding Media*: 'At some stage a machine which was previously assembled in an all-over manner may find its connexions divided into partial assemblies with a higher or lower degree of independence' (Laing 1990: 195).

Oedipus, it would appear, is inside the system but no longer on the line. The 'tonalities' heard on the soundtrack to *Forbidden Planet*, the first movie to have a completely electronic score, were the work of Bebe and Louis Barron, whose compositional approach had been heavily influenced by Wiener's writings on cybernetics. Inspired by how feedback similarly affects the behaviour of electrical and biological systems, they deliberately overloaded their electronic circuits, essentially 'torturing' them into producing random noises as they slowly expired. Meanwhile audiences attending the movie remained unaware that they were listening to the sounds of their own nervous systems collapsing.

This destructive separation of the partial subassemblies inevitably fed technological progress during the Cold War. Also published in 1964, Herbert Marcuse's *One-Dimensional Man* offered a radical critique of how technology did not so much extend the inner and social worlds as subsume them. 'The liberating force of technology – the instrumentalization of things – turns into a fetter of liberation; the instrumentalization of man,' argues Marcuse (2007: 163).

McLuhan's understanding of communications media as cybernetic 'extensions of man' has instantly flipped over into Marcuse's 'instrumentalization of man'. At the same time McLuhan joins with Marcuse in identifying something that operates through the socially organised reality of the gadget solely to perpetuate itself: 'A mass medium is one in which the message is directed not *at* an audience but *through* an audience,' McLuhan asserts (McLuhan and Carson 2003: 30–3). This self-perpetuation, according to Marcuse, extends itself 'not only through technology but as technology' (2007: 198), thereby absorbing the newly revealed subassemblies of human experience. 'Technological rationality', remarks Marcuse, 'reveals its political character as it becomes the great vehicle of better domination, creating a truly totalitarian universe in which society and nature, mind and body are kept in a state of permanent mobilization for the defense of this universe' (120). The Cold War family, isolated and huddled together in their suburban bunkers, had been transformed into an instrumentalised mass of subassemblies, whose attempts at communication have become a form of collapse. 'If the present cold war peters out into a cold peace,' Wiener had observed back in 1949, 'the time of the automatic machine age is rather difficult to determine' (6). Or, as McLuhan would note in 1964, 'The product matters less as the audience participation increases' (2001: 246).

'The Subliminal Kid Moved In'

Participation becomes a sublimated residue of the 'desiring-machine', processing human agency through a network of push-button devices that connect the nuclear home with the universe of technological and social rationality. 'Anyone leafing through a copy of *Life*, *U.S. News & World Report* or *Newsweek* during the 1950s or early 1960s', Thomas Hine recalls, 'might turn from advertisements for push-button washing machines and push-button transmissions to an article about how a push-button society was making America soft, and then to an account of a new computerized system for monitoring airplanes and missiles, under a headline like "Pushbutton Defense for Air War" ' (1986: 128). Pushing a button activates a completed system, sets a phantasy of command and control into uncontrollable action, whether for a washing machine, a television set or an atomic device. Norbert Wiener was horrified at the prospect. 'The whole idea', he declared, 'has an enormous temptation for those who are confident of their power of invention and have a deep distrust of human beings' (quoted in Conway and Siegelman 2005: 239). Wiener's subsequent refusal to share his work with the military, together with a threat to withdraw completely from scientific research, quickly brought him to the attention of the FBI.[2]

With no fixed point or residual presence, marginalisation becomes a metaphor for radical transition: a perspective on the network family that both connects and separates the like from the unlike, the complete from the incomplete, in an Oedipal 'double-bind'. While participation offers only an illusion of motion, marginalisation becomes its essence, located somewhere outside what Wiener identified as the 'power of invention' and 'a deep distrust of human beings'. The margin obliges the centre to reveal itself to itself. '"The Subliminal Kid"', William S. Burroughs noted in *Nova Express*, written during the early 1960s, 'moved in and took over bars cafés and juke boxes of the world cities and installed radio transmitters and microphones in each bar so that the music and talk of any bar could be heard in all his bars and he had tape recorders in each bar that played back and recorded at arbitrary intervals' (Burroughs 1966: 129). Here a blueprint 'for the very form of perverse artificial societies' has been clearly sketched out in a science fiction fantasy. The process of recording and playback at random inevitably scrambles meaning, creating communication without content. At the marginalised centre of the network there are boys calling girls, boys calling boys; from the early 1960s and throughout the 1970s a 'phone phreak' community of teenage boys and girls ran wild through the Bell Telephone system, taking over the switches, setting up 'party lines' in hacked exchanges and prank calling figures of authority. One such incident related by John Draper, aka 'Captain Crunch', involved getting Richard Nixon on the line at the height of the Watergate scandal using his Secret Service name, only to inform him that the West Coast office of the CIA had run out of toilet paper.[3] 'Marginality', Félix Guattari observed in 1977, 'is a place where one can discern the ruptures in social structures and emergent problematic traits in the field of the collective desiring economy. It involves analysing the margins, not as psychopathological events, but as the most vivid, the most mobile of human communities in their attempts to find responses to changes in social and material structures' (Guattari 1977: 185).[4]

After the phone phreaks' pranks and evasions, early internet explorers were treated as marginalised criminal gangs and behaved accordingly. The Masters of Deception, for example, were a notorious hacker collective that originated from teenage bedrooms in Queens and Bedford-Stuyvesant. They assumed colourful identities whose spelling reflected their passion for the phone lines they were using. Legends like 'Acid Phreak' and 'Phiber Optik' were the mysterious entities working the AT&T switches, posting philes and swapping information. Pretty soon the network family found itself under attack from both the centre and the margins of the system. Online warfare between the Masters of Deception and rival hacker collective the Legion of Doom resulted in the mass shutdown of phone lines which took place, appropriately enough, on Mother's Day 1990.

'All Other Weapons Were Discarded'

Testing and exploring, the hacker moves into the world of the system itself; this new form of interactivity regulates the relationship between the complete and the incomplete. An open network of gadgets replaces the closed push-button operating system of the nuclear family. The transistor radios, telephones and record players of the Cold War gave way to videogame consoles and personal computers as the platforms for interaction. A portable device designed for storing and manipulating data, the domestic tape recorder offered yet another metaphor for transition; William S. Burroughs considered it 'an externalised section of the human nervous system' (1984: 166), the more hands working its switches the better. Words are thereby transformed into an open system of unconnected meaning, becoming communication without content. By flipping human language over to the binary codes of the data-processing machine, hacker collectives such as the Masters of Deception and the Legion of Doom were among the first to learn how to run riot through this vast domain.

Today, as Burroughs pointed out back in the 1960s, 'any number can play' (1984: 162). The masses are now online, a self-defining network occupying digital space. They constitute what the technologically rational world had always claimed them as: an environment, a set of influences organised strategically. 'For the truth was that all the rest of the Syracusans merely provided the manpower to operate Archimedes's inventions,' Plutarch recorded, 'and it was his mind which directed and controlled every manoeuvre. All other weapons were discarded, and it was upon his alone that the city relied both for attack and defence' (Plutarch 1968: 101).

Alma Cogan was certainly not the last singer to connect dials and circuits with humans going 'wild': from rock music to techno, pop culture has if anything emphasised the relationship. Escape and evasion no longer connect the margins to the centre in the same way, however. The effect of today's portable devices is more pronounced when operating within a crowd, which occupies both the margin and the centre and where the ceaseless flow of people is wired into itself. With the introduction of multi-service handheld gadgets such as smartphones, tablets and MP3 players, this flipping of mobility and participation becomes total. The audiovisual noise generated by these devices keeps their operators blissfully unaware of their status as communication content. These networked devices work the crowd, agency being restricted solely to the connections they supply. Archimedes' arithmetical war machine, brought to bear upon the legions of Marcellus, could not have been better organised or more complete.

'Inversely,' Deleuze and Guattari argue, 'the power of the State does not rest on the war machine, but on the functioning of the binary machines that traverse us and the abstract machine that overcodes us: a whole "police force"' (1983: 102). In turn, the traversing network internalises intrusion and isolation, expelling the outsider even from the margins. 'The universe is telling me something and I'm pretty sure it's saying "get out",' Edward Snowden's girlfriend Lindsay Mills tweeted when first coming to live with him in Hawaii, where 'E' was working for the NSA as system administrator stuck 'at the end of a lot of long, thin communication pipes' (Andrews et al. 2014: 119). Lindsay, it seemed, had managed to decode the message early. Today's panics over online security and classified documents, leaked by juniors and slackers more adept at using computers than the senior agents for whom they work, are depicted and explained through the mass media in terms of evasion and instability. Snowden's online gamer name 'flashed' in his own words 'visibly in that moment of unrestrained spite' and was later revealed to be 'Wolfking Awesomefox' (Andrews et al. 2014: 114). Army intelligence analyst Chelsea Manning was formerly known in online chat rooms as 'bradass 87' (Jardin 2011). Members of the Anonymous hacker collective constitute a Society of Unknowns that can trace its origins back to the Parisian telephone system of the 1960s and 1970s. Linking these shifting identities into an uncompleted network is WikiLeaks founder Julian Assange, who has yet to leave the confines of the Ecuadorian Embassy in London. 'His legal perils have not receded,' according to one recent press account, 'but his state of diplomatic limbo means that he is no longer being hauled out of black vans and in front of screaming reporters and whirring cameras' (Ellison 2013: 187). But then Oedipus has never been out of the media for too long.

Notes

1. Alma Cogan, 'Just Couldn't Resist Her With Her Pocket Transistor', written by Jack Keller and Larry Kolber, B-side to 'Must Be Santa', His Master's Voice 7" single, 1960.
2. For a detailed account of FBI interest in Wiener and his mental condition at this time, please refer to Conway and Siegelman 2005: 262–71.
3. John Draper in conversation with the author, 11 October 2003.
4. The original reads: 'La marginalité est le lieu où peuvent se lire les points de rupture dans les structures sociales et les amorces de problématique nouvelle dans le champs de l'économie désirante collective. Il s'agit d'analyser la marginalité, non comme une manifestation psychopathologique, mais comme la partie la plus vivante, la plus mobile des collectivités humaines dans leurs tentatives de trouver des responses aux changements dans les structures sociales et matérielles.'

References

Andrews, Suzannah, Bryan Burrough and Sarah Ellison (2014), 'The Snowden Saga: A Shadowland of Secrets and Light', *Vanity Fair* 645, May, <http://www.vanityfair.com/news/politics/2014/05/edward-snowden-politics-interview> (last accessed 2 February 2016).

Bigger Than Life (1956), dir. Nicholas Ray, Twentieth Century Fox.

Burroughs, William S. (1966), *Nova Express*, London: Jonathan Cape.

Burroughs, William S. (1984), 'The Invisible Generation', in *The Job: Topical Writings and Interviews*, London: John Calder, pp. 160–70.

Conway, Flo, and Jim Siegelman (2005), *Dark Hero of the Information Age: In Search of Norbert Wiener, The Father of Cybernetics*, New York: Basic Books.

Deleuze, Gilles, and Félix Guattari (1977), 'Balance Sheet – Program for Desiring-Machines', trans. Robert Hurley, *Semiotexte* 2(3): 117–35.

Deleuze, Gilles, and Félix Guattari (1983), 'Politics', in *On the Line*, trans. John Johnston, New York: Semiotext(e), pp. 69–115.

Ellison, Sarah (2013), 'The Man Who Came to Dinner', *Vanity Fair* 638, October, <http://www.vanityfair.com/news/politics/2013/10/julian-assange-hideout-ecuador> (last accessed 2 February 2016).

Gordon, Richard E., et al. (1961), *The Split-Level Trap*, New York: B. Geis Associates.

Gregory, Danny, and Paul Sahre (2003), *Hello World: A World in Ham Radio*, Princeton: Princeton Architectural Press.

Guattari, Felix (1977), 'Gangs à New York', in *La Révolution Moléculaire*, Paris: Éditions Recherches, pp. 185–8.

Heimann, Jim (ed.) (2002), *Future Perfect: Vintage Futuristic Graphics*, Cologne: Taschen.

Hine, Thomas (1986), *Populuxe*, London: Bloomsbury.

Jardin, Xeni (2011), 'Bradley Manning's Army of One', *Boing Boing*, <http://boingboing.net/2011/07/03/bradley-mannings-arm.html> (last accessed 2 February 2016).

Laing, R. D. (1990), *The Divided Self: An Existential Study in Sanity and Madness*, Harmondsworth: Penguin.

McLuhan, Marshall (2001), *Understanding Media: The Extensions of Man*, London: Routledge.

McLuhan, Marshall, and David Carson (2003), *The Book of Probes*, Berkeley: Ginko Press.

Marcuse, Herbert (2007), *One-Dimensional Man: Studies in the Ideology of Advanced Industrial Society*, London: Routledge.

Plutarch (1968), *Makers of Rome: Nine Lives*, trans. Ian Scott-Kilvert, Harmondsworth: Penguin.

Wiener, Norbert (1949), 'The Machine Age', version 3, Massachusetts Institute of Technology, <http://libraries.mit.edu/archives/mithistory/pdf/MC0022_MachineAgeV3_1949.pdf> (last accessed 2 February 2016).

Chapter 9

The Signal-Haunted Cold War: Persistence of the SIGINT Ontology

Jussi Parikka

The Ephemeral SIGINT

The persistence of the signal marks an ephemeral yet material continuity of the Cold War. The war of signals, signal interception, spy stations, cryptology and signal intelligence had intensified since the start of World War I. Wireless cryptography became one focal point of national security during the war; national territories were guarded in signal space too, localised in concrete sites such as Tuckerton, New Jersey, or Nayville, New York, telegraph stations, owned by the German Telefunken. For obvious reasons, it was taken into American control during the war years when suspicions of German military interests over the traffic that flowed through the 500-foot aerial towers became stronger (see Wythoff 2014).

Thousands of code-breakers and radio interceptors – primarily Europeans – worked towards analyses of what was being said and to what ends, and how the obvious message could be altered with only an addition of an extra gap in patterns of Morse code. In ciphers, the persistence of the word 'ṣifr' in Arabic (and also Turkish), meaning 'zero', is a reminder of how marking 'nothing' becomes essential for coded messaging. The contemporary-seeming 'nothingness' of wireless communications that does not allow much in terms of perception of the signals crossing space between end-devices is encased in a longer history of the mathematical nothingness that stands as a key reference point for a media archaeology of the cryptographic world that we sometimes bluntly call in more popular terms 'digital culture'.

Cryptography was still limited in the early wireless days, a different situation than with the arrival of World War II some twenty-five years later. Cryptography itself of course has a longer history in written forms spanning centuries. But techniques of data analysis were even more strongly tied to the use of machines as ways to process intelligence gathered, signals intercepted. Some years later, with the advent of the Cold War, the situation had changed to one characteristic of any modern technological data situation: dealing with information that was 'often trivial in quality and overwhelming in quantity' (Ferris 2010: 167). The air and transmission waves were full of signals anyway, which made even the identification of code from everyday nonsense a task in itself. From the forefront of the hot wars, agencies specialising in this technological epistemology of signals moved to increasingly secret organisations of media analysis. In more ways than one, the perpetuation of signals is a key legacy of the Cold War and the systems thinking that it produced: both literal work in signal engineering and its use in the creation of a technically sophisticated crypto-industrial complex (Kittler 2014), and in analogous ways that prepare the discursive path to digital network culture.

The existence of the NSA and other institutions as part of the Cold War and contemporary geopolitical practice demonstrates the most significant way in which the importance of signals persists alongside that of code. Media theorist Friedrich A. Kittler wrote in 'No Such Agency', decades before the Snowden leaks, about the NSA's technical operations of surveillance and the gradual displacement of the human operator from the heroic forefront of intelligence agencies:

> Exactly because Human Intelligence or HUMINT (as spies are called in agency jargon) has been surpassed by Signals Intelligence or SIGINT according to budget and rank, in order to leave 'human understanding' to German philosophy lectures, a new Le Carré is published every year.

In other words, because the main importance of security and surveillance is in SIGINT, the romantic literature of spy novels and films flourishes as a nostalgic memory of how it used to be. The narrativisation of the heroic character persists, but so does the signal. The heroic names are nowadays mostly visible only in the remediating film and television culture types of spies, whereas the scientific and technological reality is more interested in the signals. The communication-technological world of secrets and their leaks is not limited to the number of cases new platforms – and whistleblowers – of the past years released, from WikiLeaks to Snowden, Assange to Manning. Instead of proper names, think of the importance of the signals and their interception. This is what Kittler in 'Cold War Networks' (2006) more broadly narrativises as the legacy of the Second World War and the Cold War: a geopolitical struggle for the waves, but ones that are of the electromagnetic spectrum. The specific places of signal processing and cryptoanalysis – whether the World War II huts at Bletchley Park that housed Alan Turing and his machines and human computers, or the later radar sites with their own relation to the electromagnetic spectrum – become oddly nostalgic sites of cultural heritage.[1] Future wars will be increasingly dependent on the control of the air – as spectrum, offering an interesting tension in relation to the architectural materials as ruins, increasingly domesticated as part of an aesthetic fascination (Huyssen 2006: 8).

Hence, imagine for a second that the air is a recording medium, as Charles Babbage, the developer of the Difference Engine and the Analytical Engine, did. The Difference Engine was a machine that was pitched to have a role as part of the Empire's efforts: to calculate astronomical and mathematical tables. The Analytical Engine, later in the 1830s, was planned to serve imperial ends as well. But in the midst of the plans and building that never finished, Babbage also meditated more on the cosmological dimensions:

> [W]hat a strange chaos is this wide atmosphere we breathe! Every atom, impressed with good and ill, retains at once the motions which philosophers and sages have imparted to it, mixed and combined in ten thousand ways with all that is worthless and base. The air itself is one vast library, on whose pages are forever written all that man has ever said or woman whispered. There, in their mutable but unerring characters, mixed with the earliest, as well as with the latest sighs of mortality, stand forever recorded, vows unredeemed, promises unfulfilled, perpetuating in the united movements of each particle, the testimony of man's changeful will. (1989: 36)

If air really could be a recording medium, it would be an archive of inscribed past events, documents, monuments and discussions – a rather speculative idea, but one that meditates on what is hearable by means of gods and goddesses, spirits or technical media. The constant meticulous listening that characterises the usual image of surveillance is itself increasingly shifted from human ears listening to plain messages to machinic analysis. Indeed, emblematic of recent developments, an MIT team presenting at SIGGRAPH 2014 was boasting in its new research about the even more precise techniques of capturing vibrations from 'still' things such as crisp bags, and reproducing them as sound.[2] In other words, as we have known for a longer historical period, plain 'air' or 'things' are themselves vibrations, which can be exposed as visual patterns when analysed with extremely high-frame-rate cameras able to encode much more than the eye or ear can perceive.[3]

From Babbage to MIT, let us imagine that every whisper is recorded, whether by air, celestial scribes or just the techniques of modern institutions of intelligence. 'Cold War continuity' would not be a mere discursive or ideological theme but one of material recording media: vibrations and signals from the imaginary to the machine-perceived. The ghosts of the extended silent background hum that followed the Second World War and predated the Middle East wars, not least in Iraq, are still around us. It is the ruins of the Cold War that are still such monuments that haunt us as reminders of the constant operations of interception, surveillance and recording that themselves are now the subject of new revelations regarding the same institutions – like the NSA. Of course, they are also a social media platform's business strategy of data capture, analysis and reselling. From the military to social media, the business of *information about information* (Kittler 2014) is what keeps agencies busy. Stepping into old bunkers, abandoned command centres, military barracks and intelligence centres means stepping into an archive of the Cold War. It is an archive not only of written documents and human voices but of intelligence machinery inscribing in encrypted language their machine-processed signals. The air that records the ghosts of the past inscribes both humans and non-humans; the air full of signals. This chapter is a short look, through examples such as the Teufelsberg spy station in Berlin, at signal realities that constitute the environment in which the Cold War persists.

Architectures for Signals

'Technological warfare is mathematics and the machinery of its encryption,' writes Kittler in his 1986 text on the NSA, 'No Such Agency', referring to its secrecy in terms of both architecture and the way it handles its business. Kittler's short intervention, easy to think of as 'prophetic', merely articulates what has been known for decades: we have witnessed a shift from human, manually processed signal interception to automated signal interception. Techniques of data management have extended into huge institutional settings where people are not 'agents' but merely operators maintaining machines of interception. This reflects the gradual shift from HUMINT to SIGINT. This air of the imagined archive is full of signals, undecipherable to humans, only measurable, trackable and surveillable by means similar to those by which they were created: technical media.

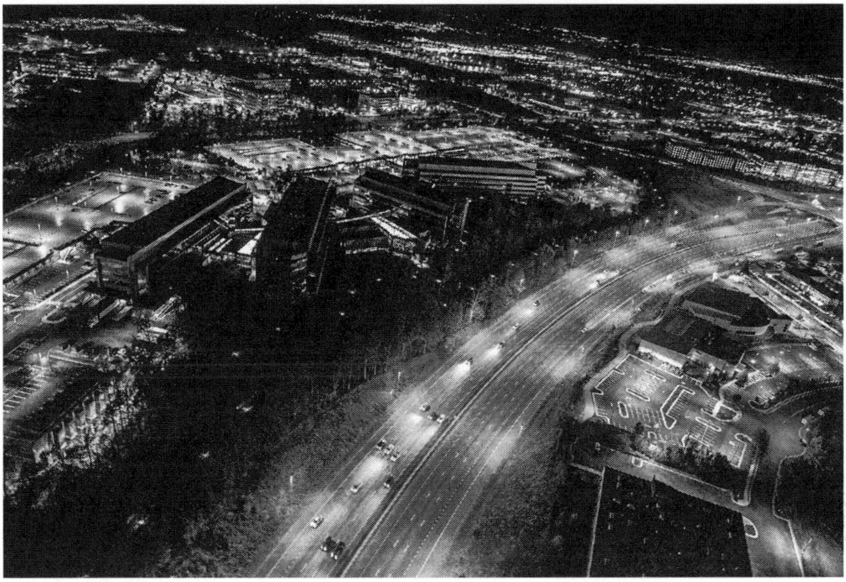

Figure 9.1 Trevor Paglen's aerial photography of the National Reconnaissance Office (NRO), in charge of developing, deploying and operating secret reconnaissance satellites.

But that is why abandoned or defunct sites of SIGINT remain interesting. They are bunkered monuments of secret operations teeming with signal activities that escape the eye and the ear as much as they seem to escape any democratic accountability. In Trevor Paglen's art, the long legacy of Cold War institutions, such as the NSA, becomes visualised. For Paglen, this visualisation is an artistic methodology relating to tracking. Even secret agencies have a physical presence that one can map in terms of their logistics, physical architectures, symbolics and other traces of their existence. Signal traffic is another thing, but at least the existence of logistical operations always by sheer physical necessity is in theory at least discoverable. Any rendition flight happens with planes following filed flight patterns governed by air control, along with departures and destinations, permissions and personnel; the materiality of the logistical operation that flies planes is what underpins Paglen's method that is, implicitly, about logistics. The 'invisibility of architectures' (see Curcio 2011) is unfolded through the operations that sustain the invisibility. These operations are technological as well as organisational, but in the end, as Paglen demonstrates in some of his work on satellites as much as on rendition flights, things need to be somewhere. In other words, even if surveillance does not necessarily look like anything particular, it is part of the real world as actions, plans, logistics and more. In other words, even images of the blank surveillance agency infrastructures, buildings that house people and primarily data traffic and analysis, have an effect when one understands their relation to a wider field where visual arts (and photographers) must understand this relation to information and logistics. In Paglen's words in *The Intercept* publication:

> My intention is to expand the visual vocabulary we use to 'see' the U.S. intelligence community. Although the organizing logic of our nation's surveillance apparatus is invisibility and secrecy, its operations occupy the physical world. Digital surveillance programs require concrete data centers; intelligence agencies are based in real buildings; surveillance systems ultimately consist of technologies, people, and the vast network of material resources that supports them. If we look in the right places at the right times, we can begin to glimpse America's vast intelligence infrastructure. (Paglen 2014)

The various architectures of secrecy – and here I am talking concretely of the buildings which house humans and technical media signals – are one such concrete spot where surveillance takes place. The imaginary of the completely ubiquitous surveillance penetrates the discussions of the key figures of twentieth-century state operations, but even ubiquity has spots where it gets enacted. Yet it is the haunted air of signals, instead of the merely human ground of dwellings, that defines SIGINT realities. Air becomes 'the groundless ground' (Irigaray 1999: 5) where contemporary versions of architectures of power are staged and need to be addressed in philosophical terms too. An anthropology of dwellings and architecture points to the primary function of such constructions since the early beginnings: a safeguard against the weather as well as living threats from others (Zinsmeister 2009: 147). But the post-anthropological security and defence constructions are measured so as to provide the signal effect and defect capacities with their material and architectural capacities.

It is not so much that the humans are missing as they are also housed as part of the surveillance machinery, security agencies and military assemblages. This means that besides the emergence of 'posthuman' scenarios from drones to automated interception, and machine-based targeting,[4] we are still somehow involved rather a lot of the time with humans. Susan Schuppli reminds us that even so-called 'unmanned' weapons take the labour of a surprisingly large number of humans: 'upwards of 165 people are required just to keep a Predator drone in the air for twenty-four hours', which accounts only for the flight logistics. If you add to that the personnel in 'multiple techno-social systems composed of military contractors, intelligence officers, data analysts, lawyers, engineers, programmers, as well as hardware, software, satellite communication, and operation centres (CAOC), and so on' (2014: 6), one starts to get to the bottom of the fallacy of the unmanned that is supported by lots of men and women, interfaced with the high-tech signal worlds.

Hence investigations of past military/surveillance architectures produce more than a psychogeographic method of analysis of the affordances of the urban lived environment; they produce a *psycho-signalgeography*: the media history of signals as they are relayed through buildings and live a life parallel to humans. Signals are sent and received by humans but at the same time phenomenologically escape us and reveal their presence only in the form of cell towers, radar architectures, signal intelligence agencies, and so on. The contemporary architecture of signals and secrecy, as well as their

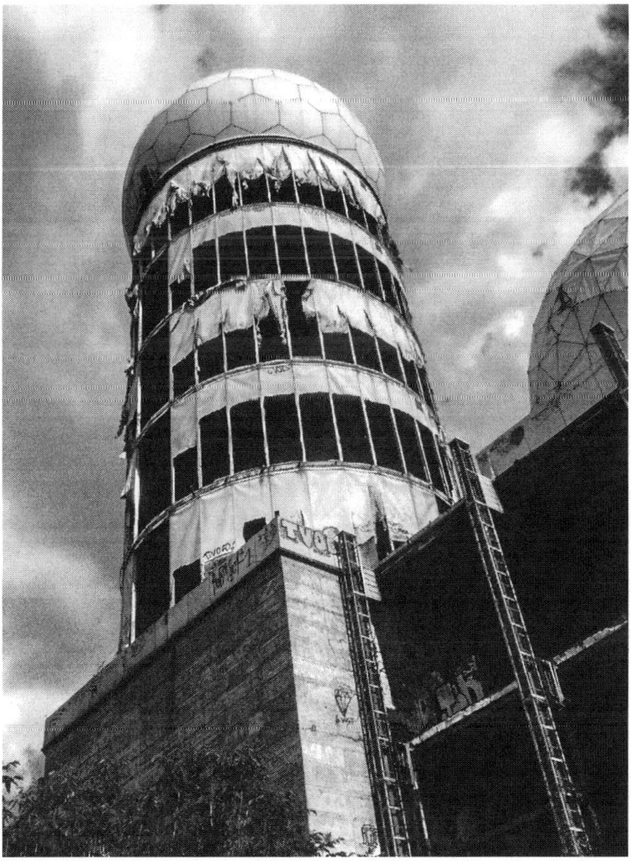

Figure 9.2 Teufelsberg, summer 2012. Image by Jussi Parikka.

ruins, are such interfaces of humans and signals. In other words, this reality is not about communication aimed at humans and decipherable with hermeneutics but is taking place at such frequencies that can be captured only at the level of the technical apparatus that goes back to the genealogy of signals and frequencies from the early nineteenth century to today: Fourier, Oersted and Faraday are some of the inventor-names that are the milestones for the scientific genealogy of this way of conducting wars in an anti-Newtonian way (see Siegert 2003: 397–8).[5]

This uncanny realisation makes military architectures and buildings so intriguing. After their time as the embodiment of high-security enforced secrecy, they open up as abandoned remainders of a war that did not go off as one big spark but as a constant low-level hum. '[T]he Cold War consisted essentially of a simulation of hot war,' argues Kittler in 'Cold War Networks' (2006: 183), continuing to underline, however, the emergence of the various accidental discoveries resulting from the various simulations such as nuclear bomb tests: the electromagnetic impulse (EMP) decapacitating the semiconductors and copper cable (183). In addition to possible human casualties, there is the EMP-induced death of advanced media infrastructure in houses, protected by materials and yet vulnerable to the non-communicating frequencies of such massive events.

The air of those abandoned buildings is this haunted archive. It is not just 'air' as an archive in the way Babbage pictured it, but the remainder of a signal intelligence air as once hosted in bunkers and sheltered by geodesic domes. During the height of the 'historical' Cold War, wars were constantly being waged indirectly through signal powers and communications. The global system established by the Western bloc was at first countered only by a much more restricted Soviet Union system of SIGINT, which, among other architectures, was sea-bound: fishing trawlers were used in the 1950s and later as mobile signal interception stations, as Knight demonstrates (2004a: 77). The ECHELON network of global spy stations was the earlier massive NSA project that lasted for some decades (developed since the late 1960s or early 1970s) and built a significant capacity to link different national stations of SIGINT. The emergence of satellite-based imagery had revolutionised intelligence gathering in the 1960s, and gradually this had an effect in terms of other capacities of SIGINT too. The ECHELON was a significant closed system with communication protocols and its own network as well as different applications for messaging, TV conferencing and mailing. The signals it gathered had to be themselves securely communicated, leading into new solutions that paralleled the gradual development of civilian 'network society'.

It emerged into wider consciousness only later in the 1990s, also in a worried EU report, demonstrating that measures of post-9/11 security surveillance systems were in place already much before. Indeed,

> Over the years, there emerged a network of listening posts and satellites intercepting cables, telephone communications, radio and microwave signals, wireless communications, e-mail, faxes, and other forms of communication traffic. Almost nothing was immune from the system that came to be known as Echelon, whether a telegram sending birthday greetings to a child in Great Britain, or walkie-talkie communications between East German guards on the Berlin Wall. (ECHELON: 371)

In Berlin, a perfect site for a geopolitical-poetic investigation of the remains of the ECHELON is that of the listening station Teufelsberg: a haunted signal ruin that is the residue of that otherwise fleetingly non-perceptible and quite mundane operational readiness that characterised this low-level hum of the Cold War. It marks an extended World War II of cryptographic intelligence, computational analysis and signal operations. Now even cryptography is becoming a widely marketed and nostalgic remnant of World War II culture (such as the 2014 Alan Turing film *The Imitation Game*).

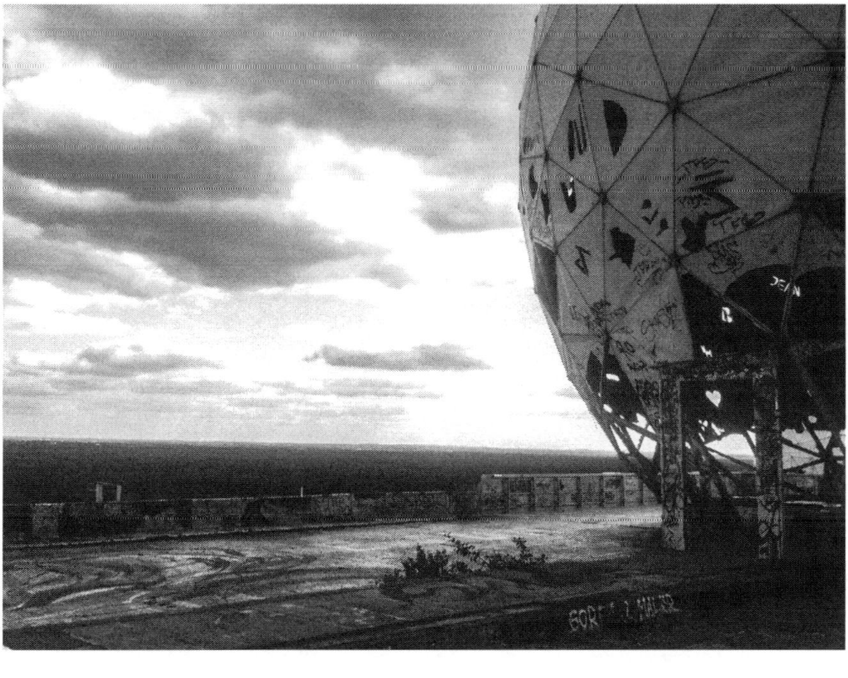

Figure 9.3 Teufelsberg, summer 2012. Image by Jussi Parikka.

My photographs from 2012 record a casual journey to the abandoned and quietly popular American station in Teufelsberg in West Berlin, easily reachable with public transport. Perhaps they are a form of hacker tourism, as Neal Stephenson coined it in one of his short stories: a form of visiting sites of infrastructures of information networks, surveillance and technology. A short walk through the woods and one has arrived next to the crumbling buildings; the entrance is not clearly marked. We did pass what looked like a makeshift ticket counter, which was, however, unattended. We saw other people, casual 'Cold War tourists', around as well and walked in, only later to be intercepted by people who claimed to be Security, asking for tickets. The private security people who eventually threw us out were preceded some forty years ago by the American Military Police when they intercepted another media and film scholar's journey to the same place. Film theorist Thomas Elsaesser shared with me his images of his own photo journey to the area in 1975. Some of these included images of him being questioned by the MPs, while in the background remained Teufelsberg in its pre-ruin state in the midst of the Cold War.

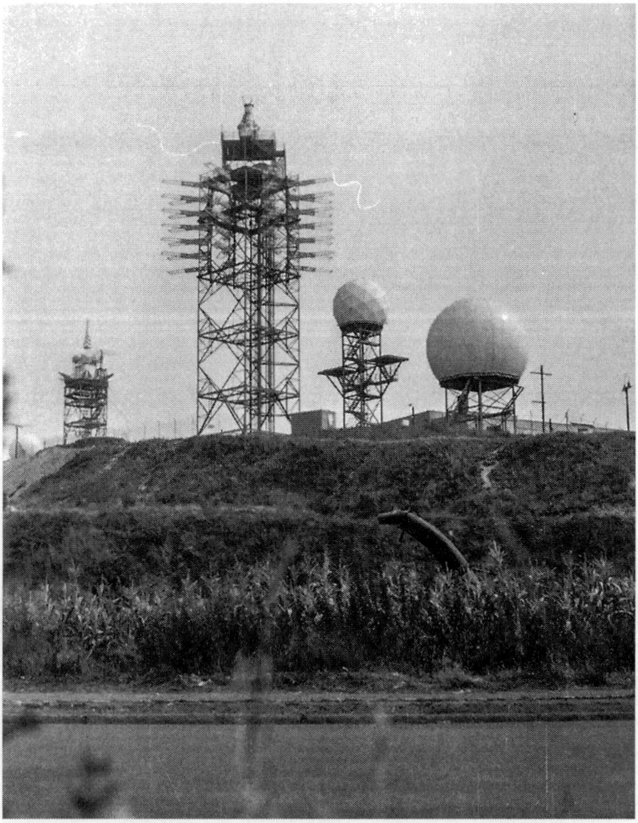

Figure 9.4 Teufelsberg, 1975. Image by and courtesy of Thomas Elsaesser.

Despite shifting from military compound to private security-controlled quasi-touristic site, Teufelsberg is a good example of the later cult status of past Cold War settlements, which were already from the start not just places for humans. Practices of spying have always been media practices, and part of a longer history of intercepting messages and adding the unwanted 'third' between the sender and the recipient of the message (see Parikka 2011). In the age of technical media, it is not only the messages we can hear or see that we spy on. Besides COMINT, we live the wider sphere of electromagnetic signalling.

Architectures become organised around their usefulness for signals, not just humans. Buildings offer enclosures for media and signal processing, a shared design task for the military and the corporate sector, as found in the interior designs of post-World War II corporate buildings such as IBM's (see Harwood 2003). In military contexts, the geodesic dome that offers a shelter to the intelligence radio posts harks back to earlier parts of the twentieth century. Buckminster Fuller pitched his earlier idea to the US Navy. Despite lightness and cheapness, the structures were stable and, importantly, because of the topology of the design, not as easily detectable by radar as other designs or structures might have been.[6] Fuller's domes were sprouting up not only at architectural showcases and international trade fairs (such as 1956 in Kabul) but were also commissioned for use by the US Air Force and the Distant Early Warning (DEW) radar system set in place to protect the nation in Northern Canada and Alaska (Anker 2007: 424). In more ways than one, Fuller and his domes became perfect symbols for architecture increasingly crafted for ecological purposes – to protect but also adapt to nature – as well as for all-out ecological demise: housings for the military and surveillance technological culture of the US Navy and Air Force as well as for the possible scenario of a post-apocalyptic mass evacuation of cities to the countryside. They implied a true posthuman architectural situation. Of course, Fuller became a countercultural hero too, with a vision of design-backed humanism (see Anker 2007). And yet, the idea of 'spaceship earth' that he promoted finds a curious twist in the idea of the electromagnetic spectrum as an alien reality for which some of the architecture is increasingly perfected.

The number of such inadvertent monuments across the globe is a concrete reminder of Cold War places that link the terrestrial and extra-terrestrial. Besides Teufelsberg, there are chains of such abandoned radar and listening posts throughout the world. In addition to being more or less abandoned buildings, part of the ruin-nostalgia of modernity, they are structures of a wider global space that had to do with the celestial vectors of signals like the famous early warning systems in Britain (Chain Home), the later North American Dew System and, for instance, the McGill Fence. In Kittler's words, from DEW to SAGE, the major decentralised system emerging was the true beginning of what we now celebrate as network society – in the 1950s case a linking of some seventy radar stations in the North with some twenty-seven command centres: 'The great decentralization now celebrated as the civilian spin-off called information society began with the building of a network that connected sensors (radar), effectors (jet planes), and nodes (computers)' (Kittler 2006: 183).

This is one sort of bunker archaeology, an investigation of the structures that relay logistics of war and remain as ruins of a different sort of cultural heritage. For Paul Virilio, this term emerged as part of his investigations of the architectural changes and remnants from the Second World War: the fortress architecture of the Atlantic Wall built to defend the German positions. Despite their solid and bulletproof concrete encasings, these bunkered architectures acted as relays in vector space; they offered a temporary home for the circulation of signals, 'a carpet of trajectories' (Virilio 1994: 19). The monumental nature of the concrete bunker, later 'naturalised' in urban geographies as Brutalism, was already during its active military period part of what Virilio terms the history of acceleration. Increasing speeds of transportation, motorised vehicles and projectiles but also of frequency-based transmissions are emblematic perhaps of how 'the time of war is disappearing' (1994: 21) but yet retains a different sort of temporality. The monolithic bunkers are part of such defence systems that had to be built into a world of signal transmissions. Virilio writes:

> Defense, in the course of the Second World War, switched from entrenchment to intelligence through the prodigious development of detection systems and telecommunications. In fact, while most of the means for acoustic detection had been created during the First World War, the improvement of optical telemetric, radiophony, and radar stem from the Second World War. (1994: 30)

In other words, the bunker and its representations also carry this implicit awareness of the other spectrums that penetrate the mute walls and open its surface to other sorts of less solid investigations. '[B]unker images are never neutral surfaces but always underwritten by concealed and murky histories,' argues John Beck (2011: 91). We can add that such murky histories are also ones that escape the solidity of the structures we perceive visually.

Urban planning and topographies have long had a close relationship with war. The specific relations of walls, constructions and designs to different techniques of war that have so far been projectile-based is of noteworthy nature (see Zinsmeister 2009). In addition, since the widespread mobilisation of the scientific discoveries of electromagnetism and frequency modulation, the architectural has been a question of intelligence architectures just as much as real-time computing has been perceived as an interior architectural task (see Harwood 2003).

This architecture is a monument to the total signal war that commenced with the advent of World War II. Signals and their interception have a longer history, of course (see Parikka 2011), but the massive mobilisation of computerised means of signal processing and interception was the significant step in terms of new architectures. These ruins – and their contemporary versions – are designed with different architectural insights and requirements: specifically to design spaces for signal transmissions and operations. The seeming stability and silence of the monumental constructions is misleading. They are teeming with the time-critical nature of signal processing, or, as Wolfgang Ernst puts it, 'the microtemporality in the operativity of data processing (synchronization) replaces the traditional macro time of the historical archive (governed by the semantics of historical discourse)' (2013: 70). Ernst's point relates to the temporal basis of digital technologies that are embedded not only in historical macrotemporalities but in the time-critical microtemporalities that are the technologically specific time of computing. This is the temporal logic of signals and signal processing that is accessible only through machines as the epistemological condition to access such a reality. It is also a shift from architectures of human bodies to those of signal processes and how certain material structures convey, filter and enhance signals.

Military planning, notes Virilio, always has a special relation to space but in terms of the geographical as well as the geophysical: the human space of troop operations as well as tectonics and geomorphological matter. War is geopolitical with an emphasis on *geo*, the earth, the soil, and I would argue, following Irigaray, that it needs to address the celestial bodies covering the ground, the air as the archive of past and future messages as Babbage in his celestial imaginary articulated. Indeed, material specialism of buildings becomes of great strategic importance for architecture that has to deal with signals: dead zones in badly designed buildings (e.g. university buildings that accidentally block mobile signal) or deliberately blocked signals in security-sensitive spaces.

War is of the earth, but it is also from the skies. It is the groundless ground of the air that increasingly determines our ontology in the SIGINT sense of existence of something that escapes direct hermeneutical meaning as it is not able to be heard by human ears unless technologically enhanced (see Siegert 2003: 398). Indeed, as Virilio continues in *Bunker Archaeology*, military space is no longer solely about the conquering of terrestrial space but focused on the non-human habitat of the skies and a sort of distancing from the earth – the speed of escape velocity to conquer earth's gravity to reach extra-terrestrial 'spaces' is paralleled by movements of war conditioned by the 'infinite small spaces of nuclear physics and in the infinitely huge outer space' (1994: 18). From actual military operations to their preparation in terms of surveillance and intercept operations, one is dealing with escape velocities of both bodies and signals. Hence an understanding of geophysics such as electromagnetism is what is of crucial interest to the continuous signal-processing operations that are themselves part of this 'outer space' too. And yet, we should not think this has evacuated the geopolitical but actually imbued it with signal territories of the sort that define new borders. Artist-Critical Engineer Julian Oliver engages with this signal reality in his 2012 project Border Bumping,[7] which deploys the signal-layered geopolitics of borders. Instead of geographical borders, telecommunication infrastructure ensures signal-hopping when mobile devices pick up signals across national territories when close to borders. Besides being a technological meditation on and at borders, the work engages with telecommunication infrastructures including 'stealth cell towers' as physical relay points of the otherwise ephemeral signal-borders. (On media studies of infrastructures, see also Starosielski 2015; Parks and Starosielski 2015.)

In terms of architecture, the ephemeral signal-realities can be approached with an emphasis on architectural remains as monumental ruins of spaces of bodies and signal vectors. These defunct infrastructures are reminders of the reality of this other sort of geopolitical territory. The architectures remain as relays to the places where signals interface with humans. They are also reminders of places where signals turn from microtemporal technical operations to human-processed decision-making and analysis. Such ruins are there as a monument to the interface between HUMINT and SIGINT. They are haunted because of their status of disuse, or as nostalgic cultural heritage possessing something mysterious about them. But the architectures were already haunted from the onset, with a slight nod towards the ways in which 'haunted media' has escorted the emergence of technical culture since the nineteenth century (see Sconce 2000). In other words, in addition to the physical objects, the air was full of signals of other sorts that connect not to human utterances but rather to a different sort of machinic *agencement* that functions

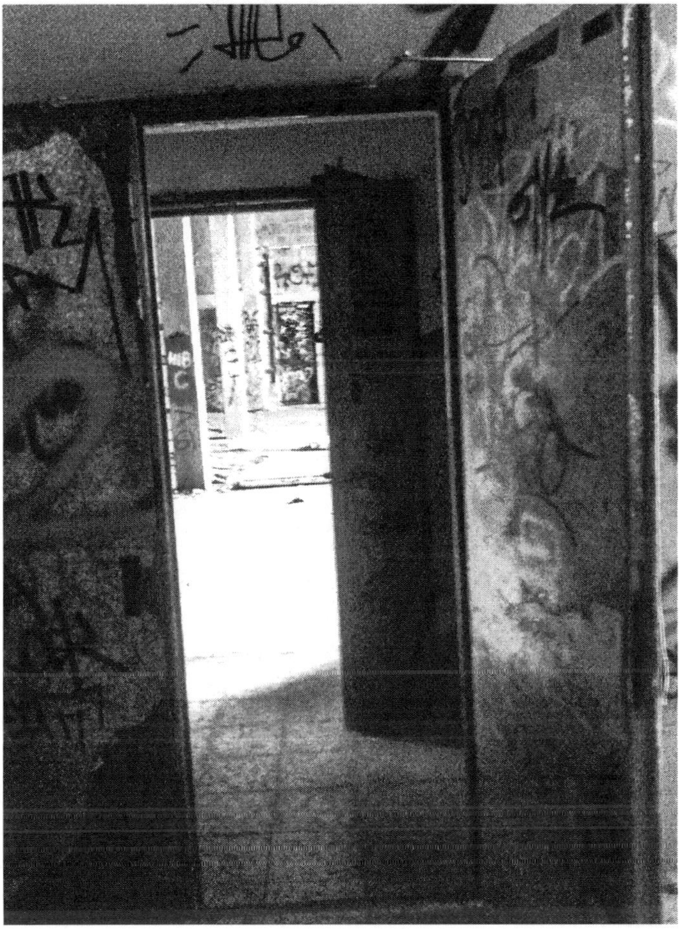

Figure 9.5 Teufelsberg, summer 2012. Image by Jussi Parikka.

by way of microtemporal signal operations or asignifying semiotics (see Lazzarato). Not all ghosts are hallucinations of the dead that try to signal to us through the aether; some ghosts are the real signals that escape our senses and seem as paranormal as any message from the human dead.

Signal Perversions

This sort of time-critical continuity that happens not on the level of macrohistorical narration but on that of microtemporal signal processing characterises another route to understand the technical basis of surveillance culture. Cold War systems perpetuate the primacy of the signal and the information theoretical framework over that of meaning-oriented analysis. Information/noise ratios, big data and statistical search for patterns take over the work of individual decrypting just like SIGINT replaces HUMINT, and just as structures must host the needs of signals as much as the needs of humans.

The surveilling state machine is one feature and legacy of the Cold War often pitched as a fear of the ubiquitous machineries that listen in on every movement in the vibrating air. Various discursive contexts offer this as a reference point when discussing government or social media corporation snooping; referring to Orwellian narratives or other forms of canonic literature works to make sense of the otherwise technically detailed ways of gathering metadata and other indexes of localisable data points.

In reality, pervasive surveillance always homes in on specific places and infrastructures. As part of the Snowden leaks, Berlin resurfaced on the map of this historical narrative. It was already a central spot for the Cold War narratives of spy thrillers as well as constant surveillance activities focused on installations in areas such as Teufelsberg. Nowadays such activities are housed more centrally, such as in the inconspicuous GCHQ spy station or the NSA facility placed on top of the US Embassy. Indeed, this 'hiding in plain sight' was one of the dozens of revelations that made it into newspaper stories after the Snowden leaks. For example, one focused on 'Britain's secret listening post in the heart of Berlin',[8] which revealed the extent of covert SIGINT operations targeting (German) politicians. Just as with the normal clandestine telecoms infrastructures investigated by Oliver, these 'concealed collection systems' utilise 'structures with fake windows'. The document said: 'Collection equipment on a building is concealed so as not to reveal SIGINT activity [. . .] antennas are sometimes hidden in false architectural features or roof maintenance sheds.'

Whereas the political response was rather blunt – no information is ever given about information (or, in British Prime Minister David Cameron's words, reacting to allegations, 'We don't comment on intelligence questions') – it merely represents one of those SIGINT stories that pervade the signal-based surveillance landscape. Such narratives point to buildings that are less to look at in terms of architecture as they are designed for signal capture, especially when situated near the Berlin Reichstag, for example.

Such SIGINT operations as revealed by Snowden and found in that brand of post-9/11 security paranoia are often labelled as 'perversions' of democratic rules and ideals. Yet, in an alternative media cultural framework, we should wonder if there is an underlying sense of perversion that actually presents a different story which underlines that this perversion is just a logical part of the state of media technologies as part of modern history of Cold War and current culture. Hence, by way of a short meta-reflection, and by way of conclusion, we need to ask if there is another sort of perversion that characterises this situation more accurately.

Thomas Elsaesser has articulated the wider significance of surveillance, science and the military as one of SM perversions in the field of cinema and media studies, perversions which offer a systematic focus on the issue of signal work in media culture. In other words, we can summarise the interest in architecture, the geophysical and the geographical, as well as the mathematical, microtemporal signal aspects of the Cold War that become the contemporary, as one of SM perversion. In this case, it is less about perversions of ideals of privacy and democracy or perversions of a sexual nature, but more about the SM variations that offer an alternative to the visual-entertainment focus of media analysis of visual culture. Instead, the SM realities are ones of science and medicine, surveillance and the military, sensory-motory coordination and perhaps also GMS and MMS (referring to mobile media signal systems). The word-play mobilised by Elsaesser reveals an underground of cinema history and visual culture dominated by an interest in the technical-material conditioning of the aesthetic, and we might want to add that it is also an above-ground of architectural ruins that are still present but in different forms. This above-ground is perhaps often located in the ruin-nostalgia of sites such as Teufelsberg, and we can also refer to them as archaeological conditions constantly present in the NSA-type operations that reterritorialise geopolitics through their SIGINT operations and transnational sharing of expertise between the NSA, GCHQ, CSEC and the Israeli ISNU.[9] This sharing was demonstrated yet again in 2014 as being party to the US-supported Israeli attack on Gaza and revealed in the Snowden-leaked files, narrated by Glenn Greenwald (2014).

Signal intelligence is another lineage in the genealogy of technical media practices that offer media analysis prior to the moment when media studies became offered as a university course. It suits the lineage of SM perversions of cinema and network media culture. It illuminates spaces of science as well as surveillance as a conceptual focus on those aspects crucial for modern technical media. The mathematical a priori is what drives an understanding of technical media and surveillance culture. Two continuities from the Cold War to our current day are parts of these perversions – normalised political perversions of everyday life in metadata that is made to reveal political, economic and diplomatic secrets, and media perversions as part of the research agenda of film, media and digital studies where the military, surveillance, science and medicine underpin so much of the supposedly entertaining media side of reality production. This sort of signal-supported perversion should not arrive with a shock and a surprise: a post-Snowden world of 9/11 insecurity cultures is just a reminder of the existence of the pre-Snowden folders of the NSA and other SIGINT operations of haunted signal worlds.

Notes

1. Paul Virilio: 'War is at once a summary and a museum . . . its own' (1994: 27). See also Beck 2011: 93–8.
2. See 'MIT researchers can listen to your conversation by watching your potato chip bag', *The Washington Post*, 4 August 2014.
3. 'When sound hits an object, it causes small vibrations of the object's surface. We show how, using only high-speed video of the object, we can extract those minute vibrations and partially recover the sound that produced them, allowing us to turn everyday objects – a glass of water, a potted plant, a box of tissues, or a bag of chips – into visual microphones' (Davis et al. 2014).
4. Machine-based targeting is taking place, for example, in Afghanistan, where drone strikes are executed based on gathered intelligence and mobile phone location signals. The HUMINT is replaced with partly automated metadata analysis and machine-targeting in the form of F3: Find, Fix, Finish. Location of a mobile phone SIM card becomes the target as a proxy of the suspect, although also in technical ways that simulate the existence of signal towers: 'The agency also equips drones and other aircraft with devices known as "virtual base-tower transceivers" – creating, in effect, a fake cell phone tower that can force a targeted person's device to lock onto the NSA's receiver without their knowledge' (Scahill and Greenwald 2014). Bishop and Phillips also address the aesthetics and operations of targeting in *Modernist Avant-Garde Aesthetics and Contemporary Military Technology* (2010).
5. More analytically, it means this: signal intelligence is often divided into COMINT (communications intelligence) and ELINT (electronics intelligence). COMINT consists of examples such as broadcasting interception (of course, having to do with signals as well) but ELINT opens up to the wider world of any intelligence-relevant signalling, whether directly transferable to human ears or not: 'All intercepts of non-communication signals sent over electromagnetic waves, excluding those from atomic detonations (which are the province of MASINT operations), fall under the heading of ELINT' (Knight 2004b: 80).
6. Many thanks to Dr Christina Vagt for explaining to me Buckminster Fuller's role and the design of the domes in this. See also Krausse and

Lichtenstein's *Your Private Sky: R. Buckminster Fuller – The Art of Design Science* (1999) and the chapter on 'Geodesics'.
7. See <http://borderbumping.net> (last accessed 2 February 2016).
8. *The Independent*, 5 November 2013.
9. Later collaboration in the field of SIGINT can be said to stem from the 1943 BRUSA Agreement between Britain and the USA, followed by expanded networks during the Cold War (ECHELON: 370).

References

Anker, Peder (2007), 'Buckminster Fuller as Captain of Spaceship Earth', *Minerva* 45: 417–34.

Babbage, Charles (1989 [1838]), *The Ninth Bridgewater Treatise: A Fragment* (2nd edn), in *The Works of Charles Babbage*, vol. 9, ed. Martin Campbell-Kelly, London: William Pickering.

Beck, John (2011), 'Concrete Ambivalence: Inside the Bunker Complex', *Cultural Politics* 7(1): 79–102.

Bishop, Ryan, and John Phillips (2010), *Modernist Avant-Garde Aesthetics and Contemporary Military Technology: Technicities of Perception*, Edinburgh: Edinburgh University Press.

Curcio, Seth (2011), 'Seeing Is Believing: An Interview with Trevor Paglen', *Dailyserving*, 24 February, <http://dailyserving.com/2011/02/interview-with-trevor-paglen> (last accessed 2 February 2016).

Davis, Abe, et al. (2014), 'The Visual Microphone: Passive Recovery of Sound from Video', SIGGRAPH 2014, <http://people.csail.mit.edu/mrub/VisualMic> (last accessed 2 February 2016).

ECHELON (2004), in *Encyclopedia of Espionage, Intelligence and Security*, vol. 1, ed. K. Lee Lerner and Brenda Wilmoth Lerner, Detroit: Thomson & Gale, pp. 370–2.

Elsaesser, Thomas (2006), 'Early Film History and Multi-Media: An Archaeology of Possible Futures?', in Wendy Hui Kyong Chun and Thomas Keenan (eds), *New Media, Old Media: A History and Theory Reader*, New York: Routledge, pp. 13–25.

Ernst, Wolfgang (2013), *Digital Memory and the Archive*, ed. with intro. by Jussi Parikka, Minneapolis: University of Minnesota Press.

Ferris, John (2010), 'Signals Intelligence in War and Power Politics, 1914–2010', in Loch K. Johnson (ed.), *The Oxford Handbook of National Security Intelligence*, Oxford: Oxford University Press, pp. 155–71.

Greenwald, Glenn (2014), 'Cash, Weapons and Surveillance: The U.S. is a Key Party to Every Israeli Attack', *The Intercept*, 4 August, <https://firstlook.org/theintercept/2014/08/04/cash-weapons-surveillance> (last accessed 2 February 2016).

Harwood, John (2003), 'The White Room: Eliot Noyes and the Logic of the Information Age Interior', *Grey Room* 12: 5–31.

Huyssen, Andreas (2006), 'Nostalgia for Ruins', *Grey Room* 23: 6–21.

Irigaray, Luce (1999), *The Forgetting of Air*, London: Athlone Press.

Kittler, Friedrich (2006), 'Cold War Networks or Kaiserstr. 2, Neubabelsberg', in Wendy Hui Kyong Chun and Thomas Keenan (eds), *New Media, Old Media: A History and Theory Reader*, New York: Routledge, pp. 181–6.

Kittler, Friedrich (2014), 'No Such Agency', trans. Paul Feigelfeld, *Theory, Culture & Society* blog, 12 February, <http://theoryculturesociety.org/kittler-on-the-nsa> (last accessed 2 February 2016).

Knight, Judson (2004a), 'Ships Designed for Intelligence Collection', in *Encyclopedia of Espionage, Intelligence and Security*, vol. 3, ed. K. Lee Lerner and Brenda Wilmoth Lerner, Detroit: Thomson & Gale, pp. 76–7.

Knight, Judson (2004b), 'SIGINT (Signal Intelligence)', in *Encyclopedia of Espionage, Intelligence and Security*, vol. 3, ed. K. Lee Lerner and Brenda Wilmoth Lerner, Detroit: Thomson & Gale, pp. 79–80.

Krausse, Joachim, and Claude Lichtenstein (1999), *Your Private Sky: R. Buckminster Fuller – The Art of Design Science*, trans. Steven Lindberg and Julia Thorson, Baden: Lars Müller Publishers.

Lazzarato, Maurizio (2014), *Signs and Machines: Capitalism and the Production of Subjectivity*, trans. Joshua David Jordan, Los Angeles: Semiotext(e).

Paglen, Trevor (2014), 'New Photos of the NSA and Other Top Intelligence Agencies Revealed for First Time', *The Intercept*, 10 February, <https://firstlook.org/theintercept/article/2014/02/10/new-photos-of-nsa-and-others> (last accessed 2 February 2016).

Parikka, Jussi (2011), 'Mapping Noise: On the Techniques and Tactics of Irregularities, Interception and Disturbance', in Erkki Huhtamo and Jussi Parikka (eds), *Media Archaeology: Approaches, Applications and Implications*, Berkeley: University of California Press, pp. 256–77.

Parks, Lisa, and Nicole Starosielski (eds) (2015), *Signal Traffic: Critical Studies of Media Infrastructures*, Champaign: University of Illinois Press.

Scahill, Jeremy, and Glenn Greenwald (2014), 'The NSA's Secret Role in the U.S. Assassination Program', *The Intercept*, 10 February, <https://firstlook.org/theintercept/article/2014/02/10/the-nsas-secret-role> (last accessed 2 February 2016).

Schuppli, Susan (2014), 'Deadly Algorithms: Can Legal Codes Hold Software Accountable for Code that Kills?', *Radical Philosophy* 187 (September/October): 2–8.

Sconce, Jeffrey (2000), *Haunted Media: Electronic Presence from Telegraphy to Television*, Durham, NC: Duke University Press.

Siegert, Bernhard (2003), *Passage des Digitalen. Zeichenpraktiken der neuzeitlichen Wissenschaften 1500–1900*, Berlin: Brinkmann und Bose.

Starosielski, Nicole (2015), *The Undersea Network*, Durham, NC: Duke University Press.

Stephenson, Neal (1996), 'Mother Earth Mother Board', *Wired* 4(12), <http://archive.wired.com/wired/archive/4.12/ffglass_pr.html> (last accessed 2 February 2016).

Virilio, Paul (1994), *Bunker Archaeology*, trans. George Collins, Princeton: Princeton Architectural Press.

Wythoff, Grant (2014), 'The Invention of Wireless Cryptography', *The Appendix* 2(3), July, <http://theappendix.net/issues/2014/7/the-invention-of-wireless-cryptography> (last accessed 2 February 2016).

Zinsmeister, Annett (2009), 'Abwehr: Urbane Topographien', in Claus Pias (ed.), *Abwehr. Modelle, Strategien, Medien*, Bielefeld: Transcript, pp. 147–67.

Chapter 10

'Bulk Surveillance', or The Elegant Technicities of Metadata

Mark Coté

> Intelligence collection programs naturally generate ever-increasing demands for new data.
>
> Church Committee Report (1976: 4)

When the Snowden revelations broke, one image that may have come to mind was that of a new digital Stasi. The former East German Ministry for State Security was, infamously, the per capita largest secret police force in the world. The open secret of the Stasi was its pervasive surveillance system, focused internally as a means of state control, what German scholars frame as the practice of *Herrschaft* or state power. One could read, for example, a Stasi file from 1989, targeting a free-lance journalist and poet, and see its practice of state power expressed in unambiguous Cold War terms. This *Operative Personenkontrolle* (OPK) file is a culmination of sustained Stasi efforts to gain insight into this target as he was under suspicion 'of intending to form a subversive group', indeed, a 'hostile group that would discredit party politics by means of public activities' (OPK Files 1989). We read of a key event that triggered Stasi suspicions: on May Day 1987 he mounted a banner on his rooftop which read 'To Learn from the Soviet Union is learning how to Win' – a slogan favoured by the East German state but seemingly used by our target with ironic intent. We read about the objectives of the OPK, which include identifying contacts and relationships, developing a character profile, and investigating plans and intentions. We read that these objectives, through on-the-ground surveillance, will be led primarily by *Inoffizieller Mitarbeiter* – that is, unofficial collaborators, or IMs – and that the investigation will seek to recruit further IMs from the target's 'social environment'. We also read that the OPK indicates the possible employment of 'operative technical methods' which include installing bugging devices.

Through these collaborative efforts, we are able to read a detailed personal history, including information about the target's schooling, where his final assessment noted 'we have rarely had a young person who fulfilled their duties with such enthusiasm, conscientiousness and calm'; yet further information indicates 'his political views began to deteriorate' as denoted by the target's subsequent comments: 'I root for an unrestrained freedom of press as Rosa Luxemburg had imagined it.' We read hand-written examples of his poetry, and learn that he is 'co-organizing so-called "house and yard parties" [. . .] [and] alternative citizens' initiatives' which the Stasi deems subversive. Finally, we read a notice dated 6 December 1989, less than a month after the fall of the Berlin Wall: 'Due to the changed political development in the GDR, as well as the abandonment of previous erroneous security policies, further pursuit of the OPK is not justified anymore.'

How should we read such files of Stasi pervasive surveillance in relation to contemporary surveillance practices? Does it stand as the template for the bulk data capture and ubiquitous surveillance of the US National Security Agency (NSA) and the UK Government Communication Head Quarters (GCHQ)? This chapter will question this by examining the technological prehistory of the kind of bulk surveillance practices illuminated by Snowden and by considering the role of metadata. Metadata – that is, *data about data* – has jumped from the specialist vernacular of the archivist and programmer to public discourse in the wake of the Snowden revelations. Yet the precise nature and import of this seemingly technical artefact remains dimly understood. It is the technicities of metadata that will help us reckon with questions of continuity. This entails a kind of Cold War technical archaeology, and following a trajectory from analogue information gathered by the East German Stasi to the born digital data accessed by the NSA and GCHQ. What are the changing affordances of metadata? For the Stasi, we see onerous practices of physical surveillance that in turn generate analogue information, including metadata which is deployed in crude but effective social network analysis. For the NSA and GCHQ, we see the bulk collection of digital metadata, generated automatically through our mediated cultural practices. To what degree is metadata a cipher, not only for surveillance practices but for our contemporary technocultural condition? To what extent do these surveillant metadata assemblages act as a case study for broader shifts in *techne* (that is, the constitutive relationship between the human and technology) and in labouring practices as afforded by our data-infused digital environment?

I will first offer a brief overview of Stasi practices, and then turn to the NSA and GCHQ, concisely historicising their practices of 'bulk data collection'. We will then turn to the earliest use of digital computers by security agencies in the US at the dawn of the Cold War. Finally, we will look at the key role metadata plays in establishing the very conditions of possibility of bulk data collection and in the discontinuities it inscribes for contemporary surveillance practices. Throughout, we will emphasise: (1) how the increasingly fine granularity of the digital human renders us data objects and facilitates a kind of shift from labour-intensive HUMINT (human intelligence) to a kind of embedded SIGINT (signal intelligence) of the mediated human; and (2) how these technicities of metadata develop through a close relationship between the security state and capital.

Analogue Metadata: Stasi

What is often deemed remarkable about the Stasi is its appetite for surveillance information, it purportedly having collected more than any bureaucracy ever: 'possibly a billion pages of surveillance records, informant accounting, reports on espionage, analyses of foreign press, personnel records, and useless minutiae' (Curry 2008). Yet what is equally striking is the Stasi's emphasis on very labour-intensive strategies of HUMINT. According to Gieseke (2014), just before its dissolution in 1989 there were more than 91,000 full-time Stasi employees. There were an additional 15,000-plus soldiers working for the Stasi. Finally, there were between 150,000 and 200,000 IMs (informants) from the mid-1970s through to the demise of the GDR. This is from an East German population of some 16 million. In stark contrast to this robust apparatus of human on-the-ground snooping and spying was the relative paucity of telephony surveillance. Fuchs (2013) draws on documentation for the Stasi's Department 26: Telephone Control, Wiretapping and Video Surveillance, demonstrating the low level of more contemporary bulk collection methods. Taking a six-month period in 1985 as a recent representative sample shows that the Stasi's Department 26 monitored only 0.3% of all telephone lines and 0.1% of all telex lines.

This is a very different kind of mass surveillance industry. For many, its quotidian banalities and horrors were made visible through the film *The Lives of Others*. What was animated therein was the backbone of Stasi surveillance: Personal Surveillance Operations (*IM-Vorgang*) undertaken by friends, families, co-workers and lovers. Such operations targeted one in four East Germans, and also functioned to simply vet potential informants, thus continuously expanding this very particular social network.[1] When this standard mass surveillance revealed any suspicious information or patterns, then the second stage kicked in, the aforementioned OPK. This was structured surveillance carried out by professionals, the full-time Stasi agents. Take the case of Ulrike Poppe, a political activist renowned as one of the most surveilled women in East Germany. It was recounted how she learned to recognise her human surveillers:

> They had crew cuts and never wore jeans or sneakers. Sometimes they took pictures of her on the sidewalk, or they piled into a white sedan and drove 6 feet behind her as she walked down the street. Officers waited around the clock in cars parked outside her top-floor apartment. After one of her neighbors tipped her off, she found a bug drilled from the attic of the building into the ceiling plaster of her living room. (Curry 2008)

The OPK still relied primarily on physically spying on targets, and gathering intelligence from informants, but also included opening mail and, on occasion, tapping telephones.

Amidst all this information we can discern a kind of analogue metadata. Indeed, while we associate metadata with digital information, it is, simply, data about data – here think of the spine of a book that contains author name, book title and publisher. Analogue metadata is ancient: Zenodotus, the Great Library of Alexandria's first librarian, attached a small dangling tag to the end of each scroll so that contents could be ascertained without having to unroll each scroll, and to allow for classification and shelf placement (Phillips 2010). Metadata, then, has always facilitated both classification and information workflow management. The Stasi, like any surveillance entity, also needed to organise and analyse its information. Thus from its meticulously recorded files it also generated analogue data categorising people, places, meetings between people, and connections of various kinds. This may have been of a rather painstakingly gathered and coarse granularity but it nonetheless enabled a kind of basic social network analysis. See, for example, the 'Operational Case Jentzsch' (Figure 10.1) that targeted the poet Bernd Jentzsch. If we look at the image we see the deployment of analogue metadata for basic social network analysis. The image shows a hand-drawn social network graph with forty-six distinct connections, between people, places and meetings (further categorised as face-to-face, by post or by phone). As it happened, the target in question, Jentzsch, was able to defect in 1976 before the Stasi could act on its intelligence analysis.

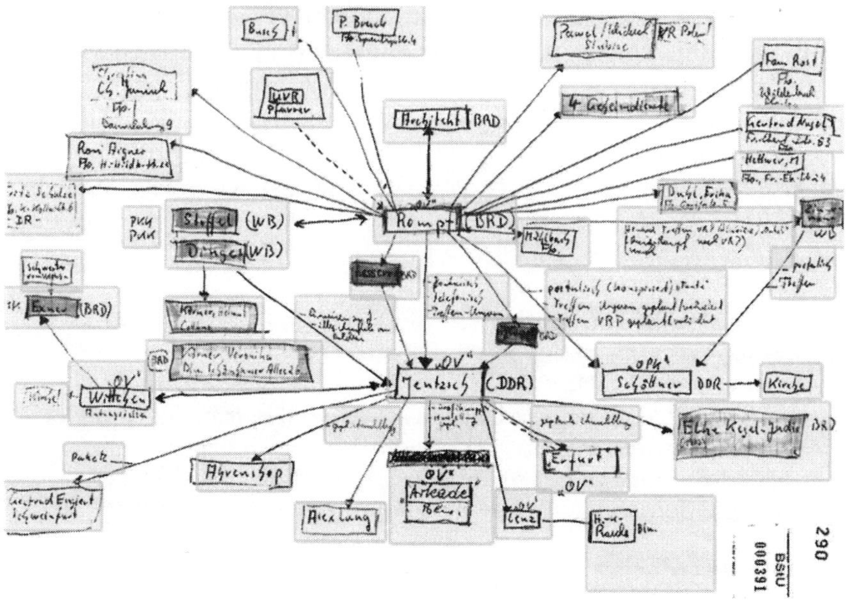

Figure 10.1 Hand-drawn social network diagram for 'Operational Case Jentzsch'.

When we look past the crudely hand-drawn social network mapping out patterns and forty-six connections linking the targets, we see the results of extensive physical surveillance. Some metadata identifies people (an 'aunt'), others places ('church'), modes of meetings ('by post, by phone, meeting in Hungary'), or people and their location ('architect, W. Germany'). What distinguishes the Stasi's surveillance practices is that they are both wholly analogue and very labour intensive. What has continued is the general practice of codifying information from target communication and social relations. Metadata, however, is now generated under radically different technological conditions. Such similarities notwithstanding, does the Stasi really stand as the historical antecedent for the NSA and GCHQ? A closer look at the historical context of US surveillance suggests otherwise.

NSA-GCHQ

When we historicise technical systems of surveillance, we see long shadows cast. 'There is indeed nothing new under the sun when it comes to contemporary surveillance technologies' (Lyon 2014: 36). Modern practices date back to US colonial administration over the

Philippines. As Lyon notes, from the late nineteenth century the occupying US Administration established an intelligence apparatus using punch cards and alpha-numeric coding, the typewriter and the telegraph to track the domestic population. There were similar developments in the exercise of British colonial power. During the Boer War at the turn of the twentieth century, the UK developed systematic postal surveillance. By World War I 'the British had evolved a highly effective system of mail monitoring and censorship, as well as cable and telephone censorship, which they passed on to their American allies' (Fiset 2001). The US developed this further during World War II, in multi-layered state and military entities. The Office of Censorship monitored radio and telegraph communication between the US and any foreign countries, while the FBI monitored all international postal activity. It was in 1945, however, that covert bulk surveillance became more permanently structured. As Bamford outlines in his groundbreaking *The Puzzle Palace*, at the war's end, US SIGINT operatives met with the three main telegraph companies – ITT World Communications, Western Union International and RCA Global (both now part of MCI Worldcom) – to gain their approval for the interception and microfilm recording of all telegraphic traffic entering, leaving or transiting the US. Here we see an example of a close surveillance partnership between leading US Information and Communications Technology (ICT) corporations and the Army Agency (ASA), a precursor to the NSA. Bamford notes the intimacy of this partnership, which enabled the comprehensive accumulation and analysis of international telegraphic communication. Both the ASA/NSA and its corporate partners had New York offices. Each day ASA couriers would call upon those corporate offices to collect microfilm copies of outgoing international telegrams. This was such a deeply covert programme that 'besides [NSA Deputy Director] Tordella and the various directors, only one lower-level managerial employee had any responsibility for the program' (Bamford 1983: 313). Project Shamrock operated in this manner unknown and uninterrupted for thirty years, from 1945 to 1975.

We can see a number of contemporary parallels with Project Shamrock. First, we see the systematic application of mass (or bulk) surveillance, enabled by a focus on information systems and the use of technological support. Even more significant is that this was surveillance of telegrams, which at that time comprised everyday mediated social communication, as opposed to encrypted geopolitical communications. Second, we see a close and abiding co-operative relationship with ICT corporations. Both of these basic dimensions are fundamental in making possible our contemporary condition of comprehensive data surveillance. Further, neither of these are prominent within the Stasi system, suggesting that continuities flowed primarily along Cold War divisions. There are three more noteworthy contemporary parallels with Project Shamrock. First, it was developed in collaboration with British intelligence. Second, it remained a secret, functioning almost wholly outside public view for nearly thirty years before being exposed in 1975 by the post-Watergate Church Committee, a Senate investigation of illegal activities by US intelligence organisations. Indeed, it was a little-known young staff lawyer who revealed what was probably the largest ever surveillance effort: 'Although the total number of telegrams read during its course is not available, NSA estimates that in the last two or three years of Shamrock's existence [1972–1975] about 150,000 telegrams per month were reviewed by NSA analysts' (Anderson 2013). The third point is the application of advanced computer technology. Until the early 1960s, Project Shamrock was operating in a manner not far removed from that of the Stasi. In addition to the physical handover of microfilmed telegraph records, these daily batches of hard copies and paper tapes were sorted manually. In 1963, however, there was a computational shift when, in parallel development, both the telegraph company RCA Global and the NSA unveiled new computer systems. As Bamford notes, 'the change in technology was also about to enable America to make a quantum leap forward in its ability to snoop' (1983: 312). RCA Global's new computer telegraph system ran on magnetic journal tapes. Now magnetic tapes were delivered to the NSA, which was able to process them on its powerful new system Harvest. This was a radical automation and augmentation of intelligence analysis capacity. It was now a matter of microseconds for the analysis of the full text of any telegram, as Harvest was programmed 'to "kick out" any telegram containing a certain word, phrase, name, location, sender or addressee, or any combination' (Bamford 1983: 313). Here one can only wonder how different the fate of the poet Jentzsch might have been had he been subjected to Harvest. But an examination of recently declassified NSA documents and other sources reveals, first, the depth of commitment to the development of ICT for both cryptanalytics and mass surveillance and, second, and even more remarkable, a deep level of technical co-operation with ICT corporations that is both parallel and recursive.

Parallelisation and Recursivity

There was nothing inevitable about the prominent role the NSA played in the development of the US computer industry. Indeed, throughout

World War II computation was still very much a mechanised process. Yet by 1964, the then classified Snyder Report comprehensively outlined the postwar zeal with which the NSA and its precursors learned to love the 'general-purpose electronic digital computer': 'The use of computers by NSA has increased considerably, beginning with one of the first machines in the country, installed in December 1950. NSA's computer installation probably ranks among the largest in the country' (Snyder 1964: 2). Snyder had been an early cryptographer with the Signal Intelligence Service, one of a number of NSA precursors. It is within these code-breaking branches that we find the military roots of computers (see Burke 1993; Flamm 1988).

Cryptography was the first branch of state security to use computers, particularly the Navy Communication Security Group OP-20-G. It is here that Louis Tordella, Deputy Director of the NSA (1958–1974), worked as a code-breaker during the war. As far back as the 1930s this prominent signal intelligence and cryptanalysis group began using 'IBM punched card machinery to process code traffic' (Flamm 1988: 35). If we briefly examine this prehistory of digital computing for surveillance we see a fundamental impetus from the challenges and demands of information management, processing and analysis. As such, we can also see a nuanced and comprehensive example of parallelisation and recursivity; that is, of shared technological interests and pursuits of information management but for differentiated military and corporate applications. This is a pattern that continues unabated to this day.

In the 1930s, computing was still carried out with mechanical devices. Technology firms, such as National Cash Register and Eastman Kodak, were thus contracted to advance mechanical approaches to cryptographic data processing and build specialised code-breakers called Rapid Analytical Machines (RAMs). In 1936, Vannevar Bush was contracted by OP-20-G to lead a project at MIT to develop a high-speed electronic analysis machine. As Norberg outlines in his excellent *Computers and Commerce*, the Navy was interested in the Comparator that Bush had developed for automating the search of scholarly content in scientific and engineering publications. The Navy recognised the polyvalence of this automation of information and Bush adjusted his machine from a tool for scientific research to one for decrypt analysis, using a technique similar to that powering the German Enigma machine (Norberg 2005: 23). Bush, however, had hoped to supersede mechanical design through the use of optical sensing, electronics and tape memory but was not successful as his approach required more memory than was technologically feasible at that time. What was successful was the informal integration of MIT graduate students into the Naval Computing

Machine Laboratory, a pattern that spread across American universities and military intelligence branches as the war commenced (24). As a coda to this prehistory, the now unclassified Burke report begins by claiming, somewhat counter-intuitively, that the OP-20-G lost its opportunity 'to be among the very first to conceive of and build a modern electronic computer' because wartime precluded the kind of stable and long-term programme necessary for its development (Burke 2002: 65). Instead, proven and reliable electromechanical machines were used for cryptology, and with considerable success, with the US breaking both Japanese diplomatic and naval code and the British famously defeating the Enigma.

It was in 1945, with the war's end nearing and the Cold War looming, that conditions of parallelisation and recursivity were further formalised. The military first sought to retain the general intellect of scientists and engineers it had gathered. A Naval intelligence memorandum on 22 February 1945, the 'Research and Development Plan', articulates three objectives: (1) to maintain close working relations with their scientists to 'enable them to form an integral part of the military services in providing instruments and equipment quickly for communications intelligence'; (2) to provide financial incentives to those scientists by enabling them to work as contractors; and (3) to provide contractors with 'laboratory facilities' or 'specialised talents' they otherwise may lack (Norberg 2005: 29–30). What this memorandum sketched out was an early model for a classified public-private partnership, that is, for a joint venture that would be both a laboratory and a financial investment group. As we will see shortly, this entity would become the exemplary Engineering Research Associates (ERA).

In addition to addressing demobilisation, the immediate demands of military intelligence were also shifting. Howard Campaigne, the technical director of OP-20-G, later noted in an oral history interview that as they no longer needed to decipher a relentless daily flow of communication traffic, they 'shifted to a longer-range view and started looking for improved ways of doing things' (Farley 1983: 53–4). What the historical documents reveal is an expansion in the SIGINT imaginary. Mechanical cipher systems were favoured because of their brute force, yet machines like the RAMs were bespoke to match enemy encryptors and thus subject to rapid obsolescence. Turing had already provided theoretical proof for a universal machine. In the summer of 1946, the technical director of the OP-20-G was able to further this pursuit of 'looking for new ways of doing things' in information management and analysis.

The real becoming digital of surveillance began in earnest when young OP-20-G officer and mathematician James T. Pendergrass was sent to the Moore School Lectures, held at the University of Pennsylvania's school of computing in the summer of 1946. The Moore School of Computing was a technological epicentre, having just made the first general-purpose computer, the ENIAC, which had been financed by the US Army Ordnance for artillery firing tables, and was subsequently used to study the feasibility of the hydrogen bomb. While less famous than the Macy Conferences, this singular event was crucial in the development of digital computers. Teachers included John von Neumann, and J. Presper Eckert and John Mauchly, who were soon to design the UNIVAC. Students included Claude Shannon, Maurice V. Wilkes and Jay Forrester, and the eight-week programme introduced participants to hardware, software, programming and machine design, along with a demonstration of the ENIAC.

Pendergrass returned to the OP-20-G as a convert, and strongly advocated the use of digital computing for all cryptanalysis. In December 1946, he issued the eponymous Pendergrass Report, which remained top secret for decades. Its key message was simple: military intelligence needs the versatility of a general-purpose machine. As NSA historian Colin Burke recalls, in the report Pendergrass had to demonstrate that a programmed computer could match all existing bespoke cryptanalytic machinery as well as the new secret cryptanalytic procedures codenamed Ultra and Magic. He also had to prove that 'the yet-to-be-born "programming", digital methods and the nonexistent general purpose computer were reasonable cryptanalytic options' (Burke 2002: 69–70). The still-redacted Pendergrass Report detailed digital solutions to the ciphering machines of the time, demonstrating to the intelligence community that practical information management and analysis needs could be met by the universal computer. The Pendergrass Report had a significant impact. As Snyder later stated: 'The potential value of electronic computers in ASA applications was recognized immediately' (1964: 14). Or, as Campaigne more colloquially recalls, upon reading Pendergrass's report: 'Gee. That's what we need. That has the flexibility that we've been looking for' (Farley 1983: 54).

While the end of the war expanded the SIGINT imaginary, actually accessing or building digital computers remained difficult: 'rigorous security clearance, the oppressive physical security, and the limited usefulness of the equipment in the marketplace made many companies shy away from the field' (Bamford 2008: 580). Flamm further underlines these challenges, noting that the OP-20-G's Washington cryptanalysis unit the Communications Supplementary Activities Washington (CSAW) had contacted seventeen different companies but all declined to partner or invest because of uncertain economic prospects (1988: 44). It is in this context that the ERA emerged out of CSAW as an exemplary classified contractor – what Burke called 'a favored captive corporation' (2002: 269). Norberg comprehensively details the technological and corporate history of ERA which lasted in its pioneering classified corporate status for six years, when the conflict between being a partner and being a captor became too great. Over time, ERA would be absorbed in turn by Remington Rand, later Sperry, and finally with Burroughs to form Unisys. But when ERA began, what is particularly noteworthy is the degree to which high-ranking military officers in OP-20-G used family and business connections to initiate contracts and financing for ERA. These ranged from meetings with American Airlines, where the need for an automated ticketing and reservation system was discussed, to IBM, to the Wall Street firm Kuhn-Loeb (Norberg 2005: 31–2).

ERA had forty-two active employees by 1946 and a contract with the Navy for communication intelligence work to 'survey of the computing field [. . .] Research looking toward the development of these new components and techniques [. . .] [and] [t]he furnishing of consulting services to the Office of Naval Research on questions concerning the development and application of computing equipment and techniques' (Norberg 2005: 44). By 1947, research had turned to development and ERA was handed 'Task 13', its thirteenth job from the Navy. It is here that the Pendergrass Report fully came to fruition, as it 'included a general description of the proposed machine's logic, its code of instructions, and coded examples of typical problem solutions' (Snyder 1964: 8). This was Task 13: an order to build the SIGINT community's first digital computer. The Snyder Report comprehensively details the technical development of Atlas, a three-year project costing $950,000 delivered at the end of 1950. Complete with its simple central processing unit, and capacious drum memory system, Atlas decisively marked the digital computing era for military intelligence.

There are three things to further note about the original Atlas. The first is the kind of privileged technology transfer ERA enjoyed. While the company possessed particular expertise in the new magnetic drum technology, this was further developed through deeply recursive relations with the military. An unpublished interview with ERA engineer Emmett Quady reveals that during the US occupation of Germany, a magnetic drum had been captured which was eventually delivered to

ERA. This marked only the first stage of military-corporate technology transfer. ERA used the technology to improve its drum memory, which became a signature component of the Atlas. Yet this military-corporate technology transfer was leveraged even further by ERA. 'In 1949 ERA entered into a design project with IBM to develop a magnetic drum computer, which, though never built, led to a technology transfer and cross-licensing arrangement with IBM that gave IBM access to ERA's extensive patents on magnetic drums' (Flamm 1988: 45). Here we can turn to the second point. What was a novel arrangement at the end of the war, while still clearly beneficial, was becoming cumbersome and awkward. IBM benefited greatly from the aforementioned exchange but ERA's privileges 'came under increasing fire as the Cold War began to turn computers and applied science into competitive industries' (Burke 2002: 269). This notwithstanding, it is worth noting the almost immediate Cold War advantage afforded by Atlas. A recently declassified document reports that the first program written for Atlas was to decrypt intercepted Soviet diplomatic communications under the long-running Venona project (1943–1980) which ultimately exposed Julius and Ethel Rosenberg, Alger Hiss and the Cambridge spy ring, among others (NSA 2002).

The third point concerns the impact ERA had on the commercial computer industry. The 1964 Snyder Report looked back and claimed 'the primary influence of NSA on industry has been felt in those instances where technical leadership or management foresight has influenced or led directly to industrial computer pioneering' (7). One year after delivering Atlas to the Navy, ERA was permitted to sell a commercial version, the ERA 1101, although only two were sold, to the Bureau of Ships. Norberg's commercial assessment is more circumspect. Examining ERA's financial ledgers, he shows that while government revenues from 1947 to 1951 increased from $1.22 m to $4.2 m, commercial revenues were stagnant, rising only from $288,220 to $295,010 (2005: 159). Even more damaging was ERA's failure to protect patentable elements of their work, like the aforementioned transfer which enabled IBM to make its own memory storage drums as opposed to buying them from ERA. This left ERA in commercial crisis. Contemporaneous was EMCC, the Eckert-Mauchly Computer Corporation which was founded by the previously mentioned builders of the EVIAC who taught at the famous Moore School Lectures. They too developed a digital computer and built the UNIVAC, which was delivered to the US Census Bureau also in 1951. They had, however, sold their company to Remington Rand in 1950. This helped give them far greater market success: 'By the end of 1952, three had been delivered to the government, and ultimately, forty-six UNIVACs were built' (Flamm 1988: 51). ERA was purchased by Remington Rand in 1952, and in recognition of the ERA-EMCC merger the computer was renamed the UNIVAC 1101. The NSA was also founded in 1952, when cryptographic and intelligence branches were consolidated.

This prehistory of contemporary surveillance illustrates a computational-data infrastructure that was composed through very particular political economic relations that emerged out of a specific military organisational form – indeed, one that adapted to the needs and demands of its composition of labour and related technicities – and in relation to emerging market conditions. In short, it provides context for the material condition of the data assemblages of surveillance.

Metadata

The Snyder Report notes that 'the role of computers at NSA can be better appreciated when considered from the viewpoint of application' and that the security agency and its predecessors were early adaptors due to their being 'useful in handling almost every class of data-processing and analytic problem' (1964: 1). Thus the perspective emphasised in the NSA's own secret *History of NSA General-Purpose Electronic Digital Computers* is that of a specialised agency of data processors. Thinking of the NSA as specialised data processors enables a more material perspective on agency surveillance practices. By widening our perspective beyond the specific data-processing application of the NSA to that of the underlying data assemblage, we can benefit from the more materialist perspective adopted by a growing body of researchers. Dourish, for example, argues that we should examine the 'fabric of information systems that constrain, shape, guide, and resist patterns of engagement and use' (2014). Kitchin also emphasises the data assemblages as a socio-technical entity wherein 'data and their assemblage are thus co-determinous and mutually constituted, bound together in a set of contingent, relational and contextual discursive and material practices and relations' (2014: 25). Here we can home in on a particular relational contingency which helps contextualise current material practices of surveillance by the NSA: metadata. There are three abiding points to make about metadata. The first is that its development transpired initially almost wholly within the realm of Library and Information Science. In the most general terms, metadata is 'structured information about an information resource of any media type or format' (Caplan 2003: 3). The second is that metadata services information workflow management, and thus it quickly spread from the specialised practices of librarians across digital domains, particularly the World Wide Web. The third is that by the turn of the millennium, metadata expanded from being structured information humans attached to objects to being something that humans automatically generated about themselves via digital devices. This contingent development allowed the NSA and other security agencies to develop new patterns of engagement and use, namely the near-ubiquitous dataveillance revealed by Snowden.

The development of metadata, then, occurred almost wholly outside of the ken and practice of the NSA and the security community in general. Yet Samuel Snyder, of the aforementioned report, stands as a curious link between these realms. He went from being one of the first cryptographers with the Signal Intelligence Service (an NSA precursor) to unofficial secret historian of the NSA to coordinator of the US Library of Congress's information system. His obituary reads: 'He was among the creators of the library's Machine Readable Cataloging system [MARC] that replaced the handwritten card with an electronic searchable database system that became the standard worldwide' (*Washington Post* 2007). What links Snyder between cryptanalysis and surveillance to Library and Information Science is the generalised need to automate searches of electronic database systems. To be clear, the MARC coding language is not metadata per se, yet, as an introduction to library metadata notes, it has 'fueled the great international effort to make catalogs electronic and to share catalog data worldwide via computer transmission' (Smiraglia 2005: 6). While MARC was developed by 1970, it was not until the late 1980s that the term 'metadata' appeared in even specialised vocabularies. An unclassified document from the National Space Science Data Center offers an early definition of metadata: 'Information describing a data set, including data user guide, descriptions of the data set in directories, catalogs, and inventories, and any additional information required to define the relationships among these' (NASA 1990: 94).

At this time, space agencies were generating increasingly large datasets that required better directory-level information management wherein metadata provided a solution. A metadata was soon developed for the related field of digital geospatial data management. Linking these early uses and the development of metadata was a common need: making increasingly large computer files useful to humans (Caplan 2003: 1). This need was most effectively addressed in Library and Information Science, and then by the internet. By the mid-1990s, librarians and internet-based information managers met and developed the Dublin Core, which became the global standard for metadata. The initial Dublin Core report asked a simple question: 'Why is it so difficult to find items of interest on the Internet or the World Wide Web?' (Weibel et al. 2005).

This was a pre-Google era of 'locator services' like Lycos and WebCrawler bereft of formal standards for electronic resource description. The actual Dublin Core is fifteen elements used for resource description which include subject, title, author, publisher, object type, data form and unique identifier. These metadata elements were designed to be both flexible and modifiable, and thus adaptable to more complex or specialised information systems. This extensibility would soon be manifested, for example, in XML and HTML. As the report notes, resource discovery was the most pressing need metadata addressed. This need was being expressed in a realm of ever-expanding digital resources which required some form of automation of information. The Dublin Core thus established a standard requiring only 'a small amount of human effort' to create an automated system of searchable databases (Weibel et al. 2005). Contrast this automation with the massive labour power necessary for the Stasi to generate rudimentary metadata for information discovery. Under the Dublin Core, authors and publishers automatically create metadata, and network publishing tools developed templates for those elements. The technicity of the Dublin Core addresses multivalent needs: from library and archive information resource managers, to capital ranging from marketing to logistics, and the state from civic records to surveillance.

The report's 'Appendix 1.0' is the first sample Dublin Core record, 'created by a subject-matter specialist who has no library cataloging expertise' – Tim Berners-Lee (Weibel et al. 2005). It described an Internet Request for Comment (RFC), regarding the development of Uniform Resource Identifiers (URI). Thus we are seamlessly taken to the second key development in metadata. Here we again see the shared needs of librarians and the internet around digital information management. Berners-Lee recognised how metadata could make the internet machine readable. He proposed an extended definition: 'Metadata is machine understandable information about web resources or other things' (1997). Even more significantly, Berners-Lee anticipated a future in which metadata would become diffused across digital culture and society: 'In the future, when the metadata languages and engines are more developed, it should also form a strong basis for a web of machine understandable information about anything: about the people, things, concepts and ideas.'

Understanding how metadata has transformed humans into machine-understandable information is crucial for understanding contemporary digital surveillance practices. Dataveillance is a strategy developed to absorb our new collective capacity to generate data in our everyday lives. The technicity of metadata is crucial, having gone from means for machine cataloguing of library and archival information to resource discovery on the World Wide Web to rendering the human condition into actionable and finely granulated data points. Datafication has been offered as an anodyne frame for this process of near-ubiquitous data generation that quantifies ourselves and the world in which we live (Mayer-Schoenberger and Cukier 2013). Others have more critically addressed how datafication expresses profoundly asymmetrical power relations in terms of the banal ideological faith of 'dataism' (van Dijck 2014) or the highly proprietary 'big social data' (Coté 2014). Here we stress how this process transforms metadata from something that gets embedded into information objects to something that is embodied in the digital human. Furthermore, we should note how metadata has shifted from making large datasets useful for humans to making them machine readable.

A quick summary of just some of the metadata generated in the data assemblages we inhabit gives a sense of the degree to which we have become embodied metadata. Through our web browsers we generate metadata about the pages we visit and when, user login details, our IP address, ISP, device hardware details, operating system, as well as cookies and cached data from websites. Through our mobiles, we generate metadata from all our callers, the time and duration of each call we make, the location of each caller, and the unique serial numbers of each phone called. Every time we use Google, metadata is generated regarding our search queries, results, and the pages we subsequently visit. When we use Facebook, metadata is generated regarding our name, birthday, home town, work history, interests, our location, device, activities, activity date, time and time zone, and our friends, likes, check-ins and events (*The Guardian* 2013).

This partial list makes clear that metadata reveals and tracks our communication devices, the people with whom we are in contact, and the location of all parties, and through social media a detailed mode of our social relations, behaviours and predilections can be easily surmised. This renders claims that it is 'only metadata' disingenuous. For example, an exposed May 2010 NSA document notes that the smartphone is furthering the 'blurring' of telecommunications, computers and the internet and gives examples of convergence in SIGINT, bringing together smartphone data, wireless data and GPRS (which provides wireless mobile internet access and SMS and messaging services). This document is often referenced for its 'Golden Nugget' page which outlines the treasure trove of metadata available to NSA analysts simply by targeting photos uploaded to a social media site. The information available matches the aforementioned summary of metadata generated: geolocation, networks connected, websites visited, friend lists, documents accessed, unique identifiers, email address, phone call log, and so on. Yet there is an even more revealing line in the document: 'Make use of fingerprints in Xkeyscore via the EXIF metadata plugin' (NSA 2010). Xkeyscore is an NSA computer system used for searching and analysing bulk surveillance. Here let us recall where things were with the NSA's Harvest computer in 1964. A declassified document recalls how 'computers were operated as stand-alone facilities; users brought their jobs to the computer or operated the computer themselves. Data was transferred between computers by punched cards or paper tape; these were eventually superseded by magnetic tape' (Hogan 1986: 2-18). That report identified an NSA goal of 'using computers as near real-time turnaround tools which are directly available to individual analysts at their work location'. Now let us compare that with Snowden reporting on the surveillant and analytical power of metadata in the Xkeyscore system:

> You could read anyone's email in the world, anybody you've got an email address for. Any website: you can watch traffic to and from it. Any computer that an individual sits at: you can watch it. Any laptop that you're tracking: you can follow it as it moves from place to place throughout the world. It's a one-stop-shop for access to the NSA's information. And what's more you can tag individuals using 'XKeyscore'. Let's say I saw you once and I thought what you were doing was interesting or you just have access that's interesting to me, let's say you work at a major German corporation and I want access to that network, I can track your username on a website on a form somewhere, I can track your real name, I can track associations with your friends and I can build what's called a *fingerprint*, which is network activity unique to you, which means anywhere you go in the world, anywhere you try to sort of hide your online presence, your identity, the NSA can find you . . . (Snowden 2014)

Accumulo

The technicities of contemporary surveillance differ fundamentally from those of the Stasi. The NSA can analyse 'trillions of data points in order to build massive graphs that can detect the connections between them and the strength of the connections' (Harris 2013).[2]

There is a disjunction between this ability to discover data patterns and generate near real-time reports and Stasi analogue social network analysis. Not only is much of the analysis automated, the metadata is generated through our everyday lives. In short, from a surveillance perspective, datafication is metadatafication and metadata translates directly into actionable intelligence.

In conclusion, consider the provenance of Accumulo, the processing power behind Xkeyscore. The NSA developed Accumulo based on Google's Big Table, which is distributed, highly scalable and fast. In short, it is based on the database innovations that enable the capture, query and analysis of massive amounts of disparate data. Accumulo took the open-source Hadoop model, developed within the non-profit Apache Software Foundation, and added to it cell-level security. This means it can manage access to individual pieces of data which effectuates different levels of access clearance for analysts and that the access management parameters are retained by a given piece of data as it migrates across datasets through processing and analysis cycles. Accumulo has been processing the massive datasets the NSA captures through Xkeyscore and elsewhere since 2010. The following year the NSA contributed Accumulo to Apache. Soon after, Adam Fuchs, a developer of Accumulo for the NSA, left the agency to commercialise the database. He founded Sqrrl with Ely Kahn, the former Director of Cybersecurity at the National Security Staff in the White House. By early 2015, Sqrrl had garnered $14.2 m in start-up funding (Jackson 2013). This fluid transition from security to capital again demonstrates the shared needs for next-generation data management. Sqrrl is targeting industries with high regulatory and data security requirements like finance, healthcare and government. Its ability to tag individual pieces of data with need-to-know access serves both privacy demands for security agencies and capital; it also brings even greater data flexibility and control to proprietary datasets.

The biggest disjuncture from the time of the Stasi is our mediated/metadata-ed condition. This has created powerful new opportunities for the kinds of bulk surveillance the NSA and its predecessors developed the better part of a century ago. By the time the Cold War commenced, the US intelligence community had already established deeply parallel and recursive relations with the ICT industry that are now even more fluid and sophisticated. Indeed, there is a fundamental multivalence to our digital infrastructures and data assemblages serving both capital and the security state. Metadata has helped render everyday life as machine-readable data that both generates economic value and is easily and comprehensively managed and analysed by state security agencies. This creates an existential condition not so different from that experienced by Bernd Jentzsch of the possibility of permanent – albeit disembodied – surveillance. Closing remarks from Ira 'Gus' Hunt, the avuncular Chief Technology Officer of the CIA, should leave us in no doubt of the permanence of this condition: 'The value of any piece of information is only known when you can connect it with something else which arrives at a future point in time. [. . .] Since you can't connect dots you don't have, it drives us into this mode of: we fundamentally try to collect everything and hang on to it forever' (Sledge 2013).

Notes

1. It is worth noting that a higher percentage of Germans – one in three – use Facebook than were under Stasi surveillance; see <https://www.searchlaboratory.com/2015/01/the-german-guide-to-social-media> (last accessed 4 February 2016).
2. It is worth noting that the NSA's Accumulo is significantly more powerful than Facebook's Graph Search. Accumulo can process a 4.4-trillion-node, 70-trillion-edge graph, while Graph Search contains only billions of nodes and low trillions of edges.

References

Anderson, Nate (2013), 'How a 30-Year-Old Lawyer Exposed NSA Mass Surveillance of Americans – in 1975', *Ars Technica*, <http://arstechnica.com/tech-policy/2013/06/how-a-30-year-old-lawyer-exposed-nsa-mass-surveillance-of-americans-in-1975> (last accessed 4 February 2016).

Bamford, James (1983), *The Puzzle Palace: Inside the National Security Agency, America's Most Secret Intelligence Organization*, Harmondsworth: Penguin.

Bamford, James (2008), *Body of Secrets: How America's NSA and Britain's GCHQ Eavesdrop on the World*, New York: Random House.

Berners-Lee, Tim (1997), 'Axioms of Web Architecture: Metadata', World Wide Web Consortium, <http://www.w3.org/DesignIssues/Metadata> (last accessed 4 February 2016).

Burke, Colin B. (1993), 'An Introduction to a Historic Document: The 1946 Pendergrass Report – Cryptanalysis and the Digital Computer', *Cryptologia* 17(2): 113–23.

Burke, Colin B. (2002), 'It Wasn't All Magic: The Early Struggles to Automate Cryptanalysis, 1930s–1960s', *United States Cryptologic History: Special Series Volume* 6, Centre for Cryptologic History, National Security Agency, <https://www.nsa.gov/public_info/_files/cryptologic_histories/magic.pdf> (last accessed 4 February 2016).

Caplan, Priscilla (2003), *Metadata Fundamentals for All Librarians*, Chicago: American Library Association.

Church, Frank (1976), 'The Church Committee: Intelligence Activities and the Rights of Americans', <https://www.law.umich.edu/facultyhome/margoschlanger/Documents/Publications/Offices_of_Goodness/%E2%80%8B2%20Select%20Comm.%20Study%20to%20Government%20Operations,%20Intelligence%20Activities%20and%20the%20Rights%20of%20Americans%20(1976).pdf> (last accessed 4 February 2016).

Coté, Mark (2014), 'Data Motility: The Materiality of Big Social Data', *Cultural Studies Review* 20(1): 121–49, <https://epress.lib.uts.edu.au/journals/index.php/csrj/article/view/3832/3962> (last accessed 4 February 2016).

Curry, Andrew (2008), 'Piecing Together the Dark Legacy of East Germany's Secret Police', *Wired* 16(2), 18 January, <http://archive.wired.com/politics/security/magazine/16-02/ff_stasi?currentPage=all> (last accessed 4 February 2016).

Dourish, P. (2014), 'No SQL: The Shifting Materialities of Database Technology', *Computational Culture* 4, <http://computationalculture.net/article/no-sql-the-shifting-materialities-of-database-technology> (last accessed 4 February 2016).

Farley, Robert D. (1983), 'Oral History Interview – Campaigne, Howard, Dr., NSA-OH-14-83', <https://www.nsa.gov/public_info/_files/oral_history_interviews/nsa_oh_14_83_campaigne.pdf> (last accessed 4 February 2016).

Fiset, Louis (2001), 'Return to Sender: U.S. Censorship of Enemy Alien Mail in World War II', *Prologue* 33(1), <http://www.archives.gov/publications/prologue/2001/spring/mail-censorship-in-world-war-two-1.html> (last accessed 4 February 2016).

Flamm, Kenneth (1988), *Creating the Computer: Government, Industry, and High Technology*, Washington, DC: Brookings Institute Press.

Fuchs, Christian (2013), 'PRISM and the Social Media-Surveillance-Industrial Complex', Christian Fuchs: Information – Society – Technology and Media, 18 June, <http://fuchs.uti.at/920> (last accessed 4 February 2016).

Gieseke, Jens (2014), *The History of the Stasi: East Germany's Secret Police 1945–1990*, New York: Berghan Books.

The Guardian (2013), 'A *Guardian* Guide to Your Metadata', 12 June, <http://www.theguardian.com/technology/interactive/2013/jun/12/what-is-metadata-nsa-surveillance#meta=0000000> (last accessed 4 February 2016).

Harris, Derrick (2013), 'Under the Covers of the NSA's Big Data Effort', Gigaom Research, <https://gigaom.com/2013/06/07/under-the-covers-of-the-nsas-big-data-effort> (last accessed 4 February 2016).

Hogan, Douglas (1986), 'General and Special-Purpose Computers: A Historical Look and Some Lessons Learned', National Security Agency, <http://www.governmentattic.org/4docs/NSAgenSpecComputers_1986.pdf> (last accessed 4 February 2016).

Jackson, Joab (2013), 'NSA's Accumulo NoSQL Store Offers Role-Based Data Access', InfoWorld, 31 October, <http://www.infoworld.com/article/2612637/nosql/nsa-s-accumulo-nosql-store-offers-role-based-data-access.html> (last accessed 4 February 2016).

Kitchin, Rob (2014), *The Data Revolution: Big Data, Open Data, Data Infrastructures and Their Consequences*, London: Sage.

Lyon, David (2014), 'Situating State Surveillance: History, Technology, Culture', in Kees Boersma et al. (eds), *Histories of State Surveillance in Europe and Beyond*, London: Routledge, pp. 32–46.

Mayer-Schoenberger, Viktor, and Kenneth Cukier (2013), *Big Data: A Revolution That Will Transform How We Live, Work and Think*, London: John Murray.

National Aeronautics and Space Administration (1990), Directory Interchange Format Manual, National Space Science Data Center, <http://ntrs.nasa.gov/archive/nasa/casi.ntrs.nasa.gov/19910021677.pdf> (last accessed 4 February 2016).

National Security Agency (2002), 'Before Super-Computers: NSA and Computer Development', <https://www.nsa.gov/public_info/_files/crypto_almanac_50th/nsa_before_super_computers.pdf> (last accessed 4 February 2016).

National Security Agency (2010), 'Converged Analysis of Smartphone Devices: Identification/Processing/Tasking – All in a Day's Work [Slides]', <https://www.documentcloud.org/documents/1009660-nsa.html> (last accessed 4 February 2016).

Norberg, Arthur Lawrence (2005), *Computers and Commerce: A Study of Technology and Management at Eckert-Mauchly Computer Company, Engineering Research Associates, and Remington Rand, 1946–1957*, Cambridge, MA: MIT Press.

OPK Files (1989), 'Illusion', <https://s3.amazonaws.com/s3.documentcloud.org/documents/1010299/stasi-file-2-translation.pdf> (last accessed 4 February 2016).

Phillips, Heather (2010), 'The Great Library of Alexandria?', *Library Philosophy and Practice*, <http://unllib.unl.edu/LPP/phillips.htm> (last accessed 4 February 2016).

Sledge, Matt (2013), 'CIA's Gus Hunt on Big Data: We "Try to Collect Everything and Hang On to It Forever" ', *Huffington Post*, 20 March, <www.huffingtonpost.com/mobileweb/2013/03/20/cia-gus-hunt-big-data_n_2917842.html> (last accessed 4 February 2016).

Smiraglia, Richard P. (2005), 'Introducing Metadata', *Cataloging & Classification Quarterly*, 40(3/4): 1–15.

Snowden, Edward (2014), 'Snowden-Interview: Transcript', *Norddeutscher Rundfunk*, <http://www.ndr.de/nachrichten/netzwelt/snowden277_page-3.html> (last accessed 4 February 2016).

Snyder, Samuel S. (1964), *History of NSA General-Purpose Electronic Digital Computers*, Washington, DC: Department of Defense, <http://www.governmentattic.org/3docs/NSA-HGPEDC_1964.pdf> (last accessed 29 February 2016).

van Dijck, José (2014), 'Datafication, Dataism and Dataveillance: Big Data between Scientific Paradigm and Ideology', *Surveillance & Society* 12(2): 197–208.

Washington Post (2007), 'Samuel Snyder, 96; Broke Codes and Designed Early Computers', 31 December, <http://www.washingtonpost.com/wp-dyn/content/article/2007/12/30/AR2007123002435.html> (last accessed 4 February 2016).

Weibel, Stuart, Jean Godby and Eric Miller (2005), 'OCLC/NCSA Metadata Workshop Report', Dublin Core Metadata Initiative, 1995–2002, <http://dublincore.org/workshops/dc1/report.shtml> (last accessed 4 February 2016).

IV Pervasive Mediations

Chapter 11

Notes from the Underground: Microwaves, Backbones, Party Lines and the Post Office Tower

John W. P. Phillips

> To isolate an ideal form is to render it independent of the empirical domain and of noise. Noise is the empirical form of the message just as the empirical domain is the noise of form.
>
> Michel Serres (1968: 45)

> She had, as young people with their charming egoism and their impromptu modes so felicitously do, taken it quite calmly for granted that I should suddenly have felt like dining on the Post Office Tower and should, since she happened to ring up, have happened to ask her to come too.
>
> Iris Murdoch (2013 [1973]: 241)

0

Interruptions, interceptions, flights, losses, holes, trapdoors . . . these figures of the motif of parasitism link the parasite to that property of communication referred to as *noise*. Following Michel Serres, we may acknowledge three broad domains in which parasitical arrangements operate: biology (tapeworms and so on), community (with, in certain communities, a special sacrificial role) and communication (noise, static, interference). As Serres observes, what was classically the biological sense involves a parasitical animal that 'lives, eats, and multiplies within the body of its host' (1980: 9). Yet this can seem to be a wide rubric: 'We adore eating veal, lamb, beef, antelope, pheasant, or grouse, but we don't throw away their leftovers. We dress in leather and adorn ourselves with feathers' (Serres 1980: 10). Serres's thought on the parasite, beginning with his multi-volume work *Hermès* (1968), and reaching a more sustained level in *Le parasite* (1980), helps to identify the paradoxical continuity of the parasitic structure across all its domains, thus transforming it in its concept.[1] Any system whatever that involves as a condition of its operation the possibility of its interruption can be said to be essentially parasitic: 'This system includes the telephone, the telegraph, television, the highway system, maritime pathways and shipping lanes, the orbits of satellites, the circulation of messages and of raw materials, of language and foodstuffs, money and philosophical theory' (Serres 1980: 11). It is with this last category that Serres begins his investigation.

The first volume of *Hermès*, *La communication*, begins with a reading of the role of mathematics for Platonic dialogue, considered as an instance of the genesis of intersubjectivity and abstraction. He makes a methodological distinction, which is quite ingenious, though mythical, between the mathematical symbol and its graphic form, which differs if sometimes only slightly with each occurrence: 'The symbol is thus an abstract being that the graphs in question only evoke' (Serres 1968: 42). Serres describes as '*cacographie*' (i.e. 'bad handwriting') the 'noise of graphic form' in relation to the abstraction of an ideal to which the form supposedly refers. The Platonic dialogue in this respect serves as an instance of the dialogic form of communication in general, in which interlocutors reach an agreement, in tune with mathematicians, to work together in the elimination of the noise that their communication inevitably produces as its essential by-product.

Serres builds on communication theory to suppose that this common enemy can be figured, in a '*prosopopée du bruit*', as a kind of 'third man' or 'demon': '*To hold a dialogue is to suppose a third man and to seek to exclude him*; a successful communication is the exclusion of the third man' (1968: 41). If dialogic communication can be figured as a struggle against the 'third man', which it inevitably produces, then this complicates in advance any question we may pose to the continuation of Cold War communications systems.

Part of this chapter concerns a plan, proposed in 1956, for a backbone radio link running north and south through Britain, with radio standby to line links to defence services along the way, avoiding large towns and designed to provide as safe a route as possible for communications vital to the prosecution of a war (GPO 1956). The plan in building on – thus making use of – existing proposals for telecoms development acts like a synecdoche for the ways in which Cold War systems operate (as another kind of 'third man') to the extent that they are hard to reliably extricate from the systems of 'peacetime' economic progress. My question concerns the bonds by which the structure of this engineering problem – situated rather precisely in a history of rapid development of telecom R&D – produces associations with relations of a more existential or ethical character.

In what follows, I trace a tendency by which a certain kind of existential fiction that both explores and instantiates the peculiar logic of the parasite connects in a parabolic way to the parasitism of Cold War communications systems. What are the implications of an ethics grounded in the attempt to deal with this logic? And where might such attempts, and the desires that drive them, eventually lead? Two of several, quite diverse, senses of the word *communication* exert a special influence on what concerns me here.

The first, appearing deceptively narrow, submits to a specific history of emergence and development. Refined by Norbert Wiener (1948, 1949) and by Claude E. Shannon (1948) as a technical term of cybernetic and mathematical theories of communication, *communication* designates a scientifically precise and limited capacity with a nonetheless broad reach and a wide range of practical applications. Shannon defines the problem exactly: 'the fundamental problem of communication is that of reproducing at one point either exactly or approximately a message selected at another point' (Shannon and Weaver 1949: 31). The breakthrough involves his framing of the problem as a telegraphic one. It concerns communications considered as *syntactical* (relations within the sphere of the message) rather than semantic (to do with meaning or reference) or pragmatic (to do with context or users). 'The semantic aspects of a message', he says, 'are irrelevant to the engineering problem' (Shannon and Weaver 1949: 31). The problem as it pertains to the reproduction of the message demands a means of calculating the capacity of a channel for transmitting information when one message is selected from a finite set of possible messages. Shannon begins with a basic application of the mathematical power law for logarithms, where the unknown variable (the capacity of information) is an exponent of the base (e.g. binary digits): $\log_b(x^y) = y \cdot \log_b(x)$. As the logarithmic function is the inverse of the exponential function it has the benefit of a seemingly 'most natural' choice: 'one feels, for example, that [. . .] two identical channels [should have] twice the capacity of one for transmitting information') (Shannon and Weaver 1949: 32). Shannon takes things considerably further than the intuitive feeling by setting mathematically the upper limit (the information capacity) beyond which it is no longer possible to obtain precise information.

Warren Weaver, in his introduction to *The Mathematical Theory of Communication*, outlines the broad implications of Shannon's solution with a generalised theory of affective transfer:

> The word *communication* will be used here in a very broad sense to include all the procedures by which one mind may affect another. This of course involves not only written and oral speech, but also music, the pictorial arts, the theatre, the ballet, and in fact all human behaviour. (Shannon and Weaver 1949: 3)

In a further revolutionary way, bypassing the question of the nature of the *human* mind, this definition of communication embraces spheres of affective information transfer that both extend and exceed the capacities of human-to-human interaction:

> In some connections it may be desirable to use a still broader definition of communication, namely, one which would include the procedures by means of which one mechanism (say automatic equipment to track an airplane and to compute its probable future positions) affects another mechanism (say a guided missile chasing this airplane). (Shannon and Weaver 1949: 3)

The mathematical theory of communication generates a calculative 'meta-language' in reference to the set of 'object languages' and evaluates conditions on which both semantic and pragmatic aspects of communication depend.[2] The entire sphere of communication in this way can be modelled on the diagrammatic form of a channel (like an electrical telegraph system) along which signals travel (Figure 11.1).

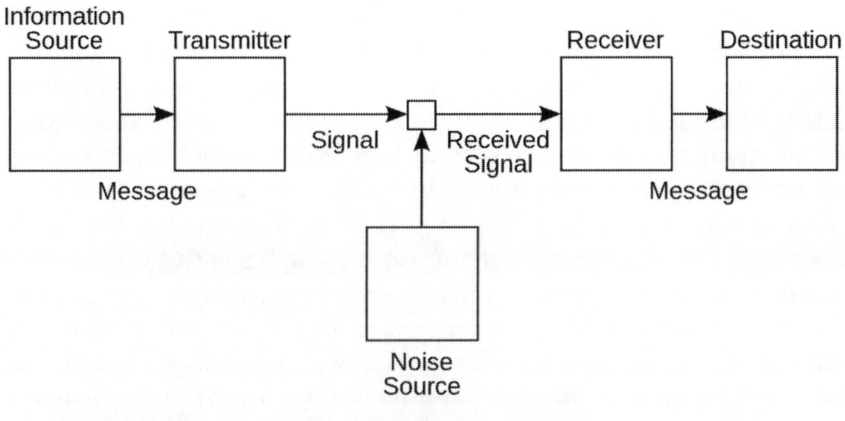

Figure 11.1 Schematic diagram of a general communication system. Source: Shannon and Weaver 1949: 7.

The expression of the limit to information capacity can be discovered in the notion of a ‘signal to noise ratio’ according to which the destructive effects of random ‘noise’ (sources of uncertainty generated by the transfer itself) can no longer be managed by engineering. On the question of this noisy signal, the prosopopeia of the third man renders the situation with further intrigue. Serres’s discussion of the Platonic dialogue suggests what may be at stake: ‘Dialectic makes the two interlocutors play on the same side; they do battle together to produce a truth on which they can agree, that is, to produce a successful communication’ (Serres 1968: 41). Some of the dialogues notoriously fail to achieve this aim and so there are times when the ferocity of the battle attests to ‘the power of the third man’ (ibid.). This evocation of the demon also applies when it comes to the second sense of *communication*.

I

Yet the second sense, in emphatic contrast to the mathematical basis of the first, takes us into broader and looser passages, or we might as well say digressions, for the treatments of the sense of *communication* in these existential philosophies and fictions resist clear definition and evade limited scope – yet it’s hard to say what exactly their practical uses might be. Garcin’s famous proclamation from Jean-Paul Sartre’s *Huis Clos* (first performed in 1944 and published in English as *No Exit* in 1947) belongs to a figure abstracted from his context but also surrounded by it in the contingency of an objective environment that pertains to him alone (‘*A drawing-room in Second Empire Style*’).[3] Hell already, then, comes to him as an externalisation of himself.[4] And although this Hell (‘L’enfer, c’est les autres’) can be interpreted, no doubt correctly, as a statement of the existential problem of other minds, it also reflects on the peculiar problem of the literary or dramatic persona, especially when the persona communicates a supposedly conceptual relation. As Sartre himself has suggested, these characters relate only negatively to a world in which change and negotiation are possible, and they exist under conditions that bar them from even the idealised transformations that traditional tragedy allows. Idealised existence in the existential drama is thus petrified. But then in what sense can a communication be said to have occurred? Transformation in a communication event can be regarded as a kind of failure. It pertains to the levels of stochastic interference (which increases with the degree of complexity of the message) that limit the capacity for the accurate reproduction of information. If we provisionally accept the definition of noise (*bruit*) proposed by Serres, as 'the set of the phenomena of interference that impede communication [l'ensemble de ces phénomènes de brouillage qui font obstacle à communication]' (1968: 40), we could say that the literary or dramatic text employs noise to open the field beyond information capacity, only to exhibit noise more clearly. Perhaps in cases like these it *performs* within the normative field of communication something like a degree zero communicative event, which strips communication bare in order to expose its inner workings, which is to say its often absurd but sometimes productive accidents and failures.

To the *mathematical* theory of communication we may therefore contrast the *existential* performance of communication, which has to do with different ways of identifying and managing the limits beyond which noise prevails. The contrast provides a setting for one of J. D. Salinger's most notable fictions, in the short tale 'A Perfect Day for Bananafish' (1948), which stands out early in the Cold War era for posing the enigma of communication in this way.[5] The opening sentence introduces the state of interpersonal telecommunications in the form of a conundrum, which might be stretched to imply an algorithm that could compute time as efficiency: 'There were ninety-seven New York advertising men in the hotel, and, the way they were monopolizing the long-distance lines, the girl in 507 had to wait from noon till almost two-thirty to get her call through' (Salinger 1953: 3). The sentence anchors the economy by which it creates its narrative context in the limitations of the system itself. The development of the story never really eclipses its background in this telecommunications-engineering puzzle, as it moves into its main existential comparison between Muriel Glass, on the phone to her mother, and her husband, Seymour Glass, home from the war and behaving in ostensibly anti-social ways.

That first sentence reads a little like one of Shannon's telegraphic problems: with a given number of phone lines, and a given number of individuals waiting to use them, how long does 'the girl in 507' have to wait to get her call through? The answer would give a power law for the capacity of the long-distance lines, by which one could calculate in this instance two and a half hours. The critical history supports a conviction that Salinger's *Nine Stories* should be understood in terms of the puzzles they pose in light of the collection's Zen koan epigraph: 'We know the sound of two hands clapping / But what is the sound of one hand clapping?' The formula 'we know × [. . .] but [. . .]' thus seems to guide the narratives at every step. Ruth Prigozy notes that 'at the heart of *Nine Stories* is a mystery' and that, 'further, within each story there lie other mysteries, some trivial, some profoundly complex, but all defying easy solutions' (1995: 114). Indeed, 'the girl in 507' (revealed at length to be Muriel Glass) begins to subtract some of 'the known' elements that help account for the calculation of time with which the story begins.

First, she fills the time required to wait for her call to go through with activities not obviously related to the call itself but which involve a more or less continuous state of attuned distraction:

> She read an article in a women's pocket-sized magazine, called 'Sex is Fun – or Hell'. She washed her comb and brush. She took the spot out of the skirt on her beige suit. She moved the button on her Saks blouse. She tweezed out two freshly surfaced hairs on her mole. When the operator finally rang her room, she was sitting on the window seat and had almost finished putting lacquer on the nails of her left hand. (Salinger 1953: 3)

The character's minute attention to this series of minor tasks and personalised entertainments suggests a negative relation to communication per se: the gathering of possessive pronouns takes her outside of communication time into a kind of ecstatic self absorption that in turn overlaps but does not coincide with the time of the telegraphic transfer. Second, by delaying answering the ringing phone once her call does come through she creates a temporal alternative to the time of communication that also establishes a spatial alternative, which she maintains.

> She was a girl who for a ringing phone dropped exactly nothing. She looked as if her phone had been ringing continually ever since she had reached puberty.
>
> With her little lacquer brush, while the phone was ringing, she went over the nail of her little finger, accentuating the line of the moon. She then replaced the cap on the bottle of lacquer and, standing up, passed her left – the wet – hand back and forth through the air. With her dry hand, she picked up a congested ashtray from the window seat and carried it with her over to the night table, on which the phone stood. She sat down on one of the made up twin beds and – it was the fifth or sixth ring – picked up the phone. (Salinger 1953: 3–4)

Surrounding the actual communication itself (intrinsically interesting as the phone call might be, I will not attempt an analysis of that here) a sphere of activities becomes theatrically visible that runs alongside those of the telegraphic transfer. The call Muriel has put through returns to her as an interruption of the activities that seemingly evolve as a function of the waiting time that the delay of the transfer causes. Muriel's attitude in general characterises this waiting time as projected from a kind of hebephrenic existential condition (since she had reached puberty) in which she has become immune to, while at the same time dependent upon, the interruptions of a ringing phone. The ringing phone can now not be extricated from the world it interrupts, which belongs to it just as it belongs to the world. Like the telephonic apparatus – when it's not in use it is, as they say, on standby – Muriel operates on standby, not fully operational but at powered-up rest until the call comes through.[6]

The fiction further functions as a kind of analysis of modes of communication: between Muriel and her mother on a long-distance phone line (phatic repetition); between the eight-year-old Sibyl Carpenter and her mother in the hotel (distracted misunderstanding); and between Seymour and Sibyl on the beach and in the sea (playful invention).[7] Stepping back, Salinger's symbolism can appear a little crude: the telephonic engineering enables banal remote conversation and awkwardly eclipses the more noisy yet fragile and elliptic kinds of communication associated with the character of Seymour Glass, whose interactions with Sibyl instantiate a discourse at once superficially playful and yet bottomless in melancholy. With Glass's symbolic and messy suicide at the close of the narrative, a seemingly unbridgeable gap opens up between the two kinds of discourse.

The sphere over which these two diverse fields of communication can be said to exert their peculiar influence emerges in a determinately historical way, as that of the kind of social relation magnetised by the advancing promise of *telecommunications*. In 1946, the year between 'the war' and the Cold War, the relation between the mathematical and existential problems of communication might not have been obvious, but its emergence guides and to an extent drives another economic relation that is more obvious and quite distinct. In the standard historical narrative, the immediate postwar economy looks forward to a period of unrestrained, even irrational, exponential growth.[8] But this looking forward takes two quite distinct forms: on the one hand reductions in government spending and in heavy manufacturing correspond to the resignation of a conservative forecasting typical of economic transitions from war to peace economies generally (a difficult peacetime projection); on the other hand, at the lower end of the economic continuum, unprecedented movement materialised by the commodities of aspirant class mobility manifests an emerging social sphere in which the cycle of economic transactions (acquisition, exchange, credit, profit, debt) can be endlessly exploited (the long easy peacetime progress).[9] It features an aspirant class that remains difficult to determine, as it introduces both alienating experiences of poverty and novel dimensions of criminality within a generally expanding economic universe.[10] If the relationship between these two kinds of forward-looking economics takes the form of a general parasitism, then the question of how to situate Cold War systems – that require expenditure for defence budgets – remains to be considered.[11]

> The requirements for secure communications cannot be met by the present cable system of this country. The main long distance cable network used at the present time to provide trunk and private wire services terminates in, or passes through, the largest cities in the country, and depends for its operation on equipment located in these cities. A heavy attack by nuclear weapons would completely disrupt this network, and physical protection of the plant, e.g. by placing it in underground accommodation, would be ineffective against groundburst megaton type weapons.
>
> GPO (1956: 5)

In Great Britain, at least, the Ministry of Defence responded to the conjectural threat the Cold War posed to vital communications systems by planning a parasite system that would operate alongside while contributing to already existing and steadily developing nationwide networks. As early as 1939 the General Post Office, experimenting with radio relays, had transmitted television signals via relay stations across the Home Counties between London and the Midlands. By 1947 the GPO had established a 900MHz system along a string of six relay stations between London and Birmingham. And by 1950 microwave links could in these ways feed BBC television across large sections of the country (London to Birmingham and Manchester to Kirk o'Shotts in Lanarkshire, Scotland).

The joint MoD/GPO project named 'Backbone' in 1956 aimed to provide a secondary core communication network (the backbone) that would bypass the major urban centres as a way of raising its chances of survival in the event of nuclear war. A top-secret GPO paper from that year outlines the plan.[12] In addition to an existing skeleton cable network, to which a multiplicity of further cables would be added over several years to bridge gaps bypassing the major cities, two further radio networks would be created: the Backbone radio link comprising fourteen relay stations running north to south, and several radio standby to line links that would connect private lines of the Defence Services (at the time entirely dependent on vulnerable cable connections) to the relay stations.

The GPO paper identifies as major concerns the various dedicated budget and funding questions for the project, which, given the long duration of its various parts, would require ‘a financial commitment in the years beyond those for which capital investment for Post Office purposes as a whole has yet been approved’ (GPO 1956: 5b). So the paper also serves as a proposal for the commitment of expenditure and investment. With reference to its interdepartmental nature (agreements arrived at between the MoD and the GPO), two related economic factors play a part: the first involves peacetime funding of defence-related expenditure, ‘funds made available for defence expenditure by civilian departments’; and the second involves the role these networks will play in ‘Post Office capital investment as a whole’, a complicated arrangement connecting national expenditure, taxation, investment and contractual engagements with shareholding companies (including, for example, Marconi, General Electric and Western Electric) whose roles in the research and development of national telecommunications technology had been set since the establishment of the BBC in 1922. The paper outlines the agreement, describes each segment of the projected plan, and enumerates each of the projected budgetary requirements. In these ways Backbone invites approval for an intertwining of economic, civilian, defence and technological interests, in support of defence expenditure, thus providing a snapshot of the ways in which Cold War systems develop in economic, dynamic and topographical negotiations with other systems.

Out of the four working channels of Backbone, the paper proposes, ‘two will be available for defence circuits, the other two being used to meet peacetime telephone trunk and television development’ (GPO 1956: 5b). The arrangement therefore implies a kind of co-operative parasitism capitalising on two powerful imaginary cultural trends: resilient communications systems responding to conjectural Cold War requirements, and the rapid evolution of client/consumer radio technology in telephone lines and television feeds. The historical development of telecommunications cable adds a complication, which we can touch on briefly here. The prohibitive size and expense of the early cables (starting in the nineteenth century) gradually gave way to progressively smaller and cheaper technologies, until the fibre-optic cable widely used by the 1980s significantly fulfilled a shift from microwaves to cable (and some might say a *revolution*) in telecommunications. Once the Backbone project reached the height of its practical establishment, relay towers cropped up as planned up and down the byways of Britain, as well as in the major cities. A nation learning the joys of private rather than party lines, and the unimagined richness of colour television, began instead to reap the benefits of vastly increased efficiency of cable performance and ultimately the mobile phone. The relay stations edged towards redundancy.

Though fibre-optic cable has replaced microwave systems for the most part, these still operate as part of the major UK communications hub, the BT Tower (formerly Post Office Tower), which performs this history iconically: a striking statement reaching upwards into the atmosphere from an otherwise unremarkable area of central London as if placed to symbolise the progress that telecommunications had already achieved by the early 1960s. The Tower's construction had incited considerable media discussion and invention, yet by the time it was operational its eventual fate as a listed building was already signalled: a concrete abstraction, as it still is in the twenty-first century, an archival symbol of the technology's tendency to operate at once before and after its time, overtaking itself and yet at once abstaining from and absorbing the drive for further development.

The TV Network Switching Centre on the second floor inherits both the Backbone-related microwave plans and contemporary packet-switching experiments that led to the networking technology of ARPANET. The development that communications would continue to take follows a trend contemporary with the Backbone plans, in various, somewhat independent, attempts to solve problems of queuing and delay in telephone switchboards and shared lines.[13] For instance, the National Physical Laboratory was partly responsible in the late 1950s for experiments with switching packets of data in systems that would become blueprints for computerised and cell communications systems.[14] Cold War concerns, as in the case of Backbone, drive these experiments, which in addition to the promise of increased performance and efficiency in telecommunications also offer systems that might better survive nuclear attack, and thus enable appropriately swift responses.

We should not lose sight of the inconsistent structure of this simultaneously temporal and spatial development. Without again getting into the question of a specifically Cold War fiction we can identify ways in which certain literary texts address communicative structures, but by doing so remove themselves from both the vagaries and the certainties of their own communicative contexts. If, as Hillis Miller has attempted to show, literature may be defined as 'a strange use of words to refer to things, people, and events about which it is impossible ever to know whether or not they have somewhere a latent existence' (2002: 45), then literature possesses properties that, like those of pure mathematics, inhabit an undecidable inexistence.[15] Furthermore the literary sphere, if it operates at all on existing models of communication, does so by its access to illimitable channels, which may seemingly be switched without constraint.

Iris Murdoch's *The Black Prince* (1973) includes an episode set on the revolving restaurant of the Post Office Tower that puts into play some of the temporal and spatial conditions that so far I have merely touched upon. Murdoch's novels have achieved an uncertain status thanks to their idiosyncratic involvement in mainstream fashions of anglophone literary history. Her familiarity with and indebtedness to the French existentialist tradition (and her teaching as a moral philosopher) mean that we expect not only Sartre and Camus but also Dostoevsky and Kierkegaard to number among her literary ancestors. That fact does not make it much easier to identify let alone analyse the techniques that characterise her novels or their significance. To start with, the 'things, people and events' that mark a Murdoch story do so as components of a structure of spatial relations and puzzling temporal consequences. Murdoch attends both to the filter of a perspective and to precise description when setting out the spatial organisation of a situation – a place, a room, for instance, or distribution of rooms in a house – and so it pays to notice properties that put into motion relations between insides and outsides and the movements of attraction and repulsion that seem like parodies of physical laws and anyway operate in an estranged and oblique relation to such laws. *The Black Prince*, most of which is narrated in the voice of its protagonist Bradley Pearson, can be read as the performance of an idealisation, though both the situation (the older man in love with a young woman) and the settings (for instance, dinner on the Post Office Tower, or a Covent Garden performance of *Der Rosenkavalier*) give rise to many episodes touched by comic absurdity.

Bradley Pearson's idealisation of Julian Baffin (the daughter of the younger and more successful author Arnold Baffin – a thinly disguised auto-satire of Murdoch herself) occurs simultaneously with his attempts to extricate himself (in order to write) from relations that he characterises as 'predatory': Julian's parents, his ex-wife, her delinquent brother, his sister recently separated from her husband, old friends, and so on. The system of parasites represented by these characters recedes as the focus of Bradley's attention becomes quickly fixated on his object.

> The restaurant at the top of the Post Office Tower revolves very slowly. Slow as a dial hand. Majestic trope of lion-blunting time.
>
> How swiftly did it move that night while London crept behind the beloved head? Was it quite immobile, made still by thought, a mere fantasy of motion in a world beyond duration? Or was it spinning like a top, whirling away into invisibility, and pinning me against the outer wall, kitten limbed and crucified by centrifugal force. (Murdoch 2013: 238)

The parasitic allusions to Shakespeare (paraphrases of idealisations of *The Sonnets*) help in the combined fictional realisations of narrative irony (characterisation) and poetic evocation (the idealisation itself). So on the one hand Bradley Pearson generates a literary jumble in what on the other hand (Murdoch's prosody) performs a classical idealisation of the courtly love sonnet. The point, however, if we pay attention to the framing of this and other supporting sequences, seems to be towards the short circuiting of communication itself, a circular operation that excludes not only the 'third man' produced in the noisy exchange (Hamlet, the Black Prince – Julian and Bradley combined or commingled) but the addressee too, which in Serres's evocation of the Platonic dialogue would have been at least an equal player in the game. The doubled union – Bradley's union with Julian, and the literary union between Bradley and his unnamed addressees – implicates the noisy signal in the aim of reducing or limiting the signal itself to zero:

> All this, and further hues and saturations of bliss which I cannot describe at all, I felt on that evening as I sat with Julian in the Post Office Tower restaurant. We talked, and our communion was so perfect that it might have been telepathic for all I could make out afterwards about how it actually occurred. (Murdoch 2013: 239)

The bathos in the characterisation is brought to a head when the host object (Julian) interrupts the parasite's (Bradley's) reveries. The peculiarity of these reported dialogues lies in their performing the more or less exact opposite of the standard communication model's aim. Instead of the reduction or limitation of noise towards an approximate repetition of the signal in question, the novel performs an increase in potential noise levels in the hopeless aim of a reduction of the signal itself. Instead of the (relatively comforting) psychoanalytic structure, in which the message returns to the sender in an inverse form, the repetition of the message establishes a milieu within which it distributes the sender and receiver as its substitutable switching points.

Interruptions therefore perform the social ethics that *The Black Prince*'s protagonist and main narrator persistently neglects. Murdoch's existential melodramas provoke the need for a typology of interruption: whether sudden, or malicious, or benign, or gradual and unfolding, interruptions often move the drama on to its next stage as if driven by a mechanical operator. Once Bradley and Julian have escaped in secret to the domestic refuge of a formulaic cottage by the sea, the quality of their disastrous conclusion (already assured by virtue of this narrative formula) unfolds across a set of telecommunication devices: a messenger, 'a man in uniform on a bicycle'; who delivers a telegram, '*Please telephone me immediately Francis*' (Murdoch 2013: 321–2); and the telephone call itself, which reveals the news of Bradley's sister's suicide. The interruption symbolises the corruption of Bradley's idealised romance by the emergent collapse of his social network (his parasites) but it does so in the persistent paraphernalia of post office services and the motifs of connection and disconnection. Murdoch tenderly explores the details of each scene and shades it with her narrator's growing alarm and his consequent disorganisation. To answer the telegram he has to drive to the nearest village in search of a phone box, inadvertently evoking the casual disruption of the distinction between public and private spheres, on the way:

> I passed the garage. I had thought of asking the garage man if I could use his telephone, but it might not be private. I drove past the church and turning a corner I saw the village street and a public telephone box.
>
> I stopped outside it. Of course the box was occupied. Inside it a girl gesticulating and smiling, turned her back on me. I waited. At last the door opened. I found I had no change. Then the operator would not answer. Finally I achieved a reverse charge call to my own number and heard Francis, who had picked up the receiver at once, babbling at the other end. (Murdoch 2013: 323)

The telephone call, taken in its entirety, involves the transmission of a message between a source (Francis) and a receiver (Bradley):

> 'Oh Bradley – it's Priscilla – '
>
> 'What?'
>
> 'She's dead.'
>
> I became suddenly and strangely conscious of the telephone box, the sunshine, somebody waiting outside, my own staring eyes in the mirror. (Murdoch 2013: 323)

But *The Black Prince* complicates the formal transfer of the message so that the first element (the telegram) merely demands a reply, such that the second element (the telephone call) reverses the roles of sender and receiver. The reverse-charge function further complicates the pattern. Whatever the actual news (Priscilla has died), Bradley has already received the effect it will have had on him (its illocutionary force):

> A postman? I have always dreaded officials. What could he want with us? Was it us he wanted? No one knew we were here. I felt cold with guilt and terror: and I thought, I have been in paradise and I have not been grateful. (Murdoch 2013: 320)

The peculiar future anterior of the message seems to signal the shock that a telecoms world has on its users, for whom the message has already been received: a queue of users in a small village each time smiling or gesticulating or staring in shock at another unseen world. This *other* world casts the world of everyday perception into a kind of surreal sharpness, a hyperreality of the everyday, dividing *the* world into two incompatible spheres. One or other of these spheres (romantic idealisation, separation from others *or* networked relationality) symbolises the death of the other.

The situation suggests a generalisable kind of relationship according to which the elements of the standard communication model, following a line between *source* and *destination*, may be replaced without loss of consistency by terms of parasitology, like *parasite* and *host* (see Figure 11.1). The 'interruptions' generated by repetition, which might seem to be imposed as further parasitical disturbances, can be reconfigured as belonging to a system of equivalent elements in a general dispersion. In Serres's diagram, the directional model is replaced such that lines now open up between three equivalent positions, thus enabling a field of play between different levels (Figures 11.2 and 11.3). The bathos of Murdoch's existential drama suggests that her protagonist remains incurably oblivious to the situation (a situation that Sartre's *No Exit* also dramatises but in a slightly different way). The sender is caught from the beginning (with only a mythical relation to a *before* of this moment) in *becoming* the 'third man' or 'demon' of communication theory's noise.

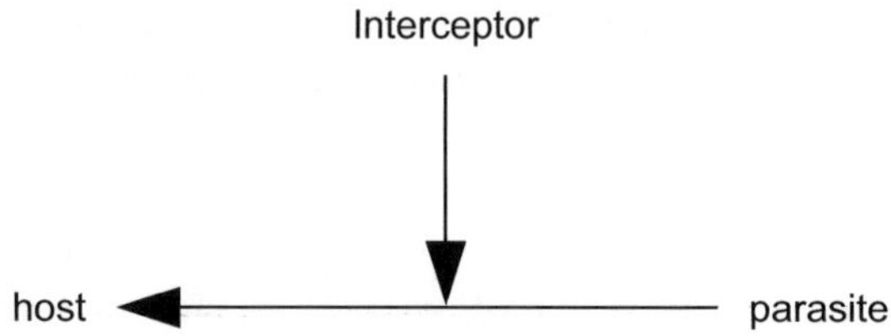

Figure 11.2 Host, parasite and interceptor. Source: Serres 1980: 44–5.

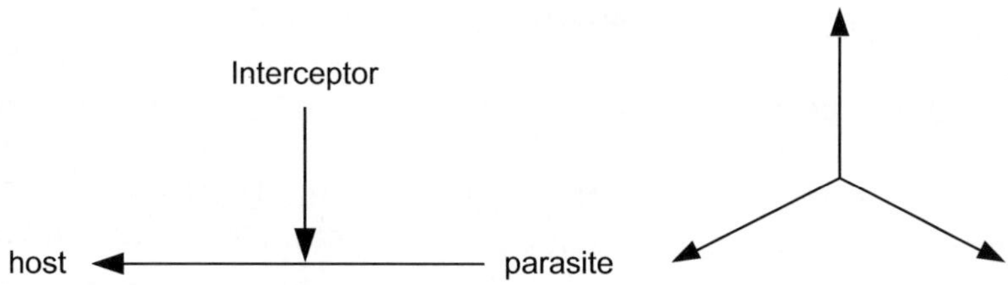

Figure 11.3 Opening into three. Source: Serres 1980: 44–5.

This way of picturing things corresponds in an admittedly quite complex manner to the kinds of world characterised by texts of the so-called existentialist tradition, according to which the formerly ontological conditions of traditional philosophy fade behind a more radical sense of having been thrown into situations beyond rational explanation. Kierkegaard's famous evocation from *Repetition* arguably captures the situation best in the form of a lament (the lament of the third man?):

> One sticks a finger into the ground to smell what country one is in; I stick my finger into the world – it has no smell. Where am I? What does it mean to say: the world? What is the meaning of that word? Who tricked me into this whole thing and leaves me standing here? Who am I? How did I get into the world? Why was I not asked about it, why was I not informed of the rules and regulations but just thrust into the ranks as if I had been bought from a peddling Shanghaier of human beings? (Kierkegaard 1983: 200)

A thoroughgoing analysis of repetition (with Kierkegaard's *Repetition* as a necessary text) would allow us at length to understand the progress of telecommunications technology in terms of that technology's main operator – repetition itself. Following Kierkegaard, Murdoch's texts – especially the darkly satirical novels of the 1970s – would reveal in the gears of repetition a paradoxical medium for understanding the role of the interrupter in the development of the interrupted sphere and the circular quality of the relations between them. Likewise, the role of Cold War systems in this development, which we regard in terms not of continuation but of repetition, leads to the following thought: while we know the Cold War is not a relatively autonomous addition to existing progress in telecommunications but a key component in how that is driven, there is more to discover in how a Cold War system functions (economically, dynamically and topographically) when considered as a component of a general parasitology. Increasing noise complicates a signal in its repetition to the point at which the signal is in peril, yet a signal without noise fails to communicate anything at all. The risk of destruction cannot be removed from the hope of a successful transfer.

This sphere of questions has shifted recently to the contemporary field of immunology, in which it is now acknowledged that defence of the organism relies on operations that put the organism in danger (although admittedly it has always been difficult to extricate discourses of biology from those of communication).[16] One of the acknowledged founders of contemporary immunology, Macfarlane Burnet, writing from the heart of the Cold War era, acknowledges the analogy between the biological immune system and national defence: 'we look on the whole function as a fail-safe system ringed around with controls to ensure that action against the "enemy" does not damage the resources of the organism, whether that organism be a political one or a mammalian body' (Burnet 1969: 255). Action against the enemy – whether in communicative or defensive systems – can risk immeasurable danger towards the body being defended, so that, as Burnet makes clear, a further layer of defence is required to act against the defences already in place: one must defend against one's defensive measures. In this way escalation threatens when one defends either too much or too little.

Notes

1. Serres can capitalise on the French idiom *bruit parasite* (background noise) in ways that remain enigmatic in anglophone contexts, though this only affects the force of the argument in translation by way of a further instance of noise (*bruit*).
2. Colin Cherry stresses this: 'The most glaring fact about this measure of information, set up by Wiener and Shannon, is that it has nothing whatever to do with meaning, nor with value, nor with usefulness of messages. The telephone and telegraph may be used equally well for the most trivial gossip, for the most tragic news, or for the most profound observations' (1956: 59).

3. The proclamation: 'So this is Hell. I'd never have believed it. You remember all we were told about the torture chambers, the fire and brimstone, the "burning marl". Old wives' tales! There's no need for red-hot pokers. Hell is – other people' (Sartre 1949: 45).
4. See also Jacques Lacan: 'Human language would then constitute a kind of communication in which the sender receives his own message back from the receiver in an inverted form' (2006: 430).
5. The category of Cold War fiction (fiction set in the context of the Cold War) does not allow finite classification of Cold War texts, which seem broadly to be an illimitable bunch, if for no other reason than that of the undecidability of the literary context itself. Nevertheless, Salinger's text and its critical history proceed conterminously with the Cold War era itself. It was published as a story in *The New Yorker* in January 1948 and then as the first of nine (with a mysterious significance in that number) in *Nine Stories* in 1953. *The New York Times* offers its own summary of the tale: 'A young man, recently returned from the Army, goes to Florida with his wife. His wife has a telephone conversation with her mother during which the mother speaks about the young man as though he were mentally deranged but the girl reassures her that she is not afraid. The husband, on the beach, goes for a dip in the ocean with a small girl, who is a guest at the hotel. He seems to get along perfectly with the child. When he gets back to his hotel room, where his wife is asleep, he calmly pulls out a gun and shoots himself.'
6. A more sustained analysis would go on to identify in the contrasting character of Seymour Glass an inability to operate on standby, like the 'bananafish' of the tale's peculiar moral fable. Cotter (1989) traces the moral message of Salinger's tale to Rainer Maria Rilke, while Anthony Fassano argues that Seymour's tale of the bananafish recreates a fable from Aesop (2010: 149).
7. For a retrospective assessment of Salinger in his time (and since) see Smith 2003: '*Nine Stories* tapped into an ambivalent milieu: the stories dealt with genius, spiritual integrity, moral corruption, and the occasional ability of innocence to transform our lives' (640). Kilicci 2008 gathers the critical evidence for reading Salinger in the existentialist tradition peculiar to the US in the 1950s.
8. See Hoselitz 1955 for an analysis of the parasitical elements of postwar urban economics.
9. Karl Marx identifies the now classical form of parasitic economics in the chapter of *Capital*, vol. 1, 'The Working Day', in which capital is characterised as reanimated labour in the metaphor of the (un)dead: 'Capital is dead labour, that, vampire-like, only lives by sucking living labour, and lives the more, the more labour it sucks. The time during which the labourer works, is the time during which the capitalist consumes the labour-power he has purchased of him' (Marx 1976: 342). The chapter goes on to document the ways in which the labouring classes are treated as parasitic on the capital to which they give their lives, in, for example, the time spent on consumption of luxuries,

and Marx notes that the 'werewolf-like hunger' for surplus labour has caused 'capital's monstrous outrages' to be at last 'bound by the chains of legal regulation' (1976: 353). The upper limit to the amount the working day can be extended might be compared to the upper limit of noise in the ideal communicative event. The law in both cases divides into what may be called a 'natural' (physical constraint of time and capacity) and a 'jurisprudential' character.

10. See Patterson 1996: 282 for the classical account of this period of American ideology and politics.
11. Empirical data abounds concerning allied defence spending. See for instance Higgs 1994 for an analysis of the US Cold War economy that shows how unprecedented peacetime defence budgets allowed the difference between growth rates of GNP and GNP* (GNP minus all defence spending) 'to diminish, becoming nearly negligible during the 1980s [the Reagan era]'. During the 1950s, the era of greatest economic prosperity, the discrepancy between growth rates of GNP and GNP* becomes much greater (Higgs 1994: 308).
12. 'Backbone Radio Link and Radio Standby to Line Links for Safeguarding Vital Communications', *The National Archives* (GPO 1956).
13. See Kleinrock 1961 for an early groundbreaking application of queue theory and packet switching to what would become network cell technology and, via ARPANET, the internet.
14. See Davies and Barber 1973.
15. Bertrand Russell had famously taught the following: 'Pure mathematics consists entirely of such asseverations as that, if such and such a proposition is true of anything, then such and such another proposition is true of that thing. It is essential not to discuss whether the first proposition is really true, and not to mention what the anything is of which it is supposed to be true [. . .] If our hypothesis is about anything and not about some one or more particular things, then our deductions constitute mathematics. Thus mathematics may be defined as the subject in which we never know what we are talking about, nor whether what we are saying is true' (1901: 84).
16. See Phillips 2012, 2013 and 2015 for preliminary attempts to mobilise this mode of questioning, on which the writings of Jacques Derrida on autoimmunity have been decisive (see especially Derrida 2002).

References

Burnet, Frank Macfarlane (1969), *Cellular Immunology*, 2 vols, Melbourne: Melbourne University Press.

Cherry, Colin (1956), '"Communication Theory" and Human Behaviour', *Studies in Communication: Contributed to the Communication Research Centre, University College, London*, London: Secker and Warburg, pp. 45–67.

Cotter, James Finn (1989), 'A Source for Seymour's Suicide: Rilke's Voices and Salinger's *Nine Stories*', *Papers on Language and Literature* 25(1): 83–9.

Davies, Donald, and Derek Barber (1973), *Communication Networks for Computers*, London: Wiley.

Derrida, Jacques (2002), 'Faith and Knowledge: The Two Sources of "Religion" at the Limits of Reason Alone', trans. Samuel Weber, in *Acts of Religion*, ed. Gil Anidjar, London: Routledge, pp. 42–101.

Fassano, Anthony (2010), 'Salinger's "A Perfect Day for Bananafish"', *The Explicator* 66(3): 149–50.

General Post Office [GPO] (1956), 'Backbone Radio Link and Radio Standby to Line Links for Safeguarding Vital Communications', *The National Archives*, <http://webarchive.nationalarchives.gov.uk/+/http://yourarchives.nationalarchives.gov.uk/index.php?title=Backbone_radio_link_and_radio_standby_to_line_links_for_safeguarding_vital_communications> (last accessed 8 February 2016).

Higgs, Robert (1994), 'The Cold War Economy: Opportunity Costs, Ideology, and the Politics of Crisis', *Explorations in Economic History* 31: 283–312.

Hillis Miller, J. (2002), *On Literature*, London: Routledge.

Hoselitz, Bert (1955), 'Generative and Parasitic Cities', *Economic Development and Cultural Change* 3(3): 278–94.

Kierkegaard, Søren (1983), *Repetition*, trans. Howard V. Hong and Edna H. Hong, Princeton: Princeton University Press.

Kilicci, Esra (2008), *J. D. Salinger's Characters as Existentialist Heroes: Encountering 1950s America*, Indiana University of Pennsylvania, ProQuest Dissertations Publishing.

Kleinrock, Leonard (1961), 'Information Flow in Large Communication Nets', *RLE Quarterly Progress Report, July*, Massachusetts Institute of Technology.

Lacan, Jacques (2006 [1966]), *Écrits*, trans. Bruce Fink in collaboration with Héloïse Fink and Russell Grigg, New York: Norton.

Marx, Karl (1976), *Capital: A Critique of Political Economy*, vol. 1, trans. Ben Fowkes, London: Penguin.

Murdoch, Iris (2013 [1973]), *The Black Prince*, London: Vintage.

Patterson, James T. (1996), *Grand Expectations: The United States 1945–1974*, New York: Oxford University Press.

Phillips, John W. P. (2012), 'Bios, Polis and the Autoimmune', *Science, Technology and Society* 17(1): 79–101.

Phillips, John W. P. (2013), '*Vox Populi*: Hölderlin and the Digital Hecatomb', *Poetica* 79: 75–90.

Phillips, John W. P. (2015), 'Force and Vulnerability in Philosophy and Science: Husserl, Derrida, Stiegler', *Cultural Politics* 11(2): 145–61.

Prigozy, Ruth (1995), '*Nine Stories*: J. D. Salinger's Linked Mysteries', in J. Gerald Kennedy (ed.), *Modern American Short Story Sequences*, Cambridge: Cambridge University Press, pp. 114–32.

Russell, Bertrand (1901), 'Recent Work on the Principles of Mathematics', *International Monthly* 4: 83–101.

Salinger, J. D. (1953 [1948]), 'A Perfect Day for Bananafish', in *Nine Stories*, New York: Little, Brown and Company.

Sartre, Jean-Paul (1949 [1944]), *No Exit and Three Other Plays*, New York: Vintage.

Serres, Michel (1968), *Hermès I: La communication*, Paris: Minuit.

Serres, Michel (1980), *Le parasite*, Paris: Pluriel.

Shannon, Claude E., and Warren Weaver (1949), *The Mathematical Theory of Communication*, Chicago: University of Urbana Press.

Smith, Dominic (2003), 'Salinger's *Nine Stories*: Fifty Years Later', *The Antioch Review* 61(4): 639–49.

Chapter 12

Insect Technics: War Vision Machines

Fabienne Collignon

> No one would have believed in the last years of the nineteenth century that this world was being watched keenly and closely by intelligences greater than man's and yet as mortal as his own; that as men busied themselves about their various concerns they were scrutinised and studied, perhaps almost as narrowly as a man with a microscope might scrutinise the transient creatures that swarm and multiply in a drop of water. With infinite complacency men went to and fro over this globe about their little affairs, serene in their assurance of their empire over matter. It is possible that the infusoria under the microscope do the same.
>
> H. G. Wells (1993: 5)

H. G. Wells's *The War of the Worlds* (1898) begins with 'man' as a 'transient creature' observed under a microscope, 'swarm[ing] and multiply[ing] in a drop of water': a fantasy or *Schwärmerei* of total control that is wielded, from above, by the other. The 'human', by contrast, is like 'infusoria', a unicellular, sedentary organism seen only through a magnification of lenses. The Martians are fungoid, glistening, tentacular: 'thin black whips [. . .] like the arms of an octopus' rise up towards 'a circular disc [spinning] with a wobbling motion'; their 'strange [bodies]' are at once metallic and abjectly organic (Wells 1993: 21, 44). What the invasion of Earth reveals, more than anything, is 'our' own abjection, the disgusting softness of 'our' being as a 'disintegrating organism' (Wells 1993: 84). The novel ends, like *The Island of Dr. Moreau* (1896), with a perspective that engulfs the narrator who, in London, notices the 'busy multitudes' that 'are but the ghosts of the past, haunting the streets that [he has] seen silent and wretched, going to and fro, phantasms in a dead city, the mockery of life in a galvanised body' (Wells 1993: 171, 172). The presiding image of 'the human', in *The War of the Worlds*, is that of an unassimilable, undifferentiated mass of (un)deadness.

The sovereign view from above that Wells's Martian perspective encourages, according to Christopher Hollingsworth in his discussion of the 'poetics of the hive', is 'a particular sort of abstraction' that opposes the individual to the collective understood as a mere mass (2001: ix, 3). What I am concerned with here is a militarised 'logistics of perception' that renders its targets insectile even as perception itself has taken the form of insect 'eye-pearls' (Connor 2006: 82) that appear at once as radically alien while realising the other as alien. In other words, I focus on a mechanics of 'seeing' that occurs by way of a war machine whose mode of 'vision' or detection aesthetically resembles the facets of an insect eye, most notably that of the fly. The notion of 'sight', however, works as metaphor and is accomplished through means other than eyes – radar, pulses of radio waves, microwaves emitted from objects. The 'viewing subject', then, is a machine that 'sees' past the limits of sight; as such, I will consider the aesthetics of the 'fly eye' in relation to the North Dakota anti-missile installation known as Safeguard (Figure 12.1) that was

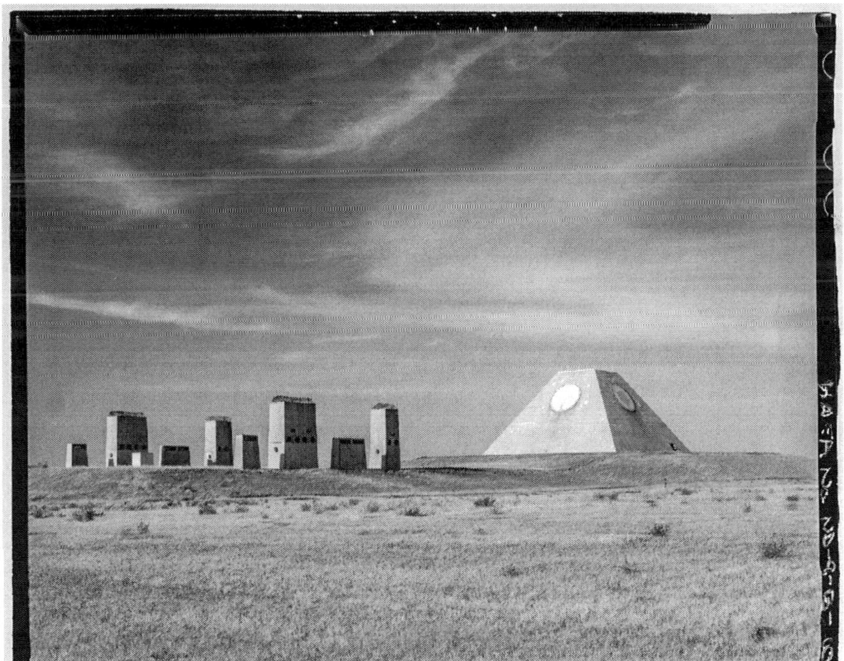

Figure 12.1 East oblique of missile site control building, with better view of exhaust (the taller columns) and intake shafts – Stanley R. Mickelsen Safeguard Complex, northeast of Tactical Road; southeast of Tactical Road South, Nekoma, Cavalier County, ND. Credit: Library of Congress, Prints & Photographs Division, HABS, Reproduction number HAER ND-9-B-10.

briefly operational in 1975. I take Safeguard as a ruined but not dead Cold War precursor to the increasingly weird and disturbing insect technics of contemporary military technofuturism.

Deep and Dead

Project Safeguard was developed in the late 1960s as a two-layer defensive system, meaning that it relied on two types of ballistic missiles – long and short range, Spartan and Sprint – to intercept enemy rockets. The complex is a 'truncated pyramid' intended to protect an adjacent Minuteman missile field and accommodated antennas, each of circular shape, thirteen feet in diameter and consisting of 5,000 phased-array elements, for the missile site radar (Baucom 1992: 91). Taken together, these elements resemble a 'gigantic, multi-lensed insect eye' (Baucom 1992: 91), whose persistent stare is repeated on the four sides of the building. Bug-eyed radar, easily a target itself and working in conjunction with diverse types of missiles – Spartan and Sprint that are electronically blind without their accompanying detection and guidance system – form 'a hedge against the uncertainties of the future', as Major General Robert C. Marshall, the Army's Ballistic Missile Defence Program Manager, stated at the Senate Hearings on Federal Year 1977 (quoted in Baucom 1992: 98). Though Safeguard was by then decommissioned, the Ballistic Missile Defence Research and Development programme, investigating not just radar but also optics, data processing and software development alongside interceptors and discrimination (the latter concerned with the isolation of decoys from warheads), maintained the quest for national closure on the basis of a scopic regime that is also occult, obscene, effectuated from the vantage point of weird sight machines.

I intend to align the notion of Safeguard's 'insect technics' with the concept of the 'weird': the insectile devices I am interested in are not the mites, tiny bionic aircraft resembling flies imagined as arriving from some military-technological dream of the future,[1] but, rather, the immense and obsolescent fly eyes of the Cold War. Installations like Safeguard anticipate the networked, invisible swarming connectivity more often associated with contemporary electronic systems. The idea of the swarm, following Bruno Latour, helps describe the coming into being of technologies and systems; it also suggests the functioning of a networked machine, where information depends on sub-systems, on 'colonial outposts', as it were, to the metropolitan brain (Pynchon 1995: 340). The networked entity is not purely technological but approximates the biological in its capacity to, swarm-like, gather and disseminate across the field of its influence.

Insect technics is 'weird' in China Miéville's sense of weirdness as an abject, indeterminate, yet 'radicalised uncanny' (2011). According to Freud, the uncanny is associated with returns and the compulsion to repeat – 'the prefix "*un*"', he writes, 'is the token of repression' (Freud 2001: 245). Miéville's 'high weird', on the other hand, 'is not the return of any repressed' but 'back-projects' an event's 'radical unremembered alterity into history' (2011). For Miéville, the 'monsters of high weird' are 'indescribable and formless *as well as being* and/or *although they are* and/or *in so far as they are* described with an excess of specificity, an accursed share of impossible somatic precision' (2011). Safeguard is insectile, then, because of its insect eyes, and it is weird because of its inscrutability and the mutable formlessness of its networked powers. While the installation is not necessarily unthinkably abject, Safeguard nonetheless represents an incomprehensible strangeness; the structure somehow exists beyond the horizon of the known – it 'sees' precisely past the horizon, senses the presence of still invisible objects. A case can, as such, be made that positions Safeguard as a thing that 'en-Weirds' (Miéville 2011) history/ontology through, yet also apart from, its weirdly insectile techno-biological machinery.

Miéville's definition of the weird informs my reading of the opening paragraph of *The War of the Worlds* in terms of an incursion that somehow pertains not only to the microscopic but also to the insectile or, at any rate, to swarms, though the latter is 'us', not the Martians, snake-like Things with faces that are not faces, masks of another order of being. It is through Miéville's insectile and cephalopodic weird, a notion that 'demand[s] a rethinking of philosophy' (ontology in particular) (Miéville 2011), that I will approach Safeguard: as a defensive formation which, as Paul Virilio notes in his analysis of the bunkers of the Atlantic Wall, resembles 'certain works of fiction[,] a spacecraft parked in the middle of an avenue announcing the war of the worlds' (1994: 12). The otherworldly materiality of military installations – too much of this world but also weirdly extra-terrestrial – positions them metaphorically and operationally as points of convergence in the weird system that combines, following Eugene Thacker, models of technological (networks), biological (swarms) and political (multitudes) organisations of the body politic (see Thacker 2004). Such overlapping models form a techno-bio-political ontology that is 'inherently dynamic, undergoing constant and variable changes' (Thacker 2004). In this chapter, concepts of network and swarm behave as figures of speech for what Sebastian Vehlken calls 'the coordination processes of an engineered present' (2013: 112) machinated into pure war.

To think of a massive, unmoving concrete thing like Safeguard as a dynamic collective or a part of a 'living' system seems, at first glance, entirely wrong. Nonetheless, the Safeguard building forms a remnant and outpost of a technologised order that not only progressively disappears but also 'proliferates' and incessantly 'improves' its processes. The endless upgrading of weapons of war also demands a constant enhancement of 'protective' installations – to safeguard the retaliatory force – that then rapidly become obsolete: ruins of fictions that keep being surpassed. Safeguard, then, is never a dead technology but a sloughed skin that reminds us to remain alert to the processes of technological development, constantly moving, as Latour argues, from 'signs to things', from paper to matter, and from matter back (and forth, to and fro) to discourse (2002: 80). The swarming, as dynamic phenomenon, refers to what Latour calls 'fiction[s] with a variable geometry', this 'capacity of a text' (or a technology) 'to weigh itself down with reality, or, on the contrary, to lighten its load of reality' in a course of coming into being that happens by degrees, and which never fully arrives at a stage beyond this 'variable-ontology world' (2002: 24, 173). Texts/technologies, fictional 'hybrid beings' (Latour 2002: 174), are then never stable, but curiously vital; Miéville's law of genre is, as such, affected by this difficult admission or impurity, let in, or just kept at bay, at the edges, or that, following Jacques Derrida, occupies the very heart of generic conventions (see Derrida 1980). This density of concrete – Safeguard as an object that has been left behind (Virilio 1994: 12) – does not strictly adhere to the law but cites it by proxy, in a 'sort of participation without belonging' (Derrida 1980: 59). In 'The Law of Genre', Derrida sees this curious 'taking part in without being part of' in terms of an 'internal pocket', an 'invagination', that harbours the 'principle of contamination' within the law itself (59, 65). Although he concentrates on the 'mark' of participation as itself – in the 'blink of an eye' (65) – preventing total belonging, total taxonomic certainty, I want to suggest that Safeguard, in a sense, functions as this pocket in Miéville's definition: its unblinking eye is a reminder that the weird unfolds and holds within itself the uncanny, the law and counter-law participating in the same 'text'.

In Safeguard – its insect eyes acting as a manifestation of the otherwise invisible swarming metaphor, all the while offering a 'vision' that seeks to make visible what remains unseen – the limits of weird are passed over: definitely uncanny, a monument to world wars, this object is simultaneously placed within and outside the 'parasitical economy' (Derrida 1980: 59) of a weird fictional/generic order. It puts to the test all boundary markers, bearing in mind the unperceived, unstable ontologies that constitute its swarming existence: (always already) outdated, this im/mobile formation gestures towards the relentless modernisation process that defined the Cold War, and defines the 'War on Terror' as/and (the psychopathology of) everyday living. It further functioned as one node in a networked system of defence that itself integrates so-called human and non-/inhuman actors interpreting the world through command grids conceptualised as tentacular: Thomas Pynchon, for one, in *Gravity's Rainbow* (first published in 1973), frequently refers to military and/or consumer capitalist strategies as cephalopodic ('octopus IG'), plastic, rubbery, yielding a 'culture of mucous' (Pynchon 1995: 339, 275).

Safeguard, then, is an iteration of the weird war machine that, post-Cold War, has mutated increasingly closer to the model of an insect technics: the titanic and concrete giving way to micro-robots, moon insects and glass bees indicative of an economy and, in Virilio's terms, an aesthetics of disappearance.[2] Even before the techniques of the microscopic and atomic – resulting in sublime, hypnotic devices like those in Ernst Jünger's novel *Gläserne Bienen* (1957) – associated with nuclear weapons, cinema had already, according to Virilio, caused the physical universe to disappear in the 'special effects of communication machines' that project the world through and as light (Virilio 1989: 60). The optic of exposure and concealment begins, for Virilio, with the soldiers 'hiding from sight in order to see', which leads to the retreat underground and from there to remote sensing and radar technology, whose installations exist at 'scattered points', where they receive and radiate information 'back into their own, defined universe' (Virilio 1989: 63, 65). The ultimate objective is, of course, total transparency, a landscape of glass – Virilio cites Jünger's most famous book in this instance, *In Stahlgewittern* (1920, translated as *Storm of Steel*), where binoculars 'distort' the field of vision. Never mind the nostalgia at work – the function of the naked eye, as if truthful, is deranged by '*Glas*' – these optical illusions point towards that derealisation of the world, rendered as spectral images by sighting and tracking arrangements as well as spaceships: light passing through a space made translucent.

If Safeguard is, in the end, insectile largely due to its bug-eyes and capacity to plug into the network-swarm, its contemporary descendant, the drone, extrapolates in its entire body the potentialities of the insect organisation of military technologies. A detached 'soul' forming part of a larger organism, like Safeguard, the drone is another sight machine, a surveillance imaging device. The drone is also a synecdoche – it implies others, in its wake, beyond the horizon – and a fantasy vehicle for 'pure', that is, precise, clean, calibrated war.[3] In contrast to the physical immobility of Safeguard, the drone exemplifies rapid deployment by small tactical units connected to command centres and media environments. There is no drone without Safeguard, however, since the ideology underpinning drone war – total surveillance capability enabled by integrated systems – has as part of its DNA the weird and mutant 'thing' (Derrida 2003: 92) of the Cold War. The perpetuation of techno-strategic operations and military-industrial governance is a continuation of Cold War thinking, articulated according to the same security myths that comprise (elsewhere and away) systematic, extra-judicial killings and (everywhere) the erosion of civil liberties, the suspension of laws: the *innere Notstand* as paradigm of state (see Agamben 2005).

These myths, as structures or machines – swarm-like in their internal disposition as well as in their outward workings – operate as networked objects, linked up to models of organisation that are equally connected, acting through constant negotiations, as movement (despite, paradoxically, the physical monumentality of those older technologies), by way of a distributed logic of control. Their functioning therefore suggests an openness or process of 'knotting into' (as Pynchon would say) between, for example, 'body' and environment, neither of which functions as a discrete entity. The network, in short, connects, but the question is whether – despite the objective of total control that comes from the God's-eye view – there is room for radical resistance inside this connectivity.

In itself, connectivity does not lead to political radicalism, as Eugene Thacker recognises when he asks whether as 'mutation in the body politic' connectivity might bring with it, automatically as it were, a collectivity (2004). From the start, though, Thacker acknowledges that such 'mutations are structurally innovative, but politically ambivalent'. As an expression of a state of emergency, a networked model is never anything but conservative; it generates a collectivity which is not defined through autonomous movement but instead directed towards sovereignty or, in other words, centralised command and control: a super-organism whose objective consists in preserving 'democracy' through its suspension – this form of government operates solely to freeze the status quo. If these phenomena continue to execute the powers of the sovereign – as part of the 'machine of command' (Hardt and Negri 2000: 393) – another tension emerges: between the dynamism of the swarm and a world frozen in its Cold War image.

The War of the Worlds ends with an imagination besieged by total death: 'And strangest of all it is to hold my wife's hand again, and to think that I have counted her, and that she has counted me, among the dead' (Wells 1993: 172). This sentiment occurs after an extraordinary passage in which the narrator describes the death-infestation of his dreams (shrouded bodies; 'distortions of humanity' (171)) that 'gutters' into waking life: 'we' so-called humans, 'busy multitudes' mocking life, are 'among the dead'. Wells's novel is less concerned, in the end, with what might invade from outside and more interested in 'our' insect-becoming and becoming-dead, which he articulates as a disintegration: 'losing coherency, losing shape and efficiency, [. . .] running at last in that swift liquefaction of the social body' (85). Insects, of course, function as memento mori; in Matthias Grünewald's painting *Dead Lovers*, for example, the corpses are 'visited' by insects that, in Nicky Coutts's reading, are invading forces that 'represent the act of breaking the body down, [. . .] causing the desired unity and wholeness of the body to fragment' (2006: 301). The insects are, in and of themselves, agents of chaos and impurity that assault codes of coherence and thereby also threaten 'our' ontological status as 'humans', premised, precisely, on myths of separation and integrity. 'We' are always caught in a process of metamorphosis that reveals 'our' impending formlessness and 'our' deadness; the insectile is about the recurring/returning impressions of thresholds crossed (over), an interiority – secret bones[4] or secret liquefaction – that gradually becomes visible, just as much as it is indicative of a momentum towards death which is at the same time always already present, within me, around me: I am among the dead.

Swarms and swarming are also occurrences associated with falling beyond borders; they are 'always living', always 'in process' (Thacker 2004). Thacker argues that these mutations 'create affects', which Jussi Parikka describes as a 'thinking beyond the signifier and the body as only an individualized entity', instead 'grasp[ing] the interconnected nature of bodies of various kinds' (2010: xxii). Affects, Parikka continues, 'are transitions, gateways, and passages between dimensions' (xxvi). Though separate, the individual units within a swarm work as autonomous wholes, as 'intelligent' systems that function in terms of temporal relations and affective assemblages. These 'living' or life-like networks 'intensify' or 'deintensify', 'understand' their surroundings: their engagements are variable as well as detached from a singular agent (Thacker 2004). Yet, this affective energy is also deeply uncanny and/or weird – because linked to softening (to recall Wells), to clotting into a mass, crossing over into other orders of being – so that the transitions and gateways that Parikka mentions also open up passages into the world of the dead.

In this vein, Vehlken argues that '[s]warms should be understood as *zootechnologies*', deriving

> less from *bios*, the concept of 'animated' life, than they do from *zoe*, the unanimated life of the swarm. *Zoe* manifests itself as a particular type of 'vivacity', for instance as the dynamic flurry of swarming individuals. It is a vivacity that lends itself to technological implementation, for it can be rendered just as well into ordered or disorderly movement. This capacity, in turn, is based on rules of motion and interaction that, once programmed and processed by computer technology, can produce seemingly lifelike behaviour among artificial agents. (2013: 113)

Following Vehlken, and also bearing in mind Laurence A. Rickels's work in *The Vampire Lectures*, I tend to see the undead everywhere and as central: technoculture conceals a death cult, whose 'vivacity' really only ever means death-transfiguration (Pynchon 1995: 197; Rickels 1999). If, then, swarming as a biological and/or techno-cultural/ontological phenomenon carries with it such attributes regardless of what it is associated with, this trajectory towards death – what Wells's narrator calls a 'mockery of life' – becomes even more evident in the context of networked war machines with which empire (that is, Pynchon's 'Deathkingdom' (1995: 857)) sustains itself. In *Gravity's Rainbow*, it is, weirdly, Walter Rathenau, the 'prophet and architect of the cartelized state', who elaborates on the notion of the death cult:

> You think you'd rather hear about what you call 'life': the growing, organic Kartell. But it's only another illusion. A very clever robot. The more dynamic it seems to you, the more deep and dead, in reality, it grows. [. . .] The persistence [. . .] of structures favouring death. Death converted into more death. (198)

Though linked to polymerisation and the 'new cosmic bombs' (198), cartelisation nonetheless remains the subject. 'Cartel' really is just another word for network, for swarming capitalism, whose realising, derealising movements through space, becoming and breaking apart, clearly function as constituent parts of a totalising system that, 'deep and dead', propels onward the technologies of market forces and of open-ended warfare. This affective relationship, consequently, between nodes or agents occurs as a '[structure] favouring death', the interconnectedness that Parikka notices as an effort to distribute death along with its dispersion of functioning. In circumstances such as these, Thacker's 'mutation in the body politic', which might imply alternatives – a radicalised political ontology, say – under different conditions, here falls short of arriving at anything other than business as usual: the catastrophe of the status quo (see Benjamin 1999: 473).

As such, and bearing in mind Hollingsworth's argument – the hive as indicative of a 'biology of seeing' (2001: xix) – the insectile here expresses an organisation whose swarm-like being perpetuates acts of violence: see, find, track, target, attack.[5] If, as Parikka argues, 'insect media' might yield a 'weird futurity' that emerges due to modes of perception that are radically other – to 'enter a plane of immanence and open oneself up to durations of animals, insects, stones, matter, technology, etc.' (Parikka 2010: 32, 74) – this ontology of enmeshment can, conversely, also function as abdication to, or immersion into, what remains a deep and (un)dead sovereign superpower. Such concerns – on the face of it a defence of 'man' against perforations – do not stem from a desire to maintain 'him', impermeable, at the centre of analysis or measure of all things, but emerge rather to query these weird assemblages as signs/things of a radically progressive or utopian politics arising through other ways of seeing, particularly if these vectors continue to give structure to a deathworld-empire already in existence. In many ways, then, this weirdness is deceptive, in that it is precisely not suggestive of new forms of embodiment: the 'mutations in the body politic' camouflage an unmoving consensus. What Parikka calls a genealogy of the weird in relation to the emergence of technics that, he argues, deterritorialises the 'human' body/eye (2010: 24, 18) only obliquely applies to the weapons systems under investigation in this essay. Safeguard – its name a clue to what it does; that is, to keep in a frozen state – executes manoeuvres that do not displace 'man' (despite its weirdness) but correct 'his' shortcomings. While, then, technology might not be 'human' but bestial (xix) – Parikka argues against the anthropocentric, narcissist model of technology as extension of 'man' proposed by Marshall McLuhan – it in this case seeks to create, through its networked systems, a closed world,[6] safeguarded, safeguarding 'man', over on 'this side', as ultimate reference point. Across, below, however – returning to the sovereign perspective that opens *The War of the Worlds* and defines drone warfare – civilians, as 'pre-insurgents', exist in an indeterminate state: they are recognised only as 'patterns of life', have tendencies, 'signatures', a trace that they might be or become members of a terrorist organisation (Chamayou 2013: 70).[7]

The 'logistics of perception', then, that sees, finds, tracks, targets, attacks and is carried out by solid bases and/or mobile systems (though the targets are different; Safeguard aims to strike at incoming missiles) is simultaneously weird and 'en-Weirds' or displaces the other, as well as totally conventional, holding fast images, politics, already long familiar. This mode of seeing might well be one of optical detachment – the radical other that 'scurries' (Tom Engelhardt quoted in Gregory 2011: 192) across the field of vision – but it is also one of immersion. To return to the concept of affect, technology as 'realm [. . .] of potentials and energetics' that folds insides and outsides (Parikka 2010: xx, xxv), the subject-operator of these devices, in such terms and with reference to McLuhan, is a gadget lover, integrated with this 'extension of himself' (McLuhan 2010: 45), servo-mechanical angel or insect, wasp-man, Brundle-fly (see David Cronenberg's *The Fly* (1986)). Derek Gregory, commenting on the 'deliberate inculcation of a "warrior culture" among UAV [Unmanned Aerial Vehicle] pilots', discusses a sense of intimacy between the 'pilot' wired to his machine and the electronic battlefield so frequently compared to the video games utilised in pre-deployment training: 'video games do *not* stage violence as passive spectacle; they are profoundly immersive, drawing players into their virtual worlds' (Gregory 2011: 197, 198). It is the contact with the machine, the close proximity to the war zone – that conversely can lead the gadget lover to experience the embrace as traumatic – which further defines this scopic regime: vision as immersion, technological extension as liquefaction but which hardens the integrated subject into sovereign, terminating being.[8] Insect media/technics, rather than offering up sights beyond the 'human', towards other forms of being, 'patterns of life' with which 'we' fold, here facet the world into 'our' angelic perspectives.

Eye, Fly

Jussi Parikka's *Insect Media* is about possibilities of seeing beyond anthropomorphic mutations of the world: compound eyes that inspire computations, digital design, navigational systems, space exploration. The seeing, or unseeing, non-human eye, though, is also one of armoured vision, even if this logistics of perception is actually blind. The war of the worlds that defensive formations indicate – recall Virilio, who describes a 'terrific atmospheric pressure' in *Bunker Archaeology* (1994: 39) – is an 'ecologized war' that began, according to Peter Sloterdijk, with gas warfare, involving the 'displacement of destructive action from the "system" (here: the enemy's body) onto his "environment"' (2009: 20, 22). War becomes about the means to create deadly climates, in more ways than one, environmental but also corporeal – an 'air force' or *Luft Waffe* that develops gas extermination, 'thermo-terrorism' (the Allied bombings of German cities between 1943 and 1945) and 'radioterrorism' inaugurated by the atom bomb (55–7). The latter is simultaneously a weapon of spectacular mass destruction and capable of imperceptible damage in sleeper cells or that gradually manifests itself on the surface of the skin. Such an environment is totally catastrophic, a 'phenomenal catastrophe' that is at the same time a 'catastrophe of the phenomenal' (59), but which already exists prior to the weapon's detonation.

In Pynchon's *Gravity's Rainbow*, the Nazi *Vergeltungswaffe Zwei* or V2 remains elusive, a clue to 'how invisible is the act of death': it is an invading spirit, a 'ghost in the sky' which avoids obstruction once in flight (1995: 25, 48). The novel is, in many ways, concerned with programmed commands engineered into the subject or slave – starved, traumatised, shocked, castrated, sent over 'into one of the transmarginal phases, past borders of their waking selves' (48) – in order to try and predict the trajectory of the missile. Slothrop's particular endowment is a hard-on, 'an instrument installed, wired by Them into his body as a colonial outpost' (285); the strategy refers to the humming erections of defensive mechanisms seeking to find shelter, an effort that began by seeking to trace the missile's paraboloid descent to its target. If the 'dawn' of the nuclear age, the Trinity detonation on 16 July 1945, produced an aesthetics linked to glass spheres – at Alamogordo, sand and the remainders of the bomb's metal tower superheated into a dish of green glass – then efforts to raise a defensive perimeter are frequently expressed in those same terms: englobing technologised fictions in which the nuclear device functions at once as weapon and armour. As boundary-breaching devices, nuclear weapons obliterate, amongst other things, the distinctions between offence and defence – over on 'our side', in official discourse, they only ever serve to ward off, not attack – while the visible and invisibility (the bodies they penetrate) exist as a continuum, the domain of the seen haunted by that which eludes it, which lies concealed, threatening to erupt from beyond the horizon.[9]

The manipulation of air – and therefore of the conditions of existence – yields 'death-worlds' that become unliveable: it is the potential destruction of the 'silent' means of life (air) through 'atmoterrorist' warfare that leads to a consumption of security in which the state of being can only ever be determined as a 'being-in' the world defined by encapsulations – integrity as a closed system (Sloterdijk 2009: 28, 23, 108). This state at once refers to both generalised circumstances – life in an atmosphere that still allows breathing but whose silence and innocence can no longer be assumed – and tactics of retreat into privileged, air-conditioned (glass) spheres (see Pynchon 1995: 857) that purport to function as 'life pods' whose architectures invariably fold, literally or metaphorically, around the ballistic missile. The art of defensive space-building, Cold War-style, began with the V2, but dream-designs are, in a way, 'phase spaces', a term perverted through its usage here. A continual, unbounded, open-ended spatiality, characterised through interdependence and flow (see Jones 2009), phase space becomes in this context a description that refers, yet again, to the momentum of technicity. These shielding projects, technicised spatialities, might stabilise for a while, but never for long – whatever mechanisms of defence are realised (if at all), once operational, they are invariably unable to cope with the latest 'generation' of intercontinental ballistic missiles (ICBMs). Each new design 'restructures' older technologies; each updated conception is also an archive in which previous incarnations survive: a 'transparent earth' approached by 'Zeus-like' (Bishop 2011: 280) formations that anticipate (total, dream-like) safeguarding.

In this vein, Nike-Zeus, a 'three-staged, solid-propellant missile' that comprises 'advanced radar equipment and communications links to tie the subsystems together' (Baucom 1992: 6–7),[10] gave way to Nike-X, a method of layered defence employing a phased-array radar apparatus, which, by the mid-1960s, was modified into Sentinel – all of which exist in terms of technologised networks or cybernetic systems as 'multitudes' of defensive arrangements executing a politics of preservation. Sentinel, to keep guard, is about keeping secret watch, but perception really means detection or a vision that is no longer simply biological: the 'catastrophe of the phenomenal' requires extra-sensory, 'synesthetic' tracking devices like radar, seeking to turn everything into surface/glass, though there is, as ever, a paradox at work because a surface is 'de facto [. . .] reliant on some other entity', always out of reach (Bishop 2011: 273, 276). The 'Looking Glass', code name for Strategic Air Command's constantly airborne craft (operational twenty-four hours a day for twenty-nine years, until 1990), has been replaced by networks of remote sensing, only some of which are visually oriented, yet the articulations of such networks – visions of sealed environments – nonetheless employ metaphors of seeing through weird eye-like organs. If the rocket, in Pynchon's novel, is an angel of death, then anti-missile missile installations are 'anti-angels', whose impassive figures overlook an illimitable war zone, a field of operations that exists outside the bounds of limited 'human' sensory perceptions; these anti-angels, though, connected as they may be, retain (safeguard) a deadly totality at their centre.

Weapons systems are sighting devices; in *War and Cinema*, Virilio argues that 'a supply of images' functions as the 'equivalent of an ammunition supply' sketching out 'a strategy of *global vision*' that, as much as it is heavily technologised, also refers back to a 'Western gun-duel, where firepower equilibrium is less important than reflex response' in an air war that is conducted as an 'optical, or electro-optical, confrontation' (1989: 1, 2): precise vision – eye-like but eyeless – leading to precision strikes. Virilio notes that 'the act of taking aim is a geometrification of looking, a way of technically aligning ocular perception along an imaginary axis that used to be known in French as the "faith line" (*ligne de foi*)' (3) – which, in time, instigates that 'catastrophe of the phenomenal' in terms of the capacities, and also 'faith', of 'human' perception. Virilio takes this 'faith' in terms of a loss – of 'interpretative subjectivity' (3) in favour of a supposed objectivity. Even in moments like these, however, which are still indicative of his own faith (in a 'human' subject that somehow exists outside/without technologisation), Virilio tends to avoid any references to what Nietzsche calls the 'illusory consciousness' of the eye gliding along the surface seeing things then 'enclosed' as 'truth' (Nietzsche 1999: 142). The point is that this 'science of "visionics"' (Virilio 1989: 3) (to see through sound, tele-technology) brings up Sloterdijk's 'new dimension of latency' (Sloterdijk 2009: 58) – erupting into view in the aftermath of Hiroshima and Nagasaki – which reveals, but at the same time keeps hidden, the electromagnetic, radiological conditions of existence and extermination: truth is surface, and surface, as Ryan Bishop notes, 'presumes [. . .] depth' (2011: 272). This crisis of seeing also prompts a crisis of being: a 'living' space can be made unbreathable, imperceptibly; being-in consequently means a 'breathing-onto-death' (Sloterdijk 2009: 42), so that half-life needs to be safeguarded by watching machines whose militarised vision is less non-human than it is super-human. 'Anti-angels' supplement a failing 'human' vision to achieve full spectrum dominance: Safeguard is a concrete expression of a desire to adopt perspectives that surpass the functions of the 'human' eye through the seeing yet simultaneously blind eyes of an anti-missile missile/anti-angel angel system looking out into a world of instantaneous threat. This intensive fly-like gaze – insects and angels form 'gracious' orders, 'wholeness, and divinity', overriding 'our' limitations (Gass 1969: 169; Parikka 2010: 4–6, 38)[11] – effectuated electronically, transposes a compulsion to perceive the latent dimensions of the earth as total vision-field through vantage points that are and aren't alien at the same time. Strange because techno-ontologically weird, that is, insectile, this installation is nevertheless a manifestation of a super-human will to power against an enemy that is, after all, so frequently configured as weird, sub-human, inhuman, formless pod-people only gradually taking on the features,

Thing-like, of something strange made almost familiar. Safeguard is not indicative of a becoming-insect; instead, it is the dreaming subject that seeks to extend 'his' failing senses via a technologised vision that, while approximating the 'eye-pearls' (Connor 2006: 82) of insects, is entirely in the service of a cyborg ontology retaining 'man', and ballistic missile, at its heart.

If Safeguard is a sight machine, it remains, now, as a relic of a still (more or less) material technoculture that is disappearing: war, while conducted under the pretence of unsanctioned nuclear weapons acquisition, is carried out through drone warfare, radiating 'quilted images', 'tiled mosaics' (Gregory 2011: 193) – the art of war – back to command centres defining the universe. A system of illumination, in terms of a light that might not be atomic but stays catastrophic – visibility means death; 'what is perceived is already lost' (Virilio 1989: 5) – drones, like ballistic machinery, are the products of an act of gadget love: an integration with machinery engaged in orgies of war. In *Gravity's Rainbow*, circulations of affect, love and death, yield maps of tenderness and hardness (Latour 2002: 140), but Safeguard, networked as it is, is nonetheless mythic, immense, a monument to a superpower progressively disembodied. The dream of interconnectivity at present – a dream, still, of total war and total vision – is the drone, which designates a remotely piloted aircraft or unmanned aerial vehicle that is, however, not 'unmanned' but functions, as Derek Gregory argues, as an 'interpellation' (2011: 197) in which the subject lovingly integrates with the machine and virtual battlefield. The device itself is not passive but, according to Jordan Crandall, an agent, a description that 'situates [it] in terms of [its] performative functions or roles'; the rescue operation, assembling the drone back together after its crash,

> suggests that what these actors *are* is what they *do* in the context of the environments in which they bond and circulate, and it defines this activity as that of *affiliation*. It describes the relational structures and organizing principles through which actors are coordinated and combined together in affiliations at various scales, magnitudes, speeds, and levels of complexity, such that they gain sufficient stability to be maintained. (Crandall 2011)

As a networked entity, the drone, though 'manned' and operating at a distance (out of the sky), acts in a functional circle of love and death distribution, an 'affiliation' that keeps the guiding/operating 'man' in place, in a loving embrace: the 'weird' futurity is the face/no face of American war machines, the impassive face of the fly. In Afghanistan, villagers have their own name for Predator drones, *unki*, meaning the buzzing of flies (Karzai 2013), an army of flies for which the proximity, and not the distance, of the enemy/non-combatant – 'obdurately Other' (Gregory 2011: 201) – threatens a world order 'friendly' to United States security principles and swarm capitalism.

Notes

1. This description comes from Tom Hillenbrand's futurist crime thriller *Drohnenland* (2014: 87).
2. For moon insects and glass bees, see Jünger 1960: 89.
3. Christopher Hollingsworth talks about the bee as 'synecdoche for social perfection'; the lone bee always provokes questions about the rest of them (2001: 23, 7).
4. In 'The Order of Insects', William Gass writes of a woman getting progressively enthralled by dead bugs she finds in her carpet: she collects them, enshrines them, leading her to thinking about her own corporeality which only in death reveals her bones, 'showing last', when everything else has already decayed. Bugs, though, decay from the inside out: the shell remains, perfectly preserved, dries out, light (1969: 166).
5. This description actually applies specifically to the drone; see Chamayou 2013: 71.
6. The reference, here, is to Paul N. Edwards's *The Closed World: Computers and the Politics of Discourse in Cold War America* (1996) but also to Marshall McLuhan's *Understanding Media*, where he writes about Narcissus adapting 'to his extension of himself' and becoming a 'closed system' (2010: 45).
7. On the indeterminacy of civilians, see also Anderson 2011.
8. The reference, here, is to Jonathan Mostow's *Terminator 3: The Rise of the Machines* (DVD, Sony Pictures Home Entertainment, 2003).
9. This discussion is heavily indebted to Ryan Bishop's 2011 'Project "Transparent Earth" and the Autoscopy of Aerial Targeting: The Visual Geopolitics of the Underground' (see, in particular, pp. 275–6).
10. Nike-Zeus itself developed out of an earlier programme simply titled Zeus, a system intended to obstruct bombers and air-breathing rockets, such as cruise missiles.
11. For more on insects as anti-angels, see Connor 2006: 15, 166.

References

Agamben, Giorgio (2005), *State of Exception*, Chicago: University of Chicago Press.

Anderson, Ben (2011), 'Facing the Future Enemy: US Counterinsurgency Doctrine and the Pre-Insurgent', *Theory, Culture & Society* 28(7/8): 216–40.

Baucom, Donald R. (1992), *The Origins of SDI, 1944–1983*, Lawrence: University of Kansas Press.

Benjamin, Walter (1999), *The Arcades Project*, Cambridge, MA: Belknap Press of Harvard University Press.

Bishop, Ryan (2011), 'Project "Transparent Earth" and the Autoscopy of Aerial Targeting: The Visual Geopolitics of the Underground', *Theory, Culture & Society* 28(7/8): 270–86.

Chamayou, Grégoire (2013), *Théorie du drone*, Paris: La Fabrique.

Connor, Steven (2006), *Fly*, London: Reaktion.

Coutts, Nicky (2006), 'Portraits of the Nonhuman', in Eric C. Brown (ed), *Insect Poetics*, Minneapolis: University of Minnesota Press, pp. 298–318.

Crandall, Jordan (2011), 'Ontologies of the Wayward Drone: A Salvage Operation', *C-Theory*, 2 November, <http://www.ctheory.net/articles.aspx?id=693> (last accessed 8 February 2016).

Cronenberg, David (dir.) (2001), *The Fly*, DVD, Twentieth Century Fox.

Derrida, Jacques (1980), 'The Law of Genre', *Critical Inquiry* 7(1): 55–81.

Derrida, Jacques (2003), 'Autoimmunity: Real and Symbolic Suicides', in Giovanni Borradori (ed.), *Philosophy in a Time of Terror*, Chicago: University of Chicago Press, pp. 85–136.

Edwards, Paul N. (1996), *The Closed World: Computers and the Politics of Discourse in Cold War America*, Cambridge, MA: MIT Press.

Freud, Sigmund (2001), 'The Uncanny', in *The Standard Edition of the Complete Psychological Works of Sigmund Freud*, vol. 17, ed. James Strachey, London: Vintage, pp. 217–56.

Gass, William (1969), 'The Order of Insects', in *In the Heart of the Heart of the Country*, New York: Harper & Row, pp. 163–71.

Gregory, Derek (2011), 'From a View to a Kill: Drones and Late Modern War', *Theory, Culture & Society* 28(7/8): 188–215.

Hardt, Michael, and Antonio Negri (2000), *Empire*, Cambridge, MA: Harvard University Press.

Hillenbrand, Tom (2014), *Drohnenland*, Cologne: Kiepenheuer & Witsch.

Hollingsworth, Christopher (2001), *Poetics of the Hive*, Iowa City: University of Iowa Press.

Jones, Martin (2009), 'Phase Space: Geography, Relational Thinking and Beyond', *Progress in Human Geography* 33(4): 487–506.

Jünger, Ernst (1960), *Gläserne Bienen*, Stuttgart: Rororo.

Jünger, Ernst (2004), *Storm of Steel*, trans. Michael Hofmann, London: Penguin.

Karzai, Anas (2013), 'Drone Warfare Seminar: Anas Karzai', Pacific Centre for Technology and Culture, 20 June, <http://pactac.net/2013/06/drone-warfare-seminar-anas-karzai/#more-865> (last accessed 8 February 2016).

Latour, Bruno (2002), *Aramis or the Love of Technology*, Cambridge, MA: Harvard University Press.

McLuhan, Marshall (2010), *Understanding Media*, London and New York: Routledge.

Miéville, China (2011), 'M. R. James and the Quantum Vampire: Weird; Hauntological: Versus and/or and and/or or?', *Weird Fiction Review*, 29 November, <http://weirdfictionreview.com/2011/11/m-r-james-and-the-quantum-vampire-by-china-mieville> (last accessed 8 February 2016).

Mostow, Jonathan (dir.) (2003), *Terminator 3: The Rise of the Machines*, DVD, Sony Pictures Home Entertainment.

Nietzsche, Friedrich (1999), 'On Truth and Lying in a Non-Moral Sense', in *The Birth of Tragedy and Other Writings*, ed. Raymond Geuss and Ronald Spiers, Cambridge: Cambridge University Press, pp. 139–53.

Parikka, Jussi (2010), *Insect Media: An Archaeology of Animals and Technology*, Minneapolis: University of Minnesota Press.

Pynchon, Thomas (1995 [1973]), *Gravity's Rainbow*, New York: Penguin.

Rickels, Laurence A. (1999), *The Vampire Lectures*, Minneapolis: University of Minnesota Press.

Sloterdijk, Peter (2009), *Terror from the Air*, New York: Semiotext(e).

Thacker, Eugene (2004), 'Networks, Swarms, Multitudes', Part One, *C-Theory*, 18 May, <http://www.ctheory.net/articles.aspx?id=422> (last accessed 8 February 2016).

Vehlken, Sebastian (2013), 'Zootechnologies: Swarming as a Cultural Critique', *Theory, Culture & Society* 30(6): 110–31.

Virilio, Paul (1989), *War and Cinema: The Logistics of Perception*, London: Verso.

Virilio, Paul (1994), *Bunker Archaeology*, trans. George Collins, Princeton: Princeton Architectural Press.

Wells, H. G. (1993 [1898]), *The War of the Worlds*, London: Everyman.

Chapter 13

Overt Research

Neal White and John Beck

Neal White is an artist whose work is broadly concerned with the production of knowledge and the physical and immaterial spaces simultaneously occupied and generated by various forms of scientific, technological, military and artistic research. Many of his projects involve investigations of institutional spaces, including archives, laboratories and installations, and the practices and values that produce them. White's work, then, is often positioned inside, adjacent to, or even resolutely outside (in the case of projects concerned with securitised or secret sites) wider networks of scientific and technological research. Key to White's work is collaboration and experiment, practices that are fundamental to science, technology and engineering, and increasingly a dominant aspect of contemporary art. Since 2004, his collaborative practice with the Office of Experiments has led a series of projects focused on experimental forms of research. In the following discussion with John Beck, White discusses the notion of art-as-research, the importance of collaboration and site-specificity, and a number of ways in which his practice has engaged with the legacies of Cold War infrastructure in Europe and the UK.

John Beck: Could you tell me something about the Office of Experiments? What is it and what does it do?

Neal White: The Office of Experiments (OoE) is a collective that reflects the shift that some artists have made away from individual studio practice and toward collaboration, not just with other artists but with others who are often concealed in the process of art making. The OoE is a network, research structure, production space, and a site for experimental encounters. It was conceived during a project with Danish architects N55 in 2004, and then formalised as a non-legal entity using the ideas of artist John Latham on event structures and the work of historian of science Hans-Jörg Rheinberger.

JB: Perhaps we could unpack these influences a little. First of all, could you say a little more about the influence of Latham?

NW: John Latham was a British conceptual artist (1922–2006) and I met him in 2003, after an introduction concerning my critical interest in the relationships between artists engaging with power structures in science. He was strongly taken by a book I had published with author Lawrence Norfolk that revisits the famous forty-five frames of W. K. L. Dickson's *Record of a Sneeze* (1894) using laser, video and computer technologies. Dickson was the inventor of the Kinetograph and the book was concerned with linking two moments in time, one hundred years apart (Norfolk and White 2002).

Latham had for many years been interested in the conceptual framing of time, ranging from quantum physics to an analysis of the material nature of the 'object'. He was interested specifically in how all objects, organisms, human or geomorphic structures are created from, but return to, matter, at varying durations. At the smallest scale – that is, the smallest scale measurable by science – is quantum physics breaking time down into the smallest moments; at the largest is cosmology, the duration of the universe and the Big Bang. The relationship among these different variations or 'time-bases' is what unites art and ideas in religious and scientific belief systems. Latham applied his ideas about time to thinking about form and also broader social structures.

JB: Is this what Latham called 'Flat Time'? The idea is to shift from 'space-based' to 'time-based' thinking, so instead of thinking about 'objects' or 'things', the emphasis is on 'fields' and 'events'. The smallest unit is what Latham calls the 'least event'; at the macro level is 'what is the case' – that is, everything. I have to admit that I find Latham's explanation of these ideas quite hard to follow, but the idea of moving from the 'least event' to the constellation of micro-events as an 'event structure' seems provocative and makes sense in terms of Latham's interest in taking art out of the studio or gallery and into other contexts where particular event structures can be examined. Art becomes a kind of experiment with everyday life.

NW: Artists could move out of the studio and into the context of institutions, the landscape, the political sphere, by examining and thinking through the concepts of time he had developed. In 1966, Latham co-founded the Artist Placement Group (APG), and along with a group of other influential artists of this period (including Barbara Steveni, Barry Flanagan, Stuart Brisley, David Toop and Ian

Breakwell) set out to place artists inside organisations. In 1989, the group folded and became O+I (Organisation and Imagination), and following John's death in 2006 I stepped in as one of the directors of this with Barbara Steveni.

Latham was very influential to my thinking about the OoE, as he was specifically interested in my work inside scientific institutions, which was often critical of the thinking and political construction of science and its power relationships with others.

JB: The APG was also important in challenging the position of the artist as a kind of prime mover, wasn't it? Latham described the artist more modestly as an 'incidental person', another aspect of the event structure or field – not without influence but no more or less so than any other node in the structure. This is a very different conception of art in the workplace or in other institutions than the common contemporary notion of the 'artist in residence', which is so often restricted to observation and lending organisations a patina of cultural legitimacy. The APG idea of placement seems more like a provocation than good PR for the institutions involved. At one point, Latham suggests that artist placement is intended to 'generate maximum public involvement and maximum enthusiasm' so as to 'release the impulse to act' (1986: 59). The 'incidental person' here sounds more like a provocateur. But how does Rheinberger fit into all of this?

NW: In 2005, following a research project at the National Institute for Medical Research that examined self-experimentation, a researcher at the Max Planck Institute for the Study of Science and Ideas invited me to present a performance at a workshop in Berlin. This is when I came across Rheinberger, who was director of the Max Planck Institute. After reading the proceedings from a conference Rheinberger organised called 'The Shape of Experiment', I realised that a connection between the event-driven nature of experimentation and the discovery of knowledge was not simply a scientific development but had parallels with Latham's own observations concerning the artist's role in society. The 'Shape of the Experiment' conference addressed taking the experiment out of the laboratory, just as Latham and APG had argued for taking art out of the studio. I started to use Rheinberger's work to develop a model of experimentation, not least because his work on 'epistemic things' (see Rheinberger 1997) provides a bridge to Latham's most critical thinking on how institutions are shaped by social, technical, personal and political systems, and also how unexpected events are part of any experimental system. It meant it was possible to imagine event structures or experiments in relation to one another, which significantly guided my practice towards a more collaborative approach.

JB: Rheinberger's notion of the epistemic thing or object seems provocative not least because it is concerned with what we don't know rather than what we do know. His point is that, as he says somewhere, science is an '*exploratory* attitude toward knowledge about the world' (2005: 409) – not about discovery or revelation, with their roots in theology, but about exploring the instability and incompleteness of what there is to know. Taken this way, scientific research seems to be as much about investigating research itself – about grasping how the processes and procedures of knowledge production do not exist wholly prior to investigation or experiment but emerge in relation to the object under analysis. Within an artistic context, this mode of enquiry seems to position the artist and the artwork as provisional, contingent participants in a process whereby the material site or object of investigation shapes and is shaped by the dynamic context of ongoing investigation.

An approach like this does sound more properly 'experimental' than what is often termed experimental in art. One of the problems, presumably, is that since the method of research is contingent, it becomes quite hard to describe the work itself or contain it within the conventions of art practice. Since the visibility of so much art is dependent on signature styles or categories of work, the idea of art-as-research that is genuinely about not knowing in advance what it is that is being investigated must position the practice in a precarious relationship to the broader structures of the art world. Is that a fair comment? Or perhaps there is no need for there to be a secure relationship to the art world?

NW: My interest in Rheinberger's description of an epistemic thing is the thing itself, that which is not the experiment's technical apparatus, but processes which are to some extent reproducible within what he terms an experimental system. As you state, this, he argues, leads to unexpected events, and discovery. To return from epistemology to something more grounded, when I asked Rheinberger about the relationship between art- and science-as-research, he emphasised their root in search, and that both the artist and the scientist look for resistance within the materials they use. This describes the process of making art in a way that is experimental, without a singular style emerging – it is a process that works with intuitive logic and often requires post-rationalisation.

JB: You seem interested in the whole idea of organisations (offices, groups, centres, etc.) that have a semi- or quasi-official ring to them. Is the idea of giving your collaborations a particular name part of a strategy of effacing the individual, like taking on the anonymity of the laboratory worker?

NW: In so much as the idea of the individual artist continues to feature in the culture as a romantic figure, yes, both Latham and the broader move towards what Gerald Raunig calls 'instituent' practices influenced a range of artists who realised that the individual producing objects or artefacts alone was the initial condition required by the system of spectacle and commodity exchange.

JB: I guess there is a broader context in which the collective project overrides the claims of individual 'creativity' – I'm thinking of educational environments like the Bauhaus and Black Mountain College, where engineers, designers and artists of various kinds collaborated, though the nature of these institutions still tended toward a hierarchical structure with 'star' staff members. The explorative dimension of Bauhaus and Black Mountain pedagogy, though, is also reproduced in Cold War-era collaborations (if that's the right word) among artists, universities and technology companies. There is György Kepes's Center for Advanced Visual Studies (founded in 1967) at MIT, where Jack Burnham and Stan Vanderbeek, among others, were brought in to work with MIT's military-industrial hardware. Kepes had previously worked with Moholy-Nagy in Berlin and London before joining him at the New Bauhaus in Chicago. Then there's Billy Klüver, Fred Waldhauer, Robert Rauschenberg and Robert Whitman's organisation Experiments in Art and Technology (E.A.T.), started in 1967, with its links to Bell Laboratories and IBM. Or the Art and Technology Program at the Los Angeles County Museum of Art, which ran between 1967 and 1971 and involved all sorts of artists, scientists and heavyweight Cold War players, from RAND's Herman Kahn to William Hayward Pickering, the director of the Jet Propulsion Laboratory at CalTech. These projects are all part of the techno-utopian wing of US Cold War thinking, where, often, huge sums of government money underwrite all manner of exploratory, interdisciplinary work. The assumption, I suppose, is that some of this R&D will yield new modes of warfare and new ways of defeating communism. The problem, of course, as many noted even at the time, is that art has become absorbed into the structure of the militarised state.

Presumably, the OoE does not have this sort of aspiration, but do you think there is a danger that you might simply be reproducing the form and 'look' of managerial control the work is concerned to critique? In other words, is there an element of the work that falls into the trap of what Benjamin Buchloh called 'the aesthetic of administration'?

NW: This history is very important indeed. I studied coding and technology-based approach to art at Middlesex University Lansdowne Centre for Electronic Arts. Here I became aware of the centres, initiatives and approaches you mention and I became particularly fascinated by them. E.A.T. in particular had links, through Klüver, to the Artist Placement Group (1966–1989). So yes, the Cold War practices which were highly experimental across such boundaries did have an influence, but they omitted in their adoption of R&D knowledge production to account for the important critical turning point in art that took a long look at such relationships; not only the APG, but including groups such as Critical Art Ensemble.

Of course, within the title of the OoE there is an element of humour in the use of official-sounding titles, but there is also a serious point to be made here. The important aspect of Buchloh's argument is not so much his critique of conceptual art but how the spaces art occupies can become restrictive spaces of management and administration. This is worth discussing because the conventional space of art – the gallery or museum – is so controlled; the artist relinquishes so much power. Anything with potential critical impact made in this space can, as a result, be neutralised. Conceptual art's institutional critique is key to the kind of thinking about art as social practice that led to organisations like the APG.

The period in American art Buchloh addresses in the 'aesthetic of administration' essay marks a key moment – a shift from the aesthetics of the (minimalist and post-minimalist) object to the work of art as a non-visual thing emphasising, in Buchloh's words, 'structural contingency and contextuality, addressing crucial questions of presentation and distribution, of audience and authorship' (1990: 123). Buchloh's article – which is, incidentally, almost entirely US focused – might be read as a moment of reflection at a point just after the dismantling of the Berlin Wall and the beginning of the end of the Cold War. In the subsequent twenty-five years, we have seen an overwhelming instrumentalisation of culture, art and society that has been driven, ironically, by the bureaucratic values and militarised fantasies put into place by the Cold War middle class: militarised cybernetic visions of a technological future that include the internet, globalisation, the monetisation of every area of life, audit culture, and so on. Buchloh's attention to the aesthetic of administration senses this development, I think. His point about the tautology of art – art that can only be about art – and the aesthetics of administration are means through which we might begin to understand the rise of a certain neoliberal sensibility.

JB: So is there an alternative way of thinking about collaborative, interdisciplinary art-as-research that neither becomes uncritically absorbed into the institutional framework (as in Kepes's CAVS) nor flirts with the 'look' of power – that is, gestures toward criticality but is in fact secretly in love with the enemy?

NW: In terms of an alternative to the neoliberal, bureaucratic direction so much culture has taken, Lucy Lippard's early work on the dematerialisation of the art object, for me, provides a strong historical reference point. Lippard's influential book *Six Years*, first published in 1973, is important partly because she takes an international view, placing US art in the context of artists' groups such as the Argentinian Rosario Group, the Situationists and the APG. Lippard's reading of the challenge to institutionalised art posed at this moment recognises the importance of the political climate and the counterculture to what is sometimes framed as the merely formal dimension of conceptual art.

JB: So reading the various challenges to art as an institution during this period as part of a broader challenge to Cold War institutions and their normative authority (the valorisation of consensus, compartmentalisation, bureaucracy, and so on) situates the radical art of the time as embroiled in Cold War politics – the assault on the art world as the producer of luxury goods for a politically reactionary official culture.

NW: It seems that the countercultural forces at play here speak directly to the questions which surround a Cold War legacy, one in which capitalism and the market are not embraced but instead utilised as a field against which the commodity or space of art is tested.

JB: This is where Latham and Rheinberger come in. Could we discuss a bit further the notion of research as a practice? What distinguishes what you are doing from some previous process-oriented practices, it seems to me, is that the self-reflexivity involved in examining method does not become inward-looking and self-legitimating. In other words, experimental research, as you understand it, is not another way of describing formalism. Rather, you seem more interested in plugging art into broader structures of power and knowledge production – scientific, corporate or military – so that proximity generates new information. Does that sound right? So, could you explain a bit further what the nature of the research is that you conduct? What methods do you use and what guides your explorations?

NW: Apart from what I have outlined already, as an artist, I have always been interested in our attraction to different forms of knowledge, which includes both academic and emotional intelligence. I am interested because I find both difficult, so after working as a visual artist, and then observing the power that is bestowed on those with certain forms of academic knowledge and institutional affiliations, I became interested in how this world was configured in terms of its epistemic concerns, but also the practices it values. Why, for example, do we in the West think that science will find all the answers when, arguably, scientific progress as realised by an industrial-scale economy has also produced so many of the problems – pollution, climate change, for example?

JB: This was the crux of the Cold War dilemma – the science that invented the bomb then had to find a way of managing it. The creation of the problem provides plenty of work for the same people in finding a solution. I suppose one of the stories often told about military research is that it produces all sorts of collateral benefits for civil society as experimental research invents new materials, processes and gadgets. The mistake might be in understanding invention as progress – new things are invented (as opposed to discovered; I'm aware of Rheinberger's resistance to the notion of discovery in science) all the time but configuring this process as an ascent is to give a narrative direction that is not necessarily there. Surely it is possible to invent things that are regressive, or, ditching the linear entirely, that occur along multiple timelines and across multiple scales? Thought of this way, science isn't progressing (though even Kuhn's notion of the paradigm shift maintains for science some sort of narrative structure), but scientific knowledge, along with everything else, is happening, interacting with materials and generating new, often unanticipated forms of understanding and organisation. The progress narrative is what continues to enable those unfazed by climate change to argue that science will figure it out, as if science is always on the upward trajectory, out of trouble and into a better future.

NW: I started looking at knowledge structures, particularly spaces in which knowledge is created, as objects of enquiry, to think of ways to observe and study them. In this respect, as an artist I have sought to engage with science. However, rather than helping science to engage a wider public, an approach to art making which has been rightly criticised as engaging in the spectacle, with art as part of science's public relations wing, I have sought instead to open up for debate questions that concern me, and which science is not always dealing with. The opportunities afforded to artists since the late 1990s have allowed some artists inside the secret spaces of science, the heterotopic or hidden places, such as laboratories that clearly represent the enclosures of science.

JB: Do you think the end of the Cold War had anything to do with this opening up of previously closed worlds in science and industry? There is certainly, in a lot of landscape photography produced during the 1990s on nuclear and other military-industrial sites, a sense that these images could not have been made only a few years previously. I'm wondering if there wasn't a ten-year window, between the dissolution of the Soviet Union and 9/11, when certain places were, if not open, at least less shut off than they had been before?

NW: Yes, I do agree that photographers in particular had found a new landscape and sites around which to base their practices. This initial fieldwork is fascinating, but specifically in relation to the other historical centres you mentioned; in the case of CAVS and E.A.T., the artist also started to work with the engineers inside the military-industrial lab, and these early approaches, which also led to the first wave of media art labs in the 1980s and 1990s, largely inside universities, followed this model. To some extent, so did I. My first project inside a scientific institution (1998) was at the Sanger Centre in Cambridge, run by the Medical Research Council, and it was an important part of the Human Genome Mapping Project. My knowledge of code at the time helped to provide a first step inside enclosures like these as it was something I had in common with scientists.

However, once inside, I found a space which, as Rheinberger, after Latour, describes, was driven by egos, power, insecurities. In other words, the activity moves from artistic engagement with the pure subjects of science, its empirical positioning, toward a social analysis whereby the question of how we construct knowledge – including the political, social and moral dimensions of research itself – is questioned. This in turn gives us another view into the power of science, due to its scale and status. So a research journey starts with an interest in experimental sites, and then the experimental, before moving forward into trying to understand what the epistemic impulse might be. There has been a great deal of work published now around artistic research as a method, and I am still greatly concerned with this, both inside and outside the context of a university. Henk Borgdorff, Stephen Scrivener and Ute Meta Bauer, et al., have drawn in figures such as Hito Steyerl to broad conversations about research within the discipline of art (see Schwab 2013).

However, art's relationship to the academy remains under close scrutiny and also under administrative pressure – to get the political conditions right. Outside of the university context, then, I am interested in art making as a form of fieldwork, which does not draw upon ethnographic or auto-ethnographic methods prescribed by the academy, but also moves into the domain of life, into experiences for art where legal, political and analytic approaches lose their grip, where things are irrational, unethical and messy. To me, this means we need multiple methods of exploring the world around us, with different registers, temporalities and languages – beyond the verbal, beyond the academic grip of knowledge. Whether the academy can cope with this position is open for discussion.

JB: Well, one of the assumptions behind what you are saying is that art sits somewhere outside the academy. Yes, there is plenty of art that exists happily without that kind of institutional framework, but one of the consequences of the absorption of art and design programmes into universities, along with the emergence of the practice-based PhD and the application of other conventional university models to art and design, is surely that the nature of art and design has become remodelled according to its new institutional setting. We might also argue that there is plenty of scientific research done outside of universities, though it might nevertheless require some sort of institutional validation through, say, peer review, that draws it back into an academic environment. I suppose what I'm saying is that there can be no clear distinction between academic and non-academic research, art and academy – one exerts a pressure on the other.

There is also, of course, the question of funding. Non-academic art may draw some of its funding from government (such as through the Arts Council) or through patronage, but these avenues are no less part of what forms the work and sets its limits than the boundaries and definitions set by university research agendas and curricular. Put briefly, I don't think the academic grip on knowledge is quite as strong as you imply. On the other hand, there is no doubt that the financial and administrative constraints placed upon universities, not least the increasing pressure to explain and justify research projects according to instrumental criteria, present a serious challenge to the kind of open-ended investigations you are interested in.

NW: I think that the points you make are right, in that the academy, like many other contexts, shapes the production of art. If research-driven practices are contributing to a body of knowledge, then for artists the questions are shaped by art practice, historical and present wherever it happens, of course. As Henk Borgdorff mentions in his own analysis, the epistemological grasp of academic research here is indeed weak, as emerging research practices less easily become instruments for measurement, for example. They often also lie outside of the restrictions of, for example, ethics committees, even if they follow a moral and ethical approach, whilst art remains philosophically engaged both within and outside the academy, examining the spaces and gaps it can occupy, topologically speaking. Artists in respect to the academy seem to create problem spaces, antagonism, into which many are entangled. There is much value to this activity, which is increasingly being recognised.

JB: The necessarily secretive nature of much military research conducted during the Cold War and since has produced, outside those agencies, a kind of paranoid sensibility that is suspicious of anything that is not out in the open. There is, of course, a whole popular culture surrounding secret military projects that registers a mixture of fascination and fear: the classic response to the sublime. At odds with the notion of covert operations is your notion of 'overt research'. Could you say something about that?

NW: As I have mentioned, I had an interest in sites and places of knowledge, some of which I had gained access to through the art/science initiatives that sprung up in the 1990s. It was fascinating to be inside places like the Human Genome Mapping Project, but I was struck by two aspects: first, the privilege afforded to artists, and second, the scale of the projects at hand – their interconnections and the sheer size of the infrastructure. It struck me that whilst a specific lab is not easily accessible to all, it is for the artist socially and epistemologically porous, interconnected and, in that respect, massive, global – a postmodern space of the experiment rendered across multiple spaces. So in starting to think about how the Office of Experiments might begin to elaborate work in this network, we started to examine, with the help of geographers led by Gail Davies from University College London, the nature and spatial practices surrounding these sites.

JB: That's an interesting observation – that artists may be more welcome inside these institutions than others. I wonder why that is the case? Is it because of residual notions of the artist as sensorially, as opposed to intellectually, responsive – the artist as witness to wonders he or she will never understand but will delight in? Or because of the cultural cachet artists may have in non-artistic environments? An artist might be able to translate esoteric labour into something beautiful or meaningful and also provide a public platform for work that is otherwise unsung? Maybe this is too sceptical but it does strike me as culturally interesting that artists might be more welcome in scientific environments than, say, journalists or anthropologists.

NW: Yes, but I think initially the reception to artists was more banal, pragmatic, driven by the need to communicate and justify the expense and scale of the projects being undertaken. It was thought artists might help explain, or communicate at a social or emotional level, the benefits of all science. But artists had their own intentions. Productive antagonism, as Chantal Mouffe has outlined, remains important for the critical practices of many artists, those who did not buy into the service-driven aims of the scientists' project as a whole, nor of science's claims to unquestioned knowledge and power.

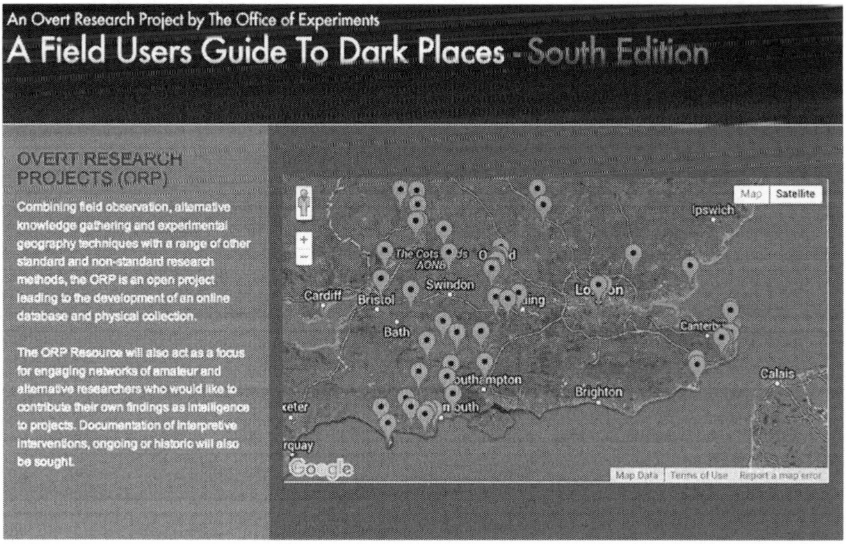

Figure 13.1 A Field User's Guide to *Dark Places*. An initial map of sites of interest for the Overt Research Project in the south of England. Credit: Office of Experiments, 2008.

What became clear to me, as an observer, was that the relationship between science and the military-industrial complex shaped this landscape. I realised that this was both a physical and a knowledge space, massive and expanding, for which there were very few observation points. So the overt research project sought to address this. Using the gallery or our website, we positioned ourselves outside of sites, looking in. Exploring the context and the information, local and institutional, our intentions became to share our observations and experiences with the passer-by, enthusiast, researcher or citizen, who also sometimes shared their own views and knowledge with us.

JB: Can you say something about the *Dark Places* exhibition held at the University of Southampton's John Hansard Gallery (November 2009 to January 2010)?

NW: The outcome of the initial wave of the 'overt' research project was realised in the exhibition *Dark Places*, which is a term already laden with notions of power, as it suggests places that are concealed or unknown and therefore prone to be feared, either because of sinister notions of what might be going on, or because it is quite simply something other than what is known or trusted (Figure 13.2).

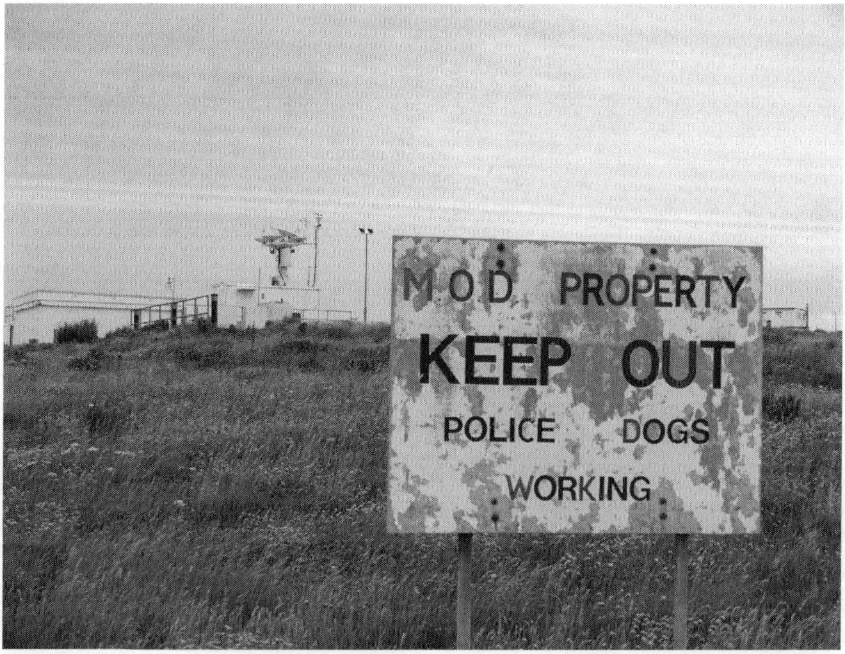

Figure 13.2 *Dark Places*. QinetiQ Facility, Portland Bill. Credit: Office of Experiments, 2008.

The overt research project underpinned this exhibition, which was co-curated with Arts Catalyst and Stephen Foster, curator at the Hansard Gallery. The OoE's original intention was to map sites of intelligence and knowledge not known or not normally accessible to the public, and to use this as a spine or resource for the exhibition. We placed this together with a range of artist projects, often based in the field, where access to sites of fear, and their subjects, has taken or is taking place. From displays of near-extinct British wildlife taken from the Natural History Museum and Horniman Museum, by Beatriz da Costa, through to Steve Rowell's study of ECHELON, NSA data surveillance and US territory in Yorkshire, in his project *Ultimate High Ground*, we were able to commission artists who were making work in the field through a political and social perspective (Figure 13.3). The exhibit and our fieldwork also provided artists and others with new research techniques, as well as working as a map that points to and literally guides the eye to spaces and places which are part of an imaginable network, a landscape we inhabit but often do not see.

JB: Another method you used for *Dark Places* was the bus tour, which took members of the public to a number of sites. What is the purpose of the bus tour?

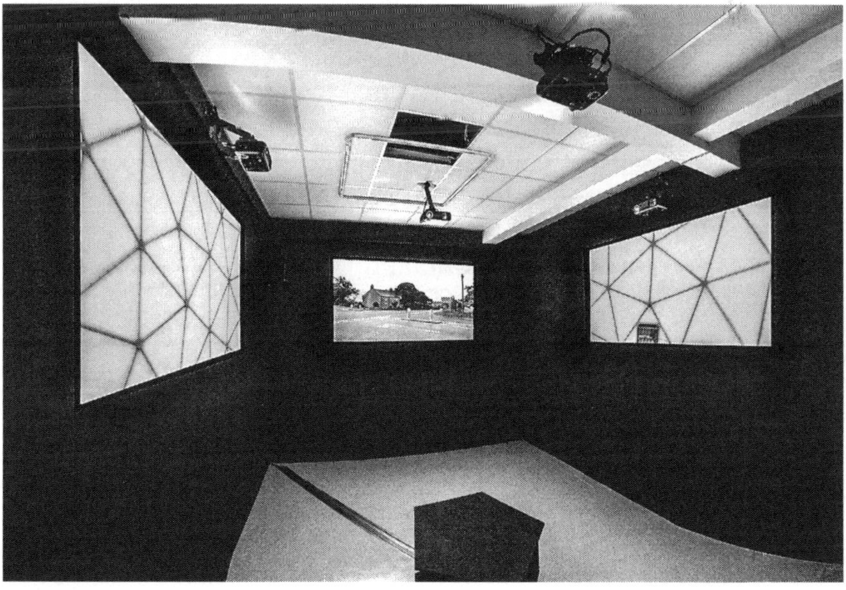

Figure 13.3 Steve Rowell, *Ultimate High Ground*. Credit: John Hansard Gallery, 2009.

NW: In defining the space of art as one of its problems, OoE work is concerned with art production in the field or in the wild. In the language of the APG, we acknowledge that 'context is half the work'. So working with Rowell, who became our International Director at this time, we developed the idea of a critical excursion (inverse to incursion) or bus tour, based on similar activity undertaken by the Center for Land Use Interpretation (CLUI), where Rowell is also a project manager (Figure 13.4). Critically, we wanted to create an event structure, a form that had the spatio-temporal dimensions that were aligned to the making of the work, which would allow media, archive footage and conspiracy films to be witnessed alongside sites of interest – in this case, Cold War spaces of secrecy and technology.

JB: I went on two of Steve's bus tours when he was in the UK a few years ago as a Visiting Artist Fellow at Newcastle University. The first one took in batteries at Tynemouth and Blyth, the military's Otterburn Range, and back into the city by way of the ship, gun and tank building history along the Tyne. The second tour took us to the remains of the Steetley Magnesitc plant on the beach at Hartlepool before lunch at RSPB Saltholme, followed by a visit to the Boulby Mine, the largest source of potash and deepest hole in the UK. The curious thing about the tours was that they were in some senses indistinguishable from any other, more conventional field trip – local points of interest, structured itinerary and expert guides – but they were also irreducibly odd since the different destinations were not of a piece but made to speak to each other by virtue of the attention we were paying to them. So industrial, military and environmental concerns started to overlap and sites that might normally be bypassed were made to converge into a fairly complex spatial and temporal network of correspondences and tensions. And the on-board viewing, a combination of instructional videos and sci-fi films, added another layer of intensity, like some sort of mind reorientation programme.

Kristoffer Gansing, the director of the German art and digital culture festival transmediale, did a similar tour of Cold War Berlin in 2014 called the Magical Secrecy Tour. It took place on 5 June, the one-year anniversary of Edward Snowden's NSA revelations. That tour was described as an investigation into the past, present and possible futures of surveillance – Berlin is obviously a prime site for this. Like your tours and the US-based CLUI tours, the point seems to be performative and immersive, not exactly random since there is a firm steer from the guide, but a kind of controlled exposure to the otherwise unknown or disregarded.

NW: On the tours – which also includes OoE Experimental Proving Grounds of Coast and Sea (2011), exploring sites in Portland, Dorset, and Experimental Ruins (London, 2012), directly exploring World War II bunkers and the Atomic Weapons Establishments and their counter sites, including women's peace camps close to London – what the public gets to experience is an unfolding set of carefully researched site visits, with films (on the bus) and interpretive texts provided by the artists and other expert witnesses and guides. The form, which takes a long time to prepare, rehearse and plan, allows for subjective interpretive analysis, as well as the potential for experimental encounters, in which structure borrows from the subject which it interrogates, even down to the mapping systems, GIS and so on used to map sites in the first place. Yes, it is performative, and has a discrete temporal register. There are no traces left, except snap shots and in the retelling of the work. The idea is close to the concept of the total artwork, and a deliberate attempt to point to a set of limitations in the visuality of art, in access to knowledge, both of the tour and of the sites themselves.

JB: Your recent show at Portikus in Germany brings together your work with Latham and your interest in the materiality of communications systems. The show places in dialogue a piece by Latham from

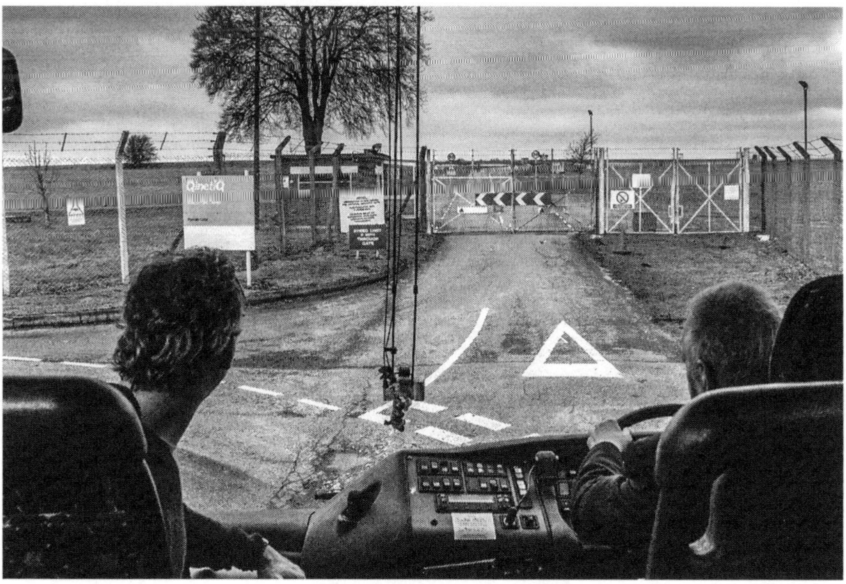

Figure 13.4 Critical excursion, Office of Experiments. Credit: Steve Rowell, 2009.

2005, *God is Great (#4)*, consisting of a field of shattered glass across the gallery floor with copies of the Bible, Koran and Talmud, and a new work by yourself that has a very long full title: *Dislocated Data Palm (in Two Parts), Guangzhou Shengjie Artificial Plants Ltd., 1/2F, Bldg. 3, No. 5 Industrial Park, Yezhuang Road, Ersche, Tangge Village, Shijing Town, Baiyun District, Guangzhou City, Guangdong, China* (Figure 13.5). The show is called *God is Great* (10^{-19}), which is a modification of Latham's interest in 'the least known amount'. Could you say something about the relationship between Latham's piece and yours in the Portikus show?

NW: John and I discussed our fascination with the void, the collapse of time and space. Both pieces are shaped by relevant belief systems in this sense, one that has a fundamental relationship to our spiritual

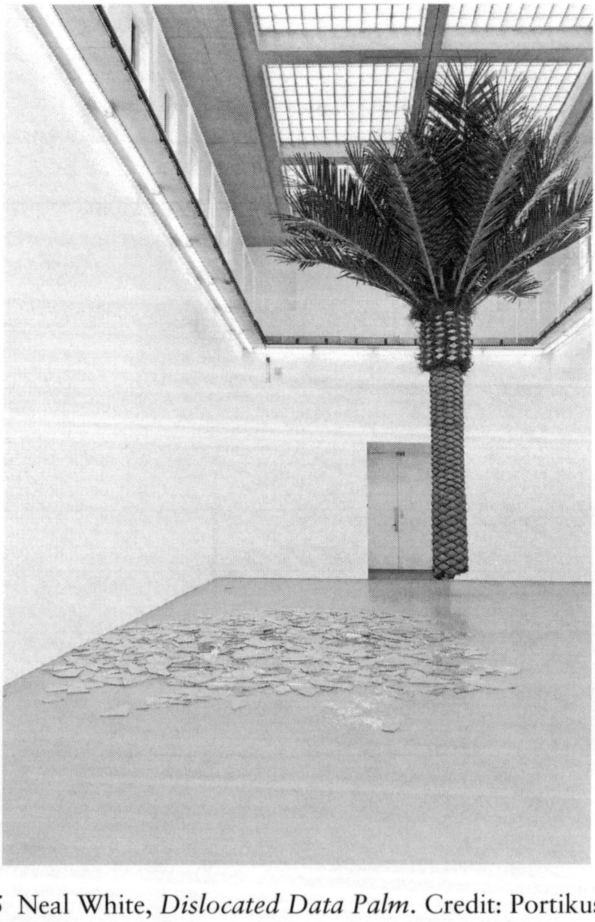

Figure 13.5 Neal White, *Dislocated Data Palm*. Credit: Portikus Gallery, Frankfurt, 2014.

encounters with the world and what unites them; *God is Great* literally embodies John Latham's ideas, with the shattered glass representing the infinite nothing that binds different religions as well as science. My piece and its title refer to the collapse of space inferred from the network which it would be part of, and the point of its origin, the title of its address, a global position in old form.

JB: There seems to be, in this interest in the least small, a concern with the threshold between the material and the immaterial – the smallest being the point beyond which something becomes nothing. One of the problems with contemporary communications technologies is that they are experienced, by and large, as immaterial forces or structures doing invisible work and, as such, are impossible to grasp, both literally and metaphorically. Presumably, this is partly the point of the palm, which conceals its true identity, as it were. It is also the material artefact that represents the absent network.

NW: *Dislocated Data Palm* was manufactured in China, and made to the specifications required for a mobile telephone communication tower or mast, disguised as a non-specific genus of coconut palm.

JB: So these 'palms' are commonly used? Mobile telecommunication masts disguised as trees?

NW: That's right. At around fifteen metres, this colossal plastic and metal object was not so much a mass-produced 'readymade' as a post-industrial networked artefact.

The original idea was to stand it amongst some local deciduous trees to the rear of the gallery, which is situated on an island in the middle of the river Main. But in the end, due to issues with the scale of the work, we needed to place a section of the palm inside. With the piece dislocated it was further deprived of its function, as a technical structure concealed amongst a natural setting, even if this was as an exotic species.

JB: Perhaps that kind of decision is itself revealing of the negotiation process that necessarily goes on between artists and other organisations and official restrictions. One of the problems I have with the popularity of the word 'intervention' in the context of artworks is that an intervention sounds like an action that has an urgency and an impact, as in an everyday situation, like an altercation on the street, where one might intervene to sort things out. Perhaps I'm being semantically over-sensitive, but I always cringe when I read about an artist's interventions because it sounds like the artist had to do something because no one else either could or would. As much as I'd like to believe in the power of art, 'intervention' has a grandiloquence to it that I find implausible. Nevertheless, as an interference or a coming between, perhaps intervention works so long as the friction and the compromise is properly factored in. It sounds like your palm tree was thwarted from intervening in the landscape but managed to negotiate a settlement in the gallery.

NW: I like the term 'incidental', which Latham and the APG developed; it is more appropriate. However, sometimes the power relationship is inverted and the gallery in this instance is incidental to the artwork. In fact, I would say that the incidental was more expansive than we see by looking at the object. The aim of this project was also to introduce students from the Städelschule to the idea of fieldwork, of working and looking at space in the real world beyond the studio, the representation of images, the world interior of capital. So the OoE worked with Portikus and conducted fieldwork around Frankfurt, taking into account some of its own unique sites, documenting quant trading and other data facilities such as the Dagger Complex, a US military base which contains the NSA's main SIGINT processing and analysis centre in Germany, the European Cryptologic Centre. We documented data exchange facilities servicing the New York Stock Exchange and the works around the new European Central Bank in Frankfurt. We visited the Geo Earth Station and other massive satellite tracking systems that form part of the European Space Agency and other global science projects, as well as broadcast media in the area.

Having identified these sites, we worked with Field Broadcast, an art technology project run by Rob Smith and Rebecca Birch, which allowed us to undertake live transmission from these field locations using simple 3G technologies. Transmissions were then streamed live to users who could download an application from the Portikus website. Live images of a landscape that revealed layers of systems were fed back through other data systems, providing new observation points and vistas – a perpetual loop of administrative and structural logistics.

All or most of these sites that were the subject of this piece, including the data palm (which itself is a movable site), deal with the material infrastructure of data. Yet, importantly, they also have geospatial and ultimately spatio-temporal qualities. Whether it is as part of the closed high-speed trading systems that demand shorter and faster transmission speeds for data, or space satellite tracking facilities, these are achieved by interventions in our urban and rural landscape. Building new physical cable/fibre networks or creating laser links with 'line of sight' capabilities also means moving facilities closer to access points.

JB: You make 'intervention' work well here, in the sense of an interruption inside the systems of communication. Perhaps the gallery, as the site of the visible, is the right place to position objects that might otherwise be imperceptible.

NW: Technological networks are not always part of the public networks we can normally access; there are also distributed nodes in the network of large-scale techno-scientific geo systems that now represent humans' most advanced forms. Both represent the development of our concerns for space beyond a single location, for communications and enquiry. As such, these sites are points of reference in a temporal or, as Latham would refer to them, evenometrical (equivalent to the geometrical) landscape. The networks serve human attempts to alter our access to other points of time, across space (live transmissions, cosmological research into dark matter) or to give it a finer granularity to work in (quantum trading algorithms operating so fast as to beat all other trading capabilities, a world inside the blink of the eye). In doing so they are a new material infrastructure for belief systems, an event structure of incredible complexity – an entanglement.

JB: I can see how this leads back to Rheinberger's point about what he calls a 'materially founded account of knowledge production' (2005: 406). The epistemic object is not an idea or a representation but a material thing that can be the conduit for all sorts of attention and use. Rheinberger says that once the relation between concept and object is no longer problematic, the thing becomes a technical object – it becomes 'transparent with respect to the concept that refers to it' (406). Your point with the palm, it seems to me, is that by working upon it in ways that go against its expected function, you keep it in the realm of the unknowable – it is not just recontextualised but its capacities are explored in ways that redefine what it might be and what it might do.

References

Buchloh, Benjamin H. D. (1990), 'Conceptual Art 1962–1969: From the Aesthetic of Administration to the Critique of Institutions', *October* 55: 105–43.

Latham, John (1986), *Report of a Surveyor*, London: Tate Gallery.

Lippard, Lucy (1997 [1973]), *Six Years: The Dematerialisation of the Art Object from 1966 to 1972*, Cambridge, MA: MIT Press.
Norfolk, Lawrence, and Neal White (2002), *Ott's Sneeze*, London: Book Works.
Rheinberger, Hans-Jörg (1997), *Toward a History of Epistemic Things: Synthesizing Proteins in the Test Tube*, Stanford: Stanford University Press.
Rheinberger, Hans-Jörg (2005), 'A Reply to David Bloor: "Toward a Sociology of Epistemic Things"', *Perspectives on Science* 13(3): 406–10.
Schwab, Michael (ed.) (2013), *Experimental Systems: Future Knowledge in Artistic Research*, Leuven: Leuven University Press.

Chapter 14

Smart Dust and Remote Sensing: The Political Subject in Autonomous Systems

Ryan Bishop

The numerous large-scale interrelated autonomous remote sensing systems operative in the present have long genealogies in military research and development and remain influential in military, civic and corporate spheres.[1] In fact, as these spheres have merged and blurred over the decades from the end of World War II to the present, the deployment and actions of these systems often become means for delineating the differences between these spheres and their priorities – this despite their being composed of the same sensor-based platforms of software and hardware regardless of deployer. Smart Dust, for example, constitutes the basis of polyscalar computer systems of remote sensing at micro-levels and relates to ubiquitous computing, 'pervasive networks' and 'utility fogs' as potentially transmitting endless streams of 'real-time' or stored data. Developed initially for DARPA, the technological R&D arm of the US Defense Department, Smart Dust started with work by Kris Pister and his team at UC Berkeley, who refer to the project as 'autonomous sensing and communication in a cubic millimetre' (Pister et al.). In a glimpse at the not-too-distant future, Hewlett-Packard intends to distribute a trillion of these micro-sensors from the bottom of the ocean and up into space in a project they are calling 'the central nervous system for the earth' (Hewlett-Packard website).

The history of remote sensing is the history of media generally, especially electric and electronic media. Remote sensing is implied in all tele-technologies and thus finds its earliest imaginary possibilities in the age of telephony, telegraphy and radio, along with the attendant avatars of subjectivity capable of experiencing sensorial phenomena at a distance. Science and technology reconfigure the imaginaries such that they can decontextualise the observing subject from the time-space constraints of the corporeal body, thus repeating Heidegger's famous dictum that the essence of technology is nothing technological: it instead resides in the immaterial, the noetic influences that render the world possible and malleable. The physical constraints of nature become those areas that certain forms of techno-scientific inquiry wish to erase or turn to their advantage, as made manifest in remote sensing systems deployed by various militaries most especially but not exclusively through opto-electronic devices operating at a distance and overcoming space to operate in a real-time of control.

With the Limited Test Ban Treaty (LTBT) signed in 1963, nuclear testing literally went underground, forcing innovations in modes of remote sensing for purposes of verification. These innovations, especially for sensing other than the visual, helped fuel a range of interrelated research leading to an immediate precursor of Smart Dust: Operation Igloo White in Vietnam, begun three years after the treaty was enacted. Scopic regimes became increasingly synaesthetic; that is, they yielded to remote sensing generally, using all of the sensorium to map or see the terrain of battle (a process begun in the early part of the twentieth century). Because so much of tele-technological development – as McLuhan, Baudrillard, Virilio and others have explored – depends on the understanding of the subject as an agent enacting its will upon a world of objects (including other subjects), the means by which we can and do imagine extensions of that sensing and acting self invariably fold into and influence the interpretation of that self. Multi-sensory tele-technologies as they pertain to the implications for the enactment of agency relate fundamentally to the constitution and expression of the political subject and the many systems in which it is embedded, formulated, constructed, subsumed and articulated. Remote sensing and tele-technologies as mobilised by the military have the potential to result in killing at a distance, which is clearly a matter of a subject controlling and manipulating objects (even unto death). However, the far greater sense of the self as agent in this scenario emerges in the belief that one possesses the power to control that distance, to alter proximity and render a plasticity to its measurable materiality that allows objects to be brought nearer or at further remove at will. The casting of the senses and the central nervous system beyond corporeal bounds, therefore, has profound ramifications for imagining the political subject as agent and further for the conditions of thinking the autonomous as concept, subject and technology. Additionally, it also is an indication of the imaginary for, as well as design of, technological systems that have no need to imitate the human form: minuscule sensory systems, insectoid, or just plain distributed in ways that bypass the imaginary of telesensors that return to or cater for the human form, as Jussi Parikka argues in *Insect Media* (2010).

Smart Dust

> And I will show you something different from either
> Your shadow at morning striding behind you
> Or your shadow at evening rising to meet you;
> I will show you fear in a handful of dust.
>
> T. S. Eliot, 'The Waste Land'

Each generation generates its own dust. Ubiquity itself, dust marks time, movement and stasis while evoking mortality. It is Aeolian, wafted on the air and carried in the atmosphere. Composed of animal and human skin and hair, industrial pollutants, fibres, particles from outer space, plant pollen, and technological and agricultural residue, dust constitutes a microscopic encyclopaedia of the minutiae of quotidian existence.

The dust we will take up here, though, is a specific kind of dust: one primarily of the imaginary at the moment but inching its way closer to actuality and implementation. Generated from and for emergent urban conditions, most specifically warfare, it is called Smart Dust. As mentioned earlier, it deploys ubiquitous computing, 'pervasive networks' and 'utility fogs' to transmit continuous streams of 'real-time' data and can be used as well to broadcast stored data for mixed reality sites. Each chip contains sensing, computing, wireless communication capabilities and autonomous power supplies within its volume of a mere few millimetres. This 'autonomous sensing and communication in a cubic millimetre' contains a host of governmental, industrial, commercial, medical and military applications, as well as multiple profound implications for understanding human positioning and intervention into the material world.

As yet another manifestation of the myriad ways in which nanotechnology is being mobilised, the concept is to distribute very large numbers of wireless micro-sensors/transmitters by scattering them across a fairly contained space. Smart Dust depends on the convergence of three technologies: digital circuitry, laser-driven wireless communications systems, and MicroElectricalMagnetic systems (called MEMS). The sensors spark off one another, detect the terrain and speak to other machines. Smart Dust, as envisioned and advertised, would work with seven different levels of coordinated networks, stretching from the ocean floor to terrestrial domains (including products), to the air and on into space. Hewlett-Packard plans, according to its own PR, to provide sensory capacities to extant IT infrastructure, so that it will no longer be inert material but active media and sensing devices. So that this infrastructure can see, feel, hear and smell, HP will in the next few years deploy a trillion sensors the size of a grain of sand that will operate under the label of the 'Central Nervous System for the Earth' (also cutely anagrammed into CeNSE). CeNSE becomes, in essence, the signature for the future of complex remote sensing systems.

HP, in a 2010 PowerPoint presentation about CeNSE generated by their Information and Quantum Lab, identified sensors as the next wave in IT and argued that they 'will impact human interaction with the earth as profoundly as the internet has revolutionized communication' (CeNSE 2010). By providing what we might call full-spectrum sensing capacities at a distance, CeNSE will extend to the deaf, dumb and blind 'brain' of networked and cloud computing the capacities of 'Taste/Touch/Smell/Sound/Sight'. Believing the Trotsky-inspired dictum related to quantity and quality, the company argues that 'Quantity of data creates quality of data', with sensors being the primary means for producing this exponential change in quantity that affects quality. In the generation of this data on variously scaled systems, as depicted on a diagram exemplifying how these various autonomous remote sensing systems could potentially interact, CeNSE provides a 'personal sensing subnet' nestled amongst and integrated into a larger set of sensing relations including, for example, 'wildlife research', 'tsunami warning system' and 'oil and gas'. The last set of relational system examples, 'oil and gas', proves important because HP has partnered its CeNSE technologies and efforts with Shell for optimising energy resource extraction, as discussed in the introduction to this volume. Clearly the individual subject is intended to find a toehold in these interconnected rapidly ramped-up remote sensing systems, and indeed can come to be defined through the node the subject occupies and accesses at the subnet level. Nonetheless, the main action entails animated objects and phenomena as non-human sensing agents speaking to and through software and hardware platforms with each other and with computing programs. Human senses now will be linked to an externalised central nervous system, as conceived by McLuhan, projected on to the earth and materialised through this projection. To this extent the claim about revolutionising human interaction with the earth in a way analogous to the internet's effects on communication might hold true: human interaction with the earth will be transposed to, mediated by and replaced by these sensing systems in much the same way that the vast majority of communication on the net occurs between machines.

Even though a leading CeNSE scientist, Peter Hartwell, has a YouTube talk entitled 'Listening to the Heartbeat of the World', the ambitions explicitly outstrip the parameters of our planet and provide an exemplar of the kind of polyscalar computing that we are building and which, by reversal and extension, is increasingly building us through a malleable imaginary of protean selves occupying a protean world in which, to paraphrase Virilio, the infosphere controls the geosphere (2008: 84; see Benjamin Bratton's excellent work on the stack in relation to related concerns). This stuff is clearly not your common household dust. Rather, it is high-end, high-tech designer dust for the information wireless city and other terrain. Some potential applications include monitoring ecosystems, traffic and population flows, and insect and vermin migration, as well as interaction with handheld devices to create interactive smart local environments, site-specific entertainment for mobile technologies, and even healthcare screenings. It can be built into bricks or woven into fabric or installed in walls and can manifest as virtual keyboards, property identification, threat detection, interactive environments for the disabled, product quality monitoring and streaming of current information for smart homes or offices. However, Smart Dust caught DARPA's imagination early, and they seeded the initial research as yet another way to expand the extant and massive defence-related sensing networks for battlefield surveillance, treaty monitoring, weapons inspection, movement detection, and so on. In this guise, Smart Dust becomes a sensorial supplement of already prosthetic tele-technologies. Smart Dust, especially as envisioned by CeNSE, constitutes an exponential expansion of the 'weapons ecosystem' (Virilio 2000: 27), as well as an expansion of the belief in the control and autonomy of that ecosystem now made *literally* ecosystem.

These fully automated machinic communications systems, programmed to track and monitor the state of circumstances, provide one of the most significant ways in which the militarisation of everyday life invisibly operates in urban environments. At the core of the operation of these tracking and sensing systems, of course, is the software that programs the conditions they are designed to sense, monitor and respond to. The politics of programs and the algorithms of urban control encode and manifest the desires of specific interests within the urban landscape. So what appears to be a machinic, objective system of observation and monitoring – just 'a view' of the cityscape or terrain that merely conveys data – is anything but. It is a view with an interest.

A key point of departure for the integrated designs for systems operative in urban sensing, tracking and targeting can be found in military plans for fighting in the tropical jungles of Southeast Asia: the response to guerrilla fighters along the Ho Chi Minh Trail known as Operation Igloo White. The operation included three separate triangulated areas: the trail laden with sensors related to almost every sense (sight, sound, touch, smell), a computer interpretation centre in Nakhon Phanom, Thailand, and the airspace above Vietnam and Cambodia. The first space was populated by guerrilla fighters and peasants, the second by US military intelligence officers and systems operators who did little except keep the automated system running and interpret data after the fact to influence future programming, and the third by fighter planes. The closed system of Operation Igloo White followed an automated set of programmed cause-and-effect actions and reactions meant to remove humans from the loop of sensing and tracking, and to reduce the gap between perception and action. The sequence went as follows: sensor detection → signal sent from sensor in Laos or Cambodia → computer analysis of sensor input → radio coordinates sent to airborne fighter planes → F-4 jets lock on target → auto guide and auto pilot of fighter planes → auto fire at target on map grid → explosion (Edwards 1997: 3–8). All of this occurred in the time-span of five minutes – jaw-dropping rapidity then but agonisingly slow now. The command and control centre 'saw' electronic information and data sent from the trail but the pilots never 'saw' the target: the entire closed system had machines reading machine-generated data to speak to other machines and automatically cause them to act on this information.

Of course, the Vietcong ascertained the interrelated and remotely related parts of the operation as well as its fully automated nature, and thus circumvented the entire operation. They even turned the system's apparent advantages against itself through a number of ploys, such as sending an unsuspecting water buffalo down a part of the trail to be blown up by the most high-tech weaponry available to the mightiest military machine on the planet while Vietcong materiel and personnel bypassed the targeted area, thus causing US forces to waste money, time and ordnance killing a non-target. The countermoves to massive attempts to incorporate horizontal diffusion into vertical control provided the Vietcong with tremendous strategic advantages, especially as the US forces continued to believe in the success of their systems. The more the US military machine believed in the autonomy and agency of its autonomous weapons systems, the more vulnerable to asymmetrical counter-tactics they became. The means by which the autonomous subject extended its agency proved to be the ways its power and control over objects in the world were undone. The more technics of control the subject/state possessed, the less control it could exercise.

Operation Igloo White prefigures all of the 'intelligent material systems' that Smart Dust promises. To pay tribute to this complexly enmeshed automated remote sensing system and progenitor of these current systems, one of the nano-chips for Smart Dust is Actel's Igloo Nano FPGA.

Smart Dust has a more stationary and urban counterpart: smart buildings (about which Jordan Crandall has written most evocatively). With buildings and infrastructure outfitted with sensors to detect stress, danger, failure, and shifts in normal states, the role of the intelligent built environment changes in numerous ways, including ways that could be mobilised for surveillance and action as on the Ho Chi Minh Trail. Previously, intelligent spaces (or mixed reality areas) and buildings have been only internally intelligent, contained entities speaking to themselves while monitoring the internal systems that observed their interior and perimeter. Now, in an effort to further safeguard the operations of the systems essential to the building or infrastructure, intelligent material systems have become externally intelligent, conversing with and tracking the environment with external machines that monitor the larger environment in a sustained engagement with the urban, natural and meteorological contexts, as well as being in conversation with other machines residing outside the integrity of the built structure or localised site. The prosthetic extensions that so constitute a range of tele-technologies for corporate, governmental and military operations for humans have now been granted to buildings, highways, water pipes, and so on, but with the same goals of maintaining specific proprietary interests of property and wealth, and influencing behaviour through the managed control of time, space and populations – along with the added threat of mobilised violence, police or military, to so manage.

When the dust settles, when this Smart Dust settles, it will have been fuelled by the desire to eliminate the event, to make sure no event occurs. It is worth noting that DARPA's website slogan is 'Creating and Preventing Strategic Surprise'. However, the elimination of the event will have been determined by an indeterminate object that senses as a subject, communicates as a subject and yet does not and cannot enact its own will: merely a node in a network shuttling data. Smart Dust will have become us: the political subject without agency.

IMS and CeNSE

> Technique has become autonomous; it has fashioned an omnivorous world which obeys its own laws and which has renounced all tradition.
>
> Jacques Ellul (1964: 14)

The LTBT provides an important moment in the development of many remote sensing systems operative in the past, present and future, including projects such as Transparent Earth, a project combining weather-hacking and artificial lightning to create the conditions in which synaesthetic tele-visual mapping of the first five kilometres under the earth's crust can occur, and the very remote sensing Mercury, Mentor, Magnum and Advanced Orion eavesdropping satellites in geosynchronous orbit that look like umbrellas the size of American football fields parked in space. The LTBT coincides with the prefix 'geo-' becoming synonymous with the earth as globe, as bounded, strategically networked and surveilled entity – a moment marked by the first issue of *The Journal of GeoElectronics* (in 1963) which included an introductory meditation on the changing understanding of the prefix 'geo-'. This journal is now called *The Journal for Geoscience and Remote Sensing*.

With the progression of the LTBT toward the Comprehensive Test Ban Treaty (CTBT), remote sensing for verification also went global with the International Monitoring System (IMS). With seismic, hydroacoustic, infrasound, radionuclide platforms for automated, global, real-time monitoring, the Comprehensive Test Ban Treaty Organization global alarm system includes 337 monitoring facilities located in eighty-nine countries covering all continents and oceans. It includes a data-processing centre in Vienna and a global satellite communications system (five satellites at a height of approximately 36,000 kilometres). When an event occurs, several stations might register it and send detection information via satellite for collection and interpretation in Vienna. The transfer of data to Vienna takes place in a matter of seconds.

The IMS is a glorified version of Operation Igloo White and a political/military version of the so-called private sector/corporate version of HP's CeNSE. Some clear differences exist, though, in that the IMS merely generates and gathers data but does not act on it, at least not automatically. Instead it plunges those who engage its mysterious traces and marks deep into the mire of interpretation and hermeneutical strategies. Even though its closed loop of automated remote sensing only gathers data, a key element in material technological development is the rapid flip of systems designed for observation to targeting, often with an automated element intended to bypass the careful hermeneutic attention provided in the IMS's considered interpretation of data in order to move as rapidly as possible to offensive engagement: the collapse of the gap between apperception and action, from sensory input to lethal engagement, that so characterises military technicity in the twentieth and twenty-first centuries.

The quotation from Jacques Ellul that serves as epigraph for this section explores productively the role of techniques and *techne* on the formation of the world and tradition. Clearly the IMS creates a new kind of world of remote sensing, a geo- out of a world, a bounded entity that is the global resulting from the strategic engagement of real-time surveillance essential to the Cold War and its enduring legacies. In this manner, then, Ellul provides a kind of paradox, for the autonomous system might well create an 'omnivorous world' of its own fashioning but it has not done so *ab nihilo*. There is a long-standing tradition – indeed, a *nomos* (which also means 'tradition' as well as 'law') – in the formulation of techniques and the autonomous. Ellul's paradoxical statement amounts to saying we have reached a stage of technological systems as autonomous but without the *nomos* yet still driven by an auto-propulsion toward some *telos* that eludes or erases us. This indeed might be the *nomos* of the earth we currently inhabit, or that we arrived at half a century ago when Ellul wrote these words, but it is by no means new or without tradition. It is tradition itself.

The Autonomous

> But, once adopted into the production process of capital, the means of labor passes through different metamorphoses, whose culmination is the *machine*, or rather, an *automatic system of machinery* (system of machinery: the *automatic* one is merely its most complete, most adequate form, and alone transforms machinery into a system), set in motion by an automaton, a moving power that moves itself; this automaton consisting of numerous mechanical and intellectual organs, so that the workers themselves are cast merely as its conscious linkages. In the machine, and even more in machinery as an automatic system, the use value, i.e. the

> material quality of the means of labor, is transformed into an existence adequate to fixed capital and to capital as such; and the form in which it was adopted into the production process of capital, the direct means of labor, is superseded by a form posited by capital itself and corresponding to it.
>
> Karl Marx, 'Fragment on Machines' (1993: 692)

> Thus, for us, *nomos* is a matter of a fundamental process of apportioning space that is essential to every historical epoch – a matter of structure-determining convergence of order and orientation in cohabitation of peoples on this now so scientifically surveyed planet. This is the sense in which the *nomos* of the earth is spoken here. Every new age and every new epoch in the coexistence of peoples, empires, and countries, of rulers and power formations of every sort, is founded on spatial divisions, new enclosures, and new spatial orders of the earth.
>
> Carl Schmitt (2003: 78–9)

When Blaise Pascal in the mid-seventeenth century crafted three documents intended to explain and provide him with exclusive control over his mechanical calculator, he relied heavily on its performativity in Lyotard's sense of the term to justify the apparatus's virtues over those of humans (see Bennington 1994: 137–51). The superiority of the machine was not simply with regard to speed and efficiency but its capacity to stand in for, to extend or even replace, the mental operations of its inventor. In fact, the user might not even possess these capacities at all. Of the machine, Pascal explains that it can 'by itself alone without any work of the mind, [perform] the operations of all the parts of arithmetic' (quoted in Bennington 1994: 138).

Pascal's machine neatly delineates a set of functions and qualities central to automation, including storage, repetition, production, substitution and performance. The inventors or programmers of any machine or set of machines reside both inside and outside the machine, for the performance of the machine depends on its inventors, to an extent, for what it performs but its performativity does not depend on its inventors once rendered operable. The performance can and usually does continue after the death of the inventors and regardless of any particular user. That it is self-operational highlights the auto- portion of automation and sets up the tension between *techne* and *logos* resident in the term 'technology'. (That what is true of the machine (*techne*) is also true of the text (*logos*) is an insight that runs throughout Derrida's work.) The death of the inventor, like the death of the author, that nonetheless allows for the survival and performativity of the machine or the text is by no means the death of the sovereign subject as numerous other pretenders to the throne stand ready and waiting. But the dispersed, distributed and automated subjectivity and agency operative in remote sensing – especially closed automated weapons systems – might well wound, perhaps mortally, the political subject as a concept.

Our common-sense narrative states that when constituting the subject (political or otherwise) we set a scene of the sensing subject solidly placed amongst objects through which we enact our agency, and any technology that helps us to so understand the scene (i.e. all sensing technology but especially visualising technologies) is also 'out there' and external to the subject. This technology is part of what helps subjects place objects in the scene, to realise their status as subjects. This reinforces a comforting story, a common-sense tale of agency, subjects, action and technology that allows us to fulfil our desire as autonomous actors, despite the division between external and internal as increasingly difficult to maintain insofar as the subject and technology are concerned – it must be noted, though, that the subject/technology divide is in fact a blurry boundary that reaches back to antiquity.

Integral to the complex remote sensing systems generated in the wake of increased tele-surveillance instigated by the LTBT is 'the auto-', that self-generating element of the machinery in its programmed engagement with the globe, its inhabitants and phenomena – which is one of the very selling points Pascal makes in the attempt to secure exclusive production rights of his calculator. The 'auto-' functions as a hinge between the event (organic/animate) and the machine (calculable/inanimate): the all-important space between the event and the machinic.

If we examine the usage of the prefix 'auto-' over time, we will notice that this prefix performs its content. This affix is self-performing, almost auto-grammatic or auto-semantic. 'Autos' in Ancient Greek was rare, but when used it was in combination with other terms and means 'self, one's own, by oneself, independently'. Its usage becomes more common and prevalent in medieval Latin. When it emerges in English, 'auto-' becomes a living element, prefixable and attachable to scientific terms to mean an action or an operation. In non-technical English, the prefix can mean: '(*a*) of oneself, one's own; self-; (*b*) self-produced or -induced (pathologically) within the body or organism; (*c*) spontaneous, self-acting, automatic' (*Oxford English Dictionary*). The self of the Greek becomes subsumed in the English action or operation of systems apparently driven by an internal machine, energy or desire constitutive of an entity resembling a subject but not necessarily a self. The 'auto-' in English, then, finds analogy in the workers as described in the Marx epigraph: causal links within a machine whose larger operational purpose they fulfil.

Remote sensing systems, as metonymically invoked by Smart Dust and CeNSE, are not only automated but also autonomous. That is, once they are set up they can and do operate on their own. These systems are self-governing, as the terms *autos* and *nomos* would imply, with *nomos* being one who deals with a set of laws and the related *nomia* indicating a field of laws or principles governing a subject.

The provocative political thinker Carl Schmitt discusses the *nomos* as the measure from which all other measures emerge, thus constituting a story of origins concerning how the division and the partitioning of the world occur – coming as it does from the verb *nemein*: to divide and thus distribute and allocate (2003: 67–72). The *nomos* is the measure that brings about other measures – the ur-measure, as it were – and is simultaneously physical, conceptual, institutional and political for it becomes constitutive of the Law and tradition. According to Schmitt, the *nomos* provides the means by which land is 'divided and situated' but 'it is also the political, social and religious order determined by the process' of dividing and conceptualising the land that 'turns a part of the earth's surface into the force field of a particular order' (2003: 70). Part of the power of the *nomos* resides in its inceptionary and generative qualities that move rapidly from materiality to immateriality, from literal divisions to conceptual and institutional justifications of them. The *nomos* begins as and operates through self-organisation, autonomous organisation as it were. The *nomos* as founding division becomes the basis for taxonomies, the division of the world into parts and wholes, including nations and states, and is therefore related to the Latin term *limes* (see Bishop, forthcoming).

It is the mark, the *gramma*, the limit, the cut: the basis for a taxonomy, the division of the world into parts and wholes, including states. The *nomos* marks the difference that makes a difference and is constitutive of difference itself. It forms the basis upon which we interpret the one and the many *as* the one and the many, and parts and wholes *as* parts and wholes. The *nomos* creates that intractable problem in Kant's 'Essay on Perpetual Peace' in which all people have equal right to the face of the earth but nonetheless are an affront to one's neighbour simply by claiming that right.

That claim to a spot on the face of the earth comes about through the division wrought by the *nomos*. The act of making this division or mark is a cultural technique that, in middle voice fashion, crafts the subject performing the act into a different kind of subject, in both grammatical and ontological senses. In an essay on the German traditions of thought surrounding *Kulturtechnik*, Geoff Winthrop-Young cites the example of the humble plough, through which the act of cutting the land establishes the farmer as subject, citizen and farmer in the same instant. The cultivation of a culture results from that incision of the land, as do claims of power, *logos*, authority and the Law. That mark in the land, that *gramma* (Gk. 'mark or cut'), is simultaneously foundational and violent. Cornelia Vismann continues the point by saying:

> One must therefore draw a distinction between persons, who *de jure* act autonomously, and cultural techniques, which *de facto* determine the entire course of action. To inquire about cultural techniques is not to ask about feasibility, success, chances and risks of certain innovations and inventions in the domain of the subject. Instead, it is to ask about the self-management or auto-praxis of media and things, which determine the scope of the subject's field of action. (2013: 84)

Such thinking on cultural techniques is related to yet different from Yeats's famous rhetorical question in his poem 'Among School Children' – 'How do we know the dancer from the dance?' – and even Ervin Goffman's performance of everyday life. It differs from these by foregrounding, as does critical theory in language studies, the productive and generative roles of media and *techne*.

The supposed autonomous capacity of the subject or the citizen continues to be produced through current *techne* and has been dispersed into the electronic and digital operations of these fully automated systems. Rather than being a threat to humans, though, perhaps they merely embody what has always been the case: the political subject as wholly constituted by those laws and technics that make people into subjects, with the failure of autonomy being the necessary condition by which the subject comes into being. That is, we have always been like these remote sensing systems that seem so alien and fearfully anti-humanist; we have always been the political subject without agency.

Coda: Autonomy and Autoscopy

> The human race owes its becoming (and perhaps even its survival) entirely to the fact that it has no end in itself, and certainly not that of becoming what it is (of fulfilling itself, of identifying itself).
>
> Jean Baudrillard (2013: 212)

The televisual capacities for remote vision have resulted in a ubiquity of aerial views of landscapes or cities in cinema and photography exhibitions, rendering them commonplace. Some kinds of aerial views, though, are rarer, indeed pathological. One of these is called 'autoscopy', that is, viewing oneself, seeing oneself as a self viewing itself: simultaneously viewing subject and viewed object. Neurologists use the term to describe out-of-body or near-death experiences, and particularly in the latter cases, when the body and the self are clearly *in extremis*, the perceiving subject sees him/herself from several feet in the air above the supine body. Autoscopy is an aerial view determined by trauma or dementia. Some neurological studies link this phenomenon of seeing oneself in extrapersonal space as a pathological response to position, movement and completeness of the body, arguing that it results from a failure to understand and process proprioceptive, visual and tactile information. The effect is almost the neurological counterpart to ghosting for analogue broadcast television, but the experience of subjective viewing of the self changes that very experience. With autoscopy, we do not see two images of the same object as in televisual ghosting; rather, we see ourselves as an object from the position of our embodied subjectivity – like looking at a hologram projection of ourselves. However rare these neurological phenomena may be, the vastly successful eye-in-the-sky opto-electronic technologies used for global surveillance and targeting have rendered us all in a state of autoscopic *extremis*, able to see ourselves simultaneously as viewed and viewing subjects, embodied in both positions simultaneously in 'real time' in two distinct spatial positions. We can call this effect 'the autoscopy of episcopy' (see Bishop and Phillips 2010: 213–28).

In this effect we project a viewing subject above, one that is not us but a simulation of us that allows us to see ourselves, and others, from above in such a powerfully mimetic manner that we can believe, as with the pathological state, that it actually is us viewing as well: the projection as actual. In the process, though, we also view and target ourselves. With the host of polyscalar remote sensing systems, we have successfully surveilled and targeted the entirety of the earth's crust and now – with projects such as 'Transparent Earth', CeNSE and IMS – we see and target that which lies below the crust as if ground and underground were somehow separate from us. We have reified a solipsistic loop of sensory projection and reception in which nothing exists outside the viewing subject, even when that viewing subject is also the object of the view. This is a trick of opto-electronic tele-technologies, however: one that makes our astral out-of-body perceiving selves seem to be or feel to be our real selves, not understanding the effects of the actions as felt and experienced on the ground, which is both where we actually dwell and what we seemingly wish to render transparent. This perceiving and hovering self is no longer a neurological anomaly or neo-necromantic epiphenomenon but rather the consolidated result of massive spending, intensive R&D, and military-driven geopolitical theorisation about and application of whiz-bang tele-technological prowess and synaesthetic manipulation. That is, it is us.

Notes

1. A similar but different version of this chapter appeared in *Cultural Politics* 11(1) (2015): 100–10.

References

Baudrillard, Jean (2013), *The Intelligence of Evil, or The Lucidity Pact*, trans. Chris Turner, London: Bloomsbury.

Bennington, Geoffrey (1994), *Legislations: The Politics of Deconstruction*, London: Verso.

Bishop, Ryan (forthcoming), '*Felo de Se*: The *Munus* of Remote Sensing', *boundary 2*.

Bishop, Ryan, and John Phillips (2010), *Modernist Avant-Garde Aesthetics and Contemporary Military Technology: Technicities of Perception*, Edinburgh: Edinburgh University Press.

Bratton, Benjamin (2016), *The Stack*, Cambridge, MA: MIT Press.

CeNSE (2010), Information and Quantum Systems Lab, <http://sites.nationalacademies.org/cs/groups/pgasite/documents/webpage/pga_056798.pdf> (last accessed 10 February 2016).

Crandall, Jordan (2010), 'The Geospatialization of Calculative Operations: Tracking, Sensing and Megacities', *Theory, Culture & Society* 27(6): 68–90.

Edwards, Paul (1997), *The Closed World: Computers and the Politics of Discourse in Cold War America*, Cambridge, MA: MIT Press.

Ellul, Jacques (1964), *The Technological Society*, London: Vintage Books.

Hewlett-Packard Intelligent Infrastructure Lab, <http://www.hpl.hp.com/research/intelligent_infrastructure_m.html> (last accessed 10 February 2016).

Marx, Karl (1993), *Grundrisse: Foundations of the Critique of Political Economy*, trans. Martin Nicolaus, London: Penguin Classics.

Parikka, Jussi (2010), *Insect Media: An Archaeology of Animals and Technology*, Minneapolis: University of Minnesota Press.

Pister, Kris, et al., 'Smart Dust: Autonomous Sensing and Communication in a Cubic Millimeter', <http://robotics.eecs.berkeley.edu/~pister/SmartDust> (last accessed 10 February 2016).

Schmitt, Carl (2003), *The Nomos of the Earth in the International Law of Jus Publicum Europaeum*, trans. G. L. Ulmen, New York: Telos Press.

Virilio, Paul (2000), *A Landscape of Events*, trans. Julie Rose, Cambridge, MA: MIT Press.

Virilio, Paul (2008), *Open Sky*, trans. Julie Rose, London: Verso.

Vismann, Cornelia (2013), 'Cultural Techniques and Sovereignty', *Theory, Culture & Society* 30(6): 83–93.

Winthrop-Young, Geoffrey (2013), 'Cultural Techniques: Preliminary Remarks', *Theory, Culture & Society* 30(6): 3–19.

Index

Page numbers in *italics* indicate illustrations.